FROM THE RENAISSANCE TO ROMANTICISM

FREDERICK B. ARTZ / *From the*

RENAISSANCE *to* ROMANTICISM

TRENDS IN STYLE IN ART, LITERATURE, AND MUSIC, 1300–1830

THE UNIVERSITY OF CHICAGO PRESS

CHICAGO & LONDON

To my students, past and present,
in History 13 and 14 at Oberlin College

The University of Chicago Press, Chicago 60637
The University of Chicago Press, Ltd., London

© 1962, 1975 by Frederick B. Artz. All rights reserved
Published 1962. Sixth Impression with Supplementary Bibliography 1975
Printed in the United States of America

ISBN: 0-226-02837-2 (clothbound); 0-226-02838-0 (paperbound)
Library of Congress Catalog Card Number: 62-20021

PREFACE

These chapters on the history of ideas are, in some degree, a continuation of my *Mind of the Middle Ages, A.D. 200–1500* (3d ed.; New York, 1958). Their purpose is to trace basic changes in style in art, literature, and music from about 1300 to 1830, from Niccolò Pisano, Petrarch, and Landino to Delacroix, Goethe, and Beethoven. Beyond this, in proceeding from a description of the styles of the Early and then of the High Renaissance through those of Mannerism and of the Baroque to conclude with the styles of Neo-Classicism and of Romanticism, there are indicated some cross-relationships in the various arts. The approach is that of a historian of ideas, not that of a specialist in the history of art, literature, or music.

The examples are chosen from some of the leading figures of each period, but no rounded history of art, letters, and music has been essayed. Throughout, some knowledge of each of these is assumed. The interest is focused on the countries where basic changes in style occurred, but no extended attempt is made to show the ramifications of a style as it later spread from the place of its origin to influence one nation after another. For example, the art of the High Renaissance first showed its fundamental forms in early sixteenth-century Italy, and attention is centered there. On the other hand, the literature of the Age of Mannerism did not have a clearly marked focus, and attention must be spread across much of western Europe if one wishes to find the varied forms that Mannerism in letters assumed. So sometimes the attention is fixed on one country, and sometimes it is dispersed widely, depending on the nature of what actually happened.

Few attempts have been made to chart such a history of the basic changes in style in the arts. There are both correspondences and divergencies in the history of art, literature, and music; an effort is made here to indicate both. This is a pioneering enterprise, and the discussion is inevitably oversimplified. The results of such an inquiry can only be incomplete and provisional. I am certain to raise as many questions as I answer, but, at this stage of the study of intellectual history, these are some of the questions that need raising.

Some of the titles in the bibliography and a number of the quotations have been shortened. I have used the commonly employed English terms for works of art, literature, and music; thus it is "Mona Lisa" and "The Last Supper" for two works of Leonardo. This is inconsistent, but it makes for a surer understanding.

The Bibliography, largely of English and French works, makes no attempt fully to cover the subjects treated herein. I hope, however, it may prove useful. Many of the works included contain bibliographies. A few titles appear under several chapter headings. Some entries, such as encyclopedias and periodicals, are intended to set the reader on the track of pertinent material.

I am greatly indebted to friends and colleagues who have read all or parts of the manuscript: Wolfgang Stechow, Henry A. Grubbs, Donald M. Love, Richard M. Murphy, Paul R. Evans, Mrs. Oscar Jászi, Richard Goldthwaite, and Wylie Sypher. Beyond this, I owe much to the authors who have written on these subjects, a debt I have tried to acknowledge in the bibliographies. I wish, also, to thank the staff of the Harvard Library and that of the Oberlin College Library for endless assistance. Finally, I wish to thank my colleague and friend Barry McGill for help on the proofs.

FREDERICK B. ARTZ

OBERLIN, OHIO

CONTENTS

Chapter I

INTRODUCTION

Many of the present views of the evolution of style in the arts date from writings of Heinrich Wölfflin, especially from his *Principles of Art History* (German ed., 1915; English ed., 1932; French ed., 1952). In this work by Wölfflin, the Baroque style in art was for the first time well analyzed in an objective fashion. From Wölfflin's study of art history, his basic concepts have spread to the analysis of stylistic changes in literature and in music. Wölfflin, however, failed to separate the Mannerism of the later sixteenth century from the Baroque of the seventeenth and eighteenth centuries. This has been corrected in the study of changes of style in the fine arts, but Wölfflin's confusion is still marked in the study of the development of literary and of musical styles, though there are indications that these confusions are beginning to be cleared up.

The characterizing of style in art, literature, and music has, by long usage, come to vary extensively, as will be shown in the discussion which follows. In these preliminary considerations, there are noted only a few factors in the analysis of styles that are common to the arts. The word "style," as used herein, represents a series of qualities in a work of art, letters, or music; it covers both the subject matter and the manner of setting it forth. Stendhal defined style as "consisting in adding to an idea all the circumstances calculated to produce the whole effect that the thought ought to produce." In trying to define style, the general terminology ordinarily used may come from any one of at least eight sources. Style may take its definition from a single artist, author, or musician (as Homeric or Mozartian), from a time or a period (as medieval or Renaissance), from a language or a medium used (as French lyric, "painterly," or polyphonic), from the subject (as philosophical, tragic, or historical), from its geographical origin (as Florentine or South American), from the audience addressed (as popular or aristocratic), from the purpose of the creator (as ironic, diplomatic, or tragic), or, finally, from a general type (as monumental or operatic). Sometimes several of these eight categories are combined, as for example, the German Romantic style. Short of a comprehensive discussion of the concept of style, these indications will suffice to show some of the ways this word is used herein. But the best way to define style is not in the abstract but in an analysis of specific works of art, literature, and music.

Phases in the history of artistic, literary, and musical styles can never be sharply cut off one from another. Everyone knows now that the Renaissance began before 1400, and the Middle Ages lasted after 1500. In all the arts, origins are often unexpectedly early, and survivals are frequently stubborn and of long duration. One phase of style not only overlaps another, but some elements of style carry over from one period to the next, and even into still later periods. Moreover, like the nationalities of central Europe and the Balkans, where some language groups are in solid blocks, but others using the same language will be found far away as enclaves in the midst of another national block, so in the history of the arts a new style will seem to have established itself when some artist, writer, or composer will appear who prefers to create partly or entirely in an older style. All is in flux; nowhere does style remain constant or unified; everywhere there are survivals from earlier styles, anticipations of succeeding styles, and interpenetrations of the past, present, and future. Every age also has a number of artistic currents running side by side. In 1911–12, there appeared such diverse compositions as Strauss's *Rosenkavalier,* Sibelius' *Fourth Symphony,* Wolf-Ferrari's *Jewels of the Madonna,* Stravinsky's *Petrouchka,* and Schönberg's *Five Orchestral Pieces.* However, in spite of all this, we shall find that often one group of style characteristics is, at any given time, dominant.

It must also be acknowledged that nearly all stylistic devices may occur at almost any time in the several arts. There are Romanesque door frames of the twelfth century that, if isolated from their buildings, could pass for fifteenth-century Italian work; some Romanesque sculpture, as that at Carpentras in southern France, looks like Roman work of the Augustan period. Similar bits of poetry and music, if taken out of context, could easily be misdated. Stylistic forms, however, cannot be understood in isolation but must be considered as parts of a whole; and they must also, in any age, be accompanied by other works of similar characteristics to be considered as symptomatic of a general trend. No one style is ever complete in a single painting, sculpture, building, poem, or musical composition. Style may be defined as a series of variations on a theme that is never given. There is, moreover, always something special that belongs to the nation, the social class, the religious group, and the personality of the artistic creator. But, again, these variations and individual differences, while they must be considered, should not obscure basic similarities of style.

The rate and extent of changes of style are different in the three arts here considered; likewise they vary from country to country. Writers often seem to make changes in style more rapidly than do artists or musicians. For example, the first two important figures in Renaissance letters and art offer much that is stylistically new, but there is a deeper penetration into the meaning of classical style in the poetry of Petrarch than in the somewhat earlier sculpture of Niccolò Pisano. Changes in style in literature also seem to be achieved more easily than in art and music. Only Michelangelo among the more important artists and Beethoven among the leading musicians made the long journey through changing styles taken by a number of writers, including Shakespeare, Milton, and Goethe. Michelangelo's work, for example, embraced the styles of the High Renaissance, Mannerism, and the Baroque, and Beethoven, in music, bridged Neo-Classicism and Romanticism. In this, each seems in his field to have been unique.

Movements in the arts reach their full expression in different countries and at different times, and the outstanding accomplishments are not the same in one nation as in another. Thus in the Renaissance the main achievements in Italy were in the plastic arts, in the Low Countries in painting and music, and in England in the drama. Some nations that made outstanding contributions to culture in certain fields produced little to parallel these accomplishments in related fields. England, in the sixteenth and seventeenth centuries—as Russia in the nineteenth century—had a striking development in literature and music but showed great backwardness in creating new forms in art. Germany, from 1750 to 1850, produced a superb body of literature, music, and philosophy, and at the same time hardly rose above mediocrity in the fine arts. So one art often pushes ahead of another. In the Romanesque and Gothic periods in England, changes in literature and music lagged behind changes in architecture and sculpture; there is little in English literature and music that is comparable to the great medieval English churches until Chaucer appeared in the fourteenth century and Dunstable in the fifteenth. In the same way, one can hardly speak of Romanticism in music before 1800, whereas, by that date, there was much Romantic literature, and some Romantic art.

Human nature and the natural world remain much the same; but the ways of looking at these phenomena differ profoundly, as do the manner and technique of presenting what is seen and felt. It is this last which brings the arts through many transformations. The story of the changing styles in the arts in the period 1300 to 1830 represents, at least well into the seventeenth century, phases of Italian artistic and literary styles and, to a less extent, of Italian musical styles as they reached across Europe and the Americas. During this period Italian paintings, sculptures, and architectural designs, and Italian books and musical compositions spread throughout the Western world. In the same period, artists, writers, and musicians flocked to Italy, while Italians found employment outside their homeland in every state from Spain to Sweden. It was a time of great cosmopolitan interchange. Among the greatest figures in the arts in northern Europe only a few, as Shakespeare, Rembrandt, and Bach, never made the pilgrimage to Italy. But Italian influences in their work are nonetheless marked. New styles usually began in Italy, but the greatest achievements in these styles were often the work of non-Italians. Italy produced no Shakespeare, Cervantes, Racine, Rembrandt, or Bach—and the list could be greatly extended—but all these geniuses bear the mark of Italian influence. What began in Italy around 1300 spread to the rest of Europe as spring moves northward from Sicily to Sweden. These changes in style in Italy affected Spain and the center and north of Europe long after they were well developed in Italy. So, while the same succession of styles observable in Italy, at least into the eighteenth century, may be found in the other countries of Europe, the changes from one style to the next inevitably occur later than in Italy. Thus, to give only approximate dates, the Early

Renaissance in Italy runs from 1300 to 1500, the High Renaissance from 1500 to 1520 or 1530, Mannerism from 1530 to 1600, Baroque from 1600 to 1750, and Neo-Classicism and Romanticism, both chiefly the creation of northern Europe, from 1750 into the nineteenth century. In the rest of western Europe, much the same succession of styles as in Italy may be observed, but·until about 1750 these always take place at later periods.

After 1650, Paris and northern France became a second center for the defining and dissemination of new styles. These styles, however, had begun earlier in Italy, and northern France played rather the role of a relay station than that of a fundamental source of change. The first new style developed north of the Alps was that of the Rococo, which appeared in France in the early eighteenth century, but this should properly be considered as a late phase of the Baroque. Not until the formation of Neo-Classicism and Romanticism, the two great styles invented by the eighteenth century, do we find northern Europe, especially Germany and England, initiating new styles and Italy becoming on the whole a follower rather than a leader. Patriotic considerations often obscure or underemphasize the common elements in European civilization. For example, most French critics still refuse to accept the idea that their art and literature in the Age of Louis XIV belong to a general Baroque movement that arose in Italy and then moved across Europe; they recognize the debt of France to Italy, but for the period after 1660 they separate the French achievement from that of the rest of Europe. To the French, their later seventeenth-century "Classicism" becomes something special and *sui generis;* and so they pull the Château de Versailles and the plays of Racine out of any essential relationship to Bernini's Colonnades of St. Peter's and Milton's *Paradise Regained.* Likewise, German "Classicism" is now generally recognized as a part of the general movement of European Romanticism despite the fact that many German literary historians still cling tenaciously to their allegedly unique "Classical Period." A less nationalistic approach would not so obscure the cultural elements that were held in common across Europe. No one would think of denying the great qualities of the art, letters, and music of the Age of Louis XIV or of the literature of the Age of Goethe, or of showing wherein they are different from the contemporary achievements of other nations; but these differences must not obscure the deeper similarities. For example—to look backward—in the fifteenth century Gothic architecture took a perpendicular form in England and a flamboyant form in France. Between these styles there are broad and striking differences, but they are both always Gothic. So we must class the Age of Louis XIV as Baroque, and that of Schiller and Goethe as fundamentally Romantic.

A better understanding of the periods in style in the arts between the Early Renaissance and Romanticism has come about through a re-estimate of Mannerism and the Baroque, first in art and, more lately, in music and in literature. Part of this is due to the scholarship of recent decades; but another and deeper cause has been the rise and spread of new styles such as Post-Impressionism and Expressionism and a number of other "isms" in the twentieth century, exemplified by the Picassos, the Eliots and Rilkes, and the Bartóks of our own time.

An extensive literature has appeared that tries to attribute most changes in style in the arts to political and economic causes. This explanation of the history of culture exists both inside and outside the range of Marxian theorizing. Without ignoring such political and economic changes which certainly create "climates of opinion," the fundamental assumption in this book is that changes in style since 1300 are chiefly due to the desire of artists, writers, and musicians to discover and then to explore and exploit new ways of artistic expression—to tap new veins of beauty. Each epoch seems to acquire new eyes and ears, and genius looks for new provinces of the imagination and for Northwest Passages to artistic oceans hitherto uncrossed. Genius moves ahead; new standards are set to which minor artists, and even major ones in their formative years, will conform. The heart of these matters is set forth by Pliny the Elder when, in speaking of the sculptor Lysippus, he says, "His chief contributions to the art of sculpture are said to consist in his rendering of the hair, in making the heads smaller, and the bodies slimmer, which makes his figures look taller, so changing the square proportions of the older artists without disturbing the harmony." This seems to contain more insight than the socio-political explanations of critics like Antal and Hauser and their school. How often artists, writers, and composers make us feel their own delight in discovering new means of expression! The excitement that Petrarch found in using the figures of speech of the Latin poets in his own verses, that the Florentines of the fifteenth century found in representing movement, that Beethoven discovered in new rhythms and harmonies, or that the Impressionists discovered in trying to master the representation of light —these are among the fundamental forces that make changes in the arts.

Art, literature, and to a less extent music do reflect the age that created them. But it is never possible to equate the arts and society; the arts are never a complete reflection of their age. Some things are left out, and others are exaggerated or distorted in the telling; and every art has an inner life of its own. There is in each of the arts an inner logic, which is made up of the accumulated experiences of earlier masters in handling motives, materials, and instruments that, in one way or another, affects every work of art, literature, and music. The artist, the writer, and the composer take up the threads of a predominant tradition of techniques and of problems and subjects which are to the fore at the time. As the young artist, writer, or musician is growing up he acquires something of the present or past vocabulary and style of his art. Sometimes there lies a choice of several currents, and the creator can decide whether he will go with the main current or against it. In tracing changes in style in the arts one must always be on the lookout for both continuity and change. While all art, literature, and music come in some degree from earlier art, letters, and music, the emphasis is continually shifting, and also new elements are constantly appearing. Everything in history is the achievement of individuals. Individuals always find themselves in a definite position in time and place; their behavior and achievement are the product of both their capacities and their situation. Included in the situation for the creator in the arts is some prevailing style; and this style shows changes in fashion as much as it shows "the spirit of the age" and economic, political, and religious changes. Thus, it is fashion that, in some degree, the artist serves as much as the tailor. Often the artist is not fully aware of the matter of style; and style is sometimes more what the artist, writer, or musician takes for granted than what he knowingly creates.

So far as political, economic, and religious conditions affect the subject matter and the style of the arts, their effects often seem to be to accelerate changes already under way. For example, Mannerism had already begun to manifest itself before the loss of independence of the Italian city-states and before the upheaval caused by the Protestant Reformation and the catastrophic Sack of Rome in 1527. All these events created deep unrest and malaise and helped to push Mannerism to extremes, but they were not its first cause. In a somewhat different application of this thought, the attempt to tie up the Baroque too closely with the Council of Trent, the Society of Jesus, and the whole movement of the Catholic Counter Reformation fails, because all of these influences were under way before the Baroque had clearly defined it-self; their influence on the Baroque style was not, as we shall see, un-important, but it was not the only element in the formation of the style.

The practical conditions surrounding the artists, writers, and com-posers, and the conditions of patronage had their effects on the subject matter of the arts and to a less extent on their style; just how this took place will be considered later. But when a new style finally was formed in Italy and then began to spread throughout Europe, the Italian style was copied and adopted with little relation to the conditions that had originally helped to shape it. For example, Caravaggio's Baroque style of painting, which was, in some degree, influenced by the desire of some of the leaders of the Counter Reformation to present a sort of revivalist sermon in painting, was passed on, already formed, to Rem-brandt, who then used it in his own way. So Rembrandt's use of dra-matic highlighting and of deep shadows is more to be explained by the influences of Italian painting on his work than by any elaborate analysis of the economic and political situation in the Netherlands in the seven-teenth century. These last matters cannot be ignored in the formation and evolution of Rembrandt's style; but more important are Rem-brandt's genius, the events of his private life, and the style of the paint-ings he saw and admired.

The best way to estimate the influence of political and economic conditions on the artists, writers, and composers of the periods herein considered is through a study of the type of patronage they received. This is most important when a new style is in formation. Here the question should be raised whether the work is created for a church, a ruler, an aristocracy of birth, a plutocracy of wealth, for a small coterie, or for the general public. Caravaggio, Tasso, and Monteverdi were nearly contemporary—as were Le Nôtre, Boileau, and Lully—but their patrons were different. The art, letters, and music of the Baroque in Italy were predominantly church-centered; the arts of the Baroque in France were king-centered. This had some effect, as we shall see, on their arts, but more on the subjects chosen than on their style, and less on both than some writers have imagined.

The transformations of style from 1300 to 1830 in art and letters, though not in music, were all deeply affected by a continual study and restudy of Roman art and Latin literature and, to a much less extent, of the art and writing of ancient Greece. There were no ancient classical models in music and few in painting, but in architecture and sculpture there was extant a superb body of Roman achievement; and after 1300 Humanists and archeologists busied themselves in unearthing more of these treasures. From the Early Renaissance on, men were widely conscious of the parallel movements in art and letters as they faced the classical past, as Filarete in his *Treatise on Architecture* (about 1455) declared, "The man who follows the ancient practice in architecture does exactly the same thing as a man of letters who strives to reproduce the classic style of Cicero and Virgil."

In seeking to explain how and why new styles arise, some critics have tried, like Henri Focillon in his *La vie des formes,* to plot a sort of natural history of stylistic changes in the arts. According to schemes of this sort, which compare chapters on the history of ideas to the life of an organism, a style begins with a primitive period of experimentation. In this tentative period, a new style slowly takes shape. This period is followed by a classical solution of the problems earlier considered, and is often paralleled by an attempt of thinkers to form a critical canon. Finally, there succeeds a third period, an age of virtuoso elaboration, where the basic elements of the style are played with, lifted out of context, and used in a purely decorative fashion. During this final period, the style grows stale, and a new style begins to evolve. In such a scheme, the final phases of one style overlap the early and experimental phases of a new style. Such an explanation, if not too rigidly held, is certainly suggestive and much more valid than the socio-political type of analysis.

A basic fact determining style is that every artist is limited by the existing materials and techniques available to him. There is much literary evidence, for example, to show that the eleventh and twelfth centuries were extremely mystical and ascetic in outlook; but it was not until the thirteenth century, when there was a rapidly growing worldly prosperity and when thinkers like Roger Bacon, Emperor Frederick II, and the authors of the *Romance of the Rose* were turning to very earthly concerns, that men mastered the engineering techniques to build in the Gothic style whose soaring lines gave full expression to the otherworldly urges of the medieval mind. Likewise, we know from the letters of Mozart and of Wagner that both men were at times in similar states of heart and mind; but Mozart did not write music that sobs and pants like Wagner's because he and his age did not think of music that way and also because Mozart did not have available the harmonic resources or the musical instruments which Wagner inherited from Beethoven, Berlioz, and others.

Painting, sculpture, and literature belong, to some extent, together in that they used—until recently—the visible and material world as a starting point, whereas music and architecture are more detached from nature, more abstract, and, hence, more concerned with subjective ideas and emotions. The attempt here is not to show the identity of art, letters, and music but to disclose certain common ideas and attitudes that manifest themselves in different media; that is, to state changes in style first in terms of general cultural attitudes, and then in terms of the technical character of the several arts. There are elements of unity in the arts; yet it would be unreasonable to go as far as Robert Schumann, when he declared, "The individual arts differ in nothing except the vehicle by which they reach the recipient." Much more to the point is the comment of Leonardo da Vinci, "Painting is poetry which is seen, not heard, and poetry is a painting which is heard but not seen. These two arts interchange the senses by which they penetrate the intellect."

Finally, what I shall note hereafter are less matters of fact than tendencies and possible relationships. In trying to simplify periods and to point out relations among the arts, there will be, as in Mercator's projection of the round globe on a flat map of the world, some distortion. Classification of styles can never cover all the individual features of a work of art, letters, or music, just as a description of the anatomy of a human face can only emphasize the general and the typical and can never identify an individual. Something always eludes and escapes the periodizer of history and the historical generalizer. It is this that led Croce and others to the belief that every work of art is a special and individual creation about which no generalizations can be made. This type of critical anarchism has in itself the fallacy of an exaggerated generalization. This is, however, a point of view to bear in mind when the summarizing statements become too neat. Also, in the separation of a series of periods in the arts, there can be nothing like a coast line in geography or like a single melodic line in music. Actually, there is everywhere both continuity and change; and the historical process is like an elaborate contrapuntal composition scored for a full orchestra. Throughout, I am attempting to be suggestive rather than definitive, to see patterns rather than to impose them.

Chapter II

THE EARLY
RENAISSANCE
1300-1500

1. The Background

The first great renewal of culture after the breakdown of the Roman Empire in the West, in the fifth century, had centered in northern France in the thirteenth century. By 1250, the whole of Latin Christendom had become a series of cultural provinces of the country about Paris. The patterns of Gothic art, of vernacular literature, of harmonized music, of philosophy, and of university education were all set by the achievements of the French. Only the renewal of the study of science, faintly foreshadowed in the work of men like Emperor Frederick II and Roger Bacon, and the revived study of Roman law, centering in Bologna and northern Italy, and the innovations in art and literature that led to Niccolò Pisano and the *dolce stil nuovo* in southern Italy form significant exceptions to this cultural concentration in northern France. At no later time in the history of Western civilization has so much of the intellectual life of the age been centered in one area as it was in the thirteenth century. This great renewal marks the real beginning of modern culture. The Occident is now no longer living on the drippings of ancient civilization but has moved ahead to create an original civilization of its own. Spengler's "Faustgeist" has returned to the West.

Beside this great renewal of the twelfth and thirteenth centuries the Italian Renaissance has less significance than our forefathers imagined, for it was only in the fields of art and literature, and to a much less extent in music, that there were really new beginnings in Italy. The Italian Renaissance, thus, does not represent a new period in the history of science or of philosophy and, as a general movement in the history of ideas, it was far less original than the "Renaissance" of the twelfth century. But in the fields of art and literature, the movements initiated by artists like Niccolò Pisano, Giotto, Brunelleschi, Donatello, and Masaccio, and by writers like Petrarch and Boccaccio represented a great new aesthetic revelation.

Wherein, exactly, did this new dispensation in the arts lie? The artists and writers of the High and Later Middle Ages, especially in northern Europe, had developed a marked taste for realism in painting, sculpture, and literature. The Gothic sculptors, the painters of miniatures and of larger compositions, and poets such as Dante, Chaucer, and Villon all reveled in vivid and realistic details sharply observed from nature. They loved to depict and to describe the warts and bumps. It was this that Ruskin admired in Gothic art and letters and that led him to declare, "Go to nature in all singleness of heart, selecting nothing, rejecting nothing." This interest in realistic details became evident in the later twelfth century, and it grew more marked thereafter. Chaucer's miller may be taken as a sort of symbol of this realistic taste in Gothic art and literature. After giving one faithfully rendered detail after another, Chaucer concentrates his attention briefly on the miller's nose, and adds, "Upon the very tip of his nose he had a wart, and on it stood a tuft of red hair like the bristles on a sow's ears, and his nostrils were black and wide." This great interest in sharp observation and a good deal of technical ability to represent it in painting, sculpture, and letters were not lost in the next age. But to them the Italian added, gradually, a reappreciation of Roman civilization and a growing interest in the stylistic forms of Roman art and literature, together with a desire to use them in new artistic and literary creations. These two currents first clearly meet in the work of Niccolò Pisano and of Petrarch before and after 1300; and in art and letters this marks as clear a division as can be found between the Middle Ages and the Renaissance. In this same period, Giotto, without classical models, began a great renewal of painting; and there was also unfolding in both Italy and France a new style of musical expression, the *ars nova of* Landino and of Guillaume de Machaut. Of these parallel currents of art, letters, and music, the most rapid advances came in literature, as may be seen in the writings of Petrarch and Boccaccio. Not until the next century—the fifteenth— did art and music come to such a new flowering as literature had already shown in the fourteenth century.

The artistic, literary, and musical styles of these two centuries of the Early Renaissance are marked by a tentative attempt to achieve new forms of expression. For sculpture, architecture, poetry, and prose there were surviving classical models; for painting almost nothing of the classical past was known directly, but the style of classical sculpture was a help for the renewal of painting as were also some surviving literary descriptions of ancient paintings. Music, in these same centuries, without the help of classical models, was launching forth on new and uncharted courses, and it rose, between 1300 and 1500, to the position of a major art. In Italy, the movement toward a new style in art and literature proceeded along two lines. One was a continuation of the Gothic desire to get realistic effects, the other was toward the representation of a classical ideal of a harmonious universe, one which in the fine arts could be represented by mathematical proportions. Alberti, our most articulate contemporary commentator, lays emphasis both on a careful observation of nature and on the necessity of selecting from nature the most beautiful elements, so as to approach a perfection toward which nature aims, but which she rarely achieves. And in this process of refining, classical examples indicate the best methods of improving on nature. Alberti's faith in the use of classical models, however, is never pedantic or slavish. He praises Vitruvius as well as surviving examples of classical art, but he never sets them up as final authorities; and he encourages the artist always to use something of his own invention.

In comparison with the Italian achievements of the High Renaissance, and later of the Baroque, the efforts of the fourteenth and fifteenth centuries seem shy, restrained, and limited. One has only to compare Brunelleschi's Pazzi Chapel with Michelangelo's Dome of St. Peter's and Bernini's Colonnades or the short poems of Petrarch with the vast plan of Ariosto's *Orlando furioso* or of Tasso's *Jerusalem Delivered;* or finally to compare a mass by Guillaume de Machaut with one by Dufay or another by Palestrina, or with the still later *B Minor Mass* by Bach. Thus one becomes aware of the relatively timid and tentative notes struck by the art, literature, and music of the Early Renaissance. It was, though, a genuine renewal of the arts that took place. This renewal was first evident in Italy, but after 1500 it affected the arts in the rest of Europe. That some renewal and refreshment was in order is seen by the style of art, letters, and music in northern Europe, where the Gothic Middle Ages held on for two centuries longer than in Italy. In spite of the work of geniuses like Claus Sluter, Jan van Eyck, François Villon, and Dufay in the fifteenth century, the arts in northern Europe were, at many points, beset with trivialities and puerilities. Even the greatest Flemish painters never developed a systematic study of anatomy and of linear perspective, and—much more significant—only a few ever learned a very effective way to compose a group. They loved to agglomerate picturesque details, which they often painted with a breath-taking realism and a craftsmanship that time seems unable to destroy; but to compose a picture like Giotto's "Flight into Egypt" or Masaccio's "Tribute Money" was beyond even the greatest northern painter of the fifteenth century. As the northern painters and sculptors often ran into sterility in the multiplication of details, the late Gothic architects in the north did the same in multiplying moldings, ribs, and decoration in their buildings. The structure of some late Gothic buildings is dematerialized into a dizzy fireworks of thin supports and writhing tracery. At the same time, the poets of the north delighted in making rules for poetry and in developing a rigid, poetic scholasticism. The ideal of the "Grands Rhétoriqueurs" in France and of the German "Meistersinger" was an ingenious multiplication of words. The result was poetry in a complicated style that was flat, didactic, and dull—bound down by rules, and smothered in allegory, personification, and verbal ingenuities. A sterile style and a more sterile logic, removed from the facts and experiences that give substance to thought, dominated the writing and teaching of scholastic nominalism in the north. Even music, which with the English composer Dunstable, and then with the Fleming Dufay, had moved toward a more varied and expressive style, became with Okeghem an art that at times meandered through endless complexities of style; Okeghem in fact wrote choral music in thirty-six parts. There was, also, through northern Europe in the fifteenth century, a strange growth of interest in the lachrymose and the macabre, as shown in the weeping Virgins and the vogue of the theme of the dance of death in both art and letters. Thus much of the thought of northern Europe in the fifteenth century is possessed with the melancholy idea that the world had grown old and stale! So the art, literature, and music of northern Europe, though still capable of producing great geniuses, do give the impression that they needed new leads in style. And certainly in art and letters Italy was, by 1500, ready to point out interesting new directions.

The genesis of the styles of the Early Renaissance in part is to be found first in a more secular attitude toward life and then in the discovery of new meanings in the art and letters of the classical world. The growth of towns and of the middle class which began in Italy as early as the tenth century, had, by the twelfth century, become a very marked feature of the society of northern Italy. The accumulation of wealth in the Italian cities and their very active civil life helped to bring a more worldly view of life. An old society that was agricultural, feudal, and ecclesiastical now had growing within it a new society that was urban, national, and secular in outlook. A new society, centered less on nobles and priests and more on bourgeois men of affairs, was coming into being. More than elsewhere in Latin Christendom, the center of civilization in Italy was moving from castle and abbey to the town. The positive and dynamic attitudes shown in business and in worldly activities came to be reflected in a new appreciation of ancient civilization, and then in a new style in arts and letters.

All this meant the gradual return to a more worldly focus in life, and so in art and letters. Man, rather than God, became for many thinkers the center of all things. And, for some, this life became an end in itself rather than a mere moment in a long adventure in eternity. There was, then, less need to go outside this world to acquire knowledge of the real. The distrust of medieval scholasticism and of the otherworldliness that lay back of it is clearly sounded by the Humanist Salutati, who, about 1390, declared in a letter to a nominalist of Padua, "The truth cannot be in all these distinctions; take away the sophistic dressing, and give us back a knowledge of reality"; and to another he wrote, "Do not believe that to avoid the sight of beautiful things, to shut one's self up in a cloister is the way of perfection. In striving and working, in caring for your family and friends, and your city, you cannot but follow the right way to please God." These new attitudes did not influence everyone, and even in many individual hearts and minds the old and the new lived side by side. So we find, as typical of the age, Lorenzo de' Medici writing both ribald drinking songs and poems of a mystical religious devotion to the saints. Likewise, the same painter would sometimes draw Bacchus in an exuberant mood, and at another time represent Mary swooning on the hill of Calvary.

The growing secular attitudes of Italian society led to a restudy of the classical past and, as early as the twelfth century, there is clear indication in the writings of students of Roman law that a fuller and more rounded understanding of Roman civilization was being achieved. This, in the end, helped to produce a new realization of the nature of Roman art and letters, together with a strong conviction that they were superior to anything then existing. Classical forms and classical stories had been used all during the Middle Ages, but in an external way, and without any real insight into their meaning, nor did the Middle Ages ever show a positive nostalgia for antiquity. So the Italian Renaissance did not discover classical art and letters—they had never been entirely lost or ignored—rather it came to believe that they represented a definitely superior civilization and that they were both beautiful and full of meaning.

The Middle Ages had regarded ancient civilization as immoral and inferior. They had, at the same time, studied the art and letters of antiquity for odds and ends they could use. Now the Renaissance looked at the ancients both for what they spoke and how they spoke it. Some medieval writers condemned all classical art and literature on the grounds of error and immorality. Even those who favored the study of classical literature did so only as a preparation for studying the Holy Scripture and the Christian writers. The classics were never supported either as the voice of a superior civilization or on the grounds of their beauty as literature. A poet like Catullus, whose matter is trivial and sometimes immoral, but whose style is exquisite, was all but lost during the Middle Ages; the Early Renaissance restored him to an eminence that would have amazed even Catullus and his contemporaries. Medieval writers used the Latin classics only for certain stories and ideas and, above all, as repositories of ethical principles and moral wisdom. Thus, to take a single example in the charming classical tale of Pyramus and Thisbe, medieval writers made the story into a religious allegory in which Pyramus is made to represent Christ, and Thisbe the human soul. In Italy, from the twelfth century on, the scales slowly fell from men's eyes, and they began to see Roman civilization plain. And they saw in the art and literature of ancient Rome a view of life that believed nature had equipped man for useful and interesting action in this world quite as much as for spiritual survival into a world to come.

The literature of the Italian fourteenth and fifteenth centuries is filled with ecstatic accounts of how the classical world was, bit by bit, being rediscovered and reappropriated. Something of the spirit of these two centuries lives in the account of Boccaccio's visit to Monte Cassino, that of Poggio to a monastery by Lake Constance, of Bruni's discovery of the glories of Greek literature, and of Brunelleschi's and Donatello's uncovering of the wonders of Roman architecture and sculpture during their stay in Rome. These artists and men of letters fell under a deep classical spell which, after 1500, passed on to the rest of Europe, a spell which, in some degree, is still with us. Unfortunately the men of the Early Renaissance also passed on the belief that Roman art and Latin letters were superior to the achievements of the Greeks in those fields. The great works of Greek art were far away and were almost inaccessible, and the Greek language, which remained a closed book even to Dante and to Petrarch, was difficult to master, whereas everyone of any education read and spoke Latin. The way these matters stood in the Early Renaissance, and the way they continued to stand, almost without exception into the eighteenth century, is shown by Petrarch's placing Cicero ahead of Plato in his "Triumph of Fame" and Alberti's conviction that Roman architecture was an improvement over Greek architecture. So, in the great classical period of European culture from Petrarch to Dr. Johnson it was, with few exceptions, Roman art and Latin literature rather than Greek art and Greek literature that were in the minds of the artists and writers.

By the fifteenth century, Italian men of art and letters reflect a new sense of the dignity of man. They presented this new view of man and of the universe not only in theoretical writings—above all in those of Alberti—but also in original works of art and literature. The harmony of man and the universe, they believed, could be presented in terms of mathematical ratios and of musical harmonies. Many of the thinkers of the Early Renaissance seem to have been possessed with the Pythagorean belief that all is numbers. Such ideas were derived partly from a revived interest in the writings of Plato and the Neo-Platonists, partly from a restudy of Pliny and Vitruvius on architecture, and partly from a reconsideration of the long poem of Horace that had come to be called the "Ars poetica." "Beauty," writes Alberti, "is the harmony of all the parts, in whatever subject, fitted together with such proportion and connection that nothing can be altered but for the worse." When Brunelleschi designed the nave of Santo Spirito, he made it just twice as high as it was wide, and with the ground story and the clerestory of equal height. Other buildings were designed with similar attention to ratios. Literature was not so ruled and measured until after 1500. But with the artists, proportion and mathematics became almost an obsession, which led Berenson to remark that the fifteenth-century Italian artist was often a man with a native gift for science who turned to architecture, painting, or sculpture for purposes of research. Certainly in some cases—one thinks especially of Uccello—the scientist seemed to have an upper hand over the artist.

At the heart of the Early Renaissance lay a new understanding of the dignity of man and the belief that he stood in the midst of a harmonious universe. This does not mean that the thought of Italy in the fifteenth century turned pagan. Indeed, the pagan side of the Humanism and culture of Early Renaissance Italy has been overemphasized. The thought of the time is less represented by sensuous worldlings like Laurentius Valla than by the Christian Humanists like Ficino. Pico della Mirandola's famous "Oration on the Dignity of Man" has been presented out of context. If Augustine and the medieval mystics and ascetics who followed him placed man "a little higher than the beasts," the Neo-Platonic Humanists—inside the same Christian framework— placed him "a little lower than the angels."

The Middle Ages had shown, in many of its works of philosophy, literature, and art, a veritable mania for order; yet it was an order that centered not in man and this world but in God and eternity. Such a search for order appears in typical works like *The City of God,* the *Divine Comedy,* and the thirteenth-century *Summas,* and in the plan and the scheme of decoration of the Gothic cathedral. The Early Renaissance was seeking for a different type of order, one that, while recognizing God, was centered on the harmonies to be found in this world. These thinkers seemed to wish to eternalize this world and the present, and to glorify God without belittling man. This accounts for their search for the perfect form of man, the perfect form of a work of art, and later the perfect form of a work of literature. Classical writers had regarded the circle as the symbol of unity and of perfection. This theory first appeared among the early Greek poets, and it goes on through Plato (especially in the *Timaeus*), Plotinus, and the Fathers of the Church, and down to some of the medieval theologians. Writers of the fifteenth century in Italy, deriving their ideas chiefly from the Neo-Platonists, gave the idea a new currency. For them, the circle was the symbol of a man-centered harmony that was an echo of a celestial harmony to which man should strive to accord himself.

According to Vitruvius the well-built man with arms outstretched and legs extended could be contained within a circle. So the perfect man, made in the image of God, was the microcosm in relation to God, and the universe the macrocosm. How could the relation of the divine and the human be better set forth than by building a church in a circular form? According to Alberti and others, a round church represented best the divine order of a universe that surrounded its supreme creation, man. This view of man and of the universe helps to explain why Brunelleschi, Donatello, Masaccio, and other artists of their age strove to impose on space a rational and integrated structure that would enable the artist to represent reality in a mode convincing to the eye and mind. At the same time, the writers were trying to place man and this world in a new ideal and harmonious cosmos of coherent moral and aesthetic values. The artists and writers of fifteenth-century Italy, while working with the technical facilities available and at the same time inventing new ones, shared many of the same ideas. Florence and the lesser centers of culture were small cities, where the intellectuals knew and influenced one another, exactly as did, later, Herder, Schiller, and Goethe in Weimar, or Hugo, Delacroix, and Berlioz in Paris. So there was in the air, especially in fifteenth-century Florence, this broad concept of a man-centered harmony that was a part of a harmony in the universe; its marks are evident in the art, literature, and music of the Early Renaissance.

The patrons of art, letters, and music in Italy during the fourteenth and fifteenth centuries were much the same as in the twelfth and thirteenth centuries: churchmen, town councils or local tyrants, landed aristocrats, and wealthy merchants and bankers. The type of patronage did not change greatly, but the cultural outlook of the patrons grew much more worldly. And the patrons wanted their more earthly interests in such subjects as classical history and mythology—and even their own portraits and the great events of their lives—set forth in painting and sculpture, and in prose and verse. The artist rose in social status during the fifteenth century. In the Middle Ages the master mason, who was also the architect, was often a man of wealth and influence; but writers were not greatly honored or rewarded; and painters, sculptors, and musicians were hardly ranked above carpenters or shoemakers. By the middle of the fifteenth century painting and sculpture were generally accepted as liberal arts. The idea had come to prevail that the practice of all the arts enriched and elevated not only the mind of the artist and writer, but also the minds of those he served to a point quite beyond the providing of material comforts or pleasures. Moreover, the artist must know mathematics; and he came to be considered as a thinker seeking laws. In all of this, the Humanist writers played a role by recalling that Pliny the Elder and other ancient writers had described the great honors paid in antiquity to leading artists, writers, and musicians. A symbol of this new status is shown in the fact that both Ghiberti and Brunelleschi held important positions in the government of Florence, that the leading artists, writers, and composers were entertained and supported by princes, and that Donatello was buried in the same vault with Cosimo de' Medici in San Lorenzo. After separating the fine arts from the manual arts, the writers then entered on extended debates as to the relative values of painting and sculpture. In the course of the fifteenth century, Italian artists and writers discussed matters of style more than these had been discussed earlier. Style came to be regarded as something created by the individual artist, writer, or composer devoted to the creation of beautiful things—creations interesting in themselves and not for some transcendental or symbolic reason. The artists, writers, and composers were aware, too, that they were creating for the art-conscious observer, reader, or listener for whom the arts were an intellectual diversion, an enhancement of life, and a stimulus to action.

Finally, the bold and brilliant innovators among the Italian artists and writers of the fourteenth and fifteenth centuries had a very prejudiced attitude toward the art and letters of the previous millennium. Medieval art and literature had, they declared, no style or a bad style. From the time of Petrarch on, scholars and artists were out in full cry against the feudal and scholastic literature, and the transcendental art of the Middle Ages. In their view, art, learning, and letters, had only begun to be revived, after nearly ten centuries of barbarism, with the writings of Petrarch and the art of Niccolò Pisano and Giotto. All this was elaborated and then repeated ad infinitum by a complacent chorus of writers down into the eighteenth century. It remained the stock-in-trade of criticism until the Romantic movement began seriously to modify it. The medieval artists and writers had not been as self-consciously aesthetic as their Renaissance successors, nor had they devoted themselves to extended critical writing. But medieval artists and writers, though they usually viewed life from a transcendental and otherworldly height, must have had a deep aesthetic sense. One has only to think of the *Book of Kells,* the Gregorian chants, the great Romanesque and Gothic churches, the poetry of the troubadours, and the *Divine Comedy* to realize how wrong were the Renaissance critics who found nothing but barbarism in the cultural achievements of the Middle Ages. An extraordinary sensitiveness to problems of style is evident in nearly every phase of medieval art and letters. Indeed, an absorption in stylistic problems was sometimes even a fault with the medieval artist. One thinks of the tracery of French Flamboyant Gothic windows, of the fan vaulting of English Perpendicular Gothic, of the hundreds of elaborate verse forms used by the troubadours, and the subtleties of the Italian writers of the *dolce stil nuovo.* Our medieval ancestors must have been profoundly conscious of problems of style in the arts. All that it is possible to say is that the styles of the Italian Renaissance were new and different. Culture was not dead before the days of Giotto and Petrarch, but the Italians liked to think it was; and so they proclaimed it to the world, and from Italy these false historical notions spread throughout Europe. The Italian innovators of the Renaissance had enough achievements to their credit; it was shabby of them to deny culture to their medieval forebears on whose shoulders they were standing.

2. Art

Vasari regarded Niccolò Pisano (d. 1287?) as a great innovator in style, as the father of Renaissance art, indeed nearly as important in sculpture as Giotto was soon to be in painting. While this view is no longer held, there is a new sculptural style foreshadowed in some of Niccolò Pisano's work. The design of his famous pulpit in the Baptistery of Pisa and the reliefs which surrounded its upper part are the first important combination of Gothic realism and classical inspiration in art. This imitation of classical models was already evident in southern Italy, the home of the earliest school of Italian vernacular poetry, in the first half of the thirteenth century. Here, a few surviving sculptures show a somewhat crude attempt to adopt the style of ancient Roman work. There is a tradition that Niccolò Pisano grew up in the South of Italy, and he may have been influenced, as a young man, by this current. Near at hand, as he was working in Pisa, were a number of Roman sarcophagi from which he borrowed details. To choose one panel of his Pisa pulpit, that of the Nativity, we see the heads of the horses at the left brilliantly depicted in a realistic Gothic fashion. Everything about these spirited beasts speaks of surprise: the curve of their necks, their bulging eyes, and their extended nostrils as they sniff the air. The human figures, on the other hand, have the thick-shouldered bodies, the poses, the facial types, the drapery, and the hair of Roman sculptures. Here, as in the rest of these sculptures, is a clear fusion of vivid Gothic realism with a deliberate and self-conscious imitation of classical models. Much of the later work of Niccolò Pisano lapsed back into the prevailing Gothic style, as did that of most of the next century of Italian sculpture; and, just as with the style of painting begun by Giotto, the innovations so interestingly begun were not taken up again before the early fifteenth century. So Niccolò Pisano's early work was less of an influence than a promise, and a prophecy of the achievement of Ghiberti and Donatello, the true founders of modern sculpture.

There has never been, since his own time, any serious question of the importance of Giotto (d. 1336) as the great innovator in style in painting. His older contemporary and friend Dante said, "First there was Cimabue, now Giotto is all the rage." Boccaccio praised Giotto in the *Decameron* (VI, 5); Ghiberti hailed him as "the discoverer of so much doctrine which has been buried for six hundred years; he led art to the greatest perfection," and the chronicler Villani declared, "Giotto can only be compared with the illustrious painters of antiquity, but he surpassed them in skill and genius; his pictures seem to live and breathe." Comments of this type could easily be multiplied into a chorus. The Byzantine style had, in painting and mosaics, preserved a few of the stylistic discoveries of the ancient Greek painters—especially in composition; in the use of modeling, that is, changing tones on faces and draperies; and in the use of foreshortening in drawing.

Additions to the prevailing Byzantine style were already evident in the thirteenth century in the large frescoes and mosaics of Cimabue of Florence, and Cavallini and Torriti of Rome. Here there were both a monumental style of wall decoration, with large majestic figures, and some observation of nature. But the great qualities of Giotto's style seem to have been mostly of his own invention. His aim was not to create in the traditional medieval style some contemplative picture that would carry the mind out of this world into an illimitable mood of otherworldliness, but to give the spectator the sense that he was actually seeing some sacred scene. Hence, his dramatic groupings and his marvelously telling postures and gestures with enough modeling and foreshortening to suggest some illusion of depth. The designing of Giotto's figures seems to indicate that the painter must have tried to think how a person would stand, and what he would do with his shoulders, head, and arms under some given circumstances.

The actors in Giotto's scenes bear no abstract symbolism, nor are they transcendental embodiments of the divine. They are, on the contrary, very human; and the spectator feels at once their joy or sorrow, their hope or despair. The stylized faces of Byzantine painting pale in comparison with the smiling or disapproving mouth or the tearful eye in a Giotto picture. Still more in contrast with the past are Giotto's vivid postures and gestures. The painter's desire to make a story from the Bible or from the life of a saint live before the beholder derives in part from the popular preaching of the friars, especially of the Franciscans, who were striving to humanize the holy stories and make them real to the masses. The birds to which St. Francis preached, both in actuality and in Giotto's portrayal, were real birds that hopped and chirped—not the mystical symbols of the Holy Ghost, or like the apocalyptic eagle of St. John.

Unlike the sculptors and architects, Giotto had no great classical models to which he could turn; and his figures lack the grace that a study of Roman sculpture helped later to bring into painting, but they are marvelously expressive. He combined his figures in large compositions that show the highest skill in grouping; in a Giotto picture everything is ingeniously combined, nothing is wasted, and everything counts. The dramatic forcefulness which Giotto achieved was aided by the fresco technique in which most of his painting was done. His vast scenes were designed for the interiors of the huge barnlike Italian Gothic churches with their slits for windows and their great expanses of bare walls. Here the paintings had to be both on a large scale and in a style that would carry at a distance. Moreover, the pictures had to be painted in a broad and rapid manner because the fresco medium (of water color on wet plaster) did not allow for repainting, or even the elaboration of small details.

The painters who followed Giotto lacked his genius—they did not possess his incisiveness, his ability to compose, and his dramatic force. They went in for rich details, and overloaded their pictures with charming non-essentials. Cennino, in his famous *Craftsman's Handbook* (early fifteenth century), the only important theoretical treatise of the time, recommended copying from nature as the most perfect guide, though he also recommended the study of good masters. But for a century Italian painters looked more to Giotto and to other earlier painters than to nature. So while it is true, as Poliziano later wrote of Giotto, "Lo, I am he by whom painting was restored to life," no great steps in advance of Giotto's style were taken until the time of Masaccio in the early fifteenth century. Thus, Niccolò Pisano and Giotto were both great innovators in style, but they had few worthy successors until a number of generations after their time. At the opening of the fifteenth century, Italian architecture, painting, and sculpture were still Gothic. But Jacopo della Quercia (d. 1438) and Ghiberti (d. 1455) were already at work in a manner that was soon to mark a great change in sculptural style. In the year 1400, Brunelleschi was twenty-three years old, Ghiberti was twenty-two, and Donatello was but a boy of fourteen. Masaccio was born the next year (1401), and within the following half-century these men revolutionized artistic styles not only for Italy but ultimately for the whole of Europe.

Ghiberti, like many artists of the fifteenth century in Italy, was trained as a goldsmith and later, besides filling commissions in sculpture, became a consultant for architectural work, a fresco painter, and a designer of stained glass windows. He tells us in his rambling *Commentaries* how he achieved his style as a sculptor: "I sought to investigate the way nature functions in art; how images come to the eye. I strove to imitate nature as closely as I could, and with all the perspective I could produce." But he also tells us how carefully he studied the style of Roman figures and reliefs, and he speaks of one Roman sculpture: "Our tongues cannot express the skill, the art, the mastery with which it was done." In his principal works, the two sets of bronze doors for the Baptistery at Florence, Ghiberti set models that deeply affected the style of both sculpture and painting. In the first set of doors he made, the interest centers in the grace and naturalness of the compositions, which are set against flat backgrounds, and the brilliant and realistic modeling of the individual figures. These are partly in a late Gothic and partly in a Roman style; their beauty lies in Ghiberti's skill in giving energy and life to figures and groups that are so small. In the scenes from the Old Testament on the final set of doors he made for the Baptistery, Ghiberti carries much further his skill in composition and in modeling separate figures, and he adds a brilliant use of perspective in backgrounds of landscape and architecture. And to heighten the sense of depth, he uses a series of planes gradually diminishing in relief. It is, of course, easier for the sculptor than for the painter to obtain a three-dimensional effect—what Berenson has called "tactile values" and Roger Fry "plasticity"—because in sculpture the figures, even in a relief, stand in real space and real light. But by the greatest skill in modeling and grouping his figures, and in the handling of his backgrounds in his later works, Ghiberti achieved effects of depth and space that fascinated sculptors and painters, and deeply affected the style of both.

While Ghiberti was turning sculpture both toward classical grace and toward a style of three-dimensional representation, Brunelleschi was creating a new architectural style, Donatello a more varied and virile style of sculpture, and young Masaccio was inventing a new manner of painting. We know something of how these men were trained. Inside the old guild system a youth was apprenticed to an artist-craftsman, who as a guild master ran a workshop, or *bottega,* where various types of commissions were executed. There were probably twenty or more of these *bottegas* in Florence in the first half of the fifteenth century. Here a boy of ten or twelve would be taught to pound gold or silver into leaf, or grind colors, or do other preparatory work for the skilled workers and the master. The boy would also be taught to draw and to model in clay. As he grew older the apprentice would be allowed to prepare a wooden panel for a painting, transfer the master's preliminary drawing to a panel, or even to paint in some of the minor figures; or to help in a carving, or in the making of a jewel-set brooch. In this way, craftsmanship and style were transmitted. A youth so trained knew something of both painting and sculpture, and later he might make his career primarily as a goldsmith, a sculptor, a painter, or even as an architect. But nearly always, the artist knew something of several arts, and he often practiced several. By the opening of the fifteenth century artists were making innumerable sketches from nature or from other works of art, and from these sketches they later drew ideas for paintings, sculptures, and buildings, for which in turn new drawings were made. Some of these drawings have been preserved and are of great interest in showing how an idea grew in the artist's mind; indeed, these sketches are often of greater interest to the student of style than are the finished products of the artists.

Brunelleschi (d. 1446), who as a sculptor had competed unsuccessfully with Ghiberti for the right to make doors for the Baptistery at Florence, lived to be the first great innovator in architectural style. His architecture grew out of a careful study and re-estimate of Roman architecture. Vasari and, earlier, his biographer, Manetti, tell of his study of ancient monuments in Rome; says Manetti:

He observed closely the supports and thrusts of the buildings, then forms, arches, and inventions, according to the function they had to serve, as, also, their ornamental detail. In these he saw wonders and beauties. He proposed to rediscover the excellent and highly ingenious building methods of the ancients and their harmonious proportions, and where such proportions could be used with ease and economy. He took notes; he studied the methods of centering the vaults and also where one could do without them to save money, and what method one would have to follow. With Donatello, they made rough drawings of almost all the buildings in Rome and in many places in the environs, with the measurements of the width, length, and height. In many places, they had excavations done in order to see the joinings of the parts of the buildings. From these observations he began to distinguish the characteristics of each style, such as Ionic, Doric, Tuscan, Corinthian, and Attic, and he used these styles as one may still see in his buildings.

The buildings Brunelleschi designed show interesting and original handling of Roman, Early Christian, Byzantine, Romanesque, and Gothic styles. The huge dome he built on the Cathedral of Florence, and which he constructed ingeniously, without centering, is the one great piece of structural designing Brunelleschi did. And the method of construction is adapted from that used on the nearby Romanesque Baptistery. In designing the Pazzi Chapel, he used Roman panels, pilasters, and moldings in a decorative but unstructural manner, as he saw them used on the Romanesque Baptistery of Florence and on certain ancient Roman buildings. He combined these, and achieved a small gem of architecture utterly unlike anything that had preceded it. His decoration is used entirely for itself, and is apart from any symbolism. The effect of the interior of the Pazzi Chapel is light and graceful, though unlike the Gothic interiors it has no high windows or slender piers. Instead, the whole area, in the form of a Greek cross surmounted by a low dome built on pendentives, is open. The white side walls are divided by gray stone pilasters, which, though they have no function in the support of the building, divide the wall surfaces with grace and elegance. This Pazzi Chapel of 1430, like the cathedral dome, is one of the most original works in the whole history of architecture. Here, as in his later designs for the basilica-like churches of San Lorenzo and Santo Spirito in Florence, Brunelleschi used the diameter of a column as the unit of measurement and proportion, and then handled the width and height of the nave and side aisles in a ratio of two to one, a careful calculation of proportions he got from the direct study of Roman buildings.

Brunelleschi was the first to work out mathematically the laws of linear perspective by which objects diminish in size as they recede into the background. In him the artist and the scientist were about equally proportioned. Brunelleschi never literally copied a Roman model, but like his contemporaries, Ghiberti and Donatello, and like Petrarch, Boccaccio, and their literary successors, he penetrated the classic style with such insight that he was able to re-create this style in a manner that is both fresh and original. He helped to set the pattern for the training of later architects in Italy, and then throughout Europe; young architects went to Rome to study and measure Roman buildings and, after Brunelleschi's time, also to study and measure the great buildings of the Italian Renaissance architects. Brunelleschi's architectural style, which employed classical proportions, used classical columns, pilasters, and round arches, and many elements of classical ornamentation such as door and window frames, and moldings. So began a type of architectural style that, with many modifications, lasted for centuries.

Donatello (d. 1466), though influenced in his sculptural style by the work of Jacopo della Quercia and Ghiberti, pushed his accomplishment beyond the range of either. Like these older masters, he too combined the realism of Gothic sculpture with a deliberate and self-conscious borrowing of stylistic devices from surviving Roman sculpture. Much of the Gothic is still evident in the harsh and angular postures of some of Donatello's figures; and in the wrinkles, protruding bones, muscles, and veins, which are ruthlessly set forth. The study of ancient sculpture, however, restrained his taste for vivid realism and curbed his high-strung energy and his emotionality. Also, it turned his attention to the study of the nude. Donatello is the first artist, in either sculpture or painting, to free the human body from its medieval bonds, to realize fully its beauty as a thing in itself, and to show clearly its value as a means of artistic expression. Likewise, he discovered the use of sculpture quite independent of architecture. His youthful "David" is the first large nude bronze sculpture made since antiquity, and certainly one of the first free-standing figures. Also, among Donatello's firsts is his "Gattamelata" at Padua, the earliest life-size equestrian statue of the Renaissance. In both the beautiful body of the young David, and in the hard and powerful figure and horse of the "Gattamelata" the classic influence is very marked.

The range of Donatello's style is very great, as are also the vitality of his figures and their warm human quality. No wonder Vasari said of his "St. George": "Life seems to move within the stone." Everything he did was marked by a close and firsthand study of nature, and by an amazing technical skill that could—in both stone and bronze—produce the softness of the flesh of children, the fine veils of headdresses, and the contrasting light and shade in the drapery of figures, especially of those in motion. As in the case of his less gifted contemporary Ghiberti, Donatello was developing new technical means in composition, in perspective, and in modeling before such discoveries in painting—discoveries from which both later sculptors and painters could borrow.

The revolution in styles accomplished in architecture by Brunelleschi and in sculpture by Ghiberti and Donatello was achieved in painting by their younger contemporary, Masaccio (d. 1428). At the end of the fourteenth and the beginning of the fifteenth century, several Florentine painters, including Masolino, had started experimentation toward producing a greater sense of three-dimensional reality in their painting. What they were feeling for in style was accomplished—so rapidly that it seemed miraculous—by a young man who died at the age of twenty-seven. In a series of frescoes, among the most notable of which are the "Adam and Eve" and "The Tribute Money" in the Brancacci Chapel of the Church of the Carmine in Florence, Masaccio achieved a great transformation in style. Inspired probably by Roman sculpture and by the fresco paintings of Giotto, he conceived of his pictures in terms of a few large figures. These were drawn with the greatest skill. Even more noteworthy innovations were the idea of lighting the whole picture from a single source of light, the use of both linear and atmospheric perspective, and the avoidance of sharp lines in the coloring, one color merging into the next. As a result, Masaccio's paintings give a sense of three dimensions on a flat wall, unlike those of any earlier painter. His figures have a great solidity; we sense their bodily structure of bone, muscle, and flesh, and they press on the ground. From earlier painters, Masaccio had learned the value of significant postures and gestures. All these discoveries are used with dramatic effectiveness in his "Expulsion of Adam and Eve." As they leave Eden, Adam, with his head lowered, shows in his whole posture hopelessness and defeat, while Eve raises her head and cries out against fate. The use of the nude here as a means of expression is even more vivid than its use by Donatello: no secondary details are introduced; the whole story is told by the two nudes. There were available for Masaccio no classical models in painting as there were Roman models in architecture and sculpture. This makes his accomplishment one of the most amazing in history. Vasari summed up his estimate of the style of Masaccio by the remark, "He recognized that painting is naught but the imitation of things as they are." Hitherto, painters were content to make references to objects and their spatial relations with only scattered attempts to model, to foreshorten, to use perspective, and to paint in shadows. No one before Masaccio had brought all these scattered devices into an organic and unified system. No wonder the Brancacci Chapel became for several generations the school for Italian painters. The advances in style made by Masaccio were not fully assimilated until the time of Leonardo da Vinci at the end of the fifteenth century; and when their potentialities were grasped painting moved from the style of the Early to that of the High Renaissance.

The study of artistic style in the fifteenth century, both in what the architects, sculptors, and painters were accomplishing and in what they desired to achieve, is greatly aided by the treatises of Leon Batista Alberti (d. 1472), the first important theoretic works on art since antiquity. The dating of Alberti's writings is uncertain, but apparently *On Painting* was written about 1436, *On Architecture* about 1450, and the last, *On Sculpture,* around 1464. All of Alberti's ideas on the fine arts are presented in terms of human reason and human activities with scarcely a trace of the theological preconceptions that dominated the thought of medieval writers. In painting and sculpture, Alberti advises the close study of nature and beyond this the selection of the most beautiful details in nature so as to form a work of art that approaches an ideal beauty. The technical equipment of the painter and sculptor should enable him to produce a three-dimensional effect. He writes, "The business of the painter is this: to draw with lines and dye with colors, on whatever panel or wall is given, the visible surface of any body, so that bodies seem to be in relief," and again, he remarks, "I shall praise those faces which seem to project out of the picture as though they were sculptured, and I shall censure those faces in which I see no art but that of an outline." Alberti warns the painter and the sculptor to avoid excess of ornament and not to crowd his paintings or reliefs with too many figures lest the plastic value of some figures be lost. Very neatly he describes his formula for perspective, by declaring, "Painting is nothing else but a cross section of a visual pyramid upon a certain surface, artificially represented with lines and colors at a given distance, with a central point of view established, and lights arranged."

Alberti was most interested in architecture, and his treatise on this subject is his most extended work. Poggio had sent him one of the few surviving copies of Vitruvius' *On Architecture*. This was the work of a mediocre Roman architect of the first century A.D. which had happened to survive. Most of its contents is concerned with building materials and practical methods of construction, but parts are devoted to aesthetic matters pertaining to the design of buildings. Some later writers on architecture looked on Vitruvius—as they had looked on Aristotle's *Poetics*—as having the validity of an infallible papal pronouncement; Alberti follows Vitruvius with great respect, but not slavishly. Alberti's own treatise has a wide range: it discusses the civic uses of architecture in both war and peace, factors to be considered in choosing a site, methods of drawing (including recipes for drawing in linear perspective), and principles of designing—both a whole town, and a single building. Beauty in architecture lies in harmonious proportion of its parts, the key to which lies in Pythagoras' system of musical harmony, and in ornament. The chief element of embellishment is the column. This idea of ornament Alberti got not from Greek but from Roman architecture, which was a wall architecture to which Greek columns (and pilasters) were added for decoration. Alberti took from Vitruvius—and from Roman buildings he had seen—the proper proportional relation of base, column, and capital for the Doric, Ionic, and Corinthian orders so as to make a canon of all architectural form. Every building must have a double aim: *commoditas* ("utility") and *voluptas* ("beauty"). In the basic design of a building, everything should be so planned that nothing could be added or removed without destroying the harmony of the whole. How utterly different from the ideas of a Gothic architect, where new parts could be added and old ones modified without destroying the beauty of the building! Alberti, like other writers of his time, praises the circle as the most perfect form, and as a favorite of nature because so many things in nature are round. All through the work, he alternates between wide-ranging aesthetic theorizing and detailed directions about building methods. So, in writing on architecture, Alberti combines aesthetics, philosophy, engineering, mathematics, and archeology.

Alberti, as a practicing architect, was a more self-conscious classicist and a man more learned in the study of antiquity than his much older contemporary, Brunelleschi. He knew the work of Brunelleschi and that of a number of other architects who were designing palaces with heavy Roman cornices, and courtyards with graceful arches borne on rows of columns. In the front that he planned for the Dominican Church of Santa Maria Novella in Florence, Alberti applied classical pilasters to define units of the façade, and, to tie fronts of the two side aisles to the higher nave in the center, he devised volutes that were endlessly copied by later architects. In churches at Mantua and Rimini, he freely used the design of a Roman triumphal arch and other Roman forms. For the Rucellai Palace in Florence, Alberti had no Roman model; instead, with great ingenuity, he initiated a new type of palace exterior by covering the façade with Roman pilasters and entablatures inspired by the outside of the Colosseum. He was an architect in the modern sense, not a medieval master mason; he was an artist who designed buildings for others to execute. Alberti's architectural style—like that of all fifteenth-century Italian architecture, with the notable exception of Brunelleschi's Dome—was primarily a decorative style where classical elements, taken from Roman ruins or from Vitruvius, supplanted Gothic types of decoration. Instead of Gothic battlements, buildings were now crowned with heavy classical cornices, designed from fragments of Roman temple cornices, with dentil, bead-and-reel, and egg-and-dart moldings. Round arches took the place of Gothic pointed ones; and Roman columns and pilasters were freely used. Above all, the elements of design and decoration in exteriors and interiors became matching and symmetrical; regular rhythms controlled all the designing, and the picturesque irregularities of Gothic were ruled out. The lessons that Italian architects learned from the study of Roman architecture were passed on not only to later generations in Italy but, after 1500, to the whole of Europe.

The advances in the style of painting inaugurated by Masaccio were continued during the fifteenth century, chiefly by Florentine painters. Pollaiuolo (d. 1498) was an intense student of anatomy, and in his painting and engraving he showed how to present nudes in movement. Uccello (d. 1475), like a modern Cubist painter, reduced the world to volumes and values, among which he tried to fix relations. His paintings give the impression of an artist searching passionately for laws and techniques in painting. Mantegna (d. 1506), who spent most of his life in his native Padua, learned as a youth to draw from ancient marbles in the studio of the artist and archeologist, Squarcione. He was, likewise, influenced by the work of Donatello, Filippo Lippi, and Uccello which he saw in Padua. Later in life, Mantegna fell under the influence of the great Venetian colorist, Giovanni Bellini, whose sister he married. No fifteenth-century artist was more Roman than Mantegna; he drew and painted in a solid, hard style which caught the harsh simplicity and austere grandeur of ancient Rome. Not only were his figures of a Roman stolidity but he loved to fill his backgrounds with Roman buildings and trappings. His "Triumph of Caesar," which Charles I of England brought to Hampton Court, is now a sadly repainted wreck. But it is as Roman as the Colosseum. Soldier trumpeters are followed by musicians playing the lyre and tambourine; then come the gods of the vanquished country, borne on chariots. Next follow battering-rams and other instruments of war, and captured trophies and emblems; then young priests bearing sacred treasures from the Roman temples, and sacrificial beasts, prisoners of war, and elephants; and finally Julius Caesar, the conquering hero, before whom a youth bears the device "Veni, vidi, vici." Parts of this vast panorama of Mantegna resemble in mood the series of *Triumphs* of Petrarch which, like it, glorify Roman antiquity. To see this huge work of Mantegna one would never guess that the Middle Ages had ever existed. Rome had indeed returned.

Piero della Francesca (d. 1492) added new elements to the style of painting by showing improved methods of using light to model his figures, and so to create the illusion of depth. He was also aware of how light modifies color. The technical problems of painting fascinated him, and he wrote an elaborate treatise on perspective. In a series of frescoes in Arezzo, he used a large and very effective style of space composition with figures of a monumental gravity and god-like nobility and dignity. In his handling of light and shadow (including a night scene) and in his style of space composition, he clearly foreshadows the High Renaissance style of Leonardo da Vinci and Raphael. At the same time, in Venice, Giovanni Bellini (d. 1516) was pushing beyond a linear vision to one of color, and he achieved a coloring with the purely emotional quality of music—a wonderful addition to the range of the painter which was passed on to the painters of the High Renaissance.

Thus two centuries of searching for new styles in the fine arts had by the close of the fifteenth century resulted in remarkable achievements in sculpture, painting, and architecture. And all this experimentation became the birthright of the Italian artists of the new generation of Leonardo da Vinci, Bramante, and Michelangelo.

3. Literature

One of the outstanding features of Renaissance literature, first in Italy, and, later, throughout western Europe, was its self-conscious emphasis on form and style. The success of the medieval epics and chivalric romances had been due to the interest of their plots rather than to their form. Much of medieval literature, like Gothic art, lacked a tightly integrated structure. At the same time, medieval writers, though they cited Cicero, Virgil, Ovid, and other classical Latin writers—and borrowed from them—usually did not understand the mentality of their models and almost universally failed to grasp their style. The Italians, beginning clearly with Petrarch and Boccaccio in the fourteenth century, began the use of the ancient writers in a new way; they tried to meet them on their own ground, both in their Latin and in their vernacular writings, to borrow their ideas, their stories, their figures of speech, and their general style, and to re-create their poetic and prose types.

With the return of secular attitudes, first clearly shown in the Latin verses of the Goliards, in the vernacular lyrics of the southern French troubadours and their successors, and in the racy tales of the authors of the *fabliaux,* writers prepared to approach in a new way the culture of classical antiquity. But it was in the writings of the Italian students of Roman law, beginning in the twelfth century, that the full meaning of Roman civilization was first clearly grasped. Here ancient civilization began to seem less a collection of books to be piously preserved from the past than a model for building a new and better civilization. All this led to a more penetrating investigation and analysis of ancient literature and art.

The results of this on Italian writers are clearly evident from the early fourteenth century. In 1314, a play, the *Eccerinis* of Mussato, furnishes a clear example for the direction in which literary taste is moving. The plot, which concerns a brutal adventurer who threatened Padua in the thirteenth century, is handled on the model of a tragedy of Seneca with five acts, and dialogue and choruses in verse. Already, what was later called Petrarchianism was under way, and Italian writers were seeking the ordered plan, the integrated structure, the symmetry, and the lofty style of Roman literature. They were coming to believe that there were locked up in classical letters the secrets of a great style that could be recaptured.

Here is the beginning of the long search of Italian writers for literary canons that would provide formal excellence in structure and style, and their efforts to reduce matters of both artistic and literary style to formulas which they believed would be certain to create a classical type of beauty. As time went on, the Italian critics, and their followers beyond the Alps, decided that an epic must begin in the middle of its plot, it must contain supernatural elements, and must end with the hero a victor. A play must have five acts and follow certain rules of plot structure; and similar laws were set down for other literary genres. What, in the end, this was to mean for the literature and art of Europe can be realized by comparing the early sixteenth-century comedies of Ariosto and Machiavelli with the rude and sprawling buffooneries of the English moralities or of the French dramatic interludes of about 1500; or by comparing a large, crowded and cluttered Gothic tapestry with the grand style of Raphael's "School of Athens." The Italian writers, like the artists, came to handle their classical enthusiasms with great creativeness, and they rarely confined themselves to mere imitation. Earlier, in the thirteenth century, the South Italian poets had invented the sonnet, a genre unknown to the ancients. They soon gave it such a polish that the form seemed to be the creation of a Horace, exactly as, later, Alberti wrote a play that passed for a work of Terence and Michelangelo carved a sculpture that passed as an ancient work. Besides the sonnet, the Italians created the *novella,* the *ottava rima* (an eight-line stanza) form, the pastoral romance and the romantic epic; and they perfected them to such a degree that the rest of Europe accepted them as classic. Typical of the Italian influence in both European letters and art is the influence of Italian storytellers. Spanish, French, English, and German writers drew hundreds of plots from Italian tales. Yet the Italians never invented a Gargantua, a Dr. Faustus, a Hamlet, or a Don Quixote. Rabelais, Montaigne, Shakespeare, Cervantes, Racine, Goethe, and a great many other writers were deeply in debt to Italian literature, but they produced utterly original work exactly as the Italian writers and artists; although they were under the spell of a glorious classical past, they ended by producing something quite different from their classical models.

The first great figure of Italian Renaissance letters, called by some historians "the first modern man," is Petrarch (d. 1374). Italian literature, which hardly existed before 1200—Latin sufficing for all types of writing in prose and poetry—had suddenly developed in the thirteenth century and, at the opening of the fourteenth century, had already produced its supreme masterpiece, *The Divine Comedy,* a development even more sudden than the appearance of "Sumer Is Icumen In" in music and Van Eyck's Ghent altarpiece in painting. Petrarch, who belonged to the next generation after Dante, was born in exile and lived in many places in northern Italy and southern France. This detached him from any homeland and from all civic responsibilities; he said of himself, "I am a pilgrim everywhere." Indeed, though he loved Italy, he never had any fatherland but the dreamland of antiquity. He accepted Christianity, but disliked the scholasticism and science of the universities; and he avoided the attraction of Dante, whose work seemed to be lacking in classical qualities. One can feel in his letters the long and deliberate attempt to pull himself out of the physical and mental world about him so as to live imaginatively in Roman antiquity. Petrarch's coronation as poet laureate on the Capitoline in Rome (1341) made him king of a new world he was helping to bring into being, a poetic kingdom on whose map the great features were Parnassus, Olympus, and the ancient City of the Seven Hills. The laws of his new kingdom and of its culture should come not only from Christianity, but also from the great heroes, writers, and artists of antiquity. Classical ways of feeling, thinking, and writing cast a deep spell upon Petrarch. Above all, he loved the polish, elegance, and perfection of form of Virgil and Horace; and he detested the un-Roman Latin of the Middle Ages and everything that had been written in it. Petrarch saw clearly the great gap between antiquity and his own times; and he strove to revive classical civilization and letters rather than merely to use bits of them in terms of contemporary culture as they had been employed by medieval writers. Petrarch helped to spread the idea that medieval civilization and its literature were barbarous and that great but neglected treasures of wisdom and beauty were to be found in classical Latin letters.

Classical culture was, to Petrarch, the model by which to judge all civilizations, and the classical-minded scholar and poet is the apostle and priest of this culture. Only under such leadership could humanity be led away from the arid scholastic rationalizing and the cultural degradation into which it had fallen since the barbarian migrations, the beginning of what Rabelais later called "the Gothic night." Locked up in the Latin classics was a magnificent cultural treasure. This attitude, which Petrarch transmitted to his followers, accounts for the passionate search for forgotten Latin books that led to the ransacking of old libraries from one end of Europe to the other. So great was Petrarch's enthusiasm for the classics, and so persuasive was his writing, that he set Italy afire for classical studies.

The style of Petrarch's writing in both Latin and the vernacular is often closely modeled on classical works. His leading Latin work, the unfinished epic, *Africa,* on Scipio Africanus and the Second Punic War, is a failure, as was later to be Ronsard's *Françiade,* chiefly because both poets tried to match the *Aeneid* incident by incident. The nearly four hundred vernacular poems of Petrarch, which he pretended to despise, but which he never ceased to polish and to circulate, show clearly his importance as the initiator of Italian and European Renaissance litera- ture. The grammar of love in his poems, most of which celebrate his de- votion to Laura, he took from the troubadours and from the masters of the thirteenth-century Italian *dolce stil nuovo.* He is, though, much more earthly and more concrete in his treatment of love than were Dante and the earlier Italian poets, and he had a more marked ability to analyze his own emotions. His Italian, though basically Tuscan, has lost all trace of dialect, and this later helped set a standard of usage in Italy. To these earlier literary currents Petrarch added stories, figures of speech, and a love of perfection of form based on his re-estimation of the work of Virgil, Horace, Ovid, and other Latin poets. The content of his poems is often less notable than the form; but he loves formal beauty and reverences words, and he has a profound feeling for mellifluous cadences, and for measure and restraint.

The verbal music of Petrarch's verses can only be suggested in transla- tion, but two sonnets will at least suggest his style.

> Oft as in pensive mood I sit and write,
> 'Mid plaint of birds and whisp'ring leafy trees,
> Where betwixt flowery banks and river bright
> Laughs back in ripples at the ruffling breeze,
> She whom heaven hath stolen from my sight,
> Whose face though mortal eye no longer sees
> Earth cannot hide, in pity of my plight

Rebukes my grief with words more sweet than these—
Celestial words not breathed by mortal breath:
"Ah why consume thy strength ere yet 'tis night
In barren tears and tempest of fierce sighs?
Weep not for me, for by the boon of death
My days were made immortal, and mine eyes,
Closing, were opened on eternal light."

The nightingale that so forlornly weeps
　　Perchance his little ones or his dear mate,
Whose fiery, tender song insatiate
With sweetness fills the air, his vigil keeps
All night with me, and never tires nor sleeps,
　　Reminding me of my unhappy fate.
　　For I, oh foolish, know it now too late,
Death the divinest blooms most quickly reaps.
How blind is he who thinks to stand secure!
　　Meseemed those fair lamps, than the sun more bright,
　　Could ne'er be quenched, and leave us plunged in night.
Now do I know my cruel destiny
　　Would have me learn in tears and agony,
　　Nought that delighteth may on earth endure.

His weaknesses lie in a taste for conceits—Laura becomes, by plays on
words, the air (*l'aura*), the laurel (*lauro*), the laurel wreath (*laurea*),
and gold (*l'oro*)—in occasional conventionalities of mood, and in a sort
of smugness. This weakness was pointed out by Shelley when he remarked that some of Petrarch's poems "begin with a sob, but end with a
simper." A life of dreams, of ecstasy, and of poetic melancholy takes the
place of the world of reality. Everything is aesthetic feeling. This self-
conscious pursuit of art for art's sake, and an overstraining for perfection
of form in writing, runs the danger of emptying a work of either literature or art of all substance. All the lover's transports are analyzed with a
fullness unmatched before in any work of vernacular literature. No hap-
pening or idea that touches his love is too slight for the poet's attention.
Every detail is explored: for example, the poet steals Laura's glove, is
made to give it up, and then is sorry he gave it back; this involves the
writing of three sonnets. At times he overuses stock metaphors as "teeth
like pearls," "hair like gold," and "lips like roses." He loves to exploit a
metaphor such as the comparison of love to a storm at sea, to a burning
fire, or to a petrifying cold. Later the Mannerist poets—Marino, Gón-

gora, Donne, and their followers—and some of the French Précieux poets carried this Petrarchian exploration of metaphors far beyond the limits set by Petrarch. Other writers, as Berni, Ben Jonson, and Malherbe, liked to parody such excesses, and drove most of them out of usage by the middle of the seventeenth century. The Romantic poets, especially those of Germany and England, revived some of the Petrarchian literary usages in the eighteenth and nineteenth centuries and rehabilitated his reputation.

For good or ill, few lyric poets have ever had so great an influence as Petrarch; his verses, in the fifteenth and sixteenth centuries, set a pattern; poets borrowed from him—his vocabulary, his figures of speech, and his methods of analyzing emotions. They loved his brilliant virtuosity, his elegance, and his perfection of form. Boscán in Spain, Wyatt and Surrey, Sidney and Spenser in England, the poets of the Pléiade in France, and Opitz in Germany all stand in Petrarch's shadow. Petrarch's place in the history of literary style lies in his emphasis on the idea that formal perfection in literature is of great value in and for itself, that no truth or insight can be dissociated from the artistic perfection of its expression, and that the best guide for the writer is the study of classical literature. In the creation of a poetry that embodies these ideas, Petrarch is one of the most important innovators in the history of European letters.

Petrarch's passionate love of classical letters was shared by his devoted friend and disciple, Boccaccio (d. 1375), who continued Petrarch's search for manuscripts of ancient Latin authors, and added something not possessed by either Dante or Petrarch—a knowledge of Greek. Both in his vernacular prose and poetry, and in the scholarly Latin writings which occupied the later part of his life, Boccaccio made new discoveries in style which carried him into fields quite beyond those known to Petrarch. As a humanist, Boccaccio wrote, in Latin, some excellent treatises on classical mythology, history, and geography, most notable of which was his encyclopedic *Genealogy of the Pagan Gods.* These Latin works, together with a number of ancient writers as Martial, Tacitus, and Ausonius, whom he unearthed and put again into circulation, dispensed materials for scholars, artists, and musicians. Indeed, Boccaccio did even more than Petrarch in furthering the craze for the search for lost Roman writers who were "lost" only in the sense that a few copies of their works had survived, hardly anyone read them, and they were out of the general stream of culture.

Both Petrarch and Boccaccio justified literature on terms that still smacked of the Middle Ages. Petrarch had earlier declared, "The task of the poet is to adorn truth with beautiful veils, so that it may be hidden from the common herd"; and he continued, "If you open your eyes you will see that the poets are resplendent with glory, and fame, and immortality, which they confer not only upon themselves but upon others whom they deem worthy of celebration." Boccaccio also held to the medieval idea that poetry is a veil that clothes truth too brilliant to be beheld by the human eye, and that it is a vehicle by which truths can be presented symbolically under the guise of literal meaning. A theoretical justification of poetry as a kind of truth in itself was not clearly set forth until the sixteenth century.

Boccaccio, as a vernacular writer, showed how to use contemporary material for fictional purposes both in his short stories and in his longer tales. He is a born storyteller, with a witty and cynical point of view and with a sharp eye for realistic details, and a keen ability to analyze the psychology of his characters. He is neither a Christian nor a stoic, nor even a convinced atheist, and he loves to speak frankly. In addition, Boccaccio also showed later writers how to handle medieval and contemporary themes together with those of classical mythology and history. Here he was a great innovator in style, and his influence went on for centuries. His *Fiammetta,* which has been called "the first modern psychological novel," is a passionate love story based on his experiences as the lover of a Neapolitan lady who deserted him. If Dante's attitude toward Beatrice is one of reverence, and that of Petrarch toward Laura one of devotion, Boccaccio's regard for his beloved is one of sensuous passion. Parts of the story are paraphrases of Ovid and Seneca; and there are passages on the poetic beauty of Roman ruins and classical scenes about the Bay of Naples. Others of his tales bring in nymphs, fauns, and satyrs, and Diana and the old pagan gods as characters in the story. This combination of the contemporary and the classical is seen not only in later literature, but in later painters such as Botticelli, Piero di Cosimo, and many others.

Boccaccio in his *Teseide* and his *Filostrato* created the romantic epic, a favorite literary form of the later Renaissance both in Italy and in the rest of Europe. Here he used amorous themes taken from medieval literature but treated in a more realistic fashion, together with classical materials such as the visits to the temples of Venus and Mars in the *Teseide.* This new literary genre, the romantic epic, was used later by

Boiardo, Ariosto, Spenser, and many others. In his *Ameto* and *Ninfale fiesolano,* Boccaccio revived the pastoral style of Theocritus, Virgil, and other ancient writers. In the *Ninfale,* the best of his long poems, Boccaccio's clarity and grace give the work almost the quality of a folk tale, and the blending of medieval, contemporary, and classical elements is complete. In both the *Ameto* and the *Ninfale* there is a happy rural setting, where country folk hold singing contests, make love to one another, and, in spite of griefs and disappointments, live an idealized existence. The whole tone is that of a sophistical love of country life on the part of weary town-dwellers. Here we are in a land of imaginative bliss, of pastoral innocence, and bucolic happiness; amid sunlit landscapes and god-haunted hills, his characters meet Damon and Pythias, Mopsus, Gallus, Thyrsis, and Corydon, and the rest of the happy company of classical Arcadia. It was all, as Lope de Vega said later, "about a shepherd's life when all is spring and flowers and trees and brooks." The pastoral was again taken up by Sannazaro in the fifteenth century, and, through him, passed on to many later poets. These, as a number of his longer stories, Boccaccio wrote in a stanza form, the *ottava rima* (*abababcc;* called in English, octave rhyme), which, though he did not invent it, he polished and popularized. The form was later used by Pulci, Boiardo, Ariosto, and Tasso, and, in a modified form, by Edmund Spenser and other northern poets. Wieland in Germany and Byron in England revived it centuries later.

Boccaccio's name is connected with many "firsts." If the *Fiammetta* may be considered the first psychological novel, the *Filocopo* the first Italian prose romance, the *Teseide* the earliest Italian romantic epic, the *Ameto* (in prose) and the *Ninfale* (in verse) the earliest Renaissance pastorals, the *Decameron* is the first collection of short stories of high literary merit in any vernacular language. In all these works, but especially in the *Decameron,* Boccaccio presents all sorts of human types; but his tendency is, like that of Ben Jonson and Molière, to treat them as types, that is, as persons dominated by a single trait, such as patience, greed, lust, or jealousy. It is interesting to see that as a storyteller Boccaccio improved. His earlier vernacular works fail to fuse the classical and contemporary material, and the writing is beset with long-windedness, with tedious, cataloguing descriptions, with passages of heavy and lumbering oratory, and with overprecious and too-studied effects. His sentences are often too long, with verbs and modifiers in positions more natural in Latin than in Tuscan. But he took his art seriously, and his style steadily became clearer and more simple. His sentences became shorter and more firm and sharply defined, and by the time he came to writing works like the *Ninfale* and the *Decameron* he had escaped from nearly all of his earlier faults.

Boccaccio's work as a Humanist furnished many new materials for literary and artistic, and, later, for musical treatment. But, in his later works, his great contribution was as innovator of an improved prose style through his skilful combination of medieval, contemporary, and classic material; his development of the *ottava rima;* and his invention of the romantic epic, the pastoral, and the highly polished short story. Most medieval prose in both Latin and the vernacular was prolix and poorly organized. Boccaccio's later prose, especially in the *Decameron* and in some of his Latin writings, which were among his most widely read works, shows the influence of a close restudy of Latin prose writers, including Cicero and the much more incisive Tacitus. Boccaccio's prose, especially in the *Decameron,* is clear, precise, tightly organized, and easy to read. The motives of the characters are sharply etched, and the backgrounds are often clearly sketched by only a few telling details. The paragraphs and the sentences move along in a steady procession inside the well-defined framework of a whole story. Many Italian critics regard Boccaccio's prose style as the best in the language. Unfortunately, the later Humanists developed in Latin, and then in the vernacular, a much more florid and artificial style of prose writing; and Boccaccio's prose style, neither in Italy nor elsewhere, had the influence of the poetic style of Petrarch. Boccaccio's stories, on the other hand, created a taste for collections of tales and these appeared in number especially in Italy, Spain, and France in the fifteenth and sixteenth centuries. And Boccaccio's individual tales were and are still widely read. Even in far-off England he influenced Chaucer, Lyly, Shakespeare, Dryden, Coleridge, Byron, Keats, and Tennyson. We see his influence in Hans Sachs in Germany, in Lope de Vega in Spain, in Rabelais and La Fontaine in France—to mention only a few of his admirers—and, far off in time, we may hear the echo of Boccaccio in some of the stories of Anatole France. Boccaccio justified the natural man and the claims of appetite against the ascetics and the mystics. He was self-centered, materialistic, skeptical, and sensuous, but he was also a great literary artist. Men were slow to forget the great storyteller who once more proclaimed the old pagan creed that man was not made only to toil and suffer, but to enjoy life.

In addition to their borrowings from classical sources of vocabulary, figures of speech, images, turns of thought, stories, and moral sentiments, Petrarch and Boccaccio also brought into the main streams of European literature stylistic devices like climax, antithesis, apostrophe, and the tricolon (as in the expression, "government of the people, by the people, and for the people"). They also showed later writers what they themselves had learned from a restudy of classical writers—how important were form and organization in a literary work. At the same time they took prose and poetry further away from everyday speech and from folk-song phraseology. Their prose and verse are thus less colloquial; more dignified, more grave, and more noble; more classical, more universal; and so written more for eternity. As Carducci pointed out, Petrarch had founded a new state within the state, the Republic of Letters; and he and Boccaccio had produced, in their writings, a kind of literary constitution for the governance of this new domain.

With Petrarch and Boccaccio, literature had, by the later fourteenth century, made more discoveries in style than had been made either by art or music. Then a strange thing happened to literature in Italy: for nearly a century after the death of Petrarch and Boccaccio all the greatest talents in Italian letters wrote in Latin; writing in the vernacular was left to a few popular writers of mediocre ability. Italian writers seem to be following Boccaccio's dictum, "Things in the vernacular cannot make a man of letters," and the strange judgment of a fifteenth-century Humanist who declared that Dante "is fit only for butchers and bakers." The practical disappearance of literature in the vernacular can hardly have been due to lack of talent in a society that produced artists like Donatello, and composers like Landino. The search for ancient Greek and Latin manuscripts, the writing of Latin verse and prose, and, beyond that, the attempt to acquire an antique soul, banded together the writers and scholars of Italy in a great cultural crusade against contemporary ignorance and ugliness.

The Humanists believed that worldly and classical beauty were reflections of the divine, and that truth should be embodied in a perfection of form that could only be grasped by a study of ancient writers. Though at first Humanism included the interests of only a few writers, it became, by the later fourteenth century, a great cultural force affecting all of Italian civilization, and it was also beginning to influence the civilization of the rest of Europe. In the fifteenth century, under the influence of the Humanists, informal groups of writers, artists, and musicians were meeting not only in the cities of Florence, Rome, Naples, Milan, and Venice, but even in such smaller centers as Ferrara, Mantua, and Urbino. Academies were formed that were half learned societies and half literary clubs. Humanism in the fifteenth century spread its ideals, as do religious and political movements, with groups forming about important patrons and writers, and with meetings and discussions which helped to carry the new ideas far and wide. So, the influence of Humanism extended into the church, the government, the schools (where the Scholastics resented it), and the workshops of artists. The aim of the Humanists was to make the earthly life a work of art along the lines of classical models, and to perfect art, letters, and scholarship. This explains why the Humanists wrote treatises on the perfect prince, the perfect family, the perfect gentleman and lady, the perfect poem, and the perfect work of art.

A great number of Latin poems, histories, biographies, and orations were written and circulated, many of them, after the middle of the fifteenth century, in a printed form. In one literary genre, the writing of history, the Humanists made an important positive contribution. They dropped the old idea of universal history in the long tradition of Augustine and Orosius, and they swept aside many old wives' tales such as the Trojan origin of certain Italian cities. They introduced the idea of natural causation in history as well as the use of source material, including archeological data derived from inscriptions, coins, and other finds. Their models were the Greek and Roman historians, especially Livy. They not only came to understand the true nature of ancient history, but they gained a perspective that improved their understanding of later history. As the classical historians had confined themselves chiefly to political events, and had largely ignored economic factors and intellectual history, so the Humanist historians are usually disappointing if one is looking for other than political history in their works. Their chief fault as historians was a tendency to oversimplify the characters of the chief actors, viewing them as representatives of traditional virtue and vices. But works like Bruni's (d. 1444) *History of the Florentine People* and Blondus' (d. 1463) *History since the Decline of the Romans* are among the earliest works on a road that led through Mabillon and Ranke to the modern study and writing of history.

The effect of this Humanist Latin literature on vernacular style was, at once, to elevate and purify it, and also to develop a type of writing that was too self-conscious, too imitative of classical models, too arti-

ficial, and too rhetorical. Erasmus loved to make fun of the pure Latin-
ists who could only call both God and Christ "deus optimus maximus."
Then, also, the Humanists showed too great a faith in mere verbal dex-
terity and a propensity to consider things said as things done. The
Humanists spread a knowledge of classical literature and civilization;
they made the classics the basis of education for centuries; and thus
brought up one generation after another to form its literary taste on
classical models. In the fifteenth century, by preparing grammars, dictionaries, and handbooks for the study of Greek and Latin civilization,
they made the classical world familiar to all intelligent readers. The
Humanists placed a new emphasis on man and on all worldly affairs,
and on knowedge of these for their own sake. So they challenged philosophy, literature, and art to consider problems and subjects that are
primarily of human significance. Many of the earlier Humanists, finding the schools closed to them, obtained positions as tutors, secretaries,
and hangers-on of the upper classes. They moved about a great deal,
had roots nowhere; their conceit was often colossal, and their morals
deplorable. Some Humanists, as Ficino, tried to combine Christian and
pagan learning; and from these Christian Humanists of Italy derived
later men like Reuchlin, Erasmus, Lefèvre d'Étaples, and Thomas
More. By 1500, nearly all the classical Greek and Latin books now
known had been recovered, many Greek works had been made more
available in Latin translations, and most were already in print.
Great libraries, like those of the Vatican, the Medici, and the Republic of Venice, were being extended, not only in Italy, but throughout
Latin Christendom, even in countries as far away as England, Bohemia,
and Hungary. The result of the efforts of the Humanists was to bring
the Greek and Latin classics and all they stood for in content and style
back into the very center of European cultural life.

In the later fifteenth century, Italian vernacular literature of a high
quality began to reappear though there were no innovators in style comparable to Petrarch and Boccaccio. Sannazaro (d. 1530) took the classical pastoral form, as it had been revived by Boccaccio, and produced a
charming picture of Neapolitan society in a classical setting in pastoral
poems about the fisher folk and common people of the region of the
Bay of Naples—works that later delighted Du Bellay in France, Spenser
in England, and writers in the other states of Latin Christendom. His
great fame and influence, however, rest on his *Arcadia* (about 1480),
first written in South Italian dialect and later recast by the author into

the Tuscan of Petrarch. It is laid in a never-never land for town-weary Neapolitans where everything is joyous and where "every man may live happily, without envy, in modest contentment with his lot." This is not the countryside described in the earlier *Vision of Piers Plowman,* where the peasants toil in dust and misery, nor are there in it any of the harsh realities that produced Wat Tyler's Rebellion in fourteenth-century England or the Peasants' Revolt in Germany in 1525. There are joyous love-making and merry songs, with lovely descriptions of nature like the backgrounds of the paintings of artists like Perugino and Mantegna. Twelve eclogues in verse alternate with passages in prose. The classical and the contemporary are charmingly mingled, with bits of Theocritus, Moschus, Bion, Ovid, Virgil, and Boccaccio woven in, just as the architects of the time loved to insert fragments of Roman architecture and sculpture into the walls of their palaces. It is a classical dreamland of beauty, an enchanted isle of nowhere like a picture by Piero de Cosimo or Giovanni Bellini, or like Mantegna's "Parnassus," or Botticelli's "Allegory of Spring." The figures are unreal, the adventures improbable, and the loves perfect. The landscape is swept and garnished for townsmen's visits where "the happy melodist" of Keats is "forever piping songs forever new." The classical pastoral genre, revived by Boccaccio, now began to sweep Europe; and in all languages pastoral tales, pastoral dramas, and masques began to appear. This was the inspiration of Tasso's *Aminta,* Montemayor's *Diana,* Sidney's *Arcadia* and Spenser's *Shepheards Calender,* Cervantes' *Galatea,* Lope de Vega's *Arcadia,* and D'Urfé's *Astrée.* The explorer Verrazano, in the sixteenth century, gave the name of Arcadia to the coast of Virginia.

The romantic epic which Boccaccio had invented was much improved and prepared for general European influence by Boiardo (d. 1494). At the aristocratic court of Ferrara, when he was in the service of the Este family, Boiardo wrote lyrics and a five-act comedy, but he was best known through his long *Orlando innamorato* ("Roland in Love"). Using the *ottava rima* which Boccaccio had perfected, Boiardo tells a tale of long ago in terms that appealed to the elegant society of his own time: The chief characters have many adventures in love and war, and the main action is broken by short tales like the old *novelle,* with which the leading persons beguile one another. There are marvelous gardens, islands of delight, rescues of fair maidens, visits to strange lands, fights with giants and dragons, and battles aplenty. It is all a fascinating mixture of old chivalric romance, of Homer and Virgil and other classical writers, and of high society in Boiardo's own time. Boiardo is an excellent storyteller, and he has a marvelous sense of form that keeps the main story clear in spite of all the complexities along the way. Here, he had moved beyond the medieval romances toward the modern novel. Boiardo's romantic epic was continued in the sixteenth century by Ariosto; and through him, after 1500, its style influenced that of every country in Europe. Boiardo is simpler, less sophisticated and much less of a thinker than his successor Ariosto. The contrast is not only between two different writers, but between two ages. Boiardo's style still belongs to the Early Renaissance and contains many echoes of the Middle Ages, and that of Ariosto is the full-blown style of the High Renaissance.

Many of the literary interests of Petrarch and Boccaccio were continued by the Florentine Humanist Poliziano (d. 1494), tutor to the children of Lorenzo the Magnificent and the teacher of Reuchlin, Linacre, and Grocyn. No other Humanist since Petrarch combined learning and fine literary taste, and wrote so graciously in both Latin and Italian. The style of his lyrics is like that of Petrarch, but in his *Orfeo,* a short play of four hundred lines, he created the first important Italian secular drama. As Boccaccio showed the way to the use of classical mythology in his short novels and stories, Poliziano showed it in the drama. And the tale of Orpheus, for centuries, was a favorite of writers of plays, operas, and masques. In the *Stanze per la giostra* ("tournament"), he started to write a kind of pastoral tale which he never completed. Botticelli's frescoes "Spring" and the "Birth of Venus" illustrate the mood of scenes in the poem.

Many of the scenes described by Poliziano remind the reader not only of Botticelli, but of scenes painted by Benozzo Gozzoli, Mantegna, and other contemporaries. A typical stanza is that on a young Florentine lady.

> White is the maid, and white the robe around her,
>   With buds and roses and thin grasses pied;
> Enwreathèd folds of golden tresses crowned her,
>   Shadowing her forehead fair with modest pride. . . .
> Reclined he found her on the swarded grass
>   In jocund mood; and garlands she had made
> Of every flower that in the meadow was,
>   Or on her robe of many hues displayed;
> But when she saw the youth before her pass,
>   Raising her timid head awhile she stayed;
> Then with her white hand gathered up her dress,
>   And stood, lap full of flowers, in loveliness.

Poliziano's verses were even more elegant in style than those of Petrarch, but they are also more frigid and without much depth of thought or emotion; their style is that of the purest decorative art. Again one may compare a writer of the Early Renaissance with one of the High Renaissance. Poliziano's descriptions of nature are much less subtle and less elaborate than those of Ariosto. Indeed, Poliziano gives sometimes a mere list of the colors of things and no more, as an Impressionist painter, and leaves it to the reader to evolve some sort of a picture, whereas the descriptions of nature in Ariosto and his English disciple, Spenser, are elaborate, detailed, and highly polished.

The poems of Poliziano's friend Lorenzo de' Medici (d. 1492) are more virile though less polished. In both men, there is introduced a strong Platonic note that came ultimately from the *dolce stil nuovo,* but more immediately from the Platonism of the Circle of Ficino. This Platonism was to play a role in the style of later Italian and European poetry. The poets describe how one mounts the ladder from love passionate to love contemplative, and from beauty carnal to beauty spiritual. The style of the poetry of Poliziano and of Lorenzo mixes the mystical and the sensuous, the Christian and the pagan, as does that of the writings of the Humanists and the work of artists of the later fifteenth century. Poliziano had far more influence on the style of later writers both inside Italy and abroad than did Lorenzo de' Medici.

A mocking and even quixotic attitude that appears in some of the verses of Lorenzo found its fullest expression in the gay spirit of Pulci (d. 1484), the jester of the fifteenth-century Renaissance. His *Morgante maggiore* borrows some of the old Charlemagne stories which Boiardo was also using at the time. But his style is very different. He is gay and ironic, and sometimes bitter and full of mockery. Pulci introduced from an earlier Italian tale a giant, Morgante, of enormous energy and appetite; and Morgante is a more important character than Orlando. Rabelais not only inherited this giant, and several other roguish characters of Pulci, but much of his spirit. No wonder Byron, who translated the first canto, said he learned the whole manner of Don Juan from Pulci. Pulci's tale reflects the gay, learned, volatile, and brittle culture of Italy on the eve of the High Renaissance. There were in this culture strange mixtures of seriousness and frivolity, of irony and pathos, of a love of dwelling in a beautiful dream world lighted by the golden sun of classical antiquity, along with a cynical fascination with intrigue and murder. It was a culture great enough to include opposites and to square the circle. By 1500 this culture had produced a whole series of original works that had transformed style in art and literature—works whose renown was now spreading beyond the Alps and beginning to fix the attention of the cultured classes from Spain to Sweden on Italy and her Renaissance. Within Italy itself three younger men who were to set the tone of the literature of the High Renaissance—Ariosto, Machiavelli, and Castiglione— were already active and on the verge of great literary achievements.

4. Music

The first great artistic style achieved by the Middle Ages in the Latin West had been in music. By about A.D. 600, long before any important new style had emerged in either art or literature, the church had, in its plain song, found a superbly expressive type of music exactly fitted to the spirit of its ritual, a musical style which added to its services a kind of incense of sound. The roots of this musical style were Jewish, and to a less extent Greco-Roman; but by the seventh century this style had moved far beyond its origins. Its mood is that of a timeless and mystical ecstasy, and for its purposes it is as glorious and original an achievement as the structure and decoration of Hagia Sophia in the Byzantine East.

This musical style had begun to be modified, in the ninth century, by the addition of a second melody at another pitch level (*organum*), a fourth or a fifth lower than the original melody (the *cantus firmus*). With this change, harmonized music in the Western world had had its beginnings. The use of any type of harmony, however, could not be carried far until staff lines came into use in the course of the eleventh century. Then, with means of indicating the pitch of the notes, harmony in more than two parts could be achieved. Changes in style came slowly, but, by the twelfth century, the harmonies were no longer confined to parallel movements. The added melodies might go down when the *cantus firmus* went up, or go up when the basic melody went down. Also, the two or three melodies combined in such polyphony (music of two or more independent melodic lines) might differ in rhythm, with several notes in one melody sung against one note in another. Sometimes, different texts were used for the different melodies that were so combined into a single composition. The *cantus firmus,* usually an old Gregorian chant, was used as a foundation, and the two or three melodies combined with it were built on top.

In the twelfth century, when northern France was beginning to set nearly all the cultural patterns of Latin Christendom, this musical style came to its most elaborate development in the music connected with the cathedral in Paris, where the leading composers were Leoninus and Perotinus. One of the chief contributions of this school of composers was the use of a metrical rhythm, resembling the stress rhythm of contemporary Latin and vernacular poetry. The musical rhythm used was all based on triple time, with three beats per unit. The resulting style is stiff and lacks flexibility, but it was a definite advance beyond the vague and less clearly defined rhythm of plain song and earlier *organum*. Motets (resembling what are now called anthems) of these composers show great ingenuity in weaving together musical lines that are both melodically and rhythmically independent. The result was, to modern ears, frequently rough and lacking euphony; but the whole development was, in the end, to result in an extraordinary enrichment of musical style.

A further advance in musical style began in northern Italy around 1300 in the time of Giotto and Petrarch and soon spread to France. A French theorist, Philippe de Vitry, writing about 1316, calls the new style *ars nova,* in contrast to the *ars antiqua* of the twelfth and thirteenth centuries. Evidently its development must have been fairly rapid, for as early as 1325, the new style was severely condemned by the Pope from his seat in Avignon. The leading changes in style of the *ars nova* were the use of duple time, with two beats per unit, the division of long notes into a greater number of short notes, and, to a less extent, the use of melodies of the type invented earlier by the troubadours, trouvères, and minnesingers of the twelfth and thirteenth centuries. These secular melodies possessed more flexibility and variety than those in plain song, and, from the early fourteenth century on, the influence of secular music on that of the church became more marked.

The masters of the *ars nova* made their greatest innovation by the range of rhythms used, and some began to compose in chords, vertically so to speak, instead of following the *ars antiqua* system where the composer had added one melodic line to another. Some compositions were now written without the use of any basic *cantus firmus;* such works were conceived as an integrated organism rather than as a structure of several successively erected layers of sound. In combining the various voice parts the composers used more thirds, increased the employment of sharps and flats, boldly and deliberately introduced dissonances, and used a variety of rhythms. The commonly used style for secular music gave the principal melody to the highest voice, and the one or two supporting voices below were often not sung but played on instruments. For all these changes, composers developed a number of new systems of notation. At the same time, the vocal and instrumental range of notes was extended both upward and downward; voices were brought in successively instead of entering simultaneously as in the *ars antiqua.* More instruments were used, and some, like the clavichord and the harpsichord, were developed, though the main effort was still directed toward writing for combinations of voices. New forms of secular part songs, as the madrigal, were invented. In these appear new rhythmic patterns, such as occasional displacement of beats; and in religious compositions isorhythmic effects were achieved—through the repetition of one part by another with the same rhythm but with different notes. Finally, the fourteenth-century composers began to exploit the use of canon, where the same melody is repeated in different voices entering at different times. One of the earliest extant examples of this is the English "Sumer Is Icumen In." All these new stylistic devices worked out in the fourteenth century by the masters of the *ars nova* were continued and elaborated on in the fifteenth century.

Most of the composers of the fourteenth century made no attempt to integrate words and music; indeed they even continued the earlier practice of using different texts for different parts of a single composition. For example, the tenor might sing French or Italian words while the bass was singing a Latin text. One fourteenth-century composer furnished an interesting recipe for words and music: "After the composition is finished, take the words of the motet and divide them into four sections, then divide the music into four sections, and set the first part of the text to the first part of the music as best you can, and, thus proceed to the end. Sometimes it is necessary to extend many notes over few words until they are all used up." On the other hand, the French composer Machaut, in his secular part songs, makes the rhythm of the music follow that of the poetry, and he wrote, "If you do not feel your song, words and melody are wrong." A closer integration of words and music, however, awaited the great flowering of the schools of music of the fifteenth century.

Guillaume de Machaut (d. 1377) is not only the greatest French master of the *ars nova,* but he is also the leading French poet of the fourteenth century. His musical works include religious motets, a complete mass (the first polyphonic mass created by one composer in all voices), and a number of secular part songs—*lais, ballades, rondeaux,* and *virelais,* all of which were, in the first instance, verse forms. In his secular compositions, Machaut shows greater melodic inventiveness and rhythmic subtlety than in his religious music. These secular songs are usually written as vocal duets with one or two purely ornamental parts that could either be sung or performed on instruments. He is one of the first composers to use syncopation, a displacement of the rhythmic accent to weak beats or to offbeats. A common method used by Machaut is to start and finish a musical passage in perfect consonants (octaves, fourths, fifths), while between cadence points the lines move with little regard for euphony. Much of his work is marked by experimentation, and a search for a new style of musical expression.

Landino (d. 1397), a friend of Petrarch and the blind organist of the Church of San Lorenzo in Florence, was, like Machaut, both a poet and a composer. He is the most gifted of the Italian composers of the fourteenth century, and his achievement shows that Florence was as important a center in music as it was at this time in literature and painting. Landino's musical style resembles that of Machaut, though his melodies are more graceful and more florid. His choral sonority and long-drawn lines of melody, now sweet and now grandiose, are unmistakably Italian. Landino's surviving works consist chiefly of secular part songs—*madrigals, ballades,* and *caccias,* all names taken from types of poetry—written for two or three voices or instruments, and some compositions for the organ which are among the earliest surviving works written for a special instrument. The musical style of Landino and his contemporary Italian composers had fewer of the older and more crude succession of fifths and octaves, and by exploiting the use of thirds and sixths produced types of harmony that were later to grow in esteem and use.

Music was used on all sorts of occasions: coronations, tournaments, baptisms, weddings, feast days, and burials. Groups of instrumentalists in the thirteenth century had rarely been larger than ten to twenty, but Machaut speaks of an orchestra where thirty-six kinds of instruments were used; and in 1397 four hundred and fifty instrumental players performed for the German Diet at Frankfort. The instruments most commonly used were recorders and viols of various sizes, harps, zithers, and beaten dulcimers; oboes, trumpets, and other brass instruments; and drums. The educated public was getting more interested in music, judging from the more frequent representation of singers and instrumental performers in painting, sculpture, and literature. Moreover, the music of men like Machaut and Landino and their contemporary composers implied a growing sophistication of musical taste at the courts of princes and nobles, among the clergy, and in the upper middle class of the growing towns. With all the changes in music style that came in the fourteenth century—and musical style changed more than it had in the preceding five centuries—the music produced was still harsh, and it remains more notable for its promise than for its achievement.

Musical style during the fifteenth century made rapid advances so that, finally, the last of the arts to develop came to attain the status of a major art. Through most of the fifteenth century Burgundy and the Low Countries (including a section of northern France) were not only united politically, but also economically and culturally; and in this century this large area furnished the leadership in musical style for the whole of Europe. The first group of composers of this area are now usually classed together as the Burgundian School, and the composers of the next generation as the Flemish School. It is interesting to remember that these great fifteenth-century musicians were the contemporaries and fellow citizens of Claus Sluter, the sculptor; of the painters of Bruges, Ghent, and Brussels; and of the Brethren of the Common Life. The same world thus produced Sluter, the Van Eycks, Rogier van der Weyden, Thomas a Kempis, Erasmus, and Dufay and Okeghem.

At the close of the fourteenth century, the style of the *ars nova* was improved and clarified by the Englishman Dunstable (d. 1453), who spent much of his adult life in northern France and Flanders. Dunstable's style exploited fully the use of intervals of thirds and sixths; and by this, and by avoiding the discords and the ineffective concords of the *ars nova* style, he moved away from both the monotony and the harshness of the older style, and so produced choral works of smoother texture. He showed great skill in handling together in one composition a group of independent melodies, each of which is of equal or nearly equal importance and yet is an essential part of the whole. Dunstable's beautiful style has been characterized as "a kind of tonal communism." He is also the first important composer to tie up such parts of the mass, as the Gloria and the Credo, and the Sanctus and Agnus Dei, by the use of the same musical theme. In the next generation, whole masses were composed which used the same theme throughout, and the theme chosen was often from some popular secular song. It is interesting to recall that Dunstable produced the earliest compositions that, today, please us harmonically at the same time that there appeared in Italy the first sculptures and paintings that satisfy us as a complete representation of natural forms. There is no connection between the two except that both are manifestations of the striking advances in style made by the fifteenth century.

The style of Dunstable was taken up by a number of Burgundian composers, the greatest of whom was Dufay (d. 1474). He spent years in Italy, both as a student, and as a choral conductor. One of his motets was written for the dedication of Brunelleschi's Dome in Florence (1436). It is composed in four parts; the two lower ones were probably played by the organ, reinforced by trombones, and the two upper parts may have been sung with accompaniment by an orchestra. Dufay is one of the first musicians to compose for a chorus. Before the fifteenth century, music in several parts was ordinarily performed by soloists, and genuine choral music was confined to plain song. In the fifteenth century, as choral music was coming into vogue, choirs became larger. In 1442 the Papal Choir had ten singers; by 1483 it had twenty-four, though choirs did not rise above thirty until after 1600.

Dufay and his contemporaries and successors developed the canon, a form long in use—where, as we have seen, each voice sings the same melody but no two voices ever sing the same phrase at the same time. In Dufay's canon, the style became more complicated, with the second voice repeating what the first voice had sung, but, sometimes, at a different interval, and even singing it backward. Music is now headed for fantastic elaboration of style—and all this in the Age of the *Meistersinger* and the *Grands Rhétoriqueurs,* and of English Decorated and French Flamboyant architecture. Dufay, like composers both earlier and later, borrowed themes from plain song, and from other composers, and even wrote masses, motets, and secular part songs on popular tunes. Exactly opposite to the practice of later periods, medieval and Renaissance composers made no particular effort to invent the melodies they used. The style was one in which the most admired composer was he who could take any theme and draw out of it rich and unexpected possibilities. The style of Dufay is gracious and ethereal to the point of being somewhat weak but it has a vague and dreamy charm; and his religious compositions convey the mood of a Rogier van der Weyden painting or of some pages of the *Imitation of Christ.*

Stemming partly from the style of Dunstable and partly from that of Dufay and his contemporaries is the writing of the Flemish School. The leading composer, Okeghem (d. 1495), though educated in Antwerp, spent much time in France and Italy. Both his secular and religious works have a greater variety and subtlety than those of Dufay, and far more complexity. Like a number of his contemporaries, Okeghem delighted to set himself elaborate problems in the technique of composition. Though hardly typical of his whole work, he actually wrote one canon in thirty-six parts. Such daring feats of musical engineering, all within the strictest logical framework, might not be very effective aesthetically; but complicated pieces of musical composition of this type supplied Josquin des Près and the composers of the High Renaissance with an arsenal of technical stylistic devices that they were to employ in works of simpler, yet grander, style.

Musical style in the fourteenth and fifteenth centuries was influenced both by the patronage from which musicians lived and by the methods of teaching the art. The patrons of music continued to be churchmen; but there were now more lay patrons than before 1300—princes, nobles, wealthy members of the upper middle class, and often the town governments. This helps to account for the large amount of secular music composed between 1300 and 1500. The chief centers of musical instruction were the choir schools of cathedrals and important churches; but, by 1400, instruction was given in connection with the chapels of princes and nobles. Private teachers in the larger towns were able to make a good living, and many a great household had a music tutor. The Fleming, Isaac, for example, was a music tutor in the household of Lorenzo de' Medici, some of whose poems he set to music. Some secondary schools in the fifteenth century, especially in Italy, gave a solid training in music, though there was almost no teaching of music in the universities. By these means, musical style was transmitted.

While there were no classical models in music, as there were in architecture, sculpture, and literature, writers of the fifteenth century, basing their ideas on passages in ancient Greek and Latin literature, did some theorizing about ancient music. The most important practical result of this development, which appeared in compositions of the later fifteenth century, was an attempt to integrate music and words, an idea derived chiefly from the writings of Plato. So the composers began to try to make the subject matter of their music visible through the tones, and to paint in music the outer world of nature and the inner world of man. This became clearly marked in some compositions of the later fifteenth century. While the painters and sculptors, especially in Italy, were developing the use of perspective and other three-dimensional devices, the composers were extending the range of harmony and of musical expression. The development of musical style in the fifteenth century was so remarkable that a Flemish composer in 1477 dared to declare that "there is no music worth hearing save only in the last forty years"; and of these Flemish composers, Guicciardini wrote in the early sixteenth century, they are "the true masters of music." In the first half of the sixteenth century, the stimulating influence of the Flemish composers spread across Europe, and helped to bring about a new era in the musical style of France, Germany, Italy, England, and Spain—a great quickening that resembles the movement across Europe in the same period of new artistic and literary styles radiating from Italy. By this time, the great figure in music had come to be Josquin des Près, with whom begins the music of the High Renaissance.

5. Conclusion

The two centuries from 1300 to 1500 found art, literature, and music all experimenting with new forms and techniques, but the ends toward which they were striving—except perhaps in some forms of literature—were only imperfectly and partially realized. The creation of new styles in art and letters and to a much less extent in music, was the work of Italians in the last two medieval centuries. Though the art and literature of northern Europe had been enriched by geniuses like Jan van Eyck, Chaucer, and François Villon, the great innovations in art and literature—innovations that were to command the future—came out of Italy. The Italian artists and writers had Romanized the styles of art and letters and a good deal of the general cultural atmosphere of their age; and they had done this without ceasing to be both fresh and original in their creations. Under Italian tutelage these new styles, after 1500, were passed on to the rest of Europe.

Cultural contacts of Italy with Christian Spain and with the center and north of Latin Christendon had gone on all during the Middle Ages; but any great flow of new ideas from Italy to the rest of Europe—except perhaps in the Franciscan Movement—was sluggish until after 1500. The first two northerners of great genius who came south to take a deep bath in the culture of the Italian Renaissance were Erasmus and Albrecht Dürer. But after 1500 Italian styles in art, literature, manners and customs, and, to a less degree in music, swept through the rest of

Europe, changing styles in every country from Portugal to Scandinavia.

The Early Renaissance thus is largely an Italian movement. In art and literature there are very close parallels in that in both, as we have seen, there is a union of Gothic realism and technical skill with a new appreciation of the possibilities of using classical elements of style. For painting and music there were available no classical models; but for the painters there was much to be learned from the study of Roman sculpture, and from the study of sculptors like Ghiberti and Donatello, who showed what could be achieved by a restudy of Roman style. In architecture and sculpture, and in poetry and prose, a complete re-estimate— first of Roman civilization and then of Roman art and literature—led to a deeper desire to fathom the secrets of Roman artistic and literary style and then to create new works that would embody these discoveries. Painting, sculpture, and imaginative literature were also alike in the new use they made of the rich stores of Greek mythology and of Greek and Roman history and legendry. And the more Roman they tried to be, the more original were their works.

At the same time, a long experimentation with new types of harmony and rhythm and with improved instruments had by 1500 brought music, the last of the arts to unfold, to a high degree of expressiveness. A new musical style had come, at last, to give music—as a highly developed art form—equality with the fine arts and literature. The music of the fourteenth century may be regarded as still medieval or, at most, transitional; and the term "Early Renaissance" is best applied only to the music of the fifteenth century. This music of northern Europe in the fifteenth century had more influence on all later music than had the art and literature of northern Europe on art and letters after 1500. For example, Heinrich Schütz owes more to Dunstable than Rubens owes to Roger van der Weyden. This is to say that the art and literature of northern Europe were in the fifteenth century still essentially medieval while its music had clearly moved ahead in the defining of a new style. So the co-ordination of periods and of styles in the arts is often only approximate. But, in any case, by 1500, art with Leonardo da Vinci, Bramante, and Michelangelo, literature with Ariosto and Machiavelli, and music with Josquin des Près were either beginning or were on the verge of starting the glorious flowering of the High Renaissance.

Finally, one may ask how did the styles of the Early Renaissance differ from those of the High Renaissance? First, the scale of the works of the Early Renaissance is usually smaller than that of the High Renaissance. Typical of the Early Renaissance are a sonnet of Petrarch, the interior of Brunelleschi's Pazzi Chapel, and a mass of Dufay. To realize this difference in scale set these against Ariosto's *Orlando furioso*, Bramante's plan for St. Peter's in Rome, and one of the great motets of Josquin des Près. A second great difference lies in the handling of all sorts of technical problems in art, letters, and music. Only in smaller and shorter works did the Early Renaissance evince the ease, competence, and sophistication that marks the works of the High Renaissance. In art and literature, also, the Early Renaissance rarely showed the insight into the style of Roman art and literature and the ability to use these styles freely in original creations as did the High Renaissance. There is almost always something tentative and not fully realized in the arts of the Early Renaissance. The High Renaissance is more concerned with idealized form and idealized composition than the Early Renaissance. And, lastly, the arts of the Early Renaissance still bear many traces of the earlier Gothic styles; and thus, like Matthew Arnold's Oxford, they still speak "with the last enchantments of the Middle Ages."

Chapter III

THE HIGH RENAISSANCE, 1500-1530 AND LATER

1. The Nature of the High Renaissance

The lofty and grand classical style toward which the Early Renaissance had been moving came to a short but glorious flowering at the end of the fifteenth and in the early part of the sixteenth century. Again, Italy took the lead in art and letters, and the Low Countries in music. The Early Renaissance had stretched over two centuries; the High Renaissance, at least in Italy, hardly extended beyond the first three decades of the sixteenth century. Of the leaders who around 1500 were either well known or were just coming into fame, nearly all were dead by 1530. Bramante died in 1514, Leonardo in 1519, Raphael in 1520, Josquin des Près in 1521, Machiavelli in 1527, Castiglione in 1529, and Ariosto in 1533. Among the giants, only Titian and Michelangelo lived on into the later sixteenth century.

The change in style between the Early and High Renaissance was due, to some extent, to changed political and social conditions in Italy. "The Renaissance," says Von Martin, "begins in the spirit of democracy and ends in the spirit of the court." The leaders of society in the fifteenth-century Italian city-states had been venturesome and daring men of the upper middle class opposed to the power of the landed aristocracy. By the close of the fifteenth century, these men had arrived, and they now wanted security for the wealth and position they had acquired. As the plutocrat grew richer, he became a *rentier*. The old emphasis given to hard work was, even before 1500, placed more on the use of leisure; leisure came to be regarded no longer as a waste of time but as a positive value and a symbol of achievement and of an assured social position. The upper middle class intermarried with the old landed aristocracy, and at the same time the democratic governments were transforming into monarchies. The princes granted titles of nobility to the great bankers and merchants, and the upper middle class increasingly invested its savings in land. Everywhere there was a new love of elegance and lavish display, a desire for security rather than for liberty, and a growing glorification of country life against that of the city. The attitudes of the Humanists showed this shift. Earlier the Humanists had been strongly bourgeois and republican; before 1500 their tone had become monarchial and aristocratic, and they snobbishly glorified country life. In the early sixteenth century, Guicciardini summed up the view commonly held by the governing classes and by most of the intellectuals when he declared, "The people are a mad beast." The story of the Medici illustrates this shift. Cosimo de' Medici was still the careful bourgeois, greatly interested in business; he lived frugally, whereas his grandson, Lorenzo the Magnificent, let his financial concerns slide almost to the point of bankruptcy while he lived in the grand style of a prince. These conditions prevailed primarily in Florence and some of the other city-states of northern Italy which had been centers of the Early Renaissance. These generalizations are less true of cities like Rome and Venice.

These changes become very evident in the later fifteenth century, and in the early sixteenth century Machiavelli denounced the leaders of Italian society for their softness and effeminacy. He found his contemporaries unwilling to face the world as it was, and he accused them of living in an imaginary world of beauty. The courts of the princely despots had by 1500 become the great centers of patronage to which cultural activities now adjusted themselves. These courts needed artists, writers, and musicians to embellish and glorify them. This changed world, which Machiavelli denounced, is exalted in Castiglione's *Book of the Courtier*. In such an atmosphere the realism of the art and letters of the Early Renaissance appeared naïve, vulgar, and plebeian. The demand in art and letters, if not in music, was for something more aristocratic, more elegant, more dignified, and more exalted. This is certainly one reason why the tone of Ariosto, Castiglione, Raphael, and Titian differs from that of the writers and artists of Italy in the fifteenth century; and it helps to explain the lofty style of the art, literature, and music of the High Renaissance.

Another cause for the shift in style was the growing importance of Rome as the great center of patronage. The popes had a huge income and a desire to rebuild and transform Rome on a grand scale. As a result, Rome became in art—and to a less degree in letters and music— the center of the High Renaissance as Florence had been for the Early Renaissance. Bramante, Raphael, Michelangelo, Ariosto, and Josquin des Près lived for extended periods in Rome. Pope Leo X's old music teacher, Isaac, composed a six-part motet to celebrate his pupil's ascending the throne of St. Peter, and Ariosto wrote his *Horatian Epistles* in Rome. Music was now considered a major art, along with painting, sculpture, architecture, and literature. Leo X loved music. He collected fine singers and instrumentalists, and even had music performed during his meals. The moving of the center of Renaissance art from Florence to Rome meant also a much greater influence on art of ancient Roman sculpture, painting, and architecture. The ruins of ancient Rome were then more extensive than they are today, while hardly a month passed without the discovery of important ancient sculptures such as the "Apollo Belvedere," and the "Laocoön," and ancient paintings, such as the frescoes in Nero's Golden House and in the Baths of Titus. These men of the High Renaissance saw the antique on equal terms; this was mainly the result of their own development as the successors of the artists and writers of the Early Renaissance. So, because of a changed social, political, and aesthetic situation, the antique in art and letters spoke differently to the men of the High Renaissance from the way it had spoken to the leaders of the Early Renaissance.

Religion still played a great role in life, though less than in the Early Renaissance. The pagan and the Christian, as in the fifteenth century, blend in the work of most of the artists and writers, who in addition to Christian subjects found a fascinating world of ideas and inspiration in Greek and Roman mythology and history. Raphael painted pagan and Christian philosophers and poets side by side on the walls of the Vatican, and Michelangelo, continuing a medieval tradition, represented pagan sibyls along with the Hebrew prophets on the Sistine ceiling. Machiavelli and Rabelais, neither of whom could ever be regarded as devout, still assumed the existence of God, but the faith of a Dante or a Savonarola was now very rare. Outright disbelief in the early sixteenth century was still unusual, though an occasional writer like Guicciardini regarded it as "nonsensical to inquire into supernatural beings and things unseen."

The influence of Platonism and Neo-Platonism, on the other hand, was more marked in the High Renaissance than it had been in the fifteenth century. This, like the influence of Roman remains and of Latin literature, led to an idealization of forms in art and literature. Leonardo da Vinci, the oldest of the painters of the High Renaissance, still laid great emphasis on an exact copying of nature. "The summit of art," he declared, "is to draw well the body of a nude man and a nude woman." At another point Leonardo said, "The painting is most praiseworthy which has the greatest conformity to the thing imitated," though he told a student, "On winter evenings, all the drawings from the nude which you have made in the summer should be brought together, and you should make a choice from among them of the best limbs and bodies, and practice these and learn them by heart." The idealization of the subject, so marked in Alberti's treatises, becomes more evident in the thought of the artists and writers of the High Renaissance. When Raphael finished his "Galatea," he was asked where he had found a model of such beauty; he replied that he never copied any specific model, but rather followed "a certain idea" he had formed in his mind. And he added, "To paint a beauty, I need to see many beauties."

Michelangelo believed it was the work of the artist to compose out of nature a second and higher nature. And he condemned the Flemish style of painting exactly a lot of unselected details of nature. Such a style would, Michelangelo believed, appeal to children and old women, but it was not truly a style. The artist and poet, he believed, must find the ideal order or essence already present, by God's grace, in the existing order. In one of his sonnets, Michelangelo wrote:

> Heaven-born, the soul a heavenly course must hold
> Beyond the visible world she soars to seek
> (For what delights the sense is false and weak)
> Ideal form, the universal mould.
> The wise man, I affirm, can find no rest
> In that which perishes; nor will he lend
> His heart to aught that doth on time depend.

Though a careful student of anatomy, Michelangelo looked beyond reality to find a beauty that is the reflection of the divine in a material world. Similarly, many of the writers of the High Renaissance sought to reflect a higher reality, and in this way they interpreted Horace's statement that poetry should teach and delight in an idealistic sense. The idealization of the subject in literature is very marked. Sir Philip Sidney said that "while the poet goeth hand in hand with nature, he groweth in effect another nature." Fracastoro, the critic, declared, "The poet is like the painter who does not wish to represent a particular man as he is with his many defects, but who, having contemplated the universal and supremely beautiful idea of his Creator, makes things as they ought to be." This tendency to idealize the subject in art and literature led to a further study of ancient sculpture and literature where the artists and writers of antiquity had shown how to select from nature to create a beauty that is beyond nature. The result of this growing tendency to idealize nature in art and poetry, which had already been evident in the fifteenth century, was a series of attempts, which increased in number during the sixteenth century, to reduce art and letters to elaborate rules. This was done with the help of treatises by Vitruvius in architecture, and by Aristotle and Horace in poetry; and by a careful study of ancient sculpture, architecture, and poetry. The great influence of such treatises, however, belongs to a period later than that of the High Renaissance.

The grand style of the High Renaissance in art, letters, and music, as has been noted earlier, owed much in each field to a greater mastery of technical means. This mastery had been won by the artists, writers, and composers of the Early Renaissance on whose shoulders the Raphaels, Ariostos, and Palestrinas were to stand. Perspective was no longer a mystery, nor were the uses of color and lighting; and the human body could be drawn or carved correctly in any position. Complicated verse forms, new literary genres, and types of musical harmony, which earlier had been handled only with difficulty and effort, had by 1500 become second nature. The techniques their predecessors had struggled to invent were a birthright to these men of the sixteenth century. This technical inheritance had not yet come to be a hindrance to creative achievement, as it had once been in Byzantine civilization and as it was later to be, in the Age of Mannerism.

For all these reasons the style of the High Renaissance in art, letters, and music had a grandeur that reached, in art and literature at least, the peak of excellence of the best of the ancients, not necessarily by following in their footsteps but by climbing the opposite side of the mountain. There is about the achievement of the High Renaissance an Olympian calm and a Sophoclean harmony. Many of the writers speak of a great harmony in the universe—a Platonic idea. At the end of *The Courtier,* Castiglione makes Cardinal Bembo discourse on this theme. In his "Four Hymns" Edmund Spenser describes this harmony:

> What time this worlds great workmaister did cast
> To make al things, such as we now behold,
> It seemes that he before his eyes had plast
> A goodly Paterne, to whose perfect mould
> He fashiond them as comely as he could;
> That now so faire and seemely they appeare,
> As nought may be amended any wheare.
> That wondrous Paterne wheresoere it bee,
> Whether in earth layd vp in secret store,
> Or else in heauen, that no man may it see
> With sinfull eyes, for feare it to deflore,
> Is perfect Beautie, which all men adore,
> Whose face and feature doth so much excell
> Al mortal sence, that none the same may tell.

The artists and writers delighted in portraying the physical strength and well-being of mature and full-blown types of men and women in contrast to the artists of the fifteenth century who preferred the slim, angular, and springy lines of youth. In painting, the narrative style of the fifteenth century, full of figures, details, and incidents, went out of style. Compositions are both larger and more simplified with greater emphasis on a few leading persons. Emotions are more restrained, there is less movement, poses are less angular. There is much more reserve, grandeur, and aloofness. Bright colors are avoided, and sculpture is no longer painted. There is a mood—as in Castiglione's description of a gentleman—of restrained gravity and a great dignity of demeanor. Della Casa in *The Gallant One* reflects this attitude when he takes Dante to task for putting into the mouth of Beatrice words which belong in the tavern. Grandeur, calmness, and harmony are the qualities that bring together works as different as Raphael's "School of Athens," Titian's "Madonna of the Pesaro Family," passages of the poetry of Ariosto, Ronsard, and Spenser, the motets of Josquin des Près, and the masses of Palestrina and William Byrd. All are characterized by a large-scale plan, by dignity, a noble simplicity, balance, and harmony, and by spaciousness and serenity, without, however, any loss of originality and vitality. The achievements of the High Renaissance in art, letters, and music make the achievements of the Early Renaissance seem timid, tentative, and limited. It was a golden moment in culture. In 1517 Erasmus declared, "Immortal God! What a world I see dawning; why can I not grow young again?"

The mood of Italian art and letters in the High Renaissance is one of great self-assurance, but also of an aristocratic understatement. The tremendous exuberance which appears in the *Autobiography* of Benvenuto Cellini is more common in northern Europe than in Italy. It appears in Marlowe's *Tamburlaine* (Part I, Act II, scene 7):

> Our souls, who faculties can comprehend
> The wondrous architecture of the world,
> And measure every wandering planet's course,
> Still climbing after knowledge infinite,
> And always moving as the restless spheres,
> Will us to wear ourselves and never rest.

In *Hamlet* (Act II, scene 2), the hero declares, "What a piece of work is a man! How noble in reason! how infinite in faculties! in form and moving how express and admirable! in action how like an angel! in apprehension how like a god! the beauty of the world, the paragon of animals." With Rabelais (Book II, chap. 8), this declaration of self-reliance and achievement becomes a sort of battle hymn of the Renaissance:

The old sciences are revived, knowledge is systematized, discipline re-established. The learned languages are restored: Greek, without which a man would be ashamed to consider himself educated, Hebrew, Arabic, Chaldean, and Latin. Printing is now in use, an art so accurate and elegant that it betrays the divine inspiration of its discovery which I have lived to witness.

Marlowe, Shakespeare, and Rabelais belong to a later period, but the mood they reflect came ultimately from the Italy of the High Renaissance. This was the attitude of mind that led Columbus to break the bonds of the world and Copernicus to break those of the universe.

As the artistic and literary styles of the High Renaissance spread beyond Italy to the rest of Latin Christendom, there was often a strange mixture of the influence of Italian styles of the High Renaissance and of Mannerism, which in Italy followed closely on the heels of the High

Renaissance. Also, in all the states beyond Italy Gothic styles in art and letters hung on, and the new forms imported from Italy were grafted onto the older styles so as to form strange and interesting hybrids. Thus, the terms High Renaissance, Mannerism, and Baroque when applied to the cultures of Spain and the states of northern Europe must be used carefully. It is difficult to separate styles in Italy, and still more difficult to differentiate them in the lands beyond Italy. By 1500, an Italian journey was beginning to be considered a necessity for all men of culture, for Italy was the point of reference against which all art and literature, and, to a less extent, music, were measured. While Spaniards and northern Europeans flocked to Italy to study, many Italians found employment as artists, teachers, and musicians in the states of western Europe.

All this resulted in an artistic, literary, and musical cosmopolitanism which resembled that created by the culture of northern France in the thirteenth and fourteenth centuries. But now, unlike the earlier situation, this cosmopolitanism, at least in literature, was accompanied by a growing nationalism. On the one hand, Humanists and poets spoke an international language, and they all shared a great enthusiasm for the culture of Greece and Rome and of Renaissance Italy. But, on the other hand, writers became aware of their national differences as never before. This helps to account for the varied treatments given literary forms, styles, and themes in different countries. This strange combination of international and national forces in letters is evident in such works as Joachim du Bellay's *Défence et illustration de la langue française* and Sir Philip Sidney's *Defence of Poesie*. In art and music, there was something of the same deep-rooted national resistance to new styles of art and music that came from outside the nation, though in neither case did this produce nationalistic manifestoes.

The influence of the styles of the High Renaissance was earliest and most deeply marked in France. Spain still held to her old-time Catholic ardor, and her medieval artistic and literary traditions as shown in her Plateresque architecture and in her picaresque novels. Germany also remained largely Gothic in art and medieval in literature, and then in 1517 became absorbed in the struggles of the Reformation. Thus in Spain and in the German Empire there is little in art and literature that belongs to the High Renaissance, for in general one proceeds in Spanish and German culture from the Gothic to Mannerism and the Baroque. England also, in art, long held onto the Gothic style, though her writers, as Sidney and Spenser, show clearly the influence of Italian

Renaissance literature. The centers of Italian Renaissance influence were in the courts of kings and the homes of important ecclesiastics and nobles, and, to a less extent, in the university centers: Salamanca in Spain, Paris in France, Oxford and Cambridge in England, Vienna, Prague, Basel, Augsburg, and Heidelberg in the German Empire. Translations of the Greek and Latin classics and of important Italian Renaissance writers into the several vernaculars appeared in the first half of the sixteenth century from the printing presses of Lyons, Paris, London, Nuremberg, and other centers, and helped to spread a taste for classical and Italian Renaissance literary subjects, forms, and general style. By the time the forms of Italian culture had begun to penetrate deeply the states beyond Italy, the Italians themselves had wearied of the Olympian grandeur of the style of the High Renaissance; they had begun a series of artistic, literary, and musical experiments that have now been given the name "Mannerism," a period, from about 1530 to 1600, that lies between the Age of the High Renaissance and that of the Baroque.

2. Art

The artists of the High Renaissance, like the writers, wished to capture the secret of classical art and literature without a mere pedantic copying which would have captured only the external aspects of ancient art and letters. Their idea was to emulate, not merely to imitate. They often made a conscious effort to get out of their actual environment which retained too much of the medieval. But the man of the Renaissance, in spite of his yearning and a deliberately conjured-up past, could never succeed in being a Julius Caesar, a Horace, or a Cicero, for he always in part still belonged to medieval Christianity. In spite of this the men of the High Renaissance did recapture some of the stately and measured composure, and something of the grandeur of the Roman past. This desire to be Romans again explains some of the reaction against localism and the picturesque in the style of the Early Renaissance; it also explains the idealization of all forms, and the love of arranging, in the arts, forms in triangles, ovals, and squares. It was an art that, though it achieved grandeur, order, and balance, lacked the charming naïveté and the freshness of the Early Renaissance and the capriciousness of Mannerism. It was a style that was stable without being static, varied without ever being confused, and clearly defined without being dull. The idealization of forms—the desire to achieve a system of proportion definable in mathematical terms and a compositional beauty derived from the total harmonization of the parts—was greatly assisted by careful observation of how ancient sculptors had adopted motifs from nature. The artist, writer, and composer of the High Renaissance, with his faith in harmonious proportions and ideal ratios, also believed there was a perfect order in a harmonious universe and a perfect order in the world of nature. As Leonardo wrote, "Our soul is composed of harmony"; and he found proportion not only in numbers and measurements, but also in sounds, weights, times, and spaces.

The Italian painting of the High Renaissance, though done with almost none of the classical models available for sculpture, architecture, and literature, has always been regarded as its greatest achievement. The Italians of the Renaissance seem to have been a seeing rather than a reading or listening folk. Their minds ran to visual images; and their literature is full of word pictures, as is evident in the *Divine Comedy* of Dante, the *Stanze* of Poliziano, and the *Orlando furioso* of Ariosto. The drama, without settings, of Elizabethan England was not for them. It was thus no mere chance that made Leonardo, Raphael, and Michelangelo the giants of the High Renaissance in Italy. Leonardo reflected this point of view when he insisted on the superiority of painting over both sculpture and poetry. Painting, he held, has a greater power and directness of appeal than poetry and, unlike poetry, presents the essence of its matter in a single instance. Painting is to poetry as reality is to a shadow; he declared, "Write up in one place the name of God, and put a figure representing him opposite, and see which will be the more deeply reverenced." Painting, he also held, is superior to sculpture because sculpture lacks the linear and aerial perspectives which bring the remote and the near together; sculpture cannot represent luminous bodies or clouds or storms; and sculpture is without the vivid appeal of color.

The painting of the High Renaissance in Italy, as we have seen, moved away from the naïve enjoyment of descriptive details and miscellaneous incidents in which the fifteenth-century painters had delighted. The interest is concentrated on a few figures; and the charming bits of local color about anything and everything, that abound in fifteenth-century paintings, disappear. Not only are homely details ruled out, but often the postures express less individual emotion than abstract qualities of dignity and grace. The figures no longer feel or do anything apart from the whole. At the same time, the accent is on maturity. The Virgin is usually no longer a girl but a woman of thirty, and Jesus is less often a baby than a small boy. Settings are frequently not localized; no time or place is represented but the universal. Human nature is elevated, and there is a new emphasis on the solemn, the grand, and the noble. In portraits—as in those of Raphael and Titian—the painter tries on the one hand to show the character of the sitter but at the same time to idealize the subject and to minimize the imperfections. Gestures and draperies become more graceful. If one compares the Three Graces in Botticelli's "Primavera," with their lingering Gothic angularity, with the small "Three Graces" of Raphael (at Chantilly) one can feel, immediately, the difference between the styles of the Early and High Renaissance. Besides this simplification and idealization, the painters desired to create a scene that could be grasped at once as a whole, and could easily be comprehended at a distance. Compositions thus became more closely integrated in such a way as to make many fifteenth-century designs seem arbitrary, meandering, and unco-ordinated. Sometimes, the figures are placed side by side across the front of the picture as in Leonardo's "Last Supper"; at other times, some of the main figures are placed farther into the composition, as in Michelangelo's "Creation of the Sun and Moon," which gives a sense of an opening up of space and depth that prefigures the Age of Mannerism. The use of bright spots of color gave way to the employment of quieter tones. Leonardo mocked at painters who sacrificed drawing and modeling to an emphasis on color, comparing them to orators who use fine phrases that mean nothing.

The chief aim of the painter or sculptor of the High Renaissance was not to copy nature. Nature should be carefully studied to provide the raw material for the artist; but nature must be transcended, and a careful, idealistic selection of materials drawn from nature must be made. The subject itself should be of an elevated sort, preferably a highly memorable event. Genre scenes from everyday life could find no place in the repertory of the grand manner. Landscape background and ornamental decoration must be reduced to a minimum, and individual peculiarities of human appearance eliminated. Draperies should be simple, and arranged so as to give an ideal and noble aspect to the figure. In spite of the growing popularity of subjects drawn from classical mythology and history, the painting, sculpture, and architecture of the High Renaissance remained primarily a religious art. Most of the great paintings of Leonardo, Raphael, Michelangelo, and Titian are still focused on religious themes though this painting glorifies the God-like qualities inherent in man. An endless number of devotional pictures were still, as in earlier centuries, painted for private devotions in city houses and in palaces; and the higher clergy and well-to-do families adorned churches with altarpieces and great cycles of wall paintings. Secular subjects, particularly those drawn from classical sources, had a growing appeal and popularity but remained secondary to religious subjects. It was, however, in this field—as in portraiture—that the painting of easel pictures, entirely apart from any architectural setting, had its first great development.

The training of artists on an apprenticeship system continued in the Age of the High Renaissance; and at the same time the status of the artist, especially of the painter, continued to rise. In 1500 most artists still were recruited from the lower middle class, and it was rare for the sons of intellectuals, government officers, bankers, or aristocrats to become artists. If a youth from a good family insisted on an artist's career, it was more honorable to apprentice him to a painter than to a sculptor, for painters belonged to the Guild of the Apothecaries, whereas sculptors ranked as bricklayers and stone masons. When the young Michelangelo, whose family belonged to the upper middle class in Florence, insisted on studying art his father finally agreed to apprentice him to a painter, Ghirlandaio. By the time Michelangelo had passed middle life, he had come to be regarded as practically a god, and the whole status of all artists was raised. The legend that Emperor Charles V picked up a paintbrush Titian had dropped is often taken as a symbol of the glorification of the artist by the men of the High Renaissance. One contemporary comments on the fact that when Michelangelo began his career his family thought he was stepping down the social ladder, yet before he died, he was hailed as "divino." As one writer remarks, "In Italy one does not care for the renown of great princes; it is only a painter that they now call divine."

The style of the High Renaissance in painting is first clearly revealed in the work of Leonardo da Vinci (d. 1519). Only in Plato was the same passionate desire for knowledge united with the same ardent love of beauty. Leonardo, being opposed to all speculation not based on experiment and experience, investigated for himself the phenomena of anatomy, physiology, botany, geology, and mechanics; and his painting and sculpture were rather the by-products of his lifework. By endless observation and experiment, he discovered that the colors of adjoining objects are not sharply cut off one from another; and he noted that if a form is left a little vague, as though disappearing into shadow, impressions of dryness and stiffness disappear, and a more lifelike effect is achieved—a discovery the Italians soon named *sfumato*. He discovered likewise the full possibilities of aerial perspective and saw that figures and objects in the distance not only change color but have edges more blurred than those in the foreground. He knew that red and yellow have their splendor in light but that blue and green have their best qualities in shade, and that shadows are often blue rather than black. All this knowledge of how to handle color in painting he combined with the most brilliant skill in drawing of human beings, animals, plants, and other objects. His notebooks are filled with hundreds of sketches which reveal his fathomless curiosity and his artistic genius. So, in his forms, he was able to represent all the mechanics of movements like walking, lifting, and climbing, as well as to depict faces that mirrored the personalities behind them.

Not only was Leonardo discovering new ways of representing three-dimensional reality but he was also discovering more penetrating means of representing various states of mind through the use of facial expressions and gestures. His drawings show his ability to present wild passions and violent movement, tender love, and the most subtle psychological states. Because his talents were so various and because of the conditions of patronage, which obliged him to move about extensively, Leonardo completed few of his writings and paintings. But the small number of his paintings that were available for everyone to see changed the course of the history of art. Leonardo was the most acute observer of nature, yet his ideal of beauty lay in the forms he saw in classical sculpture. Thus, what he wanted to represent was an ideal type of human beauty, and to it he brought a technical knowledge unmatched by any draftsman or painter of the Early Renaissance. This seems to be the explanation of both his style and the enormous fascination he had for his contemporaries. Among his paintings that have survived, several of which are unfinished, the most important are the "Adoration of the Magi" (Uffizi); "St. Jerome" (Vatican); "St. John the Baptist," "St. Anne and the Virgin," "Mona Lisa," and "The Madonna of the Rocks" (all four in the Louvre); and, most typical of all, "The Last Supper" (Milan). In "The Last Supper" the figures are lined up in a single plane and are set behind a table in front of a simple architectural background. Within the general scheme, the disciples are arranged in four triangular groups on either side of the figure of Christ, whose posture also forms a triangle. Christ has just said, "One of you shall betray me," and most of the disciples make gestures that seem to indicate each is saying, "Lord, is it I?" There is both classical repose and dramatic tension in the picture. It is all so subtly carried out that it seems inevitable and "the art that hides art," and the design is so skilful that one may compare it to the plot of Sophocles' *Oedipus Rex*. "The Last Supper" in its calm, classic simplicity and power likewise reminds one of the pediments of the Parthenon. The dream of the earlier Italian Renaissance is at last realized. What Leonardo had won through incessant personal effort was to be a birthright for Raphael, Michelangelo, Giorgione, Titian, and Correggio, for he had shown the technical means by which painting could capture and represent both nature and the most varied moods and passions of men.

The spirit of the golden age of Greek art seems to live again in the paintings of Raphael (d. 1520). As a youth, Raphael was trained in the fifteenth-century style of painting of Perugino, from whom he derived his great feeling for large compositions in space. When he was only twenty-one years old he went to Florence. Here he met Michelangelo, who was twenty-nine, and the mature Leonardo da Vinci, who had just returned to Florence after completing his "Last Supper" in Milan. After four years in Florence, where his marvelously assimilative capacities enabled him to absorb the best of Florentine art—above all that of Leonardo—Raphael went to Rome, where he did his greatest work and where he died at the age of thirty-seven. In Raphael's portraits the sitter has a reposeful and calm posture, the figure is shown at half-length, little attention is paid to the setting, and the colors are quiet; the whole is characterized by an aristocratic understatement. His madonnas are more human than pious, yet more ideal than realistic. The postures express abstract qualities of grace, dignity, and grandeur. Raphael's work is clearly in the grand style of the High Renaissance.

The greatest of his paintings are the frescoes in the Camera della Signatura in the Vatican: the "Dispute of the Sacrament," the "School of Athens," and the "Parnassus." The "Parnassus" represents the Platonic world of imagination and inspired rapture of poets and musicians who are grouped on the slopes of Parnassus about the central figure of Apollo. It is all a reflection of a superior world, a world of unruffled serenity and calm. In the "Dispute of the Sacrament," Raphael brings together prophets, saints, and theologians with God and the heavenly hosts above in a vast composition held together by its effective grouping and also by a subtly varied tonality of color. The "School of Athens" is an even greater achievement. Set against a vast architectural background based on Bramante's design for St. Peter's stands Plato, with one hand pointing upward and carrying the *Timaeus,* and beside him Aristotle, who has one hand pointing straight ahead and carries in the other his *Ethics.* Around about these two central figures are groups of other ancient philosophers and scientists. The beauty of these paintings lies not in the details but in the dovetailing of all the elements; each detail is designed with its effect on the whole kept clearly in view. Symmetry is the ruling principle but it is never made obvious; everything takes place on a plane altogether elevated above that of everyday existence. It all seems so effortless that one does not connect these frescoes with the idea of hard and relentless work. Every figure seems to correspond to some other figure, every movement to answer a countermovement. No artist of the Renaissance equaled Raphael in his skill in arranging figures in a large composition. The figures themselves are usually idealized. The "Dispute of the Sacrament" and the "School of Athens" have the same classic qualities of grandeur, simplicity, fulfilment, and inevitability that one finds in Leonardo's "Last Supper." Some of his later paintings, as the "Expulsion of Heliodorus," the "Burning of the Borgo," and the "Transfiguration," are full of movement and dramatic tension that prefigure the style of Mannerism. When Raphael died, Bembo wrote an epitaph for his tomb in the Pantheon:

> This is Raphael's tomb, while he lived he made Mother Nature
> Fear to be vanquished by him, and, as he died, to die too.

If Raphael resembles Mozart, Michelangelo (d. 1564) reminds one of Beethoven. Though Michelangelo was older than Raphael, he survived Raphael by two generations or more; and he remained active up to his death at the age of eighty-nine. Much of the work of his middle years belongs in style to the Age of Mannerism; and, finally, his design of the exterior of St. Peter's apse and dome are in the Baroque style. As a youth Michelangelo was trained both as a sculptor and as a painter, but he always regarded himself first as a sculptor. Referring to Leonardo da Vinci's view that painting is superior to sculpture, Michelangelo wrote: "Sculpture is the guide of painting; he that wrote that painting is higher than sculpture was as ignorant as a maidservant!" Michelangelo's early sculptures and paintings are in the calm style of the High Renaissance. He turned to painting on a large scale only at the behest of Pope Julius II. In the frescoes of the ceiling of the Sistine Chapel in the Vatican, he worked practically alone—refusing all assistance but a mechanic to prepare colors and a man to help transfer the designs to the plaster surface—flat on his back, on an immense scaffolding. With Raphael working only a short distance away, for four years this dizzy work of creation went on. The task undermined Michelangelo's health, but when the scaffolding was taken down men looked on this ceiling as a new wonder of the world. It covers seven hundred square yards, and contains over three hundred figures. Down the center of the ceiling is a series of panels, telling the story of the Old Testament, from the Beginning through the Flood. Here is the Creator—in skilful foreshortening—swirling through space to separate light from chaos, to create the sun and the moon, and then to give life to Adam and Eve. No artist has ever painted so powerful a vision of God or expressed the sweep of creation with comparable force. In the angles of the cornices are twelve prophets and sibyls in whom the thought seems more ponderous than the bodies are powerful. They seem to behold eternal things. No beauty seems to exist outside the human form, a thesis of Michelangelo that was deeply significant for the whole century. Many decorative nudes are thus used in the elaborate framework for the whole series of compositions. The model for these male figures seems to have been a magnificent torso, probably of Hercules, in the Vatican. Michelangelo's male figures are heavily muscled, and are in positions where nearly every muscle is under strain. These astonishing figures display all of Michelangelo's skill in drawing the human body in any position and from any angle. The movement in the figures of the ceiling and the strained muscles make the whole a very interesting transitional work between the High Renaissance and Mannerism. Here one is aware of Michelangelo's energy and uneasiness, which later in his life became an attitude of bitter defiance, and finally one of resignation.

Next to Rome as a center of painting in the High Renaissance, stood Venice. Here, in the later fifteenth century, had developed a tradition of conceiving a painting primarily in terms of masses of color. To Venetians such as Giovanni Bellini (d. 1516) color and lighting were more important than line. Not that their drawing was incorrect or inadequate, but their main interest was elsewhere. They loved to give their pictures—they painted almost entirely in oil—a warm and golden tonality such as appeared in Venetian skies. They likewise loved luscious flesh tones and luminous whites in costumes. The whole approach of the Venetian painters from the later fifteenth century on was much more sensuous than was the case with other Italian schools of painting. The style of these painters, as later their music, reflects the splendid pageants and civic celebrations of this rich, independent, and pleasure-loving city. The material world, rather than spiritual or intellectual values, was cultivated in Venice as nowhere else. It was a setting of power and glory, splendor and magnificence.

The first great Venetian painter of the High Renaissance, Giorgione (d. 1510), was a pupil of Giovanni Bellini. Giorgione died young, and the number of paintings certainly by him is small. But those that survive have a lovely quality. In rich color, he depicts a dream world close to that portrayed by the pastoral poets, Theocritus, Virgil, and Sannazaro. All sharp lines disappear, or are at least subordinated to beautiful patches of color; and the whole is bathed in a golden light. Giorgione's use of color and light to unify his pictures, and his poetic use of landscape settings were passed on to Titian and later painters of the Venetian school. He thinks of nature, the earth, the sky, the clouds, trees, buildings, and human beings as one—as great an advance in art as the earlier discovery of perspective. The charm of his pictures is in their mood rather than in action; and it is usually a mood of reverie. An elegance of form, a charm of color, and a magic of light and shade give a dreamy quality to his paintings that makes him one of the most original painters of the High Renaissance.

Giorgione died young, but his contemporary Titian (d. 1576) lived to be ninety-nine years old and was active up to the end of his life. As a young man, Titian was deeply influenced by his teacher, Giovanni Bellini, and by Giorgione. Indeed, so thoroughly did he absorb the style of Giorgione that a number of paintings have been assigned to one artist or the other without any common agreement among connoisseurs. To the dreamy and exquisite style of Giorgione, however, Titian added an inventiveness and a power and force that was his own, and most of his greatest works are in a style quite beyond anything that Giorgione painted. Titian excelled in many fields; he was a great religious painter and a great portraitist, and in his mythological paintings he brought back, as no other Renaissance painter, the charm of the world of antiquity. Titian's long life, together with his energy and originality, allowed him to try a number of styles. Vasari reproaches

Titian for his lack of skill in drawing, though this may represent Florentine jealousy of Venetian achievement. Titian himself said, "It is not bright colors but good drawing that makes figures beautiful." In his "Assumption of the Virgin" painted for the high altar of the Church of the Frari in Venice, he worked on an enormous scale with the figures larger than life size. The whole, which is over twenty feet high, is divided into three planes. Below stand the Apostles, some with arms uplifted to carry the eye upward; in the center, surrounded by seraphim, is the commanding figure of the Virgin; her face and arms are upraised toward the figure of God which fills the top of the picture. The whole is gorgeously colored. A typical classical painting by Titian is his "Sacred and Profane Love." The nude Venus represents celestial beauty; it is beauty unadorned, a beauty which is eternal and unchangeable. The costumed figure, adorned with worldly charms, represents the perishable beauty of this world. It is interesting to notice that in the High Renaissance Titian's nudes or the nudes in Shakespeare's "Venus and Adonis" are used without self-consciousness, whereas in the next age, that of Mannerism, nudity is usually used with an intent to shock. In his "Sacred and Profane Love," with its sky of an illimitable depth of blue, and its lovely flesh tones and glowing tonality, Titian evokes a golden dream of antiquity. As a colorist and as a master of composition Titian wielded tremendous influence on painters as different as El Greco, Rubens, and Delacroix, and many another. Titian's style, with certain modifications, was continued into the Age of Mannerism by his younger contemporary, Veronese (d. 1588). In his classical and religious paintings Veronese reflects the love of luxury, pomp, and ceremony of Venice in the later sixteenth century. The marble porticoes are higher and grander and the raiment and jewels more brilliant than in any other paintings of the age. There is no drama or spiritual depth; the appeal is all to the eye. Veronese was forced by the Inquisition to change the name of his "Last Supper" to "Supper in the House of Levi."

Unconnected with either Rome or Venice, the two great centers of the High Renaissance, was Correggio (d. 1534). As a youth, he was deeply influenced by the style of Leonardo da Vinci, Raphael, and Michelangelo, some of whose work he could have known only through drawings or engravings. But his own style was lighter and more graceful than that of any of these masters. He painted angels which Vasari likened to celestial rain; and he transformed the world about him into a kind of music. Correggio had a joyous and ethereal style in which, in both his religious and his mythological paintings, the forms are softened, and where the light and shade has an enchanting quality. His use of color and light is superior to his ability to draw. His paintings have a dreamlike atmosphere, a springlike freshness, and a haunting charm. He painted a number of cupolas at Parma; in these, the heavens open up, and great swirls of figures appear that anticipate the ecstatic style and the illusionism of the Baroque. Correggio's most characteristic work is seen in his smaller compositions. Here, though he lacks the structural vigor, the purity of form, and the depth of feeling of the greatest of his contemporaries, and though he was not destined to create new types and subjects in painting, he nevertheless endowed painting with a new delicacy of color and lighting and with an exquisite grace. It is these qualities of his style that make Correggio seem the faun or Ariel of the High Renaissance. His work was estimated more highly after his death, and elements of his style appear later—down through the ages of the Baroque and Rococo and of Neo-Classicism.

The first important painters to show the influence of Italian High Renaissance painting in the lands beyond the Alps were the Germans, Dürer (d. 1528), Cranach (d. 1553), and Holbein (d. 1543); and the Flemings, Mabuse (d. 1533) and Bernard van Orley (d. 1542). Here the traditional Gothic forms are modified, but not wiped out, by Italianisms. Often the northern artists did not grasp the essential qualities of Italian style. The Italian style, which aimed at idealized forms and a fixed proportion among the parts, was misunderstood by artists who fixed their attention on actuality and on the particular and were fascinated by the capricious, the unusual, and the irrational in nature. Many artists in the lands beyond Italy kept on painting in a late medieval style, with only a few odds and ends picked up from Italian paintings; for example, when Raphael was painting the "Sistine Madonna," Grünewald (d. 1530) was working on the "Isenheim Altar." Even when northern artists tried to learn from Italy, they generally failed to capture the inwardness of the Italian style; this is seen, for instance, in the nudes of German painters like Cranach and Hans Baldung (d. 1545). However, Dürer's "Four Apostles" has the simple and monumental grandeur of the Italian High Renaissance style. As time went on, and more northerners went to Italy and more Italian artists came to execute commissions outside Italy, the influences of the style of the High Renaissance in Italy came to be mixed with influences of Italian Mannerism. These were combined with elements of native tradition into a hybrid art. The result of the Italian influences outside Italy was to lay greater emphasis on symmetrical compositions, on the use of nudes (especially for Adam and Eve), on larger figures, and on details of Italian Renaissance architecture used in backgrounds of paintings. Not until the Baroque period, do we find many artists in the lands beyond the Alps who really understood the Italian style and, like Rubens, Rembrandt, and Velasquez, were able to use it freely in creations of their own. The craze for all things Italian in the lands beyond Italy dates from the early sixteenth century, and this was to continue even after the French, in the later seventeenth century, took the lead in the arts. As Dr. Johnson said, in the eighteenth century, "A man who has not been to Italy is always conscious of his inferiority."

The most essential characteristic of the sculpture of the High Renaissance, differentiating it from that of the Early Renaissance, is its increased tendency to reproduce the antique. Especially was it attracted toward the calm and elegant nudes that were everywhere being excavated, just as the next age, that of Mannerism, was particularly interested in ancient statues that showed tension and movement, as the "Laocoön" group. In the early sixteenth century, instead of the realism of a Donatello, we find, in sculpture, the idealization and generalization of the classical past. Relief lost the favor it had enjoyed earlier, and more figures in the round were produced. These stylistic changes are first clearly seen in the work of Andrea Sansovino (d. 1529). In two wall tombs in Santa Maria del Popolo in Rome—tombs which may have been designed by Bramante—the sculptures of Sansovino are done in a large style close to the antique. The sculptor had discovered the nobility of gestures and the general idealization of the whole figure of ancient sculpture, and he re-created freely in this style. He uses strong, clear contrasts; and in the drapery he creates simple, flowing lines, though he always indicates clearly the bodily structure underneath. Sansovino dropped the use of color on marble and stone, and he did no work in terra cotta. All traces of Gothic angularity and realism are gone; it is a style more elegant and graceful, and more classical than that of Donatello, but less vivid and vigorous. Sansovino, though a Florentine, worked also in Rome, and in Spain and Portugal; this helped to spread the influence of his style.

It was in sculpture that Michelangelo made his first reputation. Perhaps the most typical work in a High Renaissance style done by him is the beautiful "Pietà" in St. Peter's in Rome. The Virgin, with voluminous draperies, is seated with the limp body of her dead Son across her lap. She gazes down piteously, but with a great calm and a restrained grief. The pyramidal composition owes something to compositions of Leonardo, especially to his "Madonna with St. Anne." The Christ is a beautiful Greek god and shows clearly the idealization of the High Renaissance. On the other hand, Michelangelo's "David," which belongs to this early part of his career, shows a curious combination of idealization and realism. The beautiful body of the young David is idealized as in an antique sculpture, but the hands and feet are exaggerated in size to show the youthfulness and the still not completely developed physique of the hero. Here Michelangelo harks back to the usages of an earlier day. Though he greatly admired ancient sculpture, Michelangelo did not take his anatomy from Hellenistic figures but directly from life. At the same time, the "Bacchus," nearly contemporary with the "David," might be the work of an ancient Hellenistic sculptor. Thus, so early in his very long career, the work of Michelangelo defies classification and shows the experimental nature of his genius. In the work on sculptures for the tomb of Julius II and then on the Medici tombs in Florence, Michelangelo's style has already left that of the High Renaissance; he has become a leader in the development of Mannerism.

The tendency toward idealization and adaptation of the antique was continued by Sansovino's pupil Jacopo (d. 1570), who took his teacher's name. Through the middle of the sixteenth century and later, into the Age of Mannerism, he carried on the idealistic tradition of the High Renaissance. The younger Sansovino had great technical capacity, but he easily fell into affectation and a cold academic perfection. Much of his best work was done in Venice where he won even greater fame as an architect. Outside Italy, the High Renaissance style of sculpture, like that of painting, only began to penetrate the native styles at a time when Mannerism was well developed in Italy; and the Mannerist style of sculpture had much greater vogue in the lands beyond the Alps than that of the High Renaissance. The High Renaissance in Italy, which one must always remember was a relatively short period, produced much less remarkable results in sculpture than in painting, or even in architecture.

The architectural styles of the High Renaissance in comparison with those of the Early Renaissance show a deeper study of ancient Roman monuments and, in new creations, a nearer approach to the grandeur and monumentality of Roman architecture. The spell of Roman architecture on these new architects was very deep; what they really longed to build were temples, triumphal arches, and other Roman public buildings, but what they were commissioned to do was to build churches and city palaces. The new style shows designs on a much larger scale than in the Early Renaissance. It was a style that had dignity and repose, a fine sense of proportion, balance, and symmetry, and a feeling for clear, logical organization. Decoration was kept to a minimum, and so it avoided confusing the design with distracting ornament. Since the High Renaissance in Italy was a relatively short period, the term is applicable to a relatively small number of buildings erected during the first three decades of the sixteenth century. Thus we have the paradox that the term High Renaissance in architecture, implying the summit of achievement, is in fact very poorly represented by existing buildings; and estimates of its qualities depend in part on surviving drawings. High Renaissance architects were strongly influenced by ideas of Vitruvius and Alberti with their theories of proportion and an academic interpretation of the correct use of Roman orders, and by a mystical reverence for the circle as the symbol of divine perfection. Many of the forms used by Renaissance and by later architects were closely connected with religious symbolism. A man-created harmony was a visible echo of a celestial and universally valid harmony. In comparison with the organic nature of Gothic architecture, however, all the architecture of the various phases of the Renaissance has a papery quality; that is, it shows the influence of academic theories and it aims at great external effects, but, except for the work of Bramante, it is weak in matters of engineering and construction. Less stone and brick vaulting were used than in medieval architecture; and many buildings were roofed with wooden beams, which were sometimes exposed but were oftener covered with lath and plaster.

The great leader in High Renaissance architecture was Bramante (d. 1514), who plays something of the role of Brunelleschi in the Early Renaissance. Of Bramante, Michelangelo wrote, he "was a skilful architect and the equal of anyone from the time of the ancients until now." It is not definitely known where he acquired his knowledge of architecture and painting. He was evidently, in architecture, much influenced by the writings of Alberti, and by a profound study of surviving Roman buildings. He introduced into Italy, from Germany and France, principles of mathematics and physics as they apply to the construction of vaults; and he applied these to forms derived from the classical tradition, as the round arch, the barrel vault, the column and capital, the frieze, and the cornice. This knowledge, together with his own great inventive ability, enabled Bramante to create bold works that gave him, throughout Italy, a reputation as a leading structural engineer.

Bramante's first great building was the choir of the Church of Santa Maria della Grazie in Milan. Here he used classical forms on a larger scale than had been used by most of the architects of the Early Renaissance; and he crowned the building with a sixteen-sided dome. In 1501 he built the circular "Tempietto" in the cloister of San Pietro-a-Montorio, in Rome. The building is small and has almost no decoration, but it has the grand style of ancient Rome in its circle of Doric columns and its round dome. This building plays something of the role in the High Renaissance that the Pazzi Chapel played in the Early Renaissance. Bramante, at the order of the Pope, made a plan for the complete rebuilding of the Vatican, but the only large element built was the great Court of the Belvedere, a grandiose design with a colossal niche at one end of the court. The pope then commissioned him to draw up a new plan for St. Peter's. Here Bramante is said to have made the remark that he would place the Pantheon on top of the Basilica of Maxentius. A rough idea of his plan may be seen in the background of his friend Raphael's "School of Athens." All that Bramante lived to see finished were the four great piers and the arches that were to support the dome. Bramante's work has everywhere suffered from later rebuilding, and his theoretical writings on architecture have not survived. He was not only a great genius as an architectural designer but also a greater inspirer and teacher. The two San Gallos, Raphael, and Peruzzi were all his pupils.

San Gallo the Elder (d. 1534), a Florentine, is best known for a huge church, in the form of a Greek cross and with a large round dome, the Church of San Biagio at Montepulciano. His nephew, San Gallo the Younger (d. 1546), worked on St. Peter's, but his most famous work is the vast square Palazzo Farnese at Rome, for which the ancient Theater of Marcellus served as a model. The palace is much larger than those of the Early Renaissance and wears a very formal, grand, and monumental aspect. Michelangelo completed it and redesigned the top story and the huge cornice. Peruzzi (d. 1536), another pupil of Bramante, designed the Palazzo Farnesina, a strikingly original work and one of the most beautiful buildings in the High Renaissance style. Later, he shows in his very original and un-Roman design for the Palazzo Massini in Rome the beginnings of Mannerism in architecture. Another great architect of the High Renaissance in Italy was Jacopo Sansovino (d. 1570), a pupil of the sculptor, Andrea Sansovino. Though not a pupil of Bramante, he was deeply influenced by him. Most of his active career as an architect and also as a sculptor, was spent in Venice, where he designed a number of buildings, the finest of which is the beautiful Library of St. Mark's, one of the gems of High Renaissance architectural design. Palladio thought this library one of the most beautiful works built since the great days of ancient Rome.

Two architectural forms developed by the High Renaissance, city-planning and garden design, were passed on to later ages. In both cases the precedents were found in plans of the ancients who had, at least in the field of city-planning, tried to set off important buildings or groups of buildings so that the setting would enhance the whole and produce an effect greater than that made by any single architectural work. None of the Italian despots or the popes had either the power or wealth possessed by the French monarchs, and the first really effective city-planning on a large scale was done in France in the seventeenth century. The formal Italian garden, either on a flat surface as in the Vatican gardens or on a hillside as in the garden of the Villa d'Este at Tivoli, was one of the great creations of the High Renaissance; and from Italy this style of gardening, with local modifications, reached across Europe. Laid out in a formal plan, fountains, carefully trimmed hedges and trees, and statues were so combined as to make outdoor rooms carefully integrated with the palace or villa itself.

The High Renaissance continued the tradition of Alberti in seeking rules of proportion in architecture. The ancient Roman writer, Vitruvius, though he believed that proper proportions in the parts of a building in relation to each other and to the whole is a source of beauty, is neither clear nor explicit on just what these proportions should be. These proportions, Alberti and those who followed him believed, should be subject to reason and rules rather than to intuition. The most definite suggestion about proportion made by Vitruvius lies in his statement that the leading dimensions should be submultiples of the whole. The Renaissance also owes to Vitruvius its obsession with the analogy of the human figure with architecture. Alberti said that proportions should run in the progress of 1, 3, 9, etc. Vitruvius, for the drawing of human figures, made the face a tenth part of the whole height; others made it a ninth. This theorizing became even more extended in the period of Mannerism. But the sixteenth century never produced a single system of proportion either for the human figure or for architecture, and a number of systems existed side by side. Most theorists related their system of proportions to musical intervals and to some harmonious plan that existed in the universe. Beauty in architecture—and also in a painting or sculpture—was thought to be the result of conformity of the parts in accordance with the fundamental structure of the universe, designed by God on a system of related numbers. And this relation was revealed by the relation of harmonious musical notes to the length of strings which produce them. Both these ideas were pure conjectures, and even if accepted the analogies drawn by different theorists varied considerably. Usually, in architectural theorizing lists of ratios were given between the length and height of whole buildings and of separate rooms, and the basis of measurement was usually the diameter of a column. Not until the eighteenth century did this sort of theorizing go out of fashion.

Outside of Italy the effect of Italian High Renaissance architecture was gradually to reduce decoration and encourage more simple designs. Usually the first results of the impact of Italian style would be the addition of Italianate details to older buildings as porches, tombs, altars, doorways, choir screens, and the application of Italian decorative motifs to buildings of essentially Gothic design. Italian artists and artisans got commissions all over Europe, but they usually had to adjust their ideas to what their lay or ecclesiastical patrons would accept. At the same time, Italian drawings, prints, and books circulated throughout Europe, and these carried Italian architectural ideas far and wide. Also, many from beyond the Alps went to Italy and brought Italian ideas and ideals back home with them. In Spain the grand and simple style of the Italian High Renaissance is shown in the Escorial, the combined monastery and palace built by Philip II. The scale is very large, the proportions are classical and Roman, and there is almost no decoration. On the other hand, in Spain, as elsewhere, medieval traditions of building carried on into the middle sixteenth century and later. In Spain, for example, two large cathedrals at Segovia and Salamanca were built entirely in the Gothic style in the first half of the sixteenth century. At Granada the cathedral was begun in 1520 in the Gothic style, and a few years later the Gothic piers were covered with classical bases and Corinthian capitals. There are similar hybrids in other countries. In France, the Church of St. Eustache in Paris is entirely Gothic in structure, but all the decorative detail is of the High Renaissance Italian style. At the Château of Chambord there is the same combination in a secular building. The round towers at the corners of the building and a high pitched roof are Gothic; but there is a symmetry in the handling of architectural features and a use of decorative detail that is purely Italian. An Italian Renaissance architect would have regarded these hybrids as horrors; he would have turned away from them with some of the same views that Michelangelo had of Flemish painting—as something that could only "appeal to children and old women." As time went on, the borrowings from Italy came to be absorbed and affected the basic designs of buildings rather than surface details.

3. Literature

The first great achievements in the literature of the High Renaissance, in both verse and prose, were the work of Italians; but in the course of time the leadership of Italy in letters came to be less marked than in art, for northern Europe soon produced poets and prose writers whose accomplishments rivaled those of the Italians. Erasmus and even St. Thomas More, though they wrote in Latin, were as great prose masters as Machiavelli; Rabelais was as original a writer as any Italian; and Ronsard and Spenser were poets as pre-eminent as Ariosto.

In literature, as in art, the High Renaissance saw a growing attention to classical models. As the critic Vida wrote later, "Visit the ancients and strip them of their wealth." The Early Renaissance had initiated the classical pastoral. The High Renaissance continued this and also revived the classical comedy of Plautus and Terence; the tragedy of Seneca; the satire, especially that of Horace; the ode, particularly that of Horace, more rarely that of Pindar; and the epic of Homer and Virgil. As in art the models studied were Roman sculpture and architecture rather than Greek; so in letters, Latin rather than Greek literary works were copied and adapted. Greek works of art were rare in the West; and Latin literature was more available than Greek, as every educated man read Latin and had been brought up on the Latin classics. Ancient Rome also represented to the Italians their own national past. Petrarch seems to have thought more highly of Cicero than of the Greek philosophers—whom Petrarch, it is true, knew only at second hand. But it remained the common judgment until much later that the Roman achievements in art and literature were superior to the Greek. Quite typical of the general attitude is the critic Cinthio's comment on Seneca, "In almost all his tragedies he excelled, so far as I can judge, whatever was written by the Greeks in wisdom, gravity, decorum, and stateliness."

As in the Early Renaissance, literary as well as artistic patronage continued to come from churchmen, especially bishops, abbots, and the pope; from rulers and noblemen; and, to a less extent, from wealthy merchants and bankers. In Italy the artist, writer, and musician had, by the early sixteenth century, come to be regarded as no longer a mere craftsman or servant but as a creator in his own right, a position comparable to that held by the great Humanist scholars. After about 1530, however, the widespread influence of Spain in Italian affairs and the growth of local despotisms in the Italian states lowered the status of the artist, writer, and musician to that of servile hanger-on of the rich and powerful. A few men like Michelangelo and Titian, after 1530, were held in high regard; but in general the Age of Mannerism saw a lowering of the social status of men in the arts.

Ariosto (d. 1533) was the Orpheus of the High Renaissance and the greatest Italian literary genius since Petrarch. Born in Ferrara, he spent most of his life in service to the reigning House of Este. Ariosto's early work, in Latin and vernacular poetry, was marked by a great polish and perfection of form that shows the influence of Catullus, Horace, and Petrarch, three writers whose verses became veritable hymnbooks of the High Renaissance religion of beauty and love. In a series of *Satires,* modeled on those of Horace, Ariosto gives a revealing picture of himself, of his love of letters, and of the tedium of serving various members of the Este family. The spirit of Ariosto here is close to that of Horace; his smoothness of style and its grace, its concise elegance, its understatement, and its studied and sophisticated simplicity are all in the manner of Horace. Like Horace too he tries to make a friend of his reader, and has in what he says a charming note of intimacy. Personally, as he appears in these satires and in a famous portrait by Titian, the poet is a charming and mild-mannered man with a lively sense of humor, but easygoing and completely unheroic. He is serious about nothing except his art.

Ariosto also wrote five comedies; apart from the late medieval interludes, these were the first modern comedies of manners. Ariosto was in charge of the court theater—as later Goethe was at Weimar—and he wrote these plays for this theater. They are very skilfully constructed as to plot and action, and they show real insight into human behavior. All are marked by the evident influence of the Latin comedies of Plautus and Terence. The first two comedies were originally written in prose, and rewritten in blank verse; the last three were written initially in verse. The most notable feature of both Ariosto's satires and his comedies is their skilful construction and their smooth and polished style.

Ariosto's greatest work was his romantic epic, the *Orlando furioso,* which appeared in parts between 1516 and 1533. The poem is composed in *ottava rima,* stanzas of eight lines of eleven syllables each, rhyming *abababcc*—a verse form first extensively used by Boccaccio. The story continues the Early Renaissance tale of Boiardo. It is a long tale, longer than both the *Iliad* and the *Odyssey* together; it abounds in minor incidents, and one narrative is suspended to pass to another. But the whole is a marvel of construction, and the reader is always able to keep the threads of the tale in his grasp. Here it differs profoundly from the medieval romances of chivalry, which usually were very loosely constructed. The art of Virgil had been carefully studied by Ariosto, and the author's great emphasis on form marks it as a work of the High Renaissance. The mood of Ariosto is usually very worldly and ironic. He is condescending toward chivalric ideals and is, by his very nature, unheroic in mood; the author is always behind the scenes, gently smiling at the reader. One of the characters looks for Silence: he goes to a monastery where he finds only Discord; Silence has gone to dwell with thieves and illicit lovers. There is no profound passion or enthusiasm or serious thought in the *Orlando furioso,* and the reader never feels deeply involved with the characters. Free from illusions but struggling after no high-set ideal, and accepting the world as he found it without the impulse to affirm or deny Ariosto displayed an aspect of the High Renaissance in Italy that was to be a source of moral and political decay in that country. Yet Ariosto also embodied some strong points of his age: a sustained pursuit of beauty of form and style, a great breadth of cultural sympathy, and an urbanity of tone and delicacy of perception that characterized one of the great ages of ancient civilization.

Ariosto's greatest art lies not in character analysis but in inventing and handling the plots of stories, and in marvelous descriptions of men, events, and nature. Like his fellows, the painters, particularly those of the Venetian School, Ariosto gives the reader a continual succession of beautifully composed and colored pictures. By the music and incantation of his verses, the poet transports the reader to a fairy world filled with magic weapons, winged horses that mount through the clouds, men transformed into trees, and fortresses that dissolve at one imperious word. It is a world of beauty, a world of escape from the brutalities and shame of many of the practical affairs of his time. Though Bembo urged Ariosto to write in Latin, he wrote in an Italian more carefully Tuscan than that of Boiardo. The mood of Ariosto is that of the lovely nudes and the deep blue skies, the luminous whites and the rich flesh tones of the mythological paintings of Giorgione and Titian. It has all the golden tonality of a rapturous dream. The *Orlando furioso* became a classic in the author's own lifetime. Raphael painted the poet in his "Parnassus" alongside Homer, Virgil, Ovid, Horace, Dante, and Petrarch. The style was imitated by members of the Pléiade in France, by Spenser in England, and later by Milton. This work is the last word in the purely artistic aspect of Italian High Renaissance letters.

The great literary arbiter of the age was Cardinal Bembo (d. 1547). He was a prince of letters before he became a prince of the church, occupying a position somewhat like that of Boileau in seventeenth-century France and that of Dr. Johnson in eighteenth-century England. Bembo tried to set a Ciceronian style for Latin prose, in which he was a purist of the purists and for which he was made fun of by Erasmus. And for vernacular writings he insisted that the standard should be that of the Tuscan writers, Petrarch in poetry and Boccaccio in prose. He was greatly opposed to the use of fanciful conceits, far-fetched metaphors, and obscure references and allusions in literature, all of which were beginning to grow in Italian literature. His own poems, which he passed through many revisions, were cold and lifeless. Bembo's influence came more from his exalted social position than from his writings. He is the most important precursor of the group of Neo-Classical critics who appeared in the Age of Mannerism and whose ideas spread all across Europe. It was a movement that was to lay great stress on a conscious imitation of classical literary models and on obedience to literary rules. In the midst of political decay and moral corruption, there was being formed, as the career of Bembo and the writings of Castiglione show, an ideal of refinement adopted from antiquity and assimilated to modern modes of life. This, the most perfect bloom of the High Renaissance, was destined to be for later ages what chivalry had been for the Middle Ages. Through the continued effort of patricians and writers to acquire the tone of ancient culture, something like antique urbanity reappeared, at least among certain classes. The effect of this on visitors from the north was varied. Luther, who came to Rome to see the city of the saints, found instead the sink of all abominations. Erasmus, on the contrary, said that nothing could efface from his memory the freedom of discussion, the libraries, the large style of life, and the works of art he had found in Rome. This new civility was diffused through Europe, and became the "politesse" of the Age of Louis XIV, and the standard of social behavior in the modern world.

The first outstanding prose master of the High Renaissance, Count Castiglione (d. 1529), belonged by birth and occupation to the same elegant world of counts and princes in which Ariosto and Bembo lived. He is the perfect embodiment of the High Renaissance idea of the full development of the individual who would make of his life a work of art. A portrait of Castiglione by his friend Raphael shows him as the urbane aristocrat and man of affairs that he was. He wrote in both Latin and Italian; his best-known Latin work was an elegy, the "Alcon," which was a model later for Milton's "Lycidas." In his middle years Castiglione became involved in a discussion of the language to be used in literary works in the vernacular. Against Bembo, who would use the Tuscan dialect, Castiglione held that words from the court usage of other Italian regions and even foreign words should be employed.

Castiglione's *Book of the Courtier,* his best-known work, was one of the most characteristic and most-read books of the Italian High Renaissance. In spite of his theories, the work is written throughout in a clear and elegant Tuscan. It consists of four discourses supposed to have taken place in 1507 in the Palace of Urbino, famous for its fashionable elegance. Nineteen men and four women are the speakers; among these are a notable group of scholars, churchmen, and high aristocrats. Everything is most refined; how to please the ruler and how to act in polite society had evidently become an art in itself. The qualities and education of the courtier and the noble lady are discussed in detail. Nothing must be overdone either in emphasis on physical prowess or on intellectual accomplishments. The last book describes the noble ruler, and at the end Cardinal Bembo is made to launch forth on a rhapsodic description of the Renaissance ideal of Platonic love.

The style of the book is smooth and flowing, somewhat affected by the rhetorical devices of the Latin Humanists but better organized than any vernacular prose in Italian since that of Boccaccio. The work went through many editions both in Italian and the languages of western Europe. It was much read and highly esteemed even in faraway lands such as Sweden, Poland, and Hungary. And it was widely imitated in writings in other countries. Castiglione's work shows how the artists and writers of the High Renaissance loved to dwell in a dreamland of beauty warmed by the glow of Platonic love quite removed from the hard realities of the world about them, a world of sordid intrigues, tortures, poisonings, and assassinations.

This world of realities, which does not appear in the writings of Ariosto and Castiglione, is clearly present in the works of Machiavelli and Guicciardini. The background of their writings lies partly in the actual conditions of their time and partly in the work of the Humanist historians of the fifteenth century. These historians had dropped the idea of universal history beginning in the Garden of Eden, in the tradition of Augustine; they had abandoned the fabulous and the impossible; and they had learned to employ documents, weigh evidence, and accept the worldly point of view of the historians of classical antiquity. Machiavelli (d. 1527) learned his technique of writing history from reading the ancient historians—Plutarch, Polybius, and Livy. Polybius, especially, looked at politics, without illusions of any kind, as a play of human forces. He believed states were always changing; they never stood still. Machiavelli, as a state official, also saw the conditions of his own time, the decline of the nobility, the loss of respect for the papacy, the increase of foreign political influence in Italy, and the growth of the balance-of-power system. He came to hold a very low opinion of human nature, and he was convinced that treachery and violence are necessary to maintain governments. There is no higher law, he believed, than that of the prosperity and safety of the state. In this renunciation of divine and natural law in *The Prince* and other writings and in his isolating political issues from other questions Machiavelli was breaking new ground; he knew it, and said so. His low opinion of human nature comes out strongly in his comedy *Mandragola,* the best Italian comedy of the sixteenth century. It does not follow the models of Latin comedy, but if it has any ancestry it is that of the medieval interlude and the popular *novella.* The play is a satire on bourgeois naïveté and ecclesiastical corruption.

In his studies of history and politics, Machiavelli shows himself to be one of the greatest prose stylists of the sixteenth century. He writes clearly, vigorously, directly, and with striking metaphors. The High Renaissance ideal of a clear prose style was summed up later by Ben Jonson: "The congruent and harmonious fitting of parts in a sentence (and in a whole work) hath almost the fastening and force of connection as in stone well squared which will rise strong, a great way, without mortar." It is surprising that Machiavelli escaped both the rhetorical enthusiasm of the Humanists and the general aestheticism of the time. One characteristic of his thought is common to many of the writers of the sixteenth century: he speaks continually of the great men of classical antiquity and even of classical mythology as one might speak of contemporaries; and he drops out all consideration of or even reference to the Middle Ages. The most read of Machiavelli's books, *The Prince,* was both praised and abused; and all parties accused their enemies of being "Machiavellian." Not until the nineteenth century brought to light the whole setting of his time, was Machiavelli really understood.

Much more cynical than Machiavelli was his younger contemporary Guicciardini (d. 1540). He served the governments of Florence and the Papal States, and he was deeply read in the politics and history of antiquity. His most remarkable work, *A History of Italy,* a masterpiece of detachment and penetration, is mostly concerned with war and diplomacy. His cynicism is not relieved by the ardent Italian patriotism of Machiavelli, but his style has much of the simplicity, and force and lack of ornament that characterizes the latter's style. In a story of utter wretchedness, Guicciardini tells of brutalities and perfidy, the sack of cities, and the murder of men and the deprivation of their liberty. He hates tyrants, priests, and foreign invaders, but he sees no hope anywhere. Where Italian civilization stood at the end of the short period of the High Renaissance is forever clear in the frozen bitterness of Guicciardini's words:

I know none more disgusted than myself by the ambition, avarice, and effeminacy of the priests. Yet my relations with the popes have compelled me to love their grandeur. If it were not for this, I should have loved Martin Luther like myself. Three things I wish to see, but doubt of seeing any one of them: a well-ordered republic in our city, Italy freed from the barbarians, and the world freed from the tyranny of these vile priests.

So the art of Raphael, Titian, and Ariosto, instead of reflecting the life of the Age of the High Renaissance seems to reflect, rather, a willed classical dream of a beautiful world that existed mostly in the minds of these artists.

By the early sixteenth century all of western Europe was falling under the spell of the artistic and literary achievements of the ancients, especially those of Rome, and under the spell of Italian High Renaissance art and letters. Everywhere, in the lands beyond the Alps, classical works of art and literature and those of Renaissance Italy were being collected and studied and imitated. But, at the same time, the non-Italian nations wished to assert their own individuality. They modified ancient and Italian artistic styles and adjusted them to their own late Gothic ideas of art. In the literary field, they sought to use their own national language and to glorify it in great works of literature; and there appeared literary manifestoes like those of Du Bellay in France and Sidney in England. Thus at once in the Age of the High Renaissance Europe was swept by both international and national currents of art and letters. Everywhere in the sixteenth century there was a lengthening shadow cast upon art and literature by ancient Greece and Rome and by contemporary Italy, and at the same time a desire for original creation.

In the lands beyond Italy, the two writers who in wide influence rivaled the greatest Italian Renaissance men of letters were Erasmus and Luther. Luther's influence was largely, though by no means entirely, confined to Germany, but Erasmus of Rotterdam (d. 1536) influenced the thought and the style of writing in all the countries of western Europe from Spain to Sweden. The heralds of a new day in letters in these lands beyond Italy had been the Humanists. It was the impetus given by Italian Humanism that reactivated the classics and renewed vernacular literatures throughout western Europe. Here, beyond the Alps, the rate of change was much slower than it had been in Italy. Medieval ways of feeling and thinking continued longer, and change, when it did occur, was less thoroughgoing. Thus, Scholasticism in the schools, medieval styles in literature, and the Gothic in art lingered on well into the sixteenth century at a time when Italy had left behind most of her medieval ways.

Erasmus, the greatest of northern men of letters, came to be a towering figure in the whole intellectual life of Europe. This "father of Humanism," as Rabelais was soon to call him, helped to turn the course of scholarship; of vernacular literature; and of political, social, and religious thought. Erasmus' extraordinary influence was extended not only through such popular writings as his *Praise of Folly,* the *Colloquies,* and his edition of the New Testament—among the most-read books of the High Renaissance—but also through long sojourns he made in Italy, Germany, France, and England. Though Erasmus was the most gifted classical scholar of the whole Renaissance, his first interest lay in religious reform. He earnestly believed in a simple and undogmatic Christianity—what he called "the philosophy of Christ"—a faith founded on the "Sermon on the Mount" and the ethical teachings of the ancients. His program included the fullest study of Greek and Latin letters, a return to the Bible and the early sources of Christian faith, the suppression of abuses in the church, and the substitution of an inner piety for all mechanical schemes of salvation. He attacked scholastic sterility, the abuses of monasticism, the worship of relics, pilgrimages, and a long series of other accretions in the church. It was his fate to be hated by both Catholics and Protestants because, disliking violence and bigotry, he would not openly join either side in the Age of the Reformation.

Erasmus' Latin style—all his writing was in Latin—influenced vernacular styles wherever he was read. His style is clear, vivid, straightforward, and flexible; it has both strength and subtlety. Erasmus could be sharp in his criticism; and now and then there is a rapier thrust skilfully directed at the chosen victim. Still more effective is the quiet irony of the author as he holds up to scorn an institution or a person by a simple narrative without one word of abuse—so candid that one wonders how anything so silly or so malignant was ever allowed to exist. Erasmus was interested in classical writers, but pointed out that a slavish imitation of them was folly. The purism of Cardinal Bembo and some of the Italian Humanists, who pretended to write only the purest Ciceronian prose and who could speak of Christ only as "Jupiter optimus maximus" and of the Twelve Apostles as "the conscript fathers," disgusted him. Erasmus set forward a method of teaching writing that had a great influence on both Latin and vernacular style. Students were shown how, in reading, they should collect in their notebooks effective ways of expression, figures of speech, antitheses, epithets, synonyms, similes, anecdotes, and descriptions of places and persons—all the illustrative matter of rhetoric—and with these as a guide original writing could proceed. All of this was very influential in the clarification and enrichment of both poetic and prose styles in all the vernacular literatures.

France was more deeply penetrated with the ideas of Renaissance Italy than any country beyond the Alps. Italian scholars and artists had come into France, and French art and letters had begun to show Italian influences before the French military invasions of Italy between 1494 and 1525. These invasions, which took thousands of Frenchmen to Italy, meant that Renaissance influences from Italy began to flood the country; and art, literature, costume, and manners rapidly became more Italianate. The effect on literature was to bring a gradual change in style and subject matter. French writers imitated and adapted the classical and Italian literary forms into French writing; and they drove out of style a late medieval way of writing, that of the *Rhétoriqueurs* who wrote in a labored, mannered, and often obscure style. The first outstanding result of these changes in French letters is shown in the work of Rabelais (d. 1553), certainly one of the most original writers of the High Renaissance.

Rabelais wrote his long, meandering novel, *Gargantua and Pantagruel,* in parts as he found leisure in his career as a busy physician. As a youth, he had acquired a thorough knowledge of classical and Italian literature. He never stayed anywhere long; his curiosity, energy, and restlessness, which seem to have been without bound, always drove him on, and everywhere his consuming curiosity turned up new ideas. The bases of his tale are old stories about giants, but he manages to crowd into the work nearly all he knew about everything. He hates everything medieval and lampoons it mercilessly; especially does he despise the pedantry of the schools and the murkiness of the clergy. Satire, burlesque, sheer extravaganza, and serious discussions are all mixed together. His basic ideas are to follow nature and reason, to rely on oneself, to seek sincerely, to trust experience as the only effective guide, and to laugh the evils out of life. In his avidity for all possible kinds of experience, he reached out, as an eager child, without taste or discrimination. It is Rabelais' ideas and his gusto that is outstanding. Although he knew—and admired—the classics of Greece, Rome, and Renaissance Italy, his style of writing is diffuse and sprawling; at times, however, it can be short, direct, and vivid. Rabelais had a great effect on French prose style, moving it toward vigor and robustness and toward a larger vocabulary. In Rabelais' whole work, there is a mixture of the medieval and the modern, yet there is an elemental force in it, like the invention of printing or of gunpowder, or like the voyages of Columbus. His work is the expression of a great age; it is not out of a classical manuscript. In Rabelais we see the Triumph of Death, a favorite theme of the later Middle Ages, turned into a Triumph of Life.

In 1549 came a new trumpet call in French letters: Du Bellay's *Defense and Ennoblement of the French Language.* By this time, scholarly editions and translations of Greek and Latin authors, and critical treatises on them were available; and a number of Italian critical works on literary style were known in France. The *Defense* calls for a great renovation in French poetry which is to be invigorated by a closer study of classical and Italian verse and prose, all of which is combined with a stirring patriotic appeal. The old French literary forms must go, and French poets should write odes, elegies, eclogues, satires, epics, sonnets, tragedies, and comedies following the best classical and Italian models. In all this imitation, the poet should know his models well enough to reproduce the elements he required without resort to notebooks—as with Erasmus—and without remembering exactly from whom each gem came. Seize these classical and Italian treasures, make them your own, then create—such is his message.

It was one thing to produce a manifesto, but another to find a great poet to carry it into effect. But such was at hand in Du Bellay's cousin and collaborator, Ronsard (d. 1585), who was the leader among a group of young poets who called themselves the "Pléiade." Ronsard's output was enormous, and included verse in many forms, even an unfinished epic. But he was most effective as a writer of lyrics, especially odes, sonnets, and songs. His poetic style was at first considered so novel that it was laughed at, but gradually he came to be understood. His poems show great skill in construction and an easy command of the verse forms he used, together with movement and eloquence. He had a very subtle ear for the harmony of rhythm, rhyme, and thought, and finally a superb talent for the adjustment of his verse forms to the thought and feeling of a whole poem. Ronsard and others of the Pléiade naturalized the sonnet in France, as Boscán, and Wyatt and Surrey were doing in Spain and England. In his odes, modeled chiefly on those of Horace, Ronsard showed how to use mythology and history and elevated themes in verse. Though he rarely wrote without some germ of thought, his matchless and fluent manner in some of his verse surpasses the matter in the poem. His late sonnets are Manneristic. Though Ronsard's work is uneven his poems include some of the best not only in French literature of the High Renaissance, but in the total output of all Europe in that period.

Boscán (d. 1542) and Garcilaso de la Vega (d. 1536) spread the popularity of the Italian sonnet in Spain, and introduced forms of classical Latin poetry into the vernacular. Boscán also introduced the *terza rima,* the *ottava rima,* and blank verse from Italy, and translated Castiglione's *Courtier* into Spanish. Garcilaso de la Vega was a more gifted poet. His mastery of form, perfect finish, and careful workmanship brought Spanish verse into the full tide of the High Renaissance. These two poets played something of the same role in Spain as that of the Pléiade in France, and of Wyatt and Surrey in England. The most outstanding High Renaissance work of the Iberian Peninsula is the epic of Camoëns (d. 1580), *The Lusiads,* whose title refers to the sons of Lusus, the mythical founder of Portugal. The true hero of the epic is the Portuguese people, especially those who had launched the Portuguese Empire overseas; and though the main thread of the tale centers around the voyage of Vasco da Gama, the past, present, and future of Portugal are woven skilfully into the story. Camoëns had spent seventeen years at Goa in India and at other ports of the Portuguese commercial empire, and so knew his material at first hand. The *Aeneid* of Virgil was his model, but it is evident that Camoëns knew well much of classical Latin literature and of Italian poetry from Petrarch through Ariosto. The Portuguese people in the age of discovery and exploration are presented as a race of heroes whose accomplishment in Africa and Asia was greater than that of the heroes of antiquity. Beyond this, it is the heroic tale of Christianity against the forces of error and darkness. The epic is written in ten cantos of Italianate *ottava rima;* it is extremely musical and fluent, which has made it difficult to translate, and it has wonderful descriptions of scenery and heroic actions. Here was a true epic of the highest literary value about which the Italian writers and critics of several generations had talked and written so much, but which no Italian had produced.

In Germany, the Renaissance which began, as elsewhere, in the writing and teaching of Humanists, was soon snuffed out in the inferno of religious controversy followed by civil war that succeeded the outbreak of the Reformation in 1517. The leading German writer, Luther (d. 1546), in his treatises and sermons and in his translation of the Bible into the Saxon-German dialect, owed nothing to Italian models. The fiery and powerful vernacular he used came chiefly from the popular preaching of the time; and the Reformation hymns, for a few of which Luther wrote both words and music, were derived from folk songs and popular hymns of the church. Because of the great circulation of his translation of the Bible, he gave Germany a literary language and helped to make the Saxon dialect the national language.

A very belated representative of the literary ideals of the High Renaissance was Opitz (d. 1639), the leader of a group who wished to work reforms in German literature similar to those made in France by the Pléiade. Opitz translated plays of Sophocles and Seneca into German;

made a German version of an early Italian opera *Dafne* which was set to music by Heinrich Schütz; translated Sidney's *Arcadia,* and wrote some original poetry (of a mediocre character), using classical and Italian figures of speech and literary forms. His great influence came from his *Book of German Poetics,* the material for which was derived chiefly from Horace, Scaliger, and the writers of the French Pléiade. He wished to introduce new principles of versification into German, and new literary genres taken from the classics and from Italian and French literature. Opitz' success as a lawgiver in Germany was complete; not Bembo earlier, nor Boileau later, had such a success in winning over writers; and, until the early eighteenth century, Opitz' book remained the *ars poetica* of the German poets. On the other hand, few great literary works were produced in Germany until the eighteenth century.

England, in comparison with her close neighbor France, was both geographically and culturally a stage farther from Italy, the land of classical and Renaissance enchantments. But many of the same cultural currents appeared, though at different times, on both sides of the English Channel. In each country, the new Humanist learning and the new literary styles from Italy drew the writers toward broadened horizons. But, paradoxically, the great effect of these foreign influences was to create a literature strongly nationalistic in tone. These new currents, however, moved more slowly in Britain than in France. While Frenchmen were producing works of art in a new Renaissance style, England was either still following medieval styles of art or was importing sculptures and paintings from abroad. And before the greatest writers of the High Renaissance in England came upon the scene, France had already produced Rabelais and most of the poetry of the Pléiade. Moreover, it must be remembered that men like Spenser and Shakespeare came after the Reformation had seriously affected English thought. This helps to account for the deeper gravity and probing of conscience that one finds in the greatest English Renaissance writers in comparison with the High Renaissance writers on the Continent. Finally, in comparing the English achievement in Renaissance letters with that of France, it should be borne in mind that while much of the literature of sixteenth-century France came to be regarded all over western Europe as nearly as important as that of Renaissance Italy, English writing, on the other hand, hardly attracted any attention abroad—at least until the eighteenth century, when the early Romantics on the Continent discovered Shakespeare.

There is little in English letters between 1500 and 1570 that gives promise of the great flowering in the midst of which the century closed. The prose written in England, with some exceptions, remained clumsy and prolix, and in neither poetry nor the drama was there any outstanding achievement. Then suddenly, around 1570, poetry and drama of the highest quality appear; and, with Hooker, modern English prose is first clearly revealed. Puttenham, a late sixteenth-century critic, hails Wyatt and Surrey as "the chieftains" of a new literary movement who, "having travelled into Italy and there tasted the sweete and stately measures and stile of Italian poesie, as novices newly crept out of the schools of Dante, Petrarch, and Ariosto, they greatly polish our rude manner of poesie, and, for that cause, may be justly said the first reformers of our English numbers." Wyatt (d. 1542) introduced into English letters the sonnet (whose form he modified), *terza rima,* and *ottava rima.* His writing consists of thirty-two sonnets, seventeen of which are adopted from Petrarch; some satires; and metrical versions of certain Psalms. The most notable of his achievements was to give direct expression to virile feeling without recourse to allegory. At his best, he combines the sweetness of Horace and Petrarch with their courtly grace, and he naturalized both in English verse. Whereas the prevailing poetic style lacked form and structure, was very verbose, and was loaded with irrelevant material, Wyatt is polished, brief, direct, and clearly focused.

The Earl of Surrey (d. 1547) was a more gifted poet, who was, unfortunately, executed for treason at the age of thirty. His style was deeply indebted to that of Martial, Horace, and Virgil, and the Italian poets. Besides writing some effective sonnets, he introduced into English poetry—partly from Chaucer but more from Italy—the use of blank verse. The renovation of English verse begun by Wyatt and Surrey did not immediately bear fruit. Before their lead was again taken up by Sidney a generation later, much of the work of the Pléiade had become known in England.

Sidney (d. 1586), though he died in battle at the age of thirty-two, was the first highly gifted writer to appear in the English High Renaissance. As a youth he had acquired a wide knowledge of five foreign literatures: Greek, Latin, Italian, French, and Spanish. He was saturated with the best of European culture, and he counted among his friends, Tintoretto, Veronese, Spenser, William the Silent, and Bruno. Sidney's first important work is his pastoral novel, *Arcadia,* written in prose with verse interspersed. Here he mingles the Italian pastoral with elements drawn from old chivalric romances. His Arcadian countryside is swept and garnished for the visit of princes and nobles. It admits no noise from those stricken by the enclosure movement about which Thomas More writes in his *Utopia.* Arcadia is pictured as a poetic and enchanted land of blissful innocence, a never-never land of fabulous imaginings where the author shows his youthful and burning enthusiasm for valor, courtesy, classical and Italian culture, and beauty. The novel contains descriptions of nature in terms of line and color, and of light and shade that are new in English literature. Sidney followed this with his brilliant *Defense of Poesie,* which reflects his wide reading in ancient, Italian, and French letters, and is easily the most comprehensive work of Renaissance literary criticism. Here he analyzes what gives excellence to tragedy, comedy, the epic, and the lyric—much of which is derived from continental critics. Sidney also sounds a strong patriotic note and glorifies the use of the vernacular.

The most important original work of Sidney is in his sonnet sequence, *Astrophel and Stella.* The first sonnet sequence written outside of Italy had been one by Joachim du Bellay, followed soon by a number of sonnet sequences by Ronsard. Sidney's work consists of one hundred and eight sonnets and eleven songs. Though he borrows from the Italian and French sonneteers, there is a deep sincerity in Sidney's verses. He speaks from the heart of his unfulfilled love. Some of the sonnets follow the form used by Petrarch, and some the simplified form of Surrey. Sidney is completely master of his medium, and he writes with a surety surpassed only by some of the greatest sonnets of Spenser and Shakespeare. The publication of Sidney's sonnets after his early death caused a sensation, and seems to have started a craze for sonnet writing in England.

Sidney's friend, Edmund Spenser (d. 1599), was one of the most gifted poets of the whole High Renaissance Age in all Europe. As a youth he received a thorough Humanist education, and was early soaked in classical, Italian, and French literature; in early years he also came under strong Calvinist influence. All these currents showed up later in his writing. His first important work, *The Shepheards Calender,* consists of twelve eclogues, one for each month. Though it shows a deep knowledge of classical and continental literature, the work has great freshness and charm and exhibits a superb mastery of various verse forms unmatched in English poetry since Chaucer; it ranks as the finest pastoral poem of the whole Renaissance. Spenser's poetic output was enormous, and uneven. Among his greater achievements were the *Amoretti,* a sonnet sequence that relates the story of Spenser's courting of his second wife. They are full of echoes of classical, and Italian and French High Renaissance poetry. Closely connected in style with this great sonnet sequence are a number of wedding hymns, including the "Epithalamion," which celebrates his own wedding in what is considered the finest love poem in the English language. The verbal music of the lines is sustained and unabated. The whole is a miracle of skilful structure, and everything in it is luminous, and seems inevitable.

Spenser labored over twenty years on his never-completed masterpiece, *The Faerie Queene.* Here he intended to embody the best of Homer, Virgil, Ariosto, and Tasso; especially it was his purpose to rival Ariosto and surpass him in seriousness. In a letter to Raleigh, Spenser defines this purpose: "The general end of all the book is to fashion a gentleman or noble person in virtuous discipline." Close to Spenser's heart, also, was the desire to glorify England and Queen Elizabeth, who figures as "Gloriana." The whole was planned in twelve books, in imitation of the *Aeneid,* each to represent a virtue; but only six and a fragment of a seventh were written. Love is the prime creative force in man's existence; and earthly love and earthly beauty are only reflections of a divine love and beauty; beams from on high lodged in earthly bodies. Spenser was steeped in Platonism, which he combined with Christian ideals.

The whole poem was to supply England with a work such as Homer had given to Greece, Virgil to Rome, Ariosto and Tasso to Italy, and, by harking back to Chaucer and Malory, whom Spenser admired, to tie in with a glorious English poetic tradition. Spenser is not a great storyteller; and the fact that, from the beginning, everything is allegorized makes the work difficult to follow. We read of the Red Cross Knight (either St. George or Henry VIII) fighting with a magician, Archimago (the pope); slaying a foul witch, Duessa (either Mary Stuart or the Roman church); and finally marrying Una (the Church of England). His first name for the whole work, "Pageants," best describes it, for its series of magnificent pictures is the finest thing in the work. If the reader realizes that always to understand is unnecessary, and that it is enough to gaze and to listen to the glorious music in which the pictures are set, he will discover the essence of this great poem. As a word-painter, Spenser has few rivals in world literature. He sees nature as did the Italian Renaissance painters; single flowers, leaves, and individual rocks, and animals are sharply observed, and then all the parts are combined into one superb picture. Richness, as with Shakespeare, rather than simplicity is the note of this long, bewildering, and magnicent combination of epic, chivalric romance, and pastoral. For his verse form Spenser modified the Italian *ottava rima* into a stanza of eight five-foot, iambic lines followed by an Alexandrine line of six feet, the whole rhyming *ababbcbcc*. His stanzas flow on, one to another, as a slow-moving river; and we leave this world and listen to the harmonies of a realm of poetic illusion where there is the unhurried beauty one finds in the murmur of the wind, the roll of the sea, and the vast sweep of the sky. For Spenser is not only one of the great word-painters among the poets; he is likewise one of the great magicians. Spenser's language and his command of verse form led Lamb to call him "the poet's poet." His mastery of turning into deathless beauty words and phrases which seem only for humdrum use has never been surpassed; indeed one can hardly imagine that it ever will be.

The age of the High Renaissance in English poetry was also a great age in the drama. The public loved the theater, and to supply the demand there was a great outpouring of plays in the later sixteenth and early seventeenth centuries. The number and enormous diversity of these plays, together with the lack of dates for most of the plays, makes any classification difficult. The first highly gifted poet who turned to writing popular plays was Marlowe (d. 1593). His special contributions were to discover the effectiveness of blank verse for playwriting and the value of history as material for plays. Marlowe represents his age and the spirit of the High Renaissance in his enthusiasm for all experience—in which he especially resembles Rabelais—and his belief in life and experience. His ability to write mighty poetry that is gorgeous and electrifying is unfortunately greater than his capacity to create characters: the leading figure in each play is well portrayed, but the lesser characters have little real existence.

Among the works of Shakespeare (d. 1616), the poems "Venus and Adonis" and "Lucrece," many of his sonnets, most of his historical plays, and his romantic comedies all belong, in their spirit and style, to the Age of the High Renaissance. Shakespeare evidently knew, in translation, some of the best of classical literature—especially that of Rome and the literature of the Italian and French Renaissance—and he drew on all this literary material not only for stories but also for concepts and for figures of speech and other features of style. Through his early plays, though their exact dating is uncertain, one may follow a steady unfolding of Shakespeare's genius. The poetry becomes more varied, the mastery of the language is more marked, and the characterization of the various roles becomes much more penetrating. The leading plays of the early and middle period of Shakespeare's career that are most outstanding as poetic and dramatic achievements are: *Henry V, Romeo and Juliet, Julius Caesar, A Midsummer Night's Dream, The Merchant of Venice, As You Like It,* and *Twelfth Night.* If Shakespeare had died in 1600, he would be remembered for his poems, some of his sonnets, and for these plays. Yet a number of his best comedies and his greatest tragedies all lay in the future, and belong in their style and spirit to the Age of Mannerism, rather than to that of the High Renaissance.

Seen as a whole, Shakespeare's work is distinguished from that of his contemporaries first by its amazing variety. Of the thirty-six plays he wrote, no two are alike, or produce in us the same impression. While most other playwrights had their own distinctive area of interest, Shakespeare handled the most diverse subjects with equal ardor. He shows, too, an equal aptitude for comedy and tragedy, sentiment and mockery, lyric fantasy and character analysis—and for women no less than men. Even in the production of a single year he ranged easily from one extreme to the other. Among his greatest gifts was that of reviving figures from history and of giving life to imaginary characters. Shakespeare created a whole world of characters who have a living force greater than that of many persons among whom we pass our lives. And everything seems spontaneous and natural. The first of dramatists was also the first poet of his time; and the fusion of drama and poetry is perfect and yet escapes analysis. Truth and beauty are blended in a perfect unity.

4. Music

In its calm and grand manner the musical style of the High Renaissance resembles the parallel styles of art and literature. Music is still primarily vocal, though there begins to be more writing for solo instruments and for instrumental ensembles. The style of the Netherlands School, whose members now found employment or followers in all the states of Latin Christendom, remained dominant everywhere in both religious and secular music, though this dominance is more marked in the religious music of Catholic states and of England than in the continental states that turned Protestant in the sixteenth century. The musical style of the High Renaissance everywhere shows clarity of structure, a dignified sedateness, and calm emotion. The leading musical forms were the mass, the motet (called in England, the anthem), and the secular madrigal, chanson, and lied. All these forms were inaugurated by Netherlanders and widely accepted by composers in different nations; Netherlands music, with modifications, became Italian music in Italy, French music in France, Spanish music in Spain, German music in Germany, and English music in England.

Branching off from the dominant Netherlands style, from the middle of the sixteenth century, were new experiments in harmony and general musical style that did not supplant the Netherlands style but ran parallel with it. So for a long time in music, styles of the High Renaissance and of Mannerism overlapped. There is, however, a continuity in the lofty style of church music from Josquin des Près around 1500 through William Byrd around 1600. In secular music national differences became more marked in the course of the sixteenth century; the Italian madrigal, the English madrigal, the French chanson, and the German lied showed more variations than were evident in the prevailing styles of church music.

In the middle and later sixteenth century there appeared a shift toward an experimental and Mannerist style in both church and secular music. This change, however, did not at first set aside the traditional High Renaissance musical style but ran parallel with it; and, in addition, there was in Germany, and then in other continental lands where Protestantism grew, a new popular style of church music based on the congregational hymn or chorale. The story of sixteenth-century music is therefore much more complex than that of art or of literature, where one style succeeded another, and each new style, for all practical purposes, supplanted an earlier style.

The Netherlands style of music which had had a remarkable flowering in the fifteenth century had spread all over Latin Christendom in the sixteenth century, and the influence of its Netherlandish originators gave a wide uniformity of style to much of the music of the High Renaissance. This style showed great self-assurance and consummate mastery of counterpoint, a general tranquillity of mood, a strictly controlled use of dissonance, the absence of special parts written for instrumental accompaniment, and the use of four to eight voice parts, five parts being the most usual. Other characteristics of the style were its lofty and ethereal quality, its absence of climax, its absence of strong rhythmic accent, a lack of emphasis on originality of themes used, and a great stress on sureness of technique rather than the achievement of a markedly individual style. Contemporary writings show that music in the High Renaissance style, as much of the art and literature of the same age, was supposed to represent a harmony that existed in the universe.

The standards of performance of religious music were very high in the sixteenth century. Memberships in the Vatican Choirs for which Palestrina wrote, in the Ducal Choir at Munich where Lassus spent some of his most productive years, or in the Royal Chapel Choir in England of which Byrd was organist, were very coveted positions and were well paid. The singers, besides, had a status similar to that of performers in the best orchestras today. Just as the latter are paid to devote their whole effort to orchestral work, so choir singers in the leading choirs of the High Renaissance were paid to do nothing but sing. These choirs had elaborate rules concerning pay, absences, pensions, and many matters down to the minute details of conduct. They were highly professional bodies and were capable of an unusual polish and finish of production.

The founder of High Renaissance music, occupying a place in the development of style comparable to that held in painting by Leonardo da Vinci and in letters by Ariosto, is Josquin des Près (d. 1521). His style compared with that of his predecessors in the Netherlands School is both grander and more simple. All stark intervals of early polyphony are ruled out; few dissonances are used, and the rhythms and forms used are based on strict symmetry and mathematically regular proportions. Josquin handled all technical problems of complicated constructions with the same ease and sureness one finds in the drawings of Leonardo and Raphael. In both his religious music, masses and motets, and his secular part songs, Josquin surpassed his predecessors in the exercise of inventiveness and ingenuity, but unlike them he seems not to have regarded counterpoint as an end in itself but as a means toward a musical expression of feeling. He was the first to discover the importance of flowing melody and appropriate harmony as vehicles of such expression. In his later works he gave more attention to trying to integrate words and music.

As many of the Netherlands composers, Josquin held positions in a number of countries, in his case Italy and France; and this, together with the early publication of some of his works, helped to spread his style. The printing of music, which began in Venice in the early sixteenth century and very soon spread all over Europe, undoubtedly tended to make changes in style better and more easily known. Josquin came at a fortunate period in the development of music; by his time the art had developed a capacity for rich and varied expression. He seemed to loosen the tongue of the old polyphonic art and make it speak with unmatched eloquence in his masses, motets, and secular songs. There is no stress or strain, as with earlier Netherland masters; and he could make a tightly woven polyphony, where each part had an independent melodic and rhythmic existence but all parts were fully blended, that sounded perfectly free and natural. Much of his music— and this became more common in the High Renaissance style—is not tied to a *cantus firmus*. His music has a definite tonal center around which the whole musical structure is organized. Musical style had not shown such a focus since the Gregorian chants had been formulated. No wonder Luther declared, "Other composers do what they can with the notes; Josquin alone does what he wishes with them." And speaking of his tremendous influence, Castiglione said that no piece of music was fashionable unless it was thought to be composed by Josquin. What Josquin achieved set a standard for the great composers of the High Renaissance who succeeded him: Orlandus Lassus, Palestrina, and William Byrd.

Another great master, Orlandus Lassus (d. 1594), though born in the Low Countries, held positions all over Europe. He wrote music to texts in five languages: Latin, Italian, French, Flemish, and German; and his style takes on the mood of the language and something of the prevailing style of secular music of the particular country for whose speech he is writing. Both in his religious and in his secular music Orlandus Lassus got surprising effects by providing single voices with vigorous accents and variations in rhythm according to words of the text. He still wrote in the old modes, but his strong sense of tonalities points ahead to the time of major and minor keys. It is difficult to characterize the music of Lassus because he is the most varied of the composers of the High Renaissance. His "Penitential Psalms" are heavy with religious emotionality, and show a man shaking and crying "mea culpa"; yet some of his French songs are frivolous, witty, and worldly. He was a friend of Ronsard and set some of his poetry to music. Lassus' madrigals set to

Italian words are suave and sensitive, while his German songs reflect the heavy, clumsy humor and rough jollity of his temporarily adopted residence in Munich. Some of Lassus' motets have a great tragic intensity and others are devout but joyous; he gets all this variety, yet stays within the framework of the Netherlands polyphonic techniques. In his secular music, while Palestrina endeavored to express the general sentiment of the words by smooth and flowing melodic phrases, Lassus aimed at expressing the meaning of individual words and phrases by abrupt turns of melody or harmony, or both, and occasionally by chromatic modulations. His output was enormous, though hardly uniform in quality. It includes fifty-three masses, two hundred "Magnificats," twelve hundred motets, two hundred madrigals, and several hundred solo songs. Among his masterpieces are a number of motets that are the settings of "Seven Penitential Psalms," where the Psalmist's moods of despair at his sins and hopes for salvation are embodied in music of the highest spiritual nobility. Orlandus Lassus was indeed a whole man to whom no experience, grave or gay, came amiss, and who could turn to good account in his music every variety of human emotion. Yet it was the mysteries of sin and death that evoked his most sublime music, just as they inspired Donne's finest poetry. By 1570 Lassus was considered the prince of European music; he held a position similar to Michelangelo's in art; and pope, emperor, and kings received him as a royal personage. Though less of an innovator than Josquin des Près, Orlandus Lassus is probably the greatest musical genius of the High Renaissance; and his published religious and secular works give us the fullest musical conception of the achievements of the age.

The outstanding interpreter of the Roman liturgy was Lassus' Italian contemporary Palestrina (d. 1594). He spent most of his active years in the service of the popes. His music, though it was very traditionalist in its general aspects and quite unsensational in a propagandistic sense, was highly approved by the leaders of the Catholic church, who gave it their official sanction. Its basic quality is that of a skilful combination of a mastery of the complexities of the contrapuntal style of the age with an Italian melodic bent and grace, and clarity. Palestrina simplified the prevailing contrapuntal style and achieved a purity of effect and a coupling of ideal contents with ideal form achieved by no other church composer of the High Renaissance. The Catholic spirit has never found a more congenial or a more convincing form of musical expression. His style has a great range; he combines a seraphic mildness with passionate outcries, and soaring heights of ecstasy with deep seriousness of religious meditation. His masses were written for every liturgical occasion. His writing always seems to suit the occasion, and it is always exactly fitted to different types of voices beyond whose range he never goes. Unlike Orlandus Lassus, Palestrina does not seem to have been a facile composer, and his weaker works are heavy and monotonous in style. And unlike other composers of the High Renaissance, Palestrina only rarely used the themes of secular songs as the basis for his religious music. His secular madrigals have a seriousness of tone that make them unique in their age. Palestrina excludes worldly suggestion and sometimes even human emotions from his religious music. So absorbed does he become in his devotion that, at times, his music seems almost motionless. If there be a Paradise, the music of Palestrina must perforce resound therein.

Palestrina's Spanish follower, Victoria (d. 1611), who may have been his pupil, is less austere than Palestrina. He uses wide leaps in the individual vocal lines, a certain amount of half-step variation for the intensification of dramatic effects, and an extensive employment of suspension. Victoria used few concerted cadences except at the ends of sections, where they are handled in such a way as to create an atmosphere of ecstasy. Victoria was a very devout man; he wrote no secular music—only masses, motets, and hymns—and he used no secular themes in his compositions. His masterpiece is usually considered to be his famous *Requiem*. It is filled with the passionate mysticism of a St. Theresa or of a St. John of the Cross. There is something very Spanish in the music of Victoria with its feverish ecstasy, its dark glow, and its consuming melancholy.

The last great master of the High Renaissance style of church music was William Byrd (d. 1623), who wrote settings for both Catholic and Anglican religious services. Byrd was greatly esteemed in his own time, and he spent years as the head of Queen Elizabeth's Royal Chapel Choir. His writing is very extensive and includes not only religious works but much secular vocal music, and some fine instrumental compositions. Byrd's compositions seem to reflect the stirring times in which he lived, as do the plays of his contemporary, Shakespeare. Byrd's style of composition is more florid than that of either Orlandus Lassus or Palestrina; it shows great sensitivity to the text, great flexibility, and a complete mastery of homophony and polyphony. Byrd also employed bold dissonances, and no one ever surpassed him in the writing of canons. His greatest choral works are his three Latin masses written for three, four, and five voices, and his Anglican *Great Service* composed for a double choir of ten voices. Byrd also wrote a large number of motets and anthems set to both Latin and English words. In his madrigals he gave a subtle musical portrayal to the spirit of the text he was setting. In addition, he wrote solo songs with a carefully integrated instrumental accompaniment usually of a group of viols. Finally, Byrd is called "the father of keyboard music" because of the series of remarkable compositions he wrote for the virginal. Here, he broke away from the polyphonic tradition and wrote mostly in the form of variations. His keyboard music was influential not only in England, but all over western Europe.

The outbreak of the Reformation in Germany in 1517 soon brought in a new style of church music in the continental states that had turned Protestant all or in part. Luther was himself a good musician, and he believed strongly in the use of music and the vernacular in church services; especially did he favor congregational singing which was now rare in Catholic services. Luther hoped, thereby, to arouse the common people to interest in his movement. The first Protestant hymnbook, with only eight hymns (some of them by Luther himself), was printed in Wittenberg in 1524; and some Protestant motets were published the same year. The four-part hymn tunes were partly adaptations of ancient plain song, partly arrangements of folk songs, and partly original. The only one whose music is certainly by Luther is "A Mighty Fortress Is Our God;" whose words are based on the Forty-sixth Psalm; this became a sort of battle hymn of the Reformation. Luther certainly wrote the words, at least, to about thirty other chorales. Other hymnbooks soon appeared with more four-part chorales, with the melody in the tenor and later in the soprano. By 1600 more than two hundred books of chorales had been published in various Protestant states. In these vigorous chorales, with their simple melodies and powerful rhythm, one can still feel the fires of the Reformation, especially when one hears them sung (as they still are) in certain Protestant churches of Europe and America. These chorale tunes were seen set in polyphonic form—for from three to six parts—for singing by a choir. Later they were used by Protestant composers as the basis of organ compositions, cantatas, oratorios, and passions. So popular did these chorales become, for singing in church or in the home, that the Catholics imitated them.

Just as the Netherlands style of Josquin des Près and his contemporaries and successors dominated the style of High Renaissance church music in the Catholic states of Europe and in England, so, also, is their style in secular music everywhere marked. The Italian madrigal of the High Renaissance was not an outgrowth of the earlier Italian madrigal but of certain popular musical forms that were commonly in use in the early sixteenth century. These forms were refined and polished by sophisticated composers, who wrote in an elaborate polyphonic style. The parts at first were three or four; later on they ranged from four to six, with five being the most common. The old *cantus firmus* is given up. The linear character and the severely complicated construction of the Netherlands School are abandoned, replaced by music with more melodic grace and color. The tendency was to integrate words and music, either in words and phrases or in the mood of the whole composition. The composers all seem to have agreed that words and music should be integrated; but they differed over whether each word or phrase, or the general mood of the poem should determine the music. Zarlino, the leading theorist of the sixteenth century in Italy, believed in the former. "Plato," he writes, "puts the text as the principal element; he says that harmony and rhythm must follow the text. Therefore it would not be fitting to use a sad harmony and a slow rhythm with a gay text." Zarlino then becomes more specific: "To set each word to music in such a way that it denotes hardness, cruelty and other similar things, the music must be similar to it, however, without offending." He then went on to define sad harmony as one that combines slow movement with the use of syncopated dissonances and minor chords, whereas gay harmony prefers major chords in light and fast rhythms. Here is the foundation of a theory of tonal expression that determined in principle music from the sixteenth century on, though means and techniques changed greatly.

The Italian madrigal style was lighter and more melodic than that of their Netherlands models and predecessors. Castiglione insists in the *Courtier* that gentlemen and ladies should be able to read music, to sing, and to play some instrument. The noblest instrument is the viol and the sweetest instrumental music is that produced by a quartet of viols. He also praises keyboard instruments, and solo and ensemble singing. It does not behoove the courtier or his lady to play wind instruments. And the best occasion for music-making is when friends meet in company and no other business is at hand.

The French High Renaissance chanson differed from the religious motets in having a quicker and more marked rhythm, a leaning toward a homophonic structure (shown in an alternation of sections that are homophonic with others that are polyphonic), a sectional construction in short phrases ending simultaneously in all parts, and frequent repetition of a section of music for another line of a poem. In the early sixteenth century French part songs have the elaborate style, the dignity of expression, and the indifference to integrating words and music shown by the earlier Netherlands School. With Jannequin (d. 1560), a pupil of Josquin des Près, and his contemporaries in the middle of the century, the rhythms became more nimble and more frivolous; the rhythmic patterns also became more definite; and cadences are placed where there was punctuation in the text. Jannequin tried some experiments in descriptive music, as the "Battle of Marignano" and the "Song of the Birds," which are curious though of a mediocre artistic value. Some of the best French chansons were written by Orlandus Lassus, who also wrote Italian madrigals and German lieder. The French sixteenth-century chanson usually carried the melody in the tenor, and its general effect is lighter and livelier than that made by the Italian madrigal. Some of its finest achievements were in settings to poems of Ronsard and the Pléiade.

The influence of the Netherlands, then of Italy, is seen in the German polyphonic lied of the High Renaissance. Hassler (d. 1612) is the leading composer of German part songs, though some of his songs have Italian words. He studied for years in Italy, and his style shows Italian influence. Here, in his ability to fuse Italian and German styles of music, Hassler resembles the later Mozart. Hassler's songs mix Italian elegance and grace with German emotional depth, vigor, and solidity of workmanship. The German lied of the sixteenth century is in general characterized by a robust sense of humor, a rude vigor, and a heavy emotionality that set off this form from the elegance and refinement of the Italian madrigal and the sparkling wit and the clear form of the French chanson. After the Reformation, Germany remained divided musically as it was religiously. In northern Germany, Protestant German church music opened up new vistas and new possibilities out of which later came the music of Bach. In southern Germany and Austria, where Italian influences were strong, a musical development was under way that led later to Mozart, Haydn, and Beethoven. In Spain, polyphonic part songs called *"villancicos"* followed first Netherlands, then Italian models. Some of these songs, written as solos to be accompanied on the lute, are among the earliest examples of song in the modern sense of the word.

Nearest to the Italian madrigal in style was the English madrigal. The melody is usually in the soprano; and in England, as elsewhere, the song could be sung by one voice and the other parts performed on instruments. Many of the songs—or *ayres*—by John Dowland (d. 1626) were written for a solo voice and instruments. These songs range from a light gaiety to gloom and tragic intensity. The great madrigals of William Byrd, Orlando Gibbons, Thomas Morley, Wilkes, and Willbye were primarily intended to have all the parts sung unaccompanied. The English madrigals represent a popular movement. We hear in England of no professional madrigal singers employed by the court or the nobility, as in Italy. Instead, the vast number of madrigals that were written were intended for private use by the gentry and the rising middle class. As in Italy, the music is usually fitted either to the general mood of the words, to specific words and phrases, or to both.

Musical instruments of many types had been widely used during the whole of the Middle Ages, but only in the fourteenth century—and then only in music for the organ—had there been written compositions specifically fitted to any one instrument. The High Renaissance saw this writing of idiomatic music for various instruments carried further; and music was now written specifically for the lute, for keyboard instruments such as the organ and the virginal (an early form of the harpsichord), for solo viols, and for groups of instruments. New forms of instrumental music such as the *toccata, ricercare,* and *fugue* came in. The writing shows a growing sense for the timbre and color of various instruments. Mechanical improvements in instruments were introduced; for example, the use by Sweelinck (d. 1621) of independent pedal playing on the organ. Music for the virginal in later sixteenth-century England showed some of the most marked changes in instrumental music. Here rapid scales, arpeggio passages, and repeated chords were freely used. All over western Europe instrumental dances were arranged in series, a form which prefigures the suite. But these instrumental compositions show a development inferior to compositions written for groups of voices, and not until the seventeenth century did instrumental music have an outstanding independent development.

By the end of the sixteenth century the success of Italian music had come to be nearly as complete as the victory of Netherlands music at the opening of the century. The new Italian fashions, including those developed in Italy in the Age of Mannerism, so fascinated musicians of all countries that their national styles of music seemed old-fashioned.

Everywhere music was adopting Italian styles. The Jesuits and other agents of the Catholic Counter Reformation encouraged this and taught Italian musical styles in their schools. So the musical influence of Italy on all of Europe in the seventeenth century was to be as marked as Italy's artistic influence.

5. Conclusion

The art, literature, and music of the High Renaissance all show the calm assurance of an age that believed in itself, and believed also that a great harmony existed in the universe. Inner tensions and strain such as appear later in the ages of Mannerism and the Baroque hardly seem to exist. The achievements of the High Renaissance, with its superb self-reliance and its belief that it had successfully rivaled the ancients in its accomplishments, stands serene and untroubled in the steady light of a golden day.

In all this, as in the Early Renaissance, Italy had clearly taken the lead in art and letters, and the Netherlands in music; though, by the later sixteenth century, Italy was pushing into the position of leadership in European music. In art the Italians remained without serious rivals, but in literature and music the achievements of the lands beyond the Alps sometimes outshone those of the Italians.

It is easier to date the beginnings of High Renaissance style than its close. If one might dare to set dates when the High Renaissance went in for a transformation, if not a decline, one might choose the following: in Italy in 1527 with the Sack of Rome, and in 1530 with the fall of the Florentine Republic; in Spain in 1556 when the dour Philip II replaced his father, Charles V, as king; in France in 1572 with the gory massacre of St. Bartholomew; in England in 1603 with the death of Elizabeth and the arrival in power of the troublesome Stuarts; and, finally, in Germany in 1618 with the outbreak of the Thirty Years' War. All such dates are of course the very roughest approximations, for one period in the arts merges almost imperceptibly into another. As the old declines, the new rises within it, and there are in history no clear beginnings and no ends in the whole sequence of things.

Chapter IV

MANNERISM, 1530–1600
AND LATER

1. Introduction

The term "Mannerism," like such words as "Gothic" and "Impressionism," has had a strange history. Earlier applied to painting, it has gradually been extended to mark the Post-Renaissance Age in all the arts. The word, in one form, was first given currency by Vasari, who spoke of men who painted in the manner of some earlier master and thus did not work from nature but from details taken from earlier artists, building them up into new, strange, and complicated groupings. Vasari speaks of the "strained effects" of these painters, probably having in mind such artists as Pontormo and his pupil Bronzino. In the seventeenth century, the art historian Bellori, an admirer of the Carracci, used the term "Mannerism" in a derogatory sense. For him, it was an affected and inferior style of art. And so this term was used for a long period. In the nineteenth century, Ruskin dismissed much of the art of the later sixteenth century under the phrase, "the grotesque Renaissance," and Croce, in the twentieth century, spoke of Mannerism as "variations on ugliness." The development of Surrealism and Expressionism in the twentieth century has now led to a reappreciation of the art, letters, and music of Mannerism. So Mannerism, long considered a stage in the disintegration of the Renaissance, is now regarded as a period of invention and exploration out of which arose the Baroque, and also as a period of great value and interest in itself. Certainly any style that produced the paintings of Tintoretto, many of the works of Michelangelo, the major plays of Shakespeare, the poetry of Tasso, the *Don Quixote* of Cervantes, and the madrigals of Gesualdo and Monteverdi can never be regarded as a mere degeneration of some earlier style, or as only an unhappy age of transition from High Renaissance to the Baroque.

The origins of the new style can be found in the work of some of the artists of the High Renaissance. The gigantic nudes of Michelangelo's Sistine ceiling, with their strained muscles and contorted poses, and Raphael's "Expulsion of Heliodorus," and his last work, the "Transfiguration," both with figures in violent action, show the beginnings of change. Especially did Michelangelo's Sistine ceiling, with its "caprices" and "inventions," teach the artistic public to admire a disregard for the repose, balance, and proportion in the style of the High Renaissance. And before 1530 a number of younger painters were experimenting with new stylistic devices in composition, drawing, and color.

Soon, parallel changes appeared in literature, and later in music. The tendency in art and literature now was to refashion visible things and ordinary experiences according to fanciful patterns of the imagination. The very essence of the new style was experiment; each artist and writer seems to have been determined to express himself in an intensely personal style, which was often not in very close relation to the work of his contemporaries. The emphasis seemed to be laid on unresolved tensions, on ambiguities, and on complications for their own sake. The shift in taste around 1530 is shown in the fact that such terms as "new," "capricious," "extravagant," and "bizarre" were gradually coming to be terms of honor rather than of disapproval. Standards were shifting; as Montaigne said later in the sixteenth century, "How many ideas that we held yesterday as articles of faith are fables to us today!" After 1550, however, as a reaction to excessive individualism in the arts, critics came to lay emphasis on academic rules in art and literature. Finally, out of the latter phase, there began to arise, about 1580, the Baroque style.

From Italy, the Mannerist movement spread across western and central Europe, carried thence either by Italians who found commissions outside their own country, or by natives of countries from Spain to Sweden who traveled to Italy or at least saw Italian painting and sculpture, read Italian books, or performed Italian music. As the Mannerist style was extended beyond Italy, its influence was mixed with the simultaneous influence of the Italian High Renaissance and with native traditions in art and literature. Hence, outside Italy after 1500, it is hard to distinguish the succession of styles. Mannerism lasted longer in northern Europe than in Italy partly because it reached lands beyond Italy later and partly because Mannerism resuscitated forms of Gothic transcendence and expressionism. The style of the High Renaissance in music long outlasted the parallel styles in art and letters, though there were some composers between Josquin des Près and the early seventeenth century whose innovations were as great as those in the fields of art and literature. At no time during the Mannerist period in the arts, between about 1530 and 1600, were the dominant styles unopposed; some artists, writers, and composers continued to work in an earlier style. Veronese, for example, kept on painting in a High Renaissance style right through the Age of Mannerism.

A closer examination of the origins of Mannerism seems to indicate that by 1520 artists like Raphael, poets like Ariosto, and composers like Josquin des Près had reached a peak of perfection that made younger men despair. No technical or artistic problems seemed to be left to be solved. Their perfection, with its harmony, balance, repose, and idealized reality, came to seem tedious. Restlessness and experimentation appeared now as positive values. Artists, writers, and, later, composers appeared to have grown weary of classical serenity and poise. As Donne wrote later (in 1611):

> And new philosophy calls all in doubt
> 'Tis all in pieces, all coherence gone.

The sixteenth century was a dynamic age and one not likely to find complete aesthetic satisfaction in any one solution of its problems. At the same time, the calm classicism of the early sixteenth century was more the reflection of an artistic hope and ideal than the expression of a state of calm assurance. So, the first cause of the change from the style of the High Renaissance to that of Mannerism seems to have lain in the desire to find new worlds of beauty—unexplored continents—in art, literature, and music.

New and experimental attitudes, which appeared first in art and only later in letters and music, are found—as minor currents among younger men—in the Age of the High Renaissance. As early as 1512, the year of the completion of some of Raphael's work in the Vatican and of the finishing of the Sistine ceiling, Beccafumi made designs for the cathedral pavement of Siena that are distraught, violent, and composed of unco-ordinated details. At nearly the same time, Pontormo, a pupil of the High Renaissance painter Andrea del Sarto, was deliberately imitating the angular and elongated Gothic elements in the engravings of Dürer. These stylistic changes reflected the personalities of the artists— a spirit of revolt in some of them made their style quite different from that of their predecessors. Michelangelo was a man of violent emotional reactions; as Leo X told him, "You frighten everyone, even Popes!" The lives of painters like Pontormo, Rosso, and Parmigianino show that all these painters, who stand near the beginning of Mannerism in art, had feverish and troubled personalities. Rosso, at night, disinterred corpses from cemeteries to draw them in a state of decomposition. His life, compounded of violence and timidity, ended in suicide. And Parmigianino spent more and more of his time on experiments in alchemy and magic, and ended his life as a recluse, in a deep state of melancholia. Vasari presents Pontormo as a man who was distrustful, restless, and insecure. Similar shifts may be found in literature both before and after 1530. Instead of the smooth and elegant style of Ariosto, there appeared the sneering verses of Berni, Folengo, and Aretino, and the involved and complicated sonnets of Michelangelo. Not until late in the sixteenth century did musical style move away from the calm and exalted manner of composers like Orlandus Lassus and Palestrina to the experimental style of the Gabrielis, Gesualdo da Venosa, and Monteverdi. In each case, details of the lives of these writers and composers show that there were strong elements of restlessness in their personalities.

Alongside personal factors influencing the change of style from the High Renaissance to Mannerism were many disturbing and unsettling elements in the political, social, and religious life of the period after 1520. The Lutheran Reformation began in 1517, and soon all of western Europe was affected by dramatic religious conflicts. In 1525, Charles V took Francis I of France captive at the Battle of Pavia and upset the whole political situation. Two years later, German troops sacked Rome, ruined the city, and drove scholars, writers, and artists out of what had lately been the great center of Renaissance activity. In the meantime, Italy fell more and more under the influence of Spain, a penetration which ended in the indirect yet crushing tyranny of backward Spain over all the Italian states. A little later Copernicus destroyed the old view of the universe. His work and that of other scientists of the period greatly disturbed the faithful, both Catholic and Protestant. At the same time, heavy taxes ground down the people; the Turks increased their raids along the coasts; and brigandage in the country districts and lawlessness in the towns grew apace. The autobiography of Cellini shows the increase of duels, street brawls, murders, and rapes—not only as offenses of a few against society but as occupations of persons of culture. Economic stagnation increased as trade routes moved to the North Atlantic. As Spanish influence grew, the nobles became more haughty and removed themselves from contact with the bourgeoisie and the intellectuals. A stiff Spanish etiquette, which taught the nobles to look down on trade, banking, and the professions, also taught the upper classes to regard artists, writers, and musicians as servants and thereby changed the conditions of their patronage. Soon the heavy hand of the Counter Reformation was felt everywhere. Florence, as one chronicler wrote, "when her liberty was lost was full of such sorrow, of such terror, of such confusion that it can hardly be described or even imagined." Narrowness, formality, and intolerance took the place of the broader horizons, the democracy, and the receptiveness to new ideas of an earlier age. So the Age of Mannerism stood between a faith in a good, natural order and a growing awareness of chaos, between the High Renaissance joy in life and a growing disillusion in which men become more aware of darkness and uncertainty, though the glow of the High Renaissance still lingered in the skies.

The expansive self-assurance of the Early and High Renaissance was now dampened and deadened. As in the legend of Faust, the seeker after knowledge and experience was doomed to frustration, and a sense of the vanity and worthlessness of what had been considered the great values of the preceding age. There came to be a disbelief in the value of thought, and the very word acquired a troubled connotation, as in the expression in *Hamlet,* "sicklied o'er with the pale cast of thought." Men even raised the question, what is achievement worth?

> Imperious Caesar, dead and turn'd to clay,
> Might stop a hole to keep the wind away.

Everything seemed insecure, and it was little wonder that men felt distraught and convinced that their destiny was determined by forces beyond their control, or even their understanding. One has only to compare the calm of Castiglione's *The Courtier* with the tension and bitterness of Guicciardini's *History of Italy* to realize the great changes in the general atmosphere that came over Italy between 1520 and 1530. These changes, however, were not the first causes of the growth of Mannerism, but they undoubtedly were responsible for the deepening of tensions that appear in all the arts of the Manneristic Age, and they helped to extend the duration of this period.

The essential notes of Mannerism are extreme individualism and experimentation. Experiments in the arts mark their every phase from the Greeks down, but some ages show much more of the spirit of experimentation than others. Such a period was the Age of Mannerism. This diversity of effort makes it difficult to find common elements in the achievements of the Manneristic period. Indeed there are many more common characteristics about other ages in the arts than about the Age of Mannerism. Each artist and writer sought to express himself in an intensely personal style which often had little relationship to the style of his contemporaries. Moreover, any individual artist, writer, or composer altered his personal style quite radically within the period of a few years. Mannerism kept much of the vocabulary of High Renaissance classicism but rejected both its proportions and its spirit. At the same time, on the personal side, artists, writers, and musicians were less free creators than they had been in the Early and High Renaissance periods. They became, as we have noticed, court pets of petty despots, and worked for small, sophisticated, and intellectualized court coteries.

In High Renaissance art, letters, and music there was an orderly hierarchy of forms. The High Renaissance believed in harmony, proportion, and restraint, and it found these in the universe; as Spenser said, "God has formed the world in a goodly pattern." Mannerism lacks the calm serenity of the High Renaissance, as well as the strong sense of decision and the robustness of the Baroque. Mannerism's style is often aloof and austere when it wants to show dignity, and precious and artificial when it wants to be witty or playful. It revels in both over- and understatement; fire and ice often contend. It loves conceits, elaborate figures of speech and plays on words, obscure allusions, the piling-up of calculated surprises, movement and contrast, tensions, antitheses, paradox, hyperbole, and the occult. Dr. Johnson in his life of Cowley speaks of "the erection of an unreal wall between meaning and object." T. S. Eliot says of the Elizabethan dramatist Webster that his was "a very great literary and dramatic genius directed toward chaos," and Ben Jonson declares, "That which is tortured is counted the more exquisite; nothing is fashionable till it is deformed."

In Mannerism there is often a mere federation of forms that sometimes verges on chaos. On occasion, there is little relation in a Mannerist
painting or poem between the size and thematic importance of figures
and incidents. Motifs that seem to be of only secondary significance in
a picture or a poem are often made very prominent, and what is apparently the leading theme is devalued and depressed. Mannerism, at
times, seems to lack any general sense of structure, and gives independent organization to separate parts of a work. As Grierson says of
Donne and his school, "The poets are more aware of disintegration than
of comprehensive harmony"; or as Shakespeare puts it in Sonnet 110, "I
have look'd on truth askance and strangely"; or, finally, as Polonius
hopes in *Hamlet,* "by indirections find directions out." Mannerism often
treats its themes from unexpected points of view and eccentric angles,
sometimes hidden ones. The result resembles the arbitrary relations and
connections in a dream, or the strange relationships of details to be
found in surrealist paintings or in the novels of Kafka or James Joyce.
As Lope de Vega said of some verses of Góngora, "as if a woman who
rouges herself, instead of putting the color on her cheeks should put it
on her nose, brow, and ears." In the arts of the High Renaissance details
are submitted to one central idea. It sought effects that would be valid
for everyone. Mannerism often works from within the creator and
moves outward, and arrives at effects that are valid only for the artist or
writer or composer. If the High Renaissance broke some of the bonds
between men and God, or at least tilted the relation more to the side of
man, the Mannerists tended to break the bond between body and spirit,
and between the individual and his fellow men. Some Mannerist works
seem to be inspired by a spirit of wilful mystification. In Mannerist
painting and literature and in some Mannerist music, conflicting or un-
related modes of feeling and of action are set side by side and left un-
harmonized, as if one phase of activity had nothing to do with another
phase in which the same persons or motifs are involved. Standards certainly differed from those of the High Renaissance; the shift becomes
clear in the remark of Francis Bacon: "There is no excellent beauty that
hath not some strangeness in the proportion." The spirit of Mannerism
is that of internal conflicts and of a struggle; only in the hands of great
masters, of a Michelangelo, a Shakespeare, a Cervantes, or a Monteverdi
does it show fulfilment and conquest.

It is interesting to notice that similar attitudes prevailed in later artistic
movements. The German Romanticist Novalis declared that only "chaos

can give birth to a dancing star"; and Leo Stein, explaining Picasso, says that "tension is the requisite for a living work of art," for tension allows the artist or writer to have new experiences and to see further than the natural eye allows. The Mannerist spirit of indirection and oblique approach is well summed up by Gracián in some of the dicta of *The Oracle* (1647): "Behave sometimes disingenuously . . . sometimes with candor; . . . adapt yourself to your company; . . . know how to be evasive; . . . without lying, do not tell the whole truth. . . . Beware as if you are watched."

2. The Fine Arts

The Mannerist painters and sculptors often turned away from nature and the antique and evolved their designs from their own imagination. The artist plays tricks with space and with shapes. Drapery, while suggesting the form of the body beneath, has often an independent movement of its own. Figures strike poses without reason and without seeming to feel them. Muscles are usually not in repose, but under strain; and bodies are twisted, limbs and necks are elongated, heads are often disproportionately small, and human figures are used as abstract decoration. The composition is often crowded with figures—without any space in which the figures can move or even seem able to exist. The action in a painting or sculpture sometimes extends beyond the limits of the picture or the bronze or marble. The Mannerist painters used strange colors and color combinations. It is not unusual to find lavender, pink, and orange juxtaposed in their paintings. There is usually great virtuosity of execution but the meaning of the painting or sculpture is sometimes confused, or loaded with recherché allusions. Mannerist art loves the involved. When Giovanni da Bologna was asked the subject of one of his groups he replied that it could be given any name that suited the beholder. Vasari tells how Parmigianino had no difficulty in transforming a Venus and Cupid into a Madonna and Child when a client refused to accept the first version of the picture. In the twenty-odd rooms at the Palace of Caprarola, the frescoes are so loaded with symbolic allusions that they are quite incomprehensible without a guide to explain them. This is a not uncommon element in both Mannerist painting and sculpture. Mannerist artists loved the symbolical and the allegorical. Handbooks of emblems and symbols and other iconographical guides were very popular and much used. A good deal of Mannerist art thus reveals an impression of confusion and uncertainty. It lacks the feeling of strength and security of the art of the High Renaissance or the sense of power and triumphant force of the Baroque.

In the field of painting, besides the innovations already noted, the Mannerist artists, according to Wölfflin, began a long process of transforming style, a process that was completed only after 1600, in the Age of the Baroque. In contrast to the linear type of painting of the Early and High Renaissance, where the emphasis falls primarily on the edges of figures and objects, there was now increasing emphasis on conceiving a picture in terms of color and light—what Wölfflin calls a "painterly" style. Less frequently are figures aligned in one plane or in a sequence of planes parallel to the front of the picture; more common now is a receding and diagonal type of composition which immediately carries the eye to the back of the picture. Moreover, instead of being inclosed and self-contained within the frame of the painting, the composition now carries the eye out and beyond the limits of the picture; and instead of a single focus of interest several centers of interest are used. And, finally, the painter and the sculptor now love motion rather than repose in their compositions. Few Mannerist or, later, Baroque paintings show all these characteristic traits at once, but some of them are evinced in nearly every picture of the Mannerist and Baroque periods.

Among the early Mannerist painters, Pontormo, Rosso, and Parmigianino are the leaders. Pontormo (d. 1556), like Rosso a pupil of Andrea del Sarto, used a style of composition that is nervous, strained, and unreal; his colors do not follow nature; figures lack mass and solidity; the space is crowded; and movements are strained and affected. Vasari blames Pontormo's exaggerations on too much influence of the woodcuts and engravings of Dürer; but his style, while clearly influenced by Dürer, seems to have arisen chiefly from his own inventions. Parmigianino (d. 1540), a pupil of Correggio, likewise plays tricks with nature. As in Pontormo's "Joseph in Egypt," so in Parmigianino's "Madonna of the Long Neck," everything in the relations of the figures is confused. The painting shows no logic of structure. The scene is neither indoors nor outdoors. The angels on the left and the figure of a prophet in the background on the right are entirely out of proportion to the figures of the Madonna and Child. One cannot tell whether the Madonna is partly seated on a stool or is standing. The infant Jesus seems to be slipping off his mother's lap. The Madonna's cloak flies out at the back in defiance of all laws of gravity. Everything is bizarre and unnatural and anticanonical, at least in relation to the style of painting of the High Renaissance. Parmigianino's pupil Bronzino (d. 1572) excelled in portrait painting, where he gave his sitter a haughty and disdainful mask. His attention is centered on sharply defined linear contours, a polished, metallic surface, and small, photographically presented details.

The greatest impetus toward the spread of a Mannerist style in both painting and sculpture came from the later work of Michelangelo. His "Last Judgment" in the Sistine Chapel, painted thirty years after the ceiling, is a vast panorama of bewilderment, chaos, and despair. The space is unreal, discontinuous, and not constructed with any uniformity of scale. The figures are heavy, lumpish, and lacking in grace. The artist is no longer interested in physical beauty for its own sake; he is intent only on conveying his ideas. Michelangelo's poetry speaks the same language: "Led by long years to my last hours, too late, O world, I know your joys for what they are. You promise a peace which is not yours to give." Painting is no longer conceived of as an imitation of nature, and the artist's interest is diverted almost entirely toward an inward mental image. We know, too, that Michelangelo turned against the theories of Alberti, Leonardo, and Dürer that had laid down the proper proportions of different parts of the body to the whole. "One cannot," he declared, "make fixed rules, making figures as regular as posts." This renunciation of older ideals of beauty was, with Michelangelo, deliberate, and was not due to failing powers. In some ways, these late works remind one of Beethoven's Hammerklavier Sonata and his last quartets. The treatment is very subjective and, in terms of classic art, it is not beautiful. In his last frescoes of the "Conversion of Paul" and the "Crucifixion of Peter" all trace of the harmonious order of the High Renaissance has vanished. Empty spaces alternate with strangely cluttered areas, and there is no coherence between the figures and their setting. These frescoes go even further from classical usage than the Medici tombs; both were an impetus to Mannerist design. These late frescoes are comparable rather to Michelangelo's last two sculptured "Pietàs" where the figures are without clear articulation. They are symbols deprived of all corporeal quality, and are grouped with sharp and jagged angles. These works were all done when Michelangelo had turned to a deeper religious piety, and when he seems to have found the old means of artistic expression to be utterly inadequate.

Next to Michelangelo, the most gifted painter was the Venetian

Tintoretto (d. 1594), whom his contemporaries called "the thunderbolt of painting." As a youth, he was deeply influenced by the work of Michelangelo and of Titian, but at the same time he early came to love violent contrasts in light and movement. There is a story that he liked to work in the evening with the light of a lantern so as to study the effects of striking shadows. His earlier work resembles that of Titian, which delighted in warm flesh tones and sumptuous color; and as he proceeds, his painting grows in dramatic force and in movement. Tintoretto's output was enormous, and many of his paintings left Italy, where they influenced the painters beyond the Alps. Tintoretto's fully developed style is best shown in the huge series he painted, between 1560 and 1587, for the Scuola di San Rocco in Venice. Here, he displayed his love of deep perspective effects that carry the eye to the very back of the room, of violent movement with figures assuming uneasy and agitated poses, and of sharp contrasts of blinding light and deep shadows. His figures are seldom seen at eye level, usually being viewed either from above or from below. His rectangular forms are never parallel with the front of the picture but are sharply slanted. Often there is no center of interest, and the eye wanders back and forth amid lights and shadows and among the figures. There is no point of climax and no means of return to any center. The figures are frequently shown from the side or back, though in his draftsmanship he never loses contact with natural forms; and in his color, though he uses and abuses shadows, he maintains much of the tonal system of Titian. Tintoretto's force, his fire and passion, and sense of drama give his works an enormous vitality not possessed by the paintings of the masters of the High Renaissance. Here Mannerism has clearly conquered a new world of beauty.

Mannerism in painting spread beyond Italy in the later sixteenth century. In Spain, it appeared in Morales and El Greco; in France in the work of the Clouets and their contemporaries; and in Germany in the painting of Cranach and Hans Baldung. France showed the influence of Mannerist painting in the 1530's. Francis I brought Rosso and a number of Mannerist painters and craftsmen from Italy; and Fontainebleau became a center of Mannerist influence not only in France but in the Low Countries and other parts of northern Europe. The decoration at Fontainebleau, only part of which survives, shows a bold and daring originality. One of the decorative features that spread all through northern Europe was strapwork in stucco and wood. Here flat bands, like strips of leather, were used in folded and rolled forms, often in fantastic shapes. In this style of decoration the stucco and the painting are not subordinated to the logic of the structure but interrupt the wall and ceiling surfaces, conceal, and blur them. The figures often break over the frames. Everything tends toward a free play of ingenuity rather than of logic. The style was spread by engravings and by tapestries and paintings which pictured the rooms at Fontainebleau.

Because of the Italian School of Fontainebleau, France as well as other countries beyond the Alps skipped most of the influence of the High Renaissance of Raphael, Bramante, and Titian, and went directly from the Gothic style (modified somewhat by influences of the Early Renaissance) into Mannerism. Some of the contemporary painters of the age, as the Clouets, though they showed some Italian influence, were still essentially medieval in style. A center of Mannerist influence further east in Europe was Prague, where there came a number of Italian artists to the court of Emperor Rudolph II. The Mannerist influences that appear in the later sixteenth century in centers like Munich, Augsburg, and Nuremberg, and in Denmark and Sweden derive in part from Prague.

The most original Mannerist painter outside Italy was El Greco (d. 1614). He was born in Crete, where he learned to paint in a Byzantine style that emphasized unrealistic, flat designs; he then spent time in Venice and Rome, where he was influenced by Titian, Tintoretto, and Michelangelo; he finally settled in Toledo, in Spain, where he spent his most active years. His output was prodigious, and he must have employed assistants to fill the many commissions he received. El Greco loved distorted, twisted, and flamelike figures, which appeared in settings of strange and unnatural color and lighting, all of which appealed to the pious fervor of the Spanish. Everything is wilfully altered, deformed, and exaggerated in the interest of a heightened emotional impression. Light and color are used less to model forms than to create a rapid and restless movement across the surface. Everything is done to heighten tensions. Figures are sometimes placed one above the other in registers rather than in receding space, and they often seem to lack any physical support. By such means El Greco frequently achieves an effect of unearthly exaltation. And there is a marked dematerialization of form through which the artist seeks to arrive at the spiritual truth that lies behind the mere appearance of things. The last word in Mannerism in painting was the work of El Greco rather than of an Italian. Again, as in the case of Tintoretto, a new type of beauty is discovered.

Most gifted of the northern Mannerist painters is Pieter Brueghel the Elder (d. 1569). His was a very original talent, and, though he spent a period in Italy, most of his work stems from the traditions of painting of his native Flanders. From Italian Mannerist paintings he derived chiefly his love of deep cross diagonals and of agitated compositions. His best work is in his pictures of peasant life, to some of which he gave biblical or allegorical titles. They are painted for the sophisticated who liked to see simple conditions of life. His worthy rustics love noisy festivals and copious repasts. Brueghel had a sharp eye for details of both human beings and landscapes; he drew with delicacy and precision and was a master of rich and varied colors. There is usually also an acute criticism of morals and society.

Mannerist sculpture showed many of the same features displayed in painting. Bodies are elongated and have small heads (often turned to one side); and the figures are frequently in twisted posture, with every muscle under strain. Colossal figures are sometimes set on minute supports, like Ammannati's "Neptune" at Florence. Everywhere there is a strong reaction against the calm, harmony, and proportion of the High Renaissance. This was, in part, due to the discovery of ancient sculpture of a late Greek type like the "Niobe Group," the "Farnese Hercules," the "Apollo Belvedere," and—most important of all—the contorted and writhing "Laocoön" group.

The lead in Mannerist sculpture was taken by Michelangelo, first in the figures for the never-completed tomb of Pope Julius II, and then in the Medici tombs in San Lorenzo in Florence, for which Michelangelo also designed the architectural settings. The four gigantic figures of "Night" and "Day" and "Morning" and "Evening" are placed on the slanting sides of great sarcophagus lids, where they give the uneasy effect of being ready to slide off. These four enormous bodies, with their heavy muscles, seem to be shrines in which some melancholy rite of contemplation is perpetually performed. Of the figure of "Night," Michelangelo wrote, "Good it is to slumber, and better still to be marble. Not to see, not to feel, is fortunate in these days of shame and misery. Therefore do not wake me. Speak low, I pray you!" His "Moses," done for the tomb of Julius II, is one of the most terrifying figures in the whole history of sculpture. Moses is presented in the last moment of self-control before giving away to the impulse to rise up. The great, flowing beard and the muscles of the figure are exaggerated and out of proportion to the rest of the figure; the effect is overwhelming.

Others inspired by Michelangelo preserved the exaggeration and the outer shell of his style but were not able to give their figures the same spiritual content. His leading follower, Giovanni da Bologna (d. 1608), was born in France, and went to Italy in 1551 at the age of twenty-seven. His own work exaggerates the restlessness of Michelangelo, as in his "Rape of the Sabine Women." At the same time, he bestowed on his colossal figures a factitious elegance and an effeminate grace which seems to be ill-suited to their size. His most astounding tour de force is his "Mercury"; here a winged youth stands on one small base poised for flight. It is the work of a consummate technician who, at the same time, lacks depth of feeling. His contemporary Cellini (d. 1571) devoted himself chiefly to work as a goldsmith. His best-known large sculpture, the "Perseus," is a piece of soulless animalism all done with a brilliant technical finish. Michelangelo did not think much of Cellini's large sculptures and spoke of them as "snuff-box ornaments." The work of Giovanni da Bologna and of Cellini was much admired and imitated in Italy and, also, in the lands beyond the Alps.

In France the School of Fontainebleau had introduced Mannerist forms in sculpture, and Cellini worked in France from 1540 to 1545. The first important work done by native Frenchmen was that of the architect Lescot and the sculptor Goujon. In his "Fountain of the Innocents," with tall figures of nymphs holding urns, Goujon (d. 1568?) shows the fastidious elegance and elongated forms of Italian Mannerism handled with French restraint. Goujon and his younger contemporary, Pilon (d. 1590), helped to extend the taste for mythological subjects and Italianate style. In the Low Countries, Adriaen de Vries (d. 1627) of The Hague, introduced the style of Giovanni da Bologna to north and central Europe; he filled commissions in a number of countries, and his influence was widespread. As a result of the work of these Frenchmen and of De Vries, the sculpture of much of western Europe showed Mannerist characteristics by the end of the sixteenth century—capricious proportions, delight in agitation, and in whimsical and even grotesque shapes and poses, along with a growing interest in late antique sculpture. In sculpture, as in painting, in the lands beyond Italy, the influence of the Italian High Renaissance was usually mixed with those of Mannerism and with native traditions in the arts.

The architecture of Italian Mannerism, while it too showed much experimentation, was more tied to classical models than were painting and sculpture. This seems to have been due chiefly to two causes: to the enormous prestige of Roman architecture as represented in surviving buildings, and to the great influence of Vitruvius' *On Architecture,* for which there were no ancient parallel treatises on painting and sculpture. Sometimes, however, experimentation led to eccentricities. A common device, for example, and one much used later in the Baroque period, was to intercept sections of a round column with square blocks or to introduce raised bands of rustication inserted at intervals, thus breaking up the logic of the column. Also, whereas decoration in the High Renaissance remained subordinate to architecture, in many Mannerist buildings the decoration intrudes on the architecture without, however, assuming a successful role in its own right. The further limits of eccentric individualism mark some of the architectural work of Giulio Romano and of Michelangelo. In the Palazzo del Tè at Mantua, Giulio Romano (d. 1546) breaks up the exterior elevations into unequally spaced divisions, each of which is handled as a unit in itself; and the window and door pediments, instead of being kept as distinct features, dissolve into the wall surface. The blocks of rusticated masonry are deliberately cut in very uneven sizes and, strangest of all, some of the triglyphs slip from the entablature as though dislocated by an earthquake. Giulio Romano evidently loved to shock by intentional contradictions and malformations. In the High Renaissance edifice there had been a hierarchy of forms. Now there was a mere assemblage of forms, and one that verged on chaos.

Michelangelo did no architectural work until he was past fifty years of age; thus none of his architecture is in the style of the High Renaissance. In Michelangelo's vestibule to the Laurentian Library at Florence the artist played with older architectural forms in a whimsical fashion. The vestibule is small and very high; one feels as though one were standing in the shaft of a mine. On the sidewalls, ornaments and details are used with no relation to structural function. The attached columns, instead of standing out from the wall to support the cornice above, are set in niches; and below them are placed brackets far too small to support the columns above. Burckhardt called it all "an incomprehensible joke." Later on, in designing the square on top of the Capitoline Hill in Rome and the apse and dome of Saint Peter's, Michelangelo returned to a more structural and integrated classical style, and laid the foundations for the grandeur of the Baroque.

Somewhat less eccentric are the buildings of Peruzzi (d. 1536). In his Palazzo Massino at Rome, Peruzzi used a curved façade with a deeply inset entrance, and very small windows on the two upper floors, all seemingly designed to get away from the conventional Italian palace façade of the Early and High Renaissance styles. All in all, the later sixteenth century was very rich in original architectural achievement. Peruzzi, Vignola, and Della Porta in Rome; Sanmichele in Verona, Sansovino in Venice; and Palladio in Vicenza and Venice did work that roused the admiration of the whole of Europe. Of these, perhaps, the most gifted were Vignola and Palladio. Both were deeply under the spell of Roman architecture and of Vitruvius; and, though highly original in their creations, they thought they were working in the tradition of ancient Rome. Both wrote important treatises on how to handle, with proper proportions, the classical orders.

Vignola (d. 1573) aspired to be a second Vitruvius, yet much of his work has a restless quality, characteristic of Mannerism. In the Villa Farnese at Caprarola, he built an enormous five-sided palace with a round central court and an elaborately laid-out formal garden; and in the Gesù Church in Rome he constructed a wide nave with small side chapels in lieu of aisles—both designs being strikingly original. The Gesù, the head church of the Jesuit order, was widely copied and adopted all over western Europe. Even more gifted was Palladio (d. 1580), whose principal works are in his native Vicenza and in nearby Venice. Deeply soaked in the ancient Roman traditions of architectural design, Palladio was nevertheless highly inventive in his uses of these traditions. Typical of the experimental nature of Mannerism is his Villa Rotunda, where, on four sides of a square palace, he placed four identical façades. In his palaces and churches, he delighted in the use of colossal orders, that is, columns and pilasters extending through several stories. Palladio used very little decoration, and depended for his effects on beauty of proportion. His work has a solidity and grandeur which point toward the Baroque. If there is any exaggeration in Palladio's work it is an overemphasis on classical symmetry and balance. His buildings were widely copied and adopted throughout Europe, and he came to be especially esteemed in England; his theoretical treatise had even greater influence than his architectural creations.

As the influence of Italian Mannerist architecture spread beyond the Alps, it was usually combined with local traditions that still maintained many medieval characteristics. The Italian Serlio, a pupil of Peruzzi, introduced Italian Mannerist architecture into France, though he became best known, all over western Europe, for his theoretical treatise on architecture. The architecture of later sixteenth-century France is more or less typical of that of Europe beyond Italy. Gothic traditions are combined with classical features in strange mixtures. There is a wanton use—and abuse—of classical forms: windows or niches are cut right through entablatures; pediments are broken in varied ways, bands of heavy rustication spread over pilasters; and surfaces are covered with decoration that does violence to the basic design. Many of the features of medieval buildings survived, including high and narrow proportions, steep roofs, and defense towers, as at the Château of Chambord in France, in the Louvre, and in many other secular buildings. Gothic church structures were covered with Italian High Renaissance and Italian Manneristic decoration. Many of the same features are found in the later sixteenth-century architecture of the Low Countries and Germany where, however, decorative detail became very exuberant. The style of Floris (d. 1575) dominated the Low Countries and North Germany. Dietterlin (d. 1624) and others in Germany produced a grotesquely exaggerated version of Italian Mannerism. There was no Mannerist contortion which these German architects did not doubly contort—no conceit to which they could not add some whimsy; for example, a column must be banded with moldings, the lower part wrought with arabesques, and the upper part hung with a fringe of carved tassels. In England the Mannerist influences came mostly via Flanders; the results are often more picturesque than beautiful. In Spain various currents from Italy were seen side by side: the coldly classical, as in the Escorial, and the most agitated Mannerism. The style in Spain known as the "Churriguerresque," though it flourished in the Baroque period, is really more derived from Italian Mannerism than from the architecture and decoration of Baroque Italy. Here decorative conceits are loaded on until the design of the building is completely lost, as in the Sacristy of the Cartuga of Granada, and in many Spanish and Portuguese buildings in the Americas.

Europe beyond Italy produced no such Mannerist painters, sculptors, and architects as Tintoretto, Michelangelo, or Palladio. Not until the Baroque period do Spain and northern Europe equal or outstrip, in artistic achievement, the work of contemporary Italians.

3. Literature

The literature of Mannerism, like its art, is characterized by a strong reaction against the polished classicism of the High Renaissance. It shows everywhere marked inner tensions, contradictions, restlessness, extreme individualism, and therefore a great variety in its achievements. Within this literature there are, on the one hand, works of supreme literary merit—most of them not Italian, as those of Montaigne, Cervantes, and Shakespeare—and, on the other, writings that represent the extremes of affectation. In Mannerist literature the High Renaissance joy in life often gives place to preoccupation with dissolution, decay, and death; the tone is frequently one of cynicism, of insecurity and anxiety, and of weariness of the world; and the writers, like Shakespeare in *Othello,* delight in painting "men of measureless passion."

The style of the great writers of the Age of Mannerism was relatively direct, but the lesser men went in for all sorts of literary conceits and devices. The absorption in problems of style, which had appeared as early as Petrarch and has remained a characteristic feature of all modern literature, produced in the later sixteenth and early seventeenth centuries a kind of "left wing" of literature where, as the Italian Marino said, "to evoke wonder is the end of poetry." All across Europe, this Mannerist rage for literary conceits lasted for over a century. The stock in trade of such writers was forced antitheses, prolonged metaphors, obscure allusions, sentiments given to objects, plays on words, and a general virtuosity of language that often lost all touch with reality. The style blended passionate feeling and paradoxical ratiocination. It was also a style that mixed the trivial and things of everyday occurrence with the most recondite and remote. As in the case of Mannerist painting, the literary style disliked proportion, balance, and classical clarity and calm. In Robert Southwell's "Saint Peter's Complaint" (1598), twenty-seven stanzas are devoted to the eyes of Jesus, which are described as "sweet volumes," "nectared ambries of soul-feeding meats," "graceful quivers of love's dearest darts," "cabinets of grace," "blazing comets," "baths of grace," and "Bethlehem cisterns." This Mannerist cultivation of the obscure appears later in Symbolist poetry; writing in the 1860's, Mallarmé said, "Poetry must be an enigma; the charm of it must lie in the attempt to divine the meaning." It was an age of royal and princely culture and of the Catholic Counter Reformation, an age that loved to startle and impress by its regal and ecclesiastical splendor, an age of marble and of gildings. Manners, in the upper circles of society, were marked by elaborate bowing, hand-kissing, and cringing words at the ends of letters.

Cicero was no longer the model in prose, as he had been for the Early and High Renaissance. If any classical models were followed, they were those of Seneca and Tacitus. The author's mind seemed, at times, to follow not his reason but his whim; as Montaigne said, "I write freely without an end in view." Ciceronian prose was planned as wholes; each section reaches its height near the middle, and ends composedly. Throughout, subordinate ideas are allowed to pile up to a climax. Mannerist prose opens constantly outward, and often loses itself in a hint of infinity at the end. Mannerist prose style, also, cultivates the appearance of spontaneity and tries to avoid any effect that looks like careful preliminary planning. Actually such effects were often as carefully planned as the early Ciceronian effects. This Mannerist style often seems abrupt and jagged with a series of short independent members, irregular in length and unpredictable in order. There are constant shifts from concrete to abstract language. Words and phrases often appear in unlooked-for places, and emerge bizarrely when they are least expected. This, at its best, is the prose style of Montaigne, Pascal, and Sir Thomas Browne. Such writing gives the effect of the reader's sharing in the author's processes of thinking. Pascal said such a style "mocks at formal elegance." As in every period, a number of artists, writers, and composers do not conform to the prevailing style; so in the Age of Mannerism some of the poets, as Tasso, and a number of the prose writers, as Calvin in Geneva, Hooker in England, and Galileo in Italy, have little in their style that relates to the prevailing fashions. A series of great sixteenth-century prose writers used neither a Ciceronian nor a Mannerist style but wrote directly to convey their ideas to their readers as clearly as possible. The extreme Mannerist style in both poetry and prose was known in Italy as "Marinism," in Spain as "Gongorism," in England as "Euphuism" and later as "Metaphysical," and, finally, in France as "Préciosité."

The first clear divergence from the High Renaissance style in Italy is found in the verses of Berni (d. 1535). Cardinal Bembo had earlier tried to fix the standard of poetic style in that of Petrarch and of prose style in that of Boccaccio. Berni ridicules all this in his satiric and cynical poetry. He sneers at all conventional standards, and, because of this attitude, Saintsbury said Berni "introduced the snigger into literature." Borrowing trivial subjects like a sausage, or a paintbrush, or a dead cat, he treats them in his "Capitoli" with humorous, and, often, with obscene touches. He detests the Petrarchian style, and makes fun of it; in one poem, he speaks of a "fair lady" "of a face of gold with crinkled brow and two eyes of pearl, lips of milk and ebony teeth; hair of silver,

standing on end, and twisted around a yellow face." His younger contemporary Folengo, in his verses, but especially in a sort of mock epic,
the "Baldus," pokes fun at all the respected types in society, and ridicules the Petrarchian love lyric, the pastoral romance, and the romantic
epic, indeed, all the respected literary forms of the High Renaissance.
His principal works are written in a "macaronic" language which mixes
Latin and Italian words, of which the latter appear with Latin endings.
Though Folengo has a light touch, it is evident that he has a genuine
hatred of the clergy, the aristocracy, and the literary pedants. In both
Berni and Folengo the literary ideals of the High Renaissance, as well
as many religious, social, and political concepts of the day, are under
heavy attack.

The same mocking spirit is seen in the prose and poetry of Aretino
(d. 1556). This "scourge of princes," as Ariosto called him, respected
nothing; and he did not hesitate to get payments out of important
people to prevent his writing about them. In his obscene verses and
witty comedies, this Cesare Borgia of letters made war on Petrarchianism, and High Renaissance literary classicism. Michelangelo's poetry, of
which his sonnets represent the best-known part, though far removed
in spirit from the mocking verses of Berni, Folengo, and Aretino, is
anticlassical in style. Though Michelangelo remained a devout Catholic
and a strong Neo-Platonist, thus holding views of an earlier time, he
writes in a jagged and rugged fashion with strangely elliptical and
obscure expressions. His poetry, thus, resembles his later and unfinished
sculpture; and in style it has moved far away from the calm classicism
of the High Renaissance. Michelangelo's poetry represents one of the
most profound and original achievements of Italian Mannerist poetry.

Outstanding among the Italian poets of the later sixteenth century
were Tasso (d. 1595) and Guarini (d. 1612). Both—like the painter
Veronese—seem to belong to the earlier period of the High Renaissance
rather than to the Age of Mannerism. Guarini is best known for his
Faithful Shepherd, a pastoral drama steeped in sensuousness and written in a suave musical and felicitous style, with only a few literary
conceits. Yet the author was unhappy because of the political and religious oppressiveness of his time, and this weakens the effectiveness of
his writing. Tasso was the greatest Italian literary genius of the later
sixteenth century. His poetic output was enormous, but his two leading
works were the *Aminta,* a pastoral romance rather in the style and
spirit of the High Renaissance and his great epic *Jerusalem Delivered.*

Tasso became a restless and demented man, owing at least in part to the oppressive atmosphere of his age. In his epic, he drew materials from medieval epics and Latin histories of the First Crusade, whose story forms the heart of his tale. Mannerist features in this work, which in some ways seems to belong either to the earlier Age of the High Renaissance or to the Age of the Baroque, are to be seen in the way in which the love episodes—where Christian knights are in love with beautiful Mohammedan heroines—are more effectively handled than the main theme. Likewise in the Manneristic style, which develops details that interfere with the basic design, is his inability to sustain his poem on one level or on different levels with well-modulated transitions. He continually oscillates between warm emotion and frigid rhetoric. His descriptions are less precise and less like paintings than those of Ariosto.

Tasso is more aware of beauties of sound than of light and color; and his artistic affiliations, like those of Guarini, are more with music than with art. More than Guarini, he occasionally uses elaborate verbal conceits, rhetorical antitheses, and fine-spun subtleties. The *Jerusalem Delivered*—said to be the most-read book in the Italian language—shows how a great genius will create his own style, one that stands out from the prevailing style of his age. It is interesting to observe how far, in literature and in art, Italy was ahead of the rest of Europe; for Tasso's epic, which belongs more to Mannerism than to an earlier style, was very influential in the work of two poets whose writings are clearly marked by the characteristics of High Renaissance style—Ronsard in France and Spenser in England.

If it is difficult to classify the work of Tasso, Mannerism in a very exaggerated form appears in the work of Marino and his followers. Marino (d. 1625) had a delicate sensitivity to every form of sensuous beauty, but he could say nothing simply, and everywhere tried to astonish with unique expressions. His *Adone,* with many digressions, relates the old tale of Venus and Adonis and bristles with every sort of literary conceit. This overwrought and empty work is filled with astonishing, even stupefying, imagery. It is made up entirely of a series of episodes, each elaborately wrought, but possesses no cohesion. His images of hell and of death bring back the motifs of the Middle Ages as the mystical writings of St. Theresa and St. John of the Cross recall those of Eckhart, Suso, and Tauler. Marino's method was to call nothing by its ordinary name, and to pile on fantastic figures of speech. He wrote of "frozen fire," "scorching ice," and "cruel kindness," and of stars as "translucent

holes in the celestial sieve," until all relation to reality is lost in verbal
fireworks. In Marino, Italian amorous poetry, detached from its Platonic framework, shrank to mere gallantry and flattery. Its old ideo-
logical substance was dissolved in puns and conceits, and sensuous
eroticism. Yet it is typical of the Age of Mannerism that his work,
though placed on the *Index,* was admired all over Europe; that he was
received in Paris like a prince, and that a group of the poet's admirers,
including Queen Christina of Sweden, founded "The Arcadia," a literary academy in Rome, to award prizes for work of this type. The
continual overemphasis on matters of style by both the Italian Humanists and the vernacular writers finally ended in producing an art that is
drowned in artificiality. There is some justice in Ruskin's remark: "All
the Renaissance principles of art tended to the setting of beauty above
truth. And the proper punishment of such pursuit was that those who
thus pursued beauty should wholly lose sight of beauty."

Mannerism produced little of value for the theater except the pastoral
plays of Guarini and Tasso and the comedies of a number of minor
writers. The tragedies were written to conform to the unities as set
down by the Neo-Classical critics and were usually nothing but empty
shells of rhetoric. Typical of their frigidity is Trissino's *Sofonisba.*
Within twelve hours the heroine learns of the defeat and death of her
husband, goes into mourning, meets and is wed by a prince, is sent, a
captive in war, to Scipio's camp, receives a poisoned bowl, drinks it,
and dies. The result is so artificial and icily dull that it is hard to conceive
of an audience accepting it. Yet within these same Neo-Classical rules,
the French Baroque writers of the seventeenth century were to create
great masterpieces.

The later sixteenth century in Italy produced two new dramatic
forms, the *commedia dell' arte* and the opera, each of which were to
have widespread European influence. The most vital force in the spoken
Italian theater in the Age of Mannerism was the very popular *commedia
dell' arte.* This grew out of the work done by organized dramatic companies that toured the Italian peninsula in the second half of the sixteenth century. Their repertoire consisted at first of recently written
comedies, and then of plays which were not written out but improvised
on the basis of an outline. When the outline, with a list of the stage
properties needed, was ready, the manager read and explained it to the
company. The directions were simple, as "Isabella from her window
has a love scene with Horace; she comes down, and they promise to

marry." Most of the dramatis personae were stock characters who appeared in one play after another. The plots usually turned on love intrigues, and the action ran from love-making and witty dialogue to the most vulgar and slapstick buffoonery. The language used in these improvised plays, which were enormously popular in Italy and were carried by Italian companies all over Europe, became more and more flowery and showed thereby the vogue of Mannerism in Italian literature and life. Shakespeare, Lope de Vega, Molière, and Goldoni derived some features of their comedies from these wandering Italian players.

The appearance of Mannerism in the literature of the lands beyond the Alps was due to a number of causes: to the imitation of Italian stylistic changes, to a desire to find new means of expression and new types of effective writing different from those of the High Renaissance, to the survival or the revival of medieval forms of exprssion, and, finally, to the rapid political, economic, and religious changes of the sixteenth century. In France, a generation of writers younger than those of the Pléiade shows first an imitation of the style of Ronsard and his fellow poets, and then a movement away from their literary ideals. The long poems of Du Bartas and D'Aubigné, both of whom were strong Calvinists, reflect the turbulence and brutalities of the bitter religious wars in France. Both poets employed complex allegories, an uncontrolled use of metaphor, and a vocabulary taken partly from Old French and provincial dialects and partly from Greek and Latin. Indeed, the accusation of "speaking Greek and Latin in French" made against the poets of the Pléiade belongs still more to Du Bartas and D'Aubigné. Some of this style harks back to medieval and early Renaissance usage in France, one that had rather gone underground during the great days of the High Renaissance Pléiade. The chief work of Du Bartas (d. 1590) is his two *Semaines,* the first of which tells the story of Creation in seven books, and the second, left unfinished, was to continue the story to the birth of Christ. These works, though uneven in quality, contain some magnificent passages that, like Milton's later, combine Hebraic inspiration with Hellenic form. D'Aubigné (d. 1630) was a poet of much greater talents. Between 1577 and 1616 he wrote *Les Tragiques,* a long poem on the lurid history of his time. Like the bitter etchings of Callot's later "Miseries of War," D'Aubigné paints a powerful but wretched picture of fanaticism and misery. He rails and storms, and some of his verse smells of powder and blood. Much of his work is marred by Manneristic literary affectations, but it contains some sections of unmatched grandeur. As Lanson said, "There is nothing grander in our language than the concluding pages of 'Les Tragiques.'" Finally, the third poet of Mannerism in France, Desportes (d. 1606), is a weaker and less inspired Ronsard, and a poet much inclined to use Italianate types of literary conceits, hyberbole, exaggerated metaphors, and antitheses. As Malherbe said, he made "flattery into a fine art," and he was a great favorite at the courts of Henry III and Henry IV.

The greatest genius of the Age of Mannerism in France was Montaigne (d. 1592). The lack of certainty which had characterized the literature of the High Renaissance and, later, was to characterize that of the Baroque, is here carried to its ultimate limits. Montaigne is sure of nothing; human knowledge is a weak thing in which are wrapped ignorance, error, and inconsistency. Truth is inaccessible, and man has to act only on such partial truth as he may discover. The discovery of non-European cultures and religions beyond the seas, the triumphs of science that had found new fields of truth independent of revelation, and the disgusting spectacle of Protestants and Catholics killing each other in fanatical fighting had completely undermined Montaigne's faith. Everywhere he raises questions, though rarely does he try to answer them. There is no recourse to any religious or philosophical system. Montaigne's style is conversational and very desultory; he seems to erect digression into a system and proceeds by fits and starts. The parts of a single essay may show some organization, but the whole of an essay is almost never confined to the subject of its title. The thought opens up, stops, and then starts again. The result is chaotic, but fascinating. He is never done talking about himself, and no detail of himself is too small: he tells us, for example, that he loves salads, and can hold his water for ten hours. Both the skeptical mentality and the loose, meandering, and very experimental style of Montaigne mark him as a writer of the Age of Mannerism. His works were translated into many languages, and they were as widely read as the works of any sixteenth-century author.

The imaginative literature of French Préciosité in the first half of the seventeenth century, is strongly marked by the influence of Italian Mannerism. Henry IV and later Richelieu restored France to a peaceable and prosperous nation. The long period of civil wars in the sixteenth century, however, had coarsened manners and speech. France had seen anarchy and recoiled; and the leaders of society made a great effort to refine manners and to replace the barrack-room ways of the upper classes with Italian grace and good breeding. The queen, Maria de'

Medici, invited Marino to Paris in 1615, and, at the same time, a number of great ladies opened salons where men and women important in society and in the arts might meet and exchange ideas. Women thus came to play a great role in society and in the formation of literary taste; and since their sensibilities could easily be offended, they undertook a great refinement of the language that threw out vulgar and obscure words and expressions to an excessive degree. On the positive side, they cultivated an affected manner of speech much influenced by the conceits of Marino and of the Spaniard, Góngora. Perhaps the outstanding characteristic of French Préciosité was its linguistic purism, even prudishness, of which Molière made such fun. The leading poet of the salons was Voiture (d. 1648), a master of elegant badinage and clever conceits whose verse had no other aim than to afford a delicate pleasure to a small circle of oversophisticated people. Others, following in his footsteps, carried further the use of conceits. They loved an orgy of metaphors and seemed unable to use direct speech. In spite of their efforts to be original, their fervent use of vocabulary with images of battles, shafts, fencing, and besieged hearts, and their comparisons of persons and objects tended to become monotonous. In contrast with English Metaphysical poets, who used colloquial expressions and were usually serious, the French Précieux avoided ordinary speech and were rarely serious. In this social atmosphere, the French language narrowed its vocabulary and became more precise and polished; and literature became the expression of a small and overrefined class. The literary vocabulary, for instance, rejected "bread" and spoke of it as the "sustainer of life." Nothing must strike the ear that suggests the lower classes, that is vulgar or violent.

Some of the leading writers of the time, as Guez de Balzac, Vaugelas, and Malherbe, rejected the excesses of Préciosité and laid the foundations of the Baroque style in France. Other writers, particularly a number of novelists, popularized further this line of refinement and affectation. The pastoral romance of Italy and Spain furnished a framework for a series of French novelists. D'Urfé (d. 1625) in his pastoral romance *Astrée* tried to refine manners and speech; it is a work of much greater sincerity than Marino's *Adone* but it also contains some of the Manneristic literary devices. Mannerism reached its height in the interminable novels of Mlle de Scudéry (d. 1701), which contain little that common sense and art could approve. In the very popular *Clélie,* Mlle de Scudéry shows one of her typical "precious" fancies in a description of the

Country of Love (*Pays de tendre*), a land watered by the stream of Inclination, with the City of Friendship on its frontier; at a distance are the wastes of Oblivion, passing which one comes to "the shoreless sea of Intimacy." The psychological analysis is sound, but the expression of it is very affected. The vogue of these novels was enormous, and lasted until the combined satire of Molière and Boileau destroyed it.

It was in the days of Mannerism, at a time when Spain was beginning to go down economically and politically, that there opened her golden age of culture. The literature and art of this age were marked by the appearance of a number of great geniuses. From the Italian writers of the High Renaissance and of Mannerism, the leading Spanish writers, Cervantes, Lope de Vega, and Góngora, borrowed whole stories, incidents, and figures of speech; for the rest they built on the foundations of their own national literary traditions. These writers produced a rich and varied series of works, marked not only by a striking originality, but also by the experimentation, extreme individualism, and inner tensions that everywhere characterized the Age of Mannerism in the arts.

Cervantes (d. 1616), after a life of misfortunes and at the end of his career, wrote his *Don Quixote,* a novel that may be understood at several levels. On the surface, it is a fascinating tale of a petty nobleman, crazed with ideas derived from reading chivalric romances, who goes out to fight windmills as giants and flocks of sheep as infidels, and his servant, Sancho Panza, a peasant who thinks only of good eating and plenty of sleep. Beyond this, however, there lies a wonderful contrast between the idealist and the realist. The realist follows the visionary, grumbling and complaining; and, in the long story, each learns from the other, and the two men become slowly wise. The novel is Manneristic in representing the divided personalities of its two chief figures, in its mixture of the comic and the tragic, and of the ideal and the real. The hero is at one time sublime, at another ludicrous. The style of presentation is meandering, in turn grotesque, capricious, and extravagant, rather like a vast improvisation. *Don Quixote* is not only one of the greatest achievements of the Age of Mannerism, but according to Macaulay (and others) "the greatest novel ever written," and certainly the most read.

Góngora (d. 1627), a friend and admirer of El Greco, is now regarded by many as Spain's greatest poet. He wrote his earlier verse in the clear style of the High Renaissance, but he later turned to writing in a manner that came to be widely known as "Gongorism." His later work is filled with subtle conceits and complexities. He loved provincial, obsolete, and recondite words and turns of speech, obscure allusions, words of his own invention, inverted order of words, and strange shifts of tense in the verbs. "Spain snow" means white table cloths, and "flying snow" a white bird; "snow clad in a thousand colors" stands for peasant girls in their Sunday best, and "wandering lilies" for sheep. By the same process a considerable part of nature became a series of poetic labels: silver, gold, marble, crystal, diamonds, roses, and so forth. It is a highly metaphorical language Góngora used, but a language in which the first term of the metaphor is often omitted. When the comparison is complete, it is often strange, as when he compares a stream entering the sea to "a crystal butterfly, with waves instead of wings, seeking its death in the lantern of Thetis." Manneristic, also, is the pace of some of his poems; at one time a poem may move at a leisurely, untroubled pace, and at another it proceeds at breakneck speed. All these Manneristic elements in Góngora's style were developed before the publication of Marino's *Adone;* they are derived from earlier Spanish writers but pushed now to extremes. And his followers went even further.

Lope de Vega (d. 1635), called by Cervantes "that prodigy of nature," remade Spanish drama. He is the most prolific author in history, and besides writing over eight hundred plays, he produced a long series of other poetic works. His plays, written in verse in a variety of meters, are usually in three acts. They give great importance to women, and they cover the whole range of Spanish life from the king to the humblest peasant. Lope de Vega popularized, if he did not invent, the drama of cloak and sword, of honor injured and honor righted. He also popularized the comic, confidential servant. He is intensely loyal to the king, the protector of the humble, and devoutly Catholic; and the center of interest in his writings is usually love. He mixes tragedy and comedy freely, as did the Elizabethan writers, and the scenes shift rapidly from one place to another. He defied the classic critics, and said he only wrote to please his audience. Before sitting down to write, he declared, he always locked up the classical authors so they would not disturb him. Of covering so long a lapse of time in some of his plays, he said, "A seated Spaniard is not assuaged unless he is shown in the space of two hours everything from Genesis to the Last Judgment." Lope de Vega's style shows few literary conceits. "Poetry," he declared, "must cost great trouble to the poet, but little to the reader." But he often makes his characters speak in an equivocal way; thus, he said, each one in the audience would then think he alone was clever enough to understand what

is being said. The poetry is often very fine, and he shows great originality in adapting and in inventing plots—for which he ransacked the
literature and history of all times—and in inventing and bringing to life
new characters. The characterization is less penetrating than Shakespeare's or Molière's, and it also lacks Shakespeare's complex imagery
and introspective ruminations. Lope de Vega's work also lacks the
closely integrated structure characteristic of the High Renaissance, on
the one hand, and of the later Baroque, on the other.

Germany in the sixteenth century was so torn, first by religious controversies and then by civil wars, that her art and literature were seriously retarded. The High Renaissance style, especially that of the Pléiade,
that Opitz had tried to introduce into German lands took no hold, and
the best works of the later sixteenth and seventeenth centuries reflect, in
both their form and content, the wretched confusion of the times. The
style of the leading writers is Manneristic; it lacks a strong sense of
form, and often is full of violent and unresolved conflicts and tensions.
Grimmelshausen (d. 1676) presents a dreadful picture of German life
during the Thirty Years' War in his *Simplicissimus*. The form of this
long rambling tale is taken from Spanish picaresque novels translated
into German. The hero has many and varied adventures and finally
ends by becoming a religious hermit. The novel is hardly more than a
string of incidents; it has power but little unity. Its lack of structure and
its extended use and abuse of allegory relate it to the general tendencies
of Mannerism. More gifted was Gryphius (d. 1664), the greatest German writer of the seventeenth century. Out of a checkered career, he
drew his deep pessimism and intense religious fervor. Though the author of some effective lyric poems, he was best known as a dramatist. He
borrowed plots, as did most European writers, from the Italian storytellers; and he wrote some loosely constructed pastoral plays, and some
comedies about the common people that show, in addition to Italian influence, that of strolling English players whom he had seen in Germany
and Holland. His tragedies are very bloodthirsty, and we move through
tortures, murders, and even a nocturnal exhumation, a ghastly spectacle
that shows the love of the Age of Mannerism for the unusual. The lack
of a regular theater and a public made it difficult to present Gryphius'
plays—to which their faulty construction is in part due. Gryphius had
no worthy successor in Germany until the middle of the eighteenth
century. Also typical of the Age of Mannerism in Germany are the
rambling and mystical writings of Jakob Boehme (d. 1624), the cobbler-

prophet. Boehme's writings were known all over Protestant Europe and were subsequently rediscovered by the German Romanticists of the early nineteenth century.

Mannerism runs through English literature of the later sixteenth and early seventeenth centuries. In the sixteenth century it overlaps writing in the relatively clear and smooth style of the High Renaissance, and in the next century it parallels the unfolding of the grand style of the Baroque. The mood of the High Renaissance was one of delight in the joys and beauties of this world. Marlowe had written,

> Come live with me and be my love
> And we will all the pleasures prove
> That valleys, groves, hills, and fields,
> Woods, or steepy mountains yields,

and the rest of the poem sings along in the same happy mood. Writing only about eleven years later, on the same subject of love, Raleigh laments

> The flowers do fade and wanton fields
> To wayward winter reckoning yields,

and he asks the question

> Yet what is love? I pray thee say,
> It is a game which none doth gain.

Both the content and the style of writing changed rapidly in England at the end of the sixteenth century. Interesting innovations in prose style had earlier been made by Lyly (d. 1606) in his *Euphues,* the first English novel of manners. What Lyly has to say is trivial, and his mode of expression is highly artificial. All sorts of conceits are used: elaborate antithetical parallelism of phrases and clauses, sometimes regardless of sense; recondite allusions to mythology, history, and natural science; puns and plays on words; labored similes; crafty sentence structure; and alliteration and assonance. Lyly's aim was to supply high society with a medium of expression more fashionable than the traditional language. He overdid many of his devices; Euphuism was made fun of by Shakespeare, and it lent itself easily to caricature. But, from 1579, when the first part of *Euphues* appeared, nearly every piece of literature, almost to 1600, showed its influence. In the end, Euphuism, while subject to abuse, greatly helped to extend the scope of English style by cultivating variety and elegance in the language.

The later sonnets and some of the later plays of Shakespeare show many of the characteristics of Mannerism. In his so-called "bitter comedies," especially *All's Well That Ends Well* and *Measure for Measure,* and in his great tragedies, *Hamlet, Othello, Macbeth,* and *King Lear,* there is much inner tension in the leading characters; and in their handling there is much emphasis on the illogical, contradictory, and unfathomable elements in life, and on old age, death, and the impermanence of worldly happiness.

> Life's but a walking shadow, a poor player
> That struts and frets his hour upon the stage,
> And then is heard no more; it is a tale
> Told by an idiot, full of sound and fury,
> Signifying nothing.

The later plays furnish striking evidence of how far Shakespeare's mind has swung away from the joyous mirth and gay romance of his earlier work, and how ambiguities and complexities are multiplied. The language used shows more compression which, sometimes, as in *King Lear,* is carried to the point of obscurity. In the figure of Hamlet, Shakespeare's most complex character study, the unresolved inner tensions so characteristic of Mannerism are vividly set forth. The graveyard scene in *Hamlet,* which has little relevance to the play or to its structure, is evidence of an almost morbid preoccupation with death. In both the later plays and the later sonnets, literary conceits abound; for example, in the sonnet beginning "Mine eye hath played the painter," the heart is the "table" or canvas, the body is the "frame," and the bosom is the painter's "shop." Shakespeare's later plays, which remain unmatched for their analyses of character and of human situations, and unmatched for the poetic language in which they are clothed, represent the supreme literary achievement of the Mannerist Age.

Donne (d. 1631), even more than Shakespeare, had a deep sense of the vanity and shallowness of all created things. His poetry is a strange mixture of the significant and the inconsequential. Donne and his fellow Metaphysical poets disliked the metrical exactness of English High Renaissance poetry and its harmonious and flowing cadences. They wished to free accent and rhythm from conventional metrics, and to capture the rhythm of everyday speech. They were in revolt, too, against the sweetness of High Renaissance style; they disliked the conventions of Petrarchian love and wished to look afresh at human relations. In his

satires, epistles, elegies, and miscellaneous lyrics, Donne loved to bring
in unexpected analogies. He drew images from circles, maps, engravings, elephants, fleas, whales, new discoveries, and the like. He seems
always to have been looking for kinship in things apparently unlike.
Donne's verse usually lacks smoothness, and the expression of his ideas
is frequently oblique and lacks completeness. On the other hand, he is,
at times, unsurpassed for intensity. Donne and the other Metaphysical
poets show a great effort to present passion and thought, feeling and
ratiocination, together. The philosopher is usually behind the poet; the
result is often a feverish intellectuality, but almost no music. Donne's
subtleties, and his whimsy, are shown in his verses on the flea, which
after biting the poet, bites his mistress:

> This flea is you and I, and this
> Our marriage bed, and marriage temple is.

The strong side of Donne's poetry, on the other hand, is shown in the
unusual intensity and profundity of thought which mark his finest
verses. Much of the spirit of Mannerism is summed up in these lines:

> And new philosophy calls all in doubt,
> The element of fire is quite put out;
> The sun is lost, and th' earth, and no man's wit
> Can well direct him where to looke for it
> 'Tis all in pieces, all cohearence gone.

4. Music

The Age of Mannerism in music is shorter than in art and letters, and
it overlaps the continuance of the calm and lofty musical style of the
High Renaissance. For this reason the histories of music usually move
directly from a section on the Renaissance to one on the Baroque. However, as in art and letters, there was in the later sixteenth century a
period of extensive experimentation in music, marked by deliberate and
self-conscious attempts to find new means of expression and to move
beyond the musical style of the High Renaissance. This experimental
attitude relates changes in musical style to those in art and literature.
There is the same undoing of the balance and proportion and the same
desire for new effects; some of these were overstrained and artificial, yet
others resulted in the discovery of a new world of expression. It is, however, not possible in music, with its strict rules of harmony, to find exact

parallels to the inner tensions and the love of paradox found in art and letters. As in art, Italy took the lead in these significant changes and innovations.

Venice became one of the greatest musical centers, not only in Italy, but in all Europe, in the later sixteenth century, and here we find a series of gifted composers who undertook new ventures in music. Willaert (d. 1562), a Fleming who was choirmaster of St. Mark's, began a new development of the use of double choirs known as antiphony. This helped to extend into church music new elements of contrast and the possibility of echo effects. The contrasts were accentuated by the use of two organs, and the use of instruments either with the voices or in alternation with them. Willaert's style was continued and elaborated by the two Gabrielis, Andrea and his gifted nephew, Giovanni (d. 1612). Giovanni Gabrieli showed himself a consummate master of the effects of a many-voiced texture. Some of his compositions call for as many as eight groups interwoven in marvelous variety. His later works show dissonant effects and a use of tone color to bring out the meaning of the text— music that violated many of the rules of sixteenth-century counterpoint. Some of these changes in style had appeared first in madrigal writing, and were then taken over and developed by Giovanni Gabrieli in church music. The instruments used in his choral works sometimes doubled the voices at the octave, and sometimes moved independently. The results remind one of the glowing effects of a Tintoretto.

Giovanni Gabrieli was likewise an innovator in instrumental music, especially in separating an instrumental style from the prevailing vocal style. Among his later compositions is a *sonata pian'e forte,* one of the first uses of the term "sonata"—meaning a composition to be sounded rather than sung—and one of the first printed compositions to designate particular instruments for each part. One ensemble consists of a cornet and three trombones, the second of a viol and three trombones. The effect is rich, massive, and colorful, and of a dramatic quality quite distinct from the music of the High Renaissance. Another innovation was the printing on the score of the words "piano" and "forte," the first when one orchestra played alone, the second when they played together. Gabrieli wrote other compositions for groups of instruments. He liked to use trombones, which were available in five sizes from bass to soprano, and cornets, which at the time were made of wood. Both trombones and cornets produced milder tones than the later brass instruments that bear these names. In his organ music, Gabrieli replaced the traditional polyphony by a bold scheme of chordal progressions. Many of Giovanni Gabrieli's innovations were carried to Germany by his favorite pupil, Schütz. In the vast tonal murals of Giovanni Gabrieli and in his instrumental effects, there is an *élan,* an emotional drive, and a sensuous coloring that came to overshadow the influence and prestige of Palestrina. By transferring the technique of writing for a number of choruses to instrumental ensembles, Gabrieli laid the foundation for the Baroque orchestra. Other composers of the later sixteenth century, in writing for voices and instruments or for instrumental ensembles, tried to express in music moods of rage, defiance, tender sentiment, or pastoral tranquillity; and it became the custom to use the trumpet for heroic arias, the horn for hunting scenes, the recorder or flute for bird songs and passages of tender love-making. This sort of thing became much more developed in the seventeenth century.

In the course of the sixteenth century, a number of composers show the development of new styles of instrumental writing to exploit the musical potentialities of various instruments, especially of the lute, the virginal, the organ, and the violin. The invention of the violin proved to be an important innovation for later music. It had higher and wider shoulders than the old viols, an arched back, and four strings instead of six. Its tone was far more penetrating than that of any of the bowed instruments which preceded it. At the same time, a passion for virtuosity of performance invaded all fields of musical writing. Here an important innovator was the Spaniard Luis Milán (d. 1561), who published works for the "vihuela"—somewhat like a guitar, with five double strings and one single. Milán made no attempt to imitate either plain song or the polyphony based on it. He was also one of the earlier composers to indicate in a systematic way just how the music should be played, and he recommends the use of rubato, that is, fluctuations in tempo. His compositions demanded great technical capacity. The greatest innovator for solo instrumental playing was the Italian organist Frescobaldi (d. 1643). In the introduction to his toccatas for organ, he gave rules for playing his music that were contrary to the rules usually followed for playing organ compositions. He indicated, for example, that performances must not be subject to strict time—the tempo should be now languid and now lively in accordance with the mood of the passage; and that various sections of the composition may be played independently of one another. And he particularized, quite definitely, a style of playing he believed to be specifically fitted to the organ.

One of the new devices in writing for instruments was the use of a figured bass, a sort of musical shorthand in which chords are indicated by placing numbers below the bass notes to be played on a keyboard instrument. The part in ensemble music which carries the figures came to be known as *basso continuo,* or "thorough-bass." In an instrumental ensemble, a strong bass instrument (or group of them) would usually play the bass melody as written, and a keyboard instrument, such as an organ or a harpsichord, would play the same bass melody with the left hand and, with the right, fill in the harmonies indicated in the figured bass. This allowed considerable latitude to the performer who could do some improvising in realizing the figured bass. This use of a figured bass, which came in during the later sixteenth century, became so common in the seventeenth century that this century is sometimes called "the age of figured bass."

Much attention was given by sixteenth-century composers to the writing of secular part songs. In the earlier sixteenth century, the style of these songs—called madrigals in Italy—resembled the polyphonic style used in church music. By the latter part of the century increasing emphasis was placed on making the music fit the words of the song. Marenzio (d. 1599), the greatest of all madrigal composers, broke away from the conventional harmonies and developed a more chromatic style (use of tones extraneous to the diatonic scale); and he was one of the first to employ major and minor scales. Many of his madrigals substitute a homophonic for a polyphonic style and the *cantus firmus* of an earlier age is at last given up. Marenzio, though he used melodic figures to illustrate his text, always managed to make the whole unite in a single composition. Marenzio's published madrigals were known in France, Germany, the Low Countries, and England; and they everywhere affected the style of secular vocal music. Vecchi (d. 1605) wrote sequences of madrigals grouped into acts; he called such a sequence "madrigal comedy," an interesting forerunner of the opera.

The greatest innovator among the madrigalists was Gesualdo, Prince of Venosa (d. 1614). A man of violent temperament, passionate and excitable, he hired an assassin to murder his wife and her lover. In his madrigals he got dramatic effects by the use of a varied, free, and often complex rhythm, and by a reckless use of chordal progressions, dissonances, and chromaticism. Interested solely in expressing the content of the text, Gesualdo did not care for tonal unity. With him the madrigal becomes a free sequence of impressions, pictures, and musical outbursts. The effect is often ragged and unvocal. When the text speaks of death or pain, dissonances are introduced into the music; when joy is spoken of, the tempo is increased. The composer, for some time, had had at his disposal a set of musical figures which were classified, in an arbitrary and artificial way, to correspond with various emotions. The change now was to lay emphasis on texts that used more the figures connected with pain, death, violent emotion, and ecstatic joy, and to insist on using the musical figures no matter what might be the effect on the tonal unity. Some of Gesualdo's effects seem merely eccentric; others suggest Wagner. The logical successor of these late sixteenth-century madrigals was the Baroque *solo aria* with instrumental accompaniment. There is something desperate and frightening about some of Gesualdo's madrigals. But his six published books of madrigals were widely circulated across Europe. In his madrigals, Monteverdi (d. 1643) used some of the same devices as Gesualdo, and both composers were vigorously attacked by conservative musical theorists. Monteverdi answered that he was writing in a new style. In the later sixteenth century the new style of composition came to be known as the *nuove musiche,* a term that became a rallying point for the new forces just as *ars nova* had been in the fourteenth century. The Italian madrigal died a natural death at the end of the sixteenth century. This was partly due to the fact that, after Monteverdi, no further developments of the form seemed possible. It also ceased to be the fashion for the upper classes to consider sight-singing ability a necessary accomplishment, and at the same time musical skills became so professional that only a highly trained singer dared to give a performance.

Finally, two new musical forms, the oratorio and the opera, appeared in Italy in the later sixteenth century. Back of the oratorio were the medieval mystery and miracle plays, which had used a good deal of music in their presentation. With these in mind, in the midst of the Counter Reformation in Rome, St. Philip Neri organized services of a popular character in which were given musical works for solos and choruses, with instrumental accompaniment. In these there were presented, usually with costumes and scenery, important scenes from the Bible. More emphasis was given to the chorus than in the early operas, and a narrator was often used to connect the parts. The writing of these oratorios began as early as 1556, but the first one that is preserved is from about 1600. In the seventeenth century it became the practice to present oratorios in concert form without costumes and scenery, and the oratorio became one of the great musical forms of the Age of the Baroque. The earliest oratorio that is still often performed is Carissimi's *Jephtha* with a Latin text, in part from the Bible. Here there is a regular sequence of recitatives, arias, and choruses, all with harpsichord or orchestral accompaniments.

Opera, that is to say sung drama, made its first appearance in Florence at the very end of the sixteenth century. It was started by an aristocratic circle of amateurs, the Camerata, who met at the home of Count Bardi. Their aim was not to found a new art form, but to try out a new way of presenting Greek drama in the manner they imagined it had once been performed. Aristotle believed that tragedy, the most ennobling form of drama, should be written in poetry and enhanced with music, so that the language of tragedy should "be embellished and rendered pleasurable." The Camerata tried setting texts to music in such a way as to preserve the rhythm of the text, and in such a manner that the meaning of the words would be perfectly clear. As a background for this experimenting, they had the tradition of medieval religious dramas, and the ballets, masques, intermezzos, and madrigal cycles of the Renaissance. The members of the Florentine Camerata, and especially the musicians in the group, were opposed to the use of a polyphonic style of musical writing because it obscured the meaning of the words of the text used. At the same time, they opposed the use of a descriptive style by the madrigalists, because they believed the music should correspond in mood to a whole passage, not merely to individual words. Galilei, a member of the Camerata, in his *Dialogue on Ancient and Modern Music,* vigorously attacked the vocal counterpoint of the madrigalists. When several voices simultaneously sang different melodies and words in different rhythms, and when some voices were low and some high, some rising and some descending, some moving in slow notes and others in fast, the poetic text was lost.

An original work was written by Peri, who produced the first opera, *Dafne,* in 1597. Peri, in justification of his recitative style, declared, "I believe that the ancient Greeks and Romans (who, according to the opinion of many, sang their tragedies throughout) used a kind of music more advanced than ordinary speech, but less than the melody of singing, thus taking a middle position between the two." This work by Peri is now lost, and the earliest surviving opera is the *Eurydice* of Peri and Caccini of 1600, presented for the marriage of Henry IV of France and Maria de' Medici. Here are a series of recitatives for solos and duets and choruses with orchestra or harpsichord accompaniments. The whole work is definitely monodic; the accompaniments are always subordinated to the voice parts. The vocal line aims at close adherence to the rhythm and accent of the spoken words and lacks a melodic character. In Peri's words, "I conceived the idea of composing a harmonic speech, a sort of music in which a noble restraint was placed on singing in favor of the words." The whole movement was but a phase of the general tendency to bring words and music closer together. The effect is dry and monotonous, but ten years after Peri presented his *Dafne,* the great Monteverdi composed his *Orfeo,* the first important work of the Age of Baroque. Purists were quick to criticize the new form; Saint-Évremond, writing in the seventeenth century, complains of the mixture of music, drama, dancing, and stage design and costuming, and he described opera as "a bizarre affair of poetry and music in which the poet and the musician each equally obstruct the other, give themselves no end of trouble, and produce a wretched result."

5. The Quest for Rules

The extreme individualism and the spirit of experimentation that marked the Age of Mannerism had, from the beginning, called out a consistent effort toward restraint and toward finding rules for the artist and writer. An age of extreme individualism thus became also a great age of rule-making. The same quest for an absolute set of standards was shown in religion. Here the effort to define became first clearly marked in the Lutheran *Augsburg Confession* of 1530, soon followed by Calvin's great theological treatise, *The Institute of the Christian Religion.* On the Protestant side, other narrow statements of faith appeared as groups broke off from the Roman church, or from other Protestant groups, as, for instance, the *Six Articles,* the *Forty-two Articles,* and the *Thirty-nine Articles* of the Anglican church.

While the Protestants were busily defining their several faiths, the Catholic church, in a fight to the death with all forms of Protestantism, drew up its *Canons and Decrees of the Council of Trent.* These allowed less freedom of belief in the Catholic church than had prevailed in earlier centuries when no such specific statement of faith had been promulgated. So far as the arts were mentioned in all these statements of religious belief, both Protestant and Catholic, the emphasis was on the side of Puritanism. The Calvinists were against the use of all artworks and of organs in churches, as were some of the smaller Protestant sects. The Council of Trent accepted the work of artist, author, and composer only if these aided in bringing either the upper classes or the masses to a more fervent religious faith. The Counter Reformation, in general, was against the paganism and nudity, and luxury of the High Renaissance. Scenes of suffering must not be idealized, and, if the subject demands it, Christ must be shown "afflicted, bleeding, spat upon, with his skin torn, pale and unsightly." In 1559 Pope Paul IV ordered the nudes in Michelangelo's "Last Judgment" to have draperies painted on them. In the days of the High Renaissance, Lorenzo de' Medici's son, Leo X, had declared, "God has given us the papacy; let us enjoy it!" By the middle of the century, an atmosphere of heavy piety prevailed at Rome, and was spreading through the Catholic church everywhere. The Vatican had become like a monastery; silence was kept at table, and meat was served but twice a week. The papacy was now in close alliance with Spain, the most conservative of all Catholic states. New religious orders, including the Jesuits, were founded, the Inquisition was established in most Catholic states, books were censored, and the church even laid down rules to govern the artist in the choice and handling of subjects. Writers like Campanella, Galileo, and Bruno who were courageous enough to go on with their own speculations were silenced by the church authorities.

Religious painting and sculpture must be kept close to the realities of the biblical or traditional story, picturesque details must be avoided, and the moral of the scene represented must be emphasized. The elaborate counterpoint used in musical settings of the masses, since it obscured the words, should be simplified. No popular melodies might be used as themes in religious compositions. The objections raised to earlier works of art show the temper of the Catholic Counter Reformation. Michelangelo's "Last Judgment" was condemned, not only because of the nudes in it, but because the angels did not have wings, or the saints halos; certain of the figures have draperies blown about by the wind, in spite of the fact that at the Day of Judgment all wind and storm had ceased; and Christ is standing instead of being seated on his throne—so the bill of particulars against the painting went on and on. The Inquisition summoned Veronese (in 1573) to defend his painting of the "Feast in the House of Simon" against the charge of too many worldly elements: dogs, dwarfs, and a parrot. He was ordered to make certain alterations, which he proceeded to make, and he changed the title to

"Feast in the House of Levi." On the positive side, the Jesuits wished the artist and musician to make a definite appeal to the emotions of the worshippers without, however, introducing irrelevant or pagan elements. Religion must not be made so grim that ordinary people would be frightened away from the church. St. Philip Neri and the Oratorians had many of the same ideas about both art and music. The result of these currents was to combine religious sentiment with sensuousness in the art and music of the seventeenth century. The influence of the Counter Reformation on art, which did not become marked until after 1600, is more important on the positive than on the negative side. In Catholic lands the artist came to exalt what the Protestants attacked: the cult of the Virgin and the saints, the sacraments, the papacy, and the church militant. Such a view glorified martyrdom and religious ecstasy, and opened up the heavens. These changes gave to much of the art of the Baroque Age its essential quality.

While the discussion of religion and the arts was going on, a number of critics were trying to find rules for the arts based on ancient writings, especially those of Aristotle on literature and of Vitruvius on architecture. With these as guides, and from Greek and Latin literature and Roman models in architecture and sculpture—the Greek artistic achievements were almost unknown—the critics believed they could erect perfect sets of regulations of how to obtain beauty in art and literature. Though a few writers, as Alberti and Leonardo da Vinci, had produced theoretic works on the fine arts, and critics like Bembo had tried to lay down rules in literature, the Early and High Renaissance had not followed rules but had borrowed freely and spontaneously from the ancients. Now the critics produced rules to cover both the general structural outline of a work of art or letters and the subordinate details of all the parts. They conceived of their aesthetic rules as a kind of infallible machinery of universal order. They insisted that the artist and the writer must be learned in history, philosophy, science, and classical culture as well as versed in all the rules of his art. Artistic and literary academies were founded to give awards on the basis of such rules. The result of all this was not clearly seen before the seventeenth century. It tended then to raise standards among the lesser men, and to channel the work of the leading geniuses without, however, seeming greatly to affect the individualism and the worth of their achievements.

The first academies of art were established to try to raise the status of the artist above that of a mere artisan to one of high standing like that held by the Humanists and poets. One of the earliest of such academies was founded in Florence in the later fifteenth century by Lorenzo de' Medici for students of painting and sculpture. Here in his own palace, Lorenzo had young artists, like Michelangelo, trained, independent of all guild restrictions. In the sixteenth century, a number of groups of artists in various Italian cities met informally to discuss their problems and to draw from casts or from living models. Such groups had no formal organization and welcomed young artists and amateurs. The first regular academy, the Academy of Design, was founded about 1562 in Florence by Vasari with the backing of the reigning Medici prince. Its program was to include evening inspection of the work of young artists in studios where they were working, lectures by eminent artists, classes for young artists, and, according to a later statement, the granting of prizes. The Academy admitted thirty-six artists, thirty-two of them resident in Florence. The elaborate regulations drawn up for the Academy were never fully carried out, and it did not immediately replace the old apprentice method of training artists. Its reputation was great enough, however, that within a few years it was being consulted on artistic projects, not only by artists elsewhere in Italy, but by rulers and artists of other countries; in 1567 Philip II of Spain asked the advice of the Academy on designs for the Escorial. A similar institution, the Academy of St. Luke, was founded in Rome in 1593 under the patronage of the pope. Much more emphasis was laid here on the holding of classes for instruction of young students in anatomy and perspective. Also founded in Rome at the end of the sixteenth century was an "Academy of Drawing" that was eclectic in outlook and wished to restore painting, which it believed had declined since the days of the High Renaissance. Though the members espoused the composition and drawing of Raphael, the work of the artists who formed the academy—all men of mediocre talent—showed the usual characteristics of Mannerism. The basic difference between the old guilds and the new academies was that the academies taught theoretically as well as practically whereas the guilds had mainly aimed at passing on a technical tradition. It was not until the seventeenth century that academies played a dominant role in the training of artists and in the formation of taste.

The theoretical treatises on art of the later sixteenth century show very clear evidence of a desire to set bounds to the individualism of the artist. The critics agreed that painting had declined since the great days of Raphael, Titian, and Michelangelo—which was also the view of the first modern art historian, Vasari, in his *Lives of Eminent Artists*—and the theorists searched for means to restore art to its earlier glory. The most comprehensive treatise on painting was a book issued in 1584 by the Milanese painter Lomazzo. He laments the decline of painting and wishes to save it from descending to still lower levels by establishing rules. He agrees that a painter must be born with natural genius, but having said this, Lomazzo devotes his attention to all the minutiae of the artist's training. The earlier theorists, as Alberti and Leonardo da Vinci, believed that a student could be helped to learn the art of painting by the application of reasonable methods; the later Mannerist theorists— including Lomazzo—wish him to acquire it all by absolute rules. These rules are final, not because they are reasonable, but because they are derived from the analysis of the work of the greatest masters, including those who produced the best surviving ancient sculptures. In the seven hundred crowded pages of Lomazzo's treatise, every possible problem that can confront the painter is set forth and the proper solution given. Nothing escapes analysis; and proportion, motion, color, light, perspective, and subject matter are all covered. Under proportion, for example, details are given for drawing figures of men and women of seven, eight, nine, and ten heads in height; and similar details are given for children and horses. All human emotions and how to represent them are described. A complete Christian and classical iconography is included; to paint Apollo or St. John, the artist need only turn to the relevant passage in Lomazzo's treatise.

Lomazzo's treatise was widely read both in Italy and in the lands beyond the Alps. Besides a number of treatises on painting, published both in Italy and beyond the Alps, there were numerous works on architecture that appeared in the later sixteenth century. They were all based on the earlier Renaissance theory that every part of a building, both within and without, must be integrated into one system of mathematical ratios. These ratios, Vitruvius declared, were based on the proportions of the human body; as man is made in the image of God, the proportions used in architecture express a divine order. Further details of how to arrange proportions were not only set forth in Vitruvius but could also be studied in existing Roman buildings. These were carefully measured, and proper relations worked out for the bases and the height and diameter of columns and pilasters, for the designs of doors and windows, and the proportions of rooms. But the vagueness of Vitruvius and the variety of ancient Roman practices in the designs of buildings allowed for differing opinions on the proper proportions of buildings and their several parts.

Vignola (d. 1573), in his *Rules of the Five Orders of Architecture* (Tuscan, Doric, Ionic, Corinthian, and Composite) of 1562, and Palladio (d. 1580), in his *Four Books of Architecture* of 1570, laid their chief emphasis on the proper ratios of parts of buildings by combining the rules of Vitruvius with their own observations of Roman buildings. According to Vignola, for example, the height of a column must be seven times its diameter in the Tuscan order, eight times in the Doric order, nine times in the Ionic order, and ten times in the Corinthian and Composite orders. For an order with pedestal the total height is divided into nineteen parts, four of which are given to the pedestal, twelve to the column, and three to the entablature—and the rules go on and on. Palladio's treatise—each book was fully illustrated with woodcuts—is the more elaborate. His first book is largely a reworking of ideas of proper proportions derived from Vitruvius. In the second book, devoted to private buildings, he sets forth his own experience as an architect and shows how he reconciled the principles of Vitruvius with his own observation of Roman buildings. The third book deals with city planning; and the last takes up various forms of Roman temples, and how these could be used in modern buildings. Serlio (d. 1564), who published his *Works on Architecture* earlier, also tries to combine Vitruvius and principles derived from Roman structures, though, unlike Vignola and Palladio, he makes Vitruvius the absolute standard and holds that any Roman practice at variance with his ideas is wrong—except in cases where he allows for new inventions of Mannerism such as rusticated columns. These Italian treatises, with their numerous woodcut illustrations, circulated in the original or in translation all over Europe; and they outdistanced in influence similar architectural treatises published about the same time in France, Germany, and England.

Literary academies had first been established in Italy in the fifteenth century. These groups, like the Platonic Academy fostered by the Medici in Florence, had brought together Humanists and writers for informal discussions. Not until the second half of the sixteenth century, however, were literary academies founded that made formal statements on literary matters. Among a number of these, the most important was the Accademia della Crusca founded in Florence in the middle of the sixteenth century. Its main task was to purify and standardize the Italian language, and in 1612 it published a great dictionary of Italian. This academy has continued to exist down to the present. As early as 1570 an Academy of Poetry and Music was founded in France, but it was short-lived. Only in the seventeenth and eighteenth centuries did literary academies come to exist in numbers all over Europe and their main purpose then was to award literary prizes, to give public lectures, and to publish their proceedings and dictionaries and grammars.

Closely connected with the literary academies of sixteenth-century Italy was a long-continued controversy over the proper language to be used in literary works. A few writers, especially in the fifteenth and early sixteenth centuries, thought only Latin should be used. Among those who believed the vernacular was the proper vehicle there were sharp divisions. Some, like Bembo, wished to use the Tuscan of Dante, Petrarch, and Boccaccio as the best medium; others, like Machiavelli, preferred the contemporary Tuscan; a third group wished to combine with Tuscan words taken from other Italian areas; while a fourth group believed in using the language spoken in the princely Italian courts as the standard. By the later sixteenth century those who favored the use of the living and contemporary Tuscan usage as the national language won out. When the dictionary of the Accademia della Crusca appeared in the early seventeenth century, some Italian writers thought it had carried linguistic purism too far in that it excluded many words then in good contemporary Tuscan usage.

As with art criticism, most of the literary criticism of the middle and later sixteenth century in Italy was averse to the extreme individualism shown by the writers of the Age of Mannerism and strongly favored the setting-up of absolute rules for literature. For this, critics had recourse to four ancient treatises on literature, the *Poetics* and *Rhetoric* of Aristotle, the treatise *On the Sublime* by Longinus, and the *Ars poetica,* a long Latin epistle of Horace. The critics, however, used these treatises quite as they saw fit. Aristotle, for example, exalts tragedy above other literary forms, but all the critics, except Castelvetro, exalted the epic. Similarly, Aristotle explicitly proposed for the drama only the unity of action and merely suggests unity of time. Yet the two most important critics, Scaliger and Castelvetro, each of whom wrote a *Poetics,* insist on the three unities of action, time, and place for the drama. Aristotle made no clear class distinction in the subject matter of tragedy and comedy, whereas the critics insisted that the subject of tragedy must be royal or aristocratic and that of comedy middle and lower class. And none of the ancient writers had an elaborate theory of decorum, ascribed to them by the critics—that speech, action, costume, and setting must fit exactly the type of character presented and that this would yield the true-to-life effect that the critics called "verisimilitude." Finally, the critics, though quite absolute in their rules, did not agree among themselves in legislating for Parnassus. The effect of this sixteenth-century Italian literary criticism, first on literary criticism beyond the Alps and then on literary production in Italy, was evident well before the close of the century, but its greatest influence belonged to the Age of the Baroque.

To examine this literary theorizing more in detail, we see that during the middle and later sixteenth century it formulated—largely from Aristotle's *Poetics* and Horace's *Ars poetica*—a theory of poetry, a rigid set of rules for the drama, and a rigid form for the epic. Rules so derived from ancient writers and elaborated by Humanist theorists, together with the use of reason, were to act as a bulwark against too free an expression of the author's personality and passion, against the morbid subjectivity and individualism which is the horror of the classical temperament. No detail was too small to be covered by these theorists. In Aristotle, the critics found their own justification of imaginative literature. Literature, they declared, represents or should represent a universalizing of human experience, and it can and should allay and regulate the passions. This squares well with Horace's statement that poetry is to please and to instruct. Imaginative literature, thus, has a positive moral value. According to the critics, following a statement of Horace, "ut pictura poesis," poetry and painting should resemble one another. So painting is silent poetry, and poetry is painting in language. Hardly any treatise on art and literature, from about 1550 to about 1750, failed to cite this statement by Horace. And it could be used in contexts far removed from the idea of Horace. For instance, it was called in for the attacks on Michelangelo's "Last Judgment," where the artist was accused of serving art rather than religion and where the painting did not correspond with the theologian's picture of the Last Judgment. As in other religious pictures of the Mannerist Age there was too much individualism in Michelangelo's treatment. "Some artists," said one writer, "think they have paid their debt when they have made a saint and have put all their genius into twisting awry the legs, or the arms, or the neck, and in a violent manner that is both unseemly and ugly."

Of all Aristotle's dicta, the one most elaborated upon was his statement that poetry should imitate human life by handling actions and speech in such a manner as to reveal their significance and in such a way as to represent the universal. This came to mean that the author should imitate the way the great writers of Greece and Rome had handled these actions. Why bother with nature at all, says Scaliger, when you have everything you want in Virgil; and he adds, "Nothing was omitted by that heavenly genius; there is nothing to be added unless by fools; nothing to be changed unless by the imprudent!"

These rules of the learned critics were widely accepted but brought forth stout rejoinders from Tasso and Guarini when their works were criticized, and from Bruno, who declared, "Rules are not the source of poetry, but poetry is the source of rules; there are as many rules as there are true poets." But these proved to be no deterrent to the respect for rules in literature in the seventeenth century. The formulation of literary rules parallels the development of Jesuit ethics. Just as the Jesuits, in order to strengthen and to centralize the principle of authority were willing to multiply minute rulings even at the risk of suppressing spontaneity in the religious life, the Neo-Classical theorists exercised a centralizing influence on literature and tended to substitute purely formal precepts for spontaneous expression. And just as the Jesuits were very lenient to those who accepted their outer authority, even if they lacked the ardor of inner piety, so these literary casuists held out to those who obeyed the rules the hope that they would be able to write a good epic or drama even if they lacked any special inspiration. Chapelain, for example, declared that he hoped to show in his epic, *La pucelle,* that one who possessed the theory of the epic, might "without any special elevation of mind" put it successfully into practice. The influence of these Neo-Classical literary codifiers was much more marked in the seventeenth century than in the sixteenth.

The theorizing in music was directed less to finding rules than to justifying new experiments in musical composition, and so to defying those who still believed in holding onto the musical style of the High Renaissance. Zarlino (d. 1590), the most profound musical theorist of the sixteenth century, summed up the musical thought of the High Renaissance. He saw in music a self-contained autonomous art subject to its own laws. Much the same point of view was represented by other theorists who glorified the style of Palestrina. Toward the end of the century, Zarlino was attacked by a number of writers, including his own former student, Galilei. These writers, who represented new points of view, were mostly connected with the groups that were inaugurating the opera. In actual practice some composers were writing in the traditional High Renaissance style, now called the *stil antico,* and alongside of them others were composing in the *stil moderno.* Some composers were, so to speak, bilingual and wrote in both styles. In any case, musicians were becoming very conscious of the division. Those who wrote in the *stil moderno* used more dissonance, were greatly interested in the solo style of singing, disliked the older polyphony, and insisted that in song the music must be subordinated to the words.

In his *Dialogue on Ancient and Modern Music,* Vincenzo Galilei (d. 1591), the father of the famous physicist, attacked the elaborate polyphonic style of the High Renaissance in which, he declared, poetry was "torn to pieces" by the music. The polyphonic writers depicted words like "heaven" and "wave" by high notes and wavy lines. Galilei denounced this as "pedantry" and insisted that the sense of an entire passage rather than of a single word should be imitated by the music. He was especially interested in defending the solo recitative in which the words governed the musical rhythm and even the place of the cadences. Peri spoke of this recitative as "imitating a speaking person in song," and Caccini called it "speaking in music." In his *New Music* (1602), Caccini (d. 1618) speaks in less heated terms than those used by Galilei; he explains the new monody of a solo voice accompanied by one or more instruments in which the music is subordinated to the words. The older method of solo singing "ruins the verse by now lengthening and now shortening the syllables to match the music, a laceration of the poetry."

Monteverdi, in answering a critic of his earlier books of madrigals, asserts in his fifth book of madrigals (1605) that he deliberately did not follow the precepts of the old school but that, in his handling of dissonance and in his relating words and music, he was following the *seconda prattica,* in his view a more effective way than the older style. To one critic, who accused Monteverdi of "delighting the senses rather than satisfying the reason," and of calling "everything into question instead of following the paths of the masters," Monteverdi blandly replied that other systems of harmony existed besides those used by the "old masters."

6. Conclusion

The concept of an Age of Mannerism—from about 1530 to 1600 in Italy and later in the rest of western Europe, an age that lies between that of the High Renaissance and of the Baroque—is a concept of the twentieth century. It first appeared in the history of art, then moved into the history of literature, and is finally entering the history of music. This period of Mannerism lacks the stylistic unity of the High Renaissance which precedes it. As we have seen, it is characterized by extreme individualism and free experimentation in the arts, and the essence of the age is diversity of achievement. The artists, writers, and composers of the Age of Mannerism were striving to create new types of beauty. Their work also reflects the confused religious, political, and social conditions of the middle and later sixteenth century. For these reasons they broke up the harmony, proportion, and balance of the artistic, literary, and musical styles of the High Renaissance; and the extreme individualism displayed by artists, writers, and composers led to a tremendous effort to define excellence in the arts and to limit the range of expression in each.

Looking back, the achievements of this Age of Mannerism seem more remarkable in art and in letters than in music. Most accounts of Mannerism tend to pick out the *outré* and the bizarre in the age and emphasize "the lunatic fringe"—eccentric paintings and buildings, such currents as Euphuism and Préciosité in literature, and the musical oddities of a Gesualdo. Actually, the emphasis should be placed rather on the achievement of artists like Michelangelo, Tintoretto, and Palladio; on the accomplishment of writers like Montaigne, Cervantes, and Shakespeare; and on the compositions of Giovanni Gabrieli and the madrigals of Monteverdi. All in all, the individualism and experimentation of the age produced a superb body of achievement in the arts.

Chapter V

THE BAROQUE
1600-1750

1. The Nature of the Baroque

The word "Baroque" has had a curious history. Originally used as a term in Scholastic logic, it came, in Italy, in the sixteenth century, when Scholasticism was going out of fashion, to stand for the whole of Scholasticism. Then by the eighteenth century it was used for anything queer, overelaborate, contorted, or involved. This seems to have been the history of the word in Italy. In Portugal, Spain, France, and England, the use of the word came partly from Italy and partly from a Portuguese word meaning a rough or imperfect pearl. In the eighteenth century Milizia, a Neo-Classical art historian and critic, uses the term "baroque" for "the ultimate of the bizarre, the ridiculous carried to extremes." Another Neo-Classical critic refers to the Baroque as "a jumble of oddities and witticisms." This idea that the Baroque represented a corrupt taste, and a senseless love of novelty, was continued in the nineteenth century. Ruskin, who disliked the art both of Mannerism and of the Baroque, classed them together as the "Grotesque Renaissance" and added, "On such work it is painful to dwell." Burckhardt, at one stage of his career, speaks of the Baroque as "a corrupt dialect of the Renaissance." The term was first used in relation to architecture. As the Baroque style came to be appreciated again in the twentieth century, Wölfflin applied it to painting and sculpture, Curt Sachs to music, and a number of critics to literature. It is now commonly used to designate a period in the arts which extends from about 1600 to about 1750. Naturally, in so long a period, style underwent a number of changes in all the arts; the Early Baroque is different in quality from the High Baroque, and both were to be succeeded by a late phase, the Rococo.

The style first differentiated itself in Italy though, in many cases, the greatest achievements of the style appeared in the lands beyond the Alps. In Italy, where the Baroque style in all the arts first appeared, it was undoubtedly affected by religious and political conditions. The Counter Reformation, and the absolutism of the governments of the small Italian states—most of these came under the ultimate domination of Spain—affected the whole intellectual climate through a combination of patronage and severe censorship. The heavy hand of the Counter Reformation and of Spain was everywhere felt. The Spaniard looked on trade as disgraceful; and under Spanish influence the most stupid economic regulations were made—as that in Milan which forbade the export of raw silk in order to encourage manufacture at home when the local manufacture could use only a small fraction of the silk produced. Sheep-raising was discouraged because it might cause a scarcity of hay for the horses; as a result there was a vast oversupply of hay, but no one thought of changing the regulations. In a sonnet, Campanella makes the black dress Italians were adopting from the Spanish symbolic of the whole religious and political state of Italy. The Spanish also brought in a fantastic love of ceremonies and of all matters of social precedence. When a great Neapolitan lady died, the right to some of the coats of arms to be displayed at her funeral was called into question, and the burial had to be postponed for months so that the matter could be referred to Madrid.

The Catholic Counter Reformation of the later sixteenth century had insisted that nudes and other pagan elements should be eliminated from religious art, and that draperies and fig leaves should be added to surviving ancient sculptures. But art and music, as used in the church, must also have a positive propaganda value that would fight heresies and religious indifference and skepticism, and they should at the same time appeal to all the faithful and bring religious emotion close to all men. Religious art and music must instruct and inspire; art was to become a form of apologetics. Everything in a religious painting or sculpture must be suitable for the subject—its time, place, and meaning. Numerous theoretical treatises insist on these things. The twisted columns, the broken pediments, the billowing clouds and flying angels, the curving surfaces and serpentine lines, the cunningly concealed windows that threw dramatic sunbeams on the saints, even the sometimes eccentric ground plan of a church, were all to carry the eye of the enchanted worshipper to the host on the altar. Subjects suitable for treatment in painting and sculpture and poetry were the weeping Virgin Mary, Mary Magdalene—who combined the spiritual and the sensuous—the Slaughter of the Innocents, the Crucified Savior from whose wounds flow water and blood, the martyrdom of saints, and ecstatic saints receiving the stigmata or swooning in religious trances. Above all, art and poetry must defend what the Protestants and freethinkers attacked: the cult of the Virgin and the saints, the papacy, all the seven sacraments, good works, and prayers for the dead. Altar pieces came to be like recruiting posters. The spirit was reached through the senses, and heresy and free thought were to be overwhelmed with splendor.

In the height of the Baroque Age, Leibniz, though himself not a Catholic, lists the spectacular aspects of Catholic services: "The strains of music, the sweet concord of voices, the poetry of the hymns, the beauty of the liturgy, the blaze of lights, the fragrant perfumes, the rich vestments, the sacred vessels adorned with precious stones, the statues and pictures that awaken holy thoughts, the glorious creations of architectural genius, with their effects of height and distance, the stately splendor of public processions, the rich draperies adorning the streets, and the music of the bells." It is all a perfect picture of the life of the Catholic church in the Age of the Baroque.

The Catholic authorities denied the Calvinist theory that the senses are the enemies of the spirit. They wished the faithful to taste the salt of tears, to smell the brimstone of hell, and to feel, like a consuming fire, the love of God. In the "Spiritual Exercises" of St. Ignatius Loyola, there is presented a series of meditations which would help the initiate to see, hear, smell, taste, and feel what he contemplates; for example, the prelude to the fifth day's exercise, which is on Hell, says: "The first point consists in this, that I see with the eye of the imagination those enormous fires, and the souls in the fires; the second point consists that I hear the lamentations, howlings and cries, the blaspheming against Our Lord, and against all his saints; the third point is that I taste the bitter things, the tears, the sorrow, and the worms of conscience."

All these things were in the intentions of the leaders of the Counter Reformation, but they did not greatly affect the arts until after 1580. By that time, the Catholic church was moving into a triumphant mood. It was consolidating its position in the Catholic states of Europe, it was stopping the spread of Protestantism, and in areas like Hungary, Poland, Bohemia, and South Germany it was rolling back the bounds of Protestantism. Protestantism was now on the defensive. So the Baroque art of the Catholic states, and especially of Italy, where the style was first clearly unfolded, represents a mood of conquest. The sense of danger which had pervaded the church had passed, and with this there came not only a triumphant mood but one that was both more joyous and more relaxed. In 1622, Ignatius Loyola, Theresa, Philip Neri, and Francis Xavier were canonized. This was a kind of official acknowledgment that the regenerative forces inside Catholicism had saved the church. This triumphant mood brought an exuberant quality into the Baroque which was to characterize it for much of the rest of the century.

The artistic styles of the Baroque—in comparison with those of the High Renaissance—show the same admiration for classical Roman grandeur, the same love of harmony and symmetry, and the same self-confidence. But the Baroque is at the same time more exuberant, dynamic, and ornamented. The High Renaissance style is one of being; that of the Baroque is one of becoming. Moreover, the scale of the Baroque, in all the arts, is much larger, and the rhythmic phrase inside a whole unit is bigger than in the arts of the High Renaissance. For example, in the architecture of the High Renaissance, each story of a building formed a separate unit with a division separating one story from another. In the Manneristic style, and still more in the Baroque, the façade was regarded as a unit, and the columns and pilasters ran the whole height of the building; and the entire façade is thus bracketed into a single phase instead of being made up of a series of successive phases. Moreover, the colonnades in front of St. Peter's in Rome and the Hall of Mirrors of Versailles would have staggered any High Renaissance prelate or prince. At the same time, the air of calmness on the surface of much Baroque art has an emotional undertow that the art of the High Renaissance did not possess. As Poussin said, he had learned from Domenichino "to enter into the passion of his subject." The differences between High Renaissance and Baroque painting, which Wölfflin pointed out, have already been discussed under Mannerism, but they should be recalled here; for in these differences Baroque was a continuation of Mannerism.

The contrast of the arts of the Baroque with those of Mannerism is much more striking, though some of the great masters of the Baroque, as Caravaggio, Monteverdi, Bernini, and Milton, did some of their early work in a Manneristic style. As it developed, the Baroque took over from Mannerism its inner tensions and its experimentalism, but it resolved these tensions into a harmonious unity. In spite of twists and counter-twists in the arts, of continuing restlessness and caprice, the whole is usually resolved into a unity. There comes to be an equilibrium of religious and secular forces and of diversified artistic means. The artist, writer, or composer seems now to glory in a conflict from which he wrests decision and balance. Mannerism represented an expressive deviation from classical and realistic norms; the Baroque is a return to these norms, but with much of the emotion, tension, and color of Mannerism included in a new synthesis. The Baroque, in its love of the grand and the massive and in its cultivation of eloquence, gave up many of the contorted and precious effects of Mannerism. Unlike Mannerism, with its frequent emphasis on decay and death, the spirit of the Baroque is full of a joy in this life and of assurance of a good life in the hereafter. As Wordsworth later wrote,

> . . . The gods approve
> The depth, and not the tumult of the soul,
> A fervent, not ungovernable, love.

The audacities of the Baroque are boundless; in art, letters, and music masses are piled one on another; in literature, descriptive adjectives and declamatory nouns are heaped on; and the most exaggerated contrasts are attained. The Baroque artists loved psychological analysis of subjects like surprise, as the ecstasy of St. Theresa, and the amazement of the disciples at the supper at Emmaus. But its sweeping extravagances, its vitality, its heaven-scaling grandeur, and its complexity were usually controlled and unified. The Baroque was an artistic force that not only met the demands of its ecclesiastical, royal, and noble patrons, but spoke also to the peasant and the common man; its sumptuous and copious vision was for all men. In its desire to achieve effects of grandeur, it mingled the arts as in the opera, and as in the great ensembles of painting, sculpture, and architecture in many of the great Baroque churches and palaces. The style is, at once, robust, positive, forceful, demonstrative, exuberant, and superlative. It is addressed even more to the imagination and the emotion than to the reason, but to an imagination and emotion that recognize the order that reason can work. The love of space and of the grandiose of the Baroque may be due in part to the vastly extended concept of the universe that was the result of the discoveries of Copernicus and his followers, and to the greatly expanded view of this world that followed the exploration of the Americas and the voyages in all the Seven Seas of this earth.

The essence of the Baroque is well expressed in Macaulay's description of King William III of England: "He was born with violent passions and quick sensibilities; but the strength of his emotions was not suspected by the world. From the multitude his joy and his grief, his affection, and his resentment were hidden by a phlegmatic serenity which made him pass for the most cold-blooded of mankind. Those who brought him good news could seldom detect any sign of pleasure. Those who saw him after a defeat looked in vain for any trace of vexation. But those who knew him well were aware that under all this ice a fierce fire was constantly burning." Saint-Simon's description of Louis XIV bears a striking resemblance to this:

The king's great qualities shone more brilliantly by reason of an exterior so unique and incomparable as to lend infinite distinction to his slightest actions. He was as dignified and majestic in his dressing gown as when dressed in robes of state, or on horseback at the head of his troops. No fatigue nor stress of weather made any impression on that heroic figure; drenched with rain, pierced with cold, bathed in sweat, or covered with dust, he was always the same. Nothing could be regulated with greater exactitude than were his days and hours. In spite of all variety of places and affairs, with an almanac and a watch one might tell, three hundred leagues away, exactly what he was doing. If he administered reproof, it was in a few words. He did not lose control of himself ten times in his whole life.

The critical canons in the fine arts and literature that were developed in the Age of Mannerism had their leading effects in the Age of the Baroque. The critics and the academies had set forth rules for art and literature. In both fields great emphasis continued to be laid on "verisimilitude" and "decorum." Both were opposed to the whimsies and fantasies of some of the artists and writers of the Age of Mannerism. There must be faithful adherence to probability in the poses, manners, and language of all subjects treated. Figures must be dressed in a manner suitable to their standing and character, gestures must be appropriate, and, in literature, the language must be exactly suited to the character and status of the persons represented, and the setting must be entirely appropriate and congruent.

After 1650, the French Academy of Painting and Sculpture tried to take these earlier suggestions, and to chart a complete scheme of representing the passions. To show wrath, for example, eyebrows should be lowered, eyes should be inflamed, the forehead creased, the nostrils dilated, and the face swollen. Similar elaborate rules for literature and for acting were set forth; also, extensive files of melodic and rhythmic figures for music were circulated, each of which was supposed to correspond to a peculiar shade of feeling. In art and letters, the artist and writer must know classical art and literature, not only for their style, but also for their subject matter. While great emphasis in art and literature continued to be placed on copying and following nature, it was likewise pointed out that the best way to follow nature had been shown by the classical artists and writers. So to follow nature, in practice, meant to follow the best classical models. As Pope wrote,

> Hence learn for ancient rules a just esteem,
> To copy nature is to copy them.

Sometimes warnings were given as to copying the antique. De Piles, the French Baroque art critic, declared, "The antique is admirable, but on condition that it is treated like a book that one translates into another language, in which it suffices to transfer well the sense and the spirit without a servile attachment to the words."

And nature also could be improved upon. Writers in the later seventeenth century pointed out that the surface of the globe is unevenly divided between land and water; islands are scattered about the seas promiscuously; and hills, valleys, lakes, and deserts are distributed without any regard to regularity. The stars in the sky are carelessly scattered. The effect would have been far more beautiful if they had been placed in rank and order and disposed in regular figures. Malebranche wrote, "The visible world would be more perfect if the seas and lands made more regular figures, if the rains were more regular, if, in a word, the world had few monstrosities and less disorder." One French Catholic missionary described Niagara Falls as, "falling from a horrible precipice, foaming and boiling after the most hideous manner imaginable, and making an outrageous noise and dismal roaring, more terrible than thunder." One English traveler of the seventeenth century described the Alps as "hideous, uncouth, monstrous excrescences of nature." In the Age of the Classical Baroque, they evidently wanted to smooth and regulate all nature, and make, as it were, domestic pets of the rivers and mountains. Later the Romantic Movement reversed all this, and Chateaubriand waxed eloquent over the glories of Niagara Falls, and the Romantics became enchanted with wild and untamed scenery. On a journey through France, Dr. Johnson, while the scenery was being admired, retorted impatiently, "A blade of grass is always a blade of grass whether in one country or another. Men and women are my subjects of inquiry. As Socrates said, 'I am a lover of knowledge, and the men who dwell in the city are my teachers, and not the trees of the country.'"

Art and letters, said the critics, should not only center their attention on man, and what is universal in him, but they should also have a moral end, and Aristophanes was quoted, "For what ought we to admire the poet? Because the poet makes men better!" And Corneille declared, "Let us remember that we learned from Horace that we cannot please unless we include in our works a moral purpose." Critical canons were widely discussed and considered during the Baroque era, and they had their effect on the arts. But the art, literature, and music of this age show such a vitality and exuberance that only among the minor men do these academic rules seem to have had a stifling effect.

The interest of the Baroque Age was primarily centered—as Dr. Johnson insisted it should be—on man, though in literature descriptions of nature were given prominence, and among the painters much attention was given to landscape backgrounds, with the Dutch developing a glorious school of independent landscape painting. In depicting man, in art and literature, there was a widespread assumption that the work should represent the essential nature of man in all ages, above time and above the particular. Dr. Johnson called this "the grandeur of generality," and he represents the Baroque Age in his belief that portrayal of the essential and enduring features of human nature is more important than the representation of what is only peculiar and particular to certain men and certain times.

The Age of the Baroque, which was also a golden age of scientific discovery, returned to the High Renaissance view that there was a great plan and harmony in the universe, though it believed that the details of creation could be better arranged. As Hobbes said, the age had come to see "the picture of an orderly and knowable universe whose system of correspondences could be discovered by observation of phenomena and whose reflection of a divine order could be arrived at rationally." The writers of the Baroque are much more aware of the discoveries of science than had been the writers of the sixteenth century, and they showed likewise a great deal of interest in the ideas of the philosophers of the age. The philosophers of the seventeenth and eighteenth centuries, on the other hand, were not very favorable to the arts and regarded them as inferior to science and philosophy. Locke pays his respect to literature in grudging terms: "If we would speak of things as they are, we must allow that all the arts of rhetoric, besides order and clearness, all the artificial and figurative applications of words eloquence hath invented, are for nothing else but to insinuate wrong ideas, move the passions, and thereby mislead the judgment, and so indeed are perfect cheats." Locke compares man's fancy to a court dresser who is out with his "colors, appearances, and resemblances" to catch the unwary and divest them of truth.

The art and literary critics had more concern for philosophy than the philosophers had sensitiveness for art or understanding of it. The critics of art and letters drew from the philosophers—especially after 1650— their belief in reason, and drew up even stricter rules for the arts than those of the Age of Mannerism. They attacked the "Gothic" barbarism of earlier artists and writers, with their lack of polish and their innocence of science and reason. Above all it was Boileau (d. 1711) who assimilated poetry to Cartesian reason and order.

> Love reason, then; and let what e'er you write,
> Borrow from her its beauty, force, and light.

The music and beauty of words are secondary to clear thought. The same sort of rules was sought for art. De Piles said that often earlier artists had worked too much by habit and too little by theory. "Their science," he declared, "was in their fingers rather than in their heads." De Piles drew up a table which gives mathematical values to excellence in composition, color, design, and general expression, and thus shows exactly how painting may be estimated. To please according to the rules became the ideal in the arts. "Follow nature," as Pope said, "but nature methodized." The ultimate appeal was always back to Aristotle, who believed that a good writer (and this could also be applied to the artist) would imitate things not merely as they are, but as they ought to be. So the writer and the artist are to seek out the loveliest forms from nature's boundless store. "Though nature," as Bellori, the Italian art critic said, "always intends a consummate beauty in her productions, yet through the inequality of the matter, the forms are altered. For which reason, the artful painter and sculptor, imitating the Divine Maker, form to themselves as they are able, a model of the superior beauties; and reflecting on them, endeavor to correct and amend the common nature, and to represent it without fault." Dryden summed up the same attitude when he wrote, "Both these arts [poetry and painting] are not only true imitations of nature but of the best nature. They present us with images more perfect than the life in any individual, and we have the pleasure to see all the scattered beauties of nature united by a happy chemistry without its deformities or faults."

The rapid economic, political, and cultural development of France in the seventeenth century, and the appearance there of a great galaxy of literary, artistic, and musical geniuses gave France the leadership of the arts in the second half of the seventeenth century. As in the thirteenth century, all of Europe again became a series of cultural provinces of northern France, and Paris and Versailles became the sun around which almost all of European culture revolved. The contrast between the middle of the seventeenth century and later is shown by Milton, who looked to Italy as the home of the Muses, and Dryden, who looked for the same to France. At the time that the center was shifting from Italy to France, the Baroque style in all the arts became grander, loftier, and more reserved. So one passes from the earlier Baroque to the Classical Baroque. France, after 1650, became, par excellence, the home of polished manners, of the art of living and all the social graces, and of the greatest achievements in the arts. She poured forth a continuous stream of masterpieces; in the wake of Descartes and Corneille, came Molière, Racine, La Fontaine, Bossuet, and Boileau. And literature was paralleled by great French accomplishments in art and music.

The French language was, at the same time, supplanting Latin as the language of diplomacy and learning, and it was coming to be everywhere spoken by the upper classes. Writing in the early eighteenth century, an Italian declared: "French has become the most widely spoken language in Europe. This is either because the political power of France has brought about the spread of the French tongue, just as in ancient days the might of Rome carried the Latin speech into all the countries of the known world; or else it is that the French language, highly refined as it is, possesses a charm in the precision, the delicacy, and naturalness for which it is widely celebrated." The crusty father of

Frederick the Great complains bitterly over the universal dominion of French culture. "It is, alas, but too plain that the French devil has come to rule the Germans. In the past, Frenchmen have not been greatly esteemed in Germany, but nowadays we cannot live without them; everything must be French—French speech, French clothes, French music. The German courts are ordered on a French plan. Before our children have mastered any sort of speech they are introduced to French gallantries, and the parents must see about a French dancing master."

It was in France of the early eighteenth century that there arose the Rococo phase of the Baroque. Rococo is not a separate style; it is part of the Baroque as Decorated is part of the Gothic. It is light where the earlier was grand, delicate where the earlier was forceful, playful where the earlier was passionate. Grandeur is replaced by finesse, and a virile attitude by a feminine grace. It is a light, sophisticated, and frivolous style of interior decoration, painting, and sculpture, paralleled in literature by writers like Pope and Marivaux, and in music, by Couperin. "In the interval," says one critic, "between Velasquez in the seventeenth century and Goya in the early nineteenth, a fundamental word had dropped out—'majesty'—and the whole of Europe had put 'charm' in its place." The new decorative style of the Rococo loved novelties and gathered them from China, Persia, Turkey, India, and the Americas. Most of its decorative details were detached from any historic association with the ancient world, or with the Middle Ages or the Renaissance. The Rococo feared boredom and heaviness and loved curves, mirrors, gildings, and light and gracefully decorated porcelains. Its favorite mythological figures were Pan and Venus. All is charm and grace. The vogue of Chinese motifs was partly engendered by the attraction of a culture whose philosophy was not encumbered with metaphysics and was combined with the refinement of sensuous enjoyment. The Rococo world was a world of make-believe, all rendered with superb verve and almost incredible virtuosity.

The great wave of reappreciation of Baroque achievements that has characterized historical writing on the arts in the twentieth century may be carried too far, for the Baroque in its various phases, from early Baroque, through Classical Baroque into the Age of the Rococo, was not without faults. In it lies, often, exaggeration, overintensity, lack of sincerity, affectation, and bombast. Prince Colonna in Rome had made for his beautiful wife a unique bed, in which she received visits from the leading members of the Sacred College, and important noblemen.

It was in the form of an enormous seashell supported on the backs of four sea horses ridden by sirens, and below were carved sea waves. The canopy over the bed had a curtain held up by twelve cupids. The lady received in an elegant costume with a necklace made by Benvenuto Cellini. It all caused a sensation and was talked about all over Europe. The caryatids on a funeral monument at San Prassede in Rome cry into enormous marble handkerchiefs. It was quite Baroque, but absurdly overdone. For the dizzy limits of Baroque sensationalism, some of the stage effects of the age are typical. When the curtain rose on a play written by Bernini, there appeared beyond the scene a second audience, partly real and partly painted, and so arranged that it seemed a replica of the audience that had come to see the play. The play turned on the confusion of the actors as to which audience they were to address. In the sky were moving stars, and from time to time clouds scudded over the face of the moon. Toward the end of the comedy, grooms came on the stage, and coaches and horses, all behaving exactly as the real audience would on leaving the theater. Then Death appeared with a scythe, and the leader of the comedy announced that the final curtain would be drawn to end the grisly sight. Trifling trickery and affectation could hardly be carried further. All this is the reverse of an age that produced Rembrandt, Racine, Milton, and others who were their peers.

2. Art

When we think of the Baroque in art our minds first conjure up sumptuous interiors of churches and palaces where architecture, painting, and sculpture flow into one grand ensemble; and, beyond this, one thinks of the vast city plans and squares, and the huge gardens that formed an integral part of the layout of a palace. The Baroque loved complicated and colossal ensembles which had been brought into a harmonious unity. In the splendid church interiors where the prince or the filthiest beggar from the streets might worship or, should we say, bargain with his favorite saint, there angels and cherubs, in paintings or in stone, marble, or stucco filled the vaults and the aisles with the unrest of their wings. And the beholder is stimulated to participate actively in the supernatural manifestations rather than to look at them from the outside. The vision is pressed home with all the resources of illusionism, and supported by drama, light, and gesture. Nothing is left undone to draw the beholder into the orbit of the works of art. So miracles and all sorts of supernatural phenomena are given the air of verisimilitude. The improbable is rendered plausible and convincing. The same effects were achieved in palace interiors where the spectator is drawn into the very presence of the gods of Olympus and of the great of this earth. Everywhere, instead of forms that press down, the Baroque sought, in both religious and secular art, forms that mount and soar and, as they soar, unfold into an agitated and often swirling grandeur. To add to the whole effect, details are carefully observed and are usually painted or carved with all sorts of naturalistic details. Such carefully observed realistic details, however, are usually subordinated to a larger whole. Naturalism and complexity, both of which fascinated the Baroque painter and sculptor, were usually swept into a large unification.

The beginnings of Baroque art were seen in Rome at the close of the sixteenth century. Rome was rapidly growing in size; it was twice as large in 1600 as in 1500, and half again as large in 1700 as in 1600. This rapid growth offered tremendous building and decorating programs for artists. At the same time, many foreigners came for longer or shorter sojourns in the city, and among these were artists from all over Europe. Down to 1660, Rome played something of the role among European artists that Paris played in the nineteenth century. As the seventeenth century passed its middle, Frenchmen, likewise, were widely commissioned to execute all sorts of art works from one end of Europe to the other. In the later seventeenth century, though still a magnet for talents, Rome came to be outshone by Paris as the great art center of the Baroque. At the same time that artists were flocking to Rome, many Italians found employment in all the countries of Europe including Russia.

Toward the end of the sixteenth century, members of the Carracci family of Bologna showed a strong reaction against the Mannerist style. They returned to the grand style of the High Renaissance, borrowing ideas of drawing from Michelangelo, of space composition from Raphael, and of color from Titian and Correggio. Especially did they go back to the formal pictorial structure—the greater simplicity, restraint, and love of harmony of High Renaissance painting. The most notable achievement of the Carracci was the ceiling, by Annibale Carracci (d. 1609), in the Palazzo Farnese at Rome. The series of paintings, with decorative figures somewhat in the style of Michelangelo's Sistine ceiling, relates stories of Ovid's *Metamorphoses*. The whole shows mar-

velous planning and organization on a colossal scale. Here was a style
that offered a release from the tight space, tense poses, and strange coloring of the preceding Mannerist style. The artist strikes a balance between exuberance and restraint; between classical forms and structure,
and imaginative invention; and between High Renaissance models and
studies made directly from life and nature. The human figures show an
idealization that resembles that of the High Renaissance, and they are
without the exaggerations and distortions often shown in Manneristic
painting. These decorations of Annibale Carracci combine architecture,
sculpture, and painting on a grand scale. For the first time, there is in
the whole decorative scheme a vast and free spatiality that was to characterize much of the art of the Baroque Age. Among the chief followers
of the Carracci were the typical Baroque painters, Guido Reni, Domenichino, and Guercino. Berenson finds the drawing of the Carracci "conventional and lifeless," and Guido Reni's color "like a grate with no
fire," though he cannot deny that they started a new movement against
the prevailing trends of Mannerism, a movement that lasted through
the eighteenth century.

While the Carracci and their followers were starting in Rome a movement toward classical idealization, and a partial return to the ideals of
the High Renaissance, Caravaggio (d. 1610) was initiating a more vivid
and more realistic style of painting that was a reaction both against the
eccentricities of the Mannerist style and the archeological romanticism
of the Classicists. Caravaggio went through an extraordinary evolution
in his thirty-six years. Some of his earliest paintings were done in a
hard, polished, Manneristic style, but he steadily moved from this to
greater realism, and to a dramatic system of lighting that represented a
new dispensation in painting. Through his plebeian types he tried to
bring the Christian stories close to the masses, and he often shocked the
church authorities by his extreme realism. The artist was clearly influenced by the teaching of Loyola, who wished Christian mysteries to be
contemplated in terms of the actual, and of Philip Neri, who wanted
painting in terms of the common man. Caravaggio's was a healthy
down-to-earth spirit which brought into painting a renewed contact
with nature and with living reality. Like the scientists of his age, Caravaggio had a burning passion for reality, a desire to pierce through appearances to the essence of things, and a dislike of formalism and
decorum. He came to destroy the artifices of Mannerism and to avoid
the romantic view of the past as represented by the Carracci. His only

link with the revived classicism of his age was in his fine sense of composition, and in his great interest in the human form. In his later works,
Caravaggio used striking contrasts of light and shadow that give his
painting a highly dramatic quality. His work effected a revolution in
painting whose repercussions were seen in the course of the seventeenth
century in Rembrandt, Velasquez, George de la Tour, and many others.
Indeed much of the painting of the seventeenth century proceeds from
the two currents started in Rome by the Carracci and by Caravaggio.

Proceeding further into Italian painting of the seventeenth century,
we come to painters like Pietro da Cortona, Pozzo, and others who executed vast wall and ceiling decorations that painted away all sense of
inclosing space and, especially in their huge ceiling paintings, carried the
spectator out of this existence into a swirling world of clouds and rank
on rank of floating figures. The style of these painters is massive, dynamic, spectacular, illusionist, and full of movement. It works on the
senses and the emotions by all the visual deceptions of the stage. To a
static grandeur and a confined space it opposes a vast vision of the infinite
—and the Baroque, in all the arts, loves the infinite. Many of the
Baroque ceilings executed by these Italian painters, and later by their
followers all over Europe, are so handled that it is impossible to tell
where the wall leaves off and the ceiling begins. All sense of a limiting
space is swept away in a vast vision of the beyond. The figures surge up
into the air, the heavens open, and, in a golden blaze of light, the eye
reaches into infinity. Here painting, sculpture, and architecture flow together to produce a vast illusionist vision and the last borders between
painted and real architecture are wiped out. Nowhere is the grandilo-
quence of the Baroque so evident.

The Italian painters established the Baroque style of painting, but the
greatest achievements of Baroque painting were to be made in the lands
beyond the Alps, for Italy produced no Rubens, no Velasquez, and no
Rembrandt. These achievements of the Italians in the early and middle
seventeenth century, however, attracted attention all over Europe, and
the currents of Italian influence in painting appear in one country after
another. The two leading French painters of the seventeenth century,
Poussin and Claude Lorrain, spent most of their active years in Italy,
and they closely reflect the currents of Italian painting though they both
show a French restraint in reaction against the more exuberant forms
of the Baroque. The Italian painter Domenichino and the French
painter Poussin, like the sculptors Algardi and Duquesnoy, favored a

simplification of designs, with fewer figures, more gravity, and less movement and contrast than that of either Caravaggio or Pietro da Cortona. Their work dates from the 1630's and initiates the High Baroque period. Though the paintings of Poussin (d. 1665) were based on a profound study of nature, he was likewise deeply influenced by High Renaissance and early Baroque painting, especially that of Titian, Raphael, and the Carracci. Poussin's great interest was in solid forms and their careful arrangement in formal patterns. And it was not chance that led Picasso, in a time of great tension when the Germans were being driven out of Paris in 1944, to calm himself by copying a composition by Poussin. Poussin returned to the closed designs of the High Renaissance, though his style went through a long evolution, and his later work shows his belief that painting should represent the most noble human actions and must present these in the logical orderly fashion nature would produce them if she were perfect. Poussin's work forms an interesting counterpart to the plays of Corneille. His landscapes could easily be visualized as stage settings for Corneille's stately tragedies. The artist must seek the typical and the general, and rule out the trivial. He often built up his pictures in geometric forms which give them an abstract, but often cold, grandeur.

Claude Lorrain (d. 1682) was an important innovator in establishing landscape painting as a means of artistic expression of great variety and subtlety. His compositions have much of the formality and logic of those of Poussin. Of his pictures Goethe said: "There is not a trace of reality in his pictures, but the highest poetic truth. He knew the real world down to the smallest details, but he used it as a means of expressing the cosmos of his beautiful soul." He idealized the Italian landscape as the High Renaissance painters had idealized the human form. He loved to paint landscapes suffused with a soft atmosphere and containing a few classical ruins. Behind his concept of nature are a Baroque love of infinite space and a desire to paint unusual effects of light. There is, also, an emphasis on landscape apart from any human figures the scene may contain. Above all, he is the incomparable master of sunsets and their golden sheen on the waters of quiet harbors.

The tendency of Baroque painting in France was to reduce everything to rules and laws, and France produced a large theoretical literature on painting. This renewed old Italian controversies over the relative merits of color and drawing in painting. In the long run those who emphasized color as above drawing won the day and prepared the way for the style of French painting in the eighteenth century. The emphasis of the French on rules in art led one seventeenth-century Italian critic to declare that "the French judge art independently of the qualities of sensibility and confuse the progress of philosophy with that of art." The official patronage given by the French Academy of Sculpture and Painting, which arranged exhibitions and gave out scholarships, prizes, and commissions, left its mark on French art of the later seventeenth century. This academic tradition in the seventeenth century is best represented by Le Brun (d. 1690). He was not a great artist but was a fine organizer who knew how to get the best out of those whom he directed. His interests were wide-ranging; he could design a whole interior or a painting, the lock of a door, the border of a tapestry, or a piece of garden sculpture. His position as head of the Academy of Sculpture and Painting and as director of the decoration of Louis XIV's palaces, including Versailles, gave him a large influence on the arts, not only in France, but in all the states that, after 1660, looked to France as the headquarters of artistic culture. Because of the efforts of Louis XIV, Colbert, and Le Brun, Paris came to replace Rome as the artistic capital of Europe. The other French painters of the seventeenth century mostly followed Italian models. Only the Le Nain brothers struck out on a line of their own, painting humble peasant types with great insight, and affection. These pictures of peasant life have great dignity and solid composition and quiet color. No attempt is made to idealize the peasants; however, unlike the Dutch peasant pictures, the Le Nains painted nothing that was either hilarious or grotesque. This current of naturalism, with its love of representing the common man, runs right through the Baroque Age from Caravaggio to Hogarth and Chardin, and is reflected in the art of every state in western Europe. At times even the greatest painters turned from religious and theological subjects and from court life and rich patrons to portray peasants, laborers, tavern loungers, vagabonds, and the gamins of the street.

In Spain, the influences of Italy were very marked, but the influences of Italian High Renaissance, Mannerism, and Baroque were all active at once. In the love of deep rich colors and of deep shadows, as shown especially in Zurbarán and Ribera, the influence of Caravaggio's style is evident. Murillo, called the "Raphael of Seville," in his sweet religious pictures likewise shows the Caravaggio influence, but also that of Correggio. The most gifted Spanish Baroque painter, Velasquez (d. 1660), drew much from the Italian painters of several ages, yet went far toward inventing his own style, especially in the matter of lighting. Instead of the golden tonality that one found in many Italian pictures Velasquez loved a full daylight effect and showed a consummate mastery in achieving it. Velasquez, like Hals in Holland, painted rapidly and with broad brush strokes, a technique that achieves a sense of spontaneity that seems the very essence of life. In a subtle handling of light, he portrays textures and atmospheres as do few others. He is always more concerned with the experiences of the eye than with any inner world of the spirit. No painter was ever more successful in painting what he could see; when he deals with the world of imagination his inspiration falls off. The Spanish painters were entirely occupied with commissions in their own country, and their great discoveries in lighting and color had little influence outside Spain until their work, especially that of Velasquez, was restudied by the Impressionists in the later nineteenth century.

While Poussin was painting in Italy, and Velasquez in Spain, their older contemporary, Rubens (d. 1640), was at work in Antwerp. In his twenties Rubens had spent years of study in Italy, where he seems to have absorbed something of the styles of all the Italian painters since Leonardo. On his return to Flanders, he opened a studio where he came to employ as many as two hundred assistants and students; out of this studio came an enormous production supervised by Rubens, but often partly painted by others. He made a fortune, lived in grand style, and was sent, from time to time, on diplomatic missions for the Spanish government that controlled the southern half of the Low Countries. Rubens' style was catholic, classical, monarchical, and aristocratic. Through his vast designs he showed the most masterly handling of complex details and striking contrasts of color and light, which he swung into a dramatic unity. No Italian or northern painter ever equaled the rich, exuberant effects he obtained, and through all his work there pulsates a vibrant life. He is so accomplished in his general conceptions and in his technique that most painters seem a little amateurish beside him. He was master of one of the most perfect instruments of pictorial expression that the world has ever seen. On the other hand, he never reached, as did Rembrandt, the supreme heights of imagination, nor does he plumb the greatest depths of feeling. Grandiose and alive as are his huge compositions, he always remained the master of the commonplace, but the commonplace realized in its fullest intensity. It was an art that loved dramatic contrasts, and was peculiarly fitted to enhance the interiors of Baroque churches and palaces. Rubens' range was enormous and he excelled at once in religious pictures, mythological and allegorical pieces, portraits, hunting scenes, and beautiful landscapes. He shows his enormous ingenuity in the series he did for Queen Maria de' Medici of France in the Luxembourg Palace in Paris. The series begins with the Three Fates spinning a brilliant web of destiny for the Queen; Minerva then teaches her to read, Apollo is her music teacher, she learns eloquence from Mercury, and acquires her fascination from the Three Graces; and so on through the rest of her life, the worlds of gods and men are interwoven. In his exuberance, his ability to make dramatic unity out of the most diverse material, his glowing color, and his bravura and plenitude, Rubens is one of the most characteristic of Baroque artists. His pupil Van Dyck (d. 1641), who specialized in aristocratic portraits and the painting of rich fabrics, is far more reserved, less vigorous, and less inventive than his teacher, but for the North of Europe he set the style of portraiture for his age and the next.

Few countries, in one century, ever produced so many first-rate painters as did Holland in the seventeenth century. After the long struggle against Spain for their freedom, the Dutch turned away from an art that was monarchical, aristocratic, classical, and catholic, and produced an art that reflected the life of their towns and countryside. In landscape painting and the painting of still lifes they produced the first great school of painters, who regarded the landscape and still life as things worth painting in themselves. Jacob van Ruysdael (d. 1682) and others discovered the poetry of northern landscapes as Claude Lorrain discovered that of the Italian countryside. Among the painters of domestic scenes, the greatest master was Vermeer (d. 1675) of Delft. The Dutch painters of genre scenes bring us close to the life of the prosperous middle class, while other painters portrayed the vital life of the masses. These Dutch genre painters had an extraordinary capacity to elicit in the beholder the poetic qualities of a simple scene. Hals (d. 1666), whose style of rapid execution resembles that of Velasquez, left a series of brilliant single and group portraits of the substantial bourgeoisie of his time. So a long series of Dutch painters added, in both their subjects and the way they handled them, what were essentially whole new provinces to the realm of the imagination.

Only Rembrandt (d. 1669), in his later works, rose to that very highest level of the arts where it seems that the secrets of the universe are revealed. In his handling of light and shade, in which he was greatly influenced by the style of Caravaggio and his followers, Rembrandt was able to suggest a physical and spiritual depth and a continuation of the picture beyond its frame. Soft and velvety shadows usually play about the faces of his subjects; these encourage the beholder to discover the mood for himself. Everything he touched—individual portraits, groups of men, religious subjects, and landscapes—was invested with an unsuspected inner life. Rembrandt always seemed to be painting the soul that lies within persons and even things. Like Shakespeare, Rembrandt knew how to penetrate all types of personalities. He is never theatrical, as were Rubens and many others of the Baroque painters, but the inner meaning of a scene is never lost. His drawings and etchings have a magical quality; no other master ever conveyed more in a few strokes, but he always leaves something for the beholder to fill in.

In the early eighteenth century, the arts moved into a later phase of the Baroque, the Rococo, a word seemingly derived from "rocailles" and "coquillages," rock and shell forms used in decoration. The word may have been derived from "Barocco." It is a lighter, less grandiose, more delicate and intimate and a gayer style than the Baroque, though it is closely related to the later Baroque. Watteau (d. 1721) is the first highly gifted master of the Rococo. His paintings are small, the very antithesis of the vast canvases of Le Brun. They are pictures for the intimate drawing room rather than for a huge Baroque gallery. The mood is one of an exquisite sensitiveness and a delicate eroticism. The men, dressed in light, gay satins—like the ladies—seem ready to drop to their knees or perform a pirouette. Fans flutter, and there is a general atmosphere of some graceful minuet in a fairy play. Watteau's pictures usually portray a landscape background with dark trees, or the faint tint of a distant and elusive horizon. His colors are reminiscent of those of the great Venetians, and in both color and mood he sometimes seems close to Giorgione. His lighthearted gaiety is always tempered with a certain wistfulness, and even melancholy; he is almost the only Rococo artist who can also be serious.

Boucher (d. 1770), the favorite painter of Mme de Pompadour, loved to paint mythological or pastoral scenes with a sensuous frivolity. He is essentially a decorative painter, and his pictures belong as parts of a Rococo room. Nothing delighted him more than to paint an exquisite female nude. His colors are light and opaque, and he used much pink, pale blue, and pale yellow. His pupil, Fragonard (d. 1806), who spent several years in Rome, had an even more delicate sense of color. He delighted in painting genre pictures of the frivolous life of the upper classes and lovely landscapes, in which he was influenced by the Dutch landscape painters. Fragonard's techniques are typical of those of Rococo painting; his trees and mountains are no heavier than his clouds, and the mood of his landscapes is that of an exquisite and delicately colored dream. His light, pearly colors are put on with rapid strokes, and some of his landscapes remind one of those of the nineteenth-century Impressionists.

The Rococo style, as it spread from France, affected painting all over western Europe, though the results varied according to the local traditions of painting. Hogarth (d. 1764) used the same light, opaque colors employed by the French Rococo painters, but his subjects are often moral and satirical. He loved to paint series of narrative pictures, like the chapters of a novel; these follow one or more characters through successive involvements in increasingly evil situations. His satire is biting like that of Goya and Daumier. Hogarth was a brilliant technician in handling light and color and composition; indeed he is the first great English painter. One of the very greatest painters of the eighteenth century was the Venetian Tiepolo (d. 1770). His vast pictures were filled with the echoes of the golden age of Venetian painting. His compositions were usually large, and he excelled in the painting of huge ceilings. Tiepolo's colors, however, are much lighter and cooler than those of Titian and Veronese and his drawing is more mannered and less vigorous. The Rococo aspects of his art are shown in his color and drawing. In his vast ceilings, the weightless figures float, effortless and ethereal, on clouds against a silvery and pale blue sky. His output was enormous, and he took important commissions as far afield as Würzburg and Madrid. Tiepolo's influence was felt in all the countries of western Europe.

The styles of sculpture of the Baroque and Rococo resemble very much the parallel styles of painting. The passion and the tension of Mannerism were now resolved, but not set aside. And the scale of sculpture became larger, with more theatrical effects. Stone, marble, and bronze were forced to represent movement; striking contrasts of light and shade were sought; and architectural and scenic settings, with fabrics, rocks, and clouds, were emphasized more than in earlier styles. Combinations of marble of various colors, and the use of stone, marble, and bronze in the same work became common. In place of the small and sometimes expressionless heads and elongated bodies of Mannerist sculpture, much more naturalism is shown. As in painting, the sculptor strives for grandiose impressiveness and for effects that will bring the subject treated close to the spectator. The serene tombs of the Early and High Renaissance, where one finds children's dimpled laughter and gracious angels, are now replaced by skeletons crawling out of burial vaults. As Donne said, "We must all pass this posthumous death, this death after death, this death of corruption and putrefaction, when these bodies must say with Job, 'Corruption thou art my father,' and to the worm, 'Thou art my mother.' "

Over the whole of Baroque and Rococo sculpture towers the great figure of Bernini (d. 1680), who stood to his age and the next as a new Michelangelo. He was a man of most varied talents. In 1644 John Evelyn wrote, "Bernini gave a public opera, wherein he painted the scenes, cut the statues, invented the engines, composed the music, wrote the comedy, and built the theater." From his youth, Bernini found lavish patrons. As an architect and sculptor he, more than any other artist, gave Rome its Baroque character, and through his handling of religious subjects, of fountains, tombs and portrait busts set his stamp on European sculpture for over a century. His earliest works, done before he was twenty, show extraordinary technical skill in composition, and in the rendering of various types of surfaces in marble. Bernini was an acute observer of nature, and also of the great works of ancient and Renaissance art, which early rid his style of any vestiges of Mannerism. He excelled in designing fountains with naturalistic settings of marine deities and accessories of vegetation, animals, shells, and rocks, and vast tombs of complicated design, where all the details are swung together to make a dramatic whole. Bernini's portrait busts incisively stress the salient points of a sitter's character. His most ambitious works include the great "Throne of St. Peter" in the apse of St. Peter's in Rome, where an enormous ensemble of sculpture, painting, and stained glass produces as grandiose an impression as was ever created by the Baroque. Equally dramatic is his "Ecstasy of St. Theresa," where painting, sculpture, and architecture are united and where realism, with agitated drapery, clouds, golden rays, and theatrical lighting from an unseen source, sweep the beholder in a great emotional wave. Here, too, is an erotic mysticism—a blend of the religious and the sensuous that is of the very essence of Baroque Catholic art.

No other Baroque sculptor approached Bernini in genius; and all who came after him for several generations were, in one way or another, his followers. Duquesnoy and Algardi, both somewhat younger than Bernini, were much more restrained and less agitated in style than Bernini. In the later seventeenth century, the center for all the arts moved to Paris and northern France where, among a large group of gifted sculptors, the most notable was Coysevox (d. 1720), much of whose work was done at Versailles. His designs are quieter and more simplified than those of Bernini; he uses fewer figures, more gravity, and less movement. The variety and vehemence of Italian Baroque style were modified in France by rationalism and by an academism that strove to set limits and rules to art, as well as to letters. The establishment in 1648 of the Academy of Painting and Sculpture, in whose hands lay the right to grant prizes and to assign commissions, had the same effect on art that the founding of the French Academy, a little earlier, in 1635, had on letters. Indeed French seventeenth-century classicism in general is very clearly a part of general European Baroque, but there is always an emphasis on restraint and on the observance of rules. Within the limits of this classicism, many of the sculptors in France, and other states of western Europe influenced by the art of Italy and France, show much vigor and invention. Only in Spain, was the influence of Baroque Italian and French sculpture of slight importance. Here the sculptural styles of the High Renaissance and Mannerism continued through the whole Baroque period. In German-speaking lands, the Baroque kept some of the dramatic qualities of the style of Bernini, but no sculptor of the originality and stature of Bernini appeared there, or, for that matter, elsewhere.

The Rococo phase of the Baroque in painting, sculpture, and architecture began in France early in the eighteenth century, and spread from there over most of western Europe. The sculpture of the Rococo, especially that of France, has a light and frivolous air. In its variety and elegance, in its feminine grace and soft sensuality, and in its marvelous skill in reproducing the texture of fabrics, skin, and hair, French Rococo sculpture, which was imitated all over Europe, resembles the painting of Boucher and Fragonard. The Rococo is loath to leave any part of an interior undecorated; compared to the Baroque it is much airier in spirit, more graceful in its motifs, and more averse to straight lines. The forms are much slighter than in Baroque, and the dainty, the pretty, and the carefree are always cultivated. The

Rococo excelled in the decorative arts. Its furniture, silver, and porcelain are still more highly regarded by collectors and decorators than
the decorative art of any other period. Many of the French Rococo
sculptors furnished small models for the manufacture of Sèvres porcelain. Perhaps the most characteristic French Rococo sculptor is
Clodion (d. 1814), who continued the Rococo tradition into a period
when Neo-Classicism was the dominant style. His favorite subjects
were nymphs and satyrs and romping *putti* which he executed in small
statuettes and terra cottas.

The most notable feature of Baroque architecture is the enormous
scale of its buildings and its striving to achieve fully the grandeur and
monumentality of ancient Roman architecture. The garden front of
the Palace of Versailles is a quarter of a mile long, and the famous
Hall of Mirrors is two hundred and forty feet in length. At the same
time, the experimentation in design that had characterized the Age of
Mannerism continues, and the architectural results of these currents
appear in buildings of great originality and of a bewildering variety
of forms. Emphasis was laid on designing ensembles of churches and
palaces with squares or gardens about them. These vast groupings often
assume a symphonic quality; by means of calculated spaces and curves,
by strong contrasts of light and shade, of big and small, of the complicated and the simple, there is built up a vast unified effect that
reaches a tremendous climax. It was a style that demanded extravagance and deliberate ostentation with an opera producer's sense of
the sublime. Its works were to impress men in general, not just a circle
of intellectuals. There is often in this architecture, as in the Baroque
arts in general, a delight in "kicking over the traces," and the sheer
joy of being impressive, and at times even fantastic. The love of contrast is everywhere. Pediments are broken and their sides are curved
or in scrolls, great coats of arms or urns are placed in between, columns
are twisted, moldings and columns are duplicated to give sharp emphasis, and decorative sculpture and painting on a colossal scale are
freely employed. Often all feeling for materials is lost; painting, plaster
work, stone, marbles of various colors, and bronze are freely mixed
together. Architecture, painting, and sculpture are all combined in vast
and organic ensembles. In such combinations, many Baroque churches
seem to become one vast monstrance.

The Baroque usually played up the facade in order to make its primary impact at first sight. Sometimes, especially on churches, the

façade is carried far above the level of the roof, and such a building, when viewed from the side, may look ridiculous. The style favored oval ground plans of churches and oval rooms in palaces and public buildings. To get a sense of movement, curves were freely introduced in both exteriors and interiors; convex or concave walls were used in façades; and, to vary the effect, niches were often introduced. These and other devices give a remarkably plastic quality to both exteriors and interiors. In secular buildings, much attention was paid to blending rooms of various shapes, and to linking the building with the square or garden about it. Individual elements, especially in the interiors, are no longer sharply delimited but flow into each other. Among the most striking features of Baroque buildings are the vast, sweeping staircases, veritable triumphs of rhythm in stone. Baroque buildings admirably fitted the splendor of church services and the grand scale of entertainment that characterized the age. In 1580 Montaigne, at the dawn of the Baroque Age, wrote of life in Rome: "The city is all for courts and nobility. There are no main streets of trade; palaces and gardens take up all the space. In the palaces, the apartments are huge, and there is one great room after another." The taste of the Baroque for fountains with water trickling from basin to basin, or spouting upward in vertical jets or forming arcs as it rushed out of pipes, and huge formal gardens, and elaborate city plans was very marked. In the designing of each of these, emphasis was laid on creating the illusion of motion. Long avenues were laid out both in the cities and in the country to give elaborate settings to churches, palaces, and public buildings. In 1585 Pope Sixtus V commissioned an architect to lay out a network of streets connecting the most important churches of Rome. The center of the plan was Santa Maria Maggiore with five streets leading up to it. From this plan, similar city planning spread all over Europe, even as far as Bath and Edinburgh in Britain. In gardens and public squares, the designers multiplied colonnades, staircases, balconies, balustrades, and free-standing sculptures.

Baroque architecture, like Baroque painting and sculpture, was first unfolded in Rome; but before the style had run its course, some of its greatest achievements appeared in lands beyond the Alps. The Baroque style in Rome is foreshadowed in the later sixteenth century by Vignola's vast interior of the Gesù and by Michelangelo's redesigning of the square on top of the Capitoline Hill, and his plan for the outside of the apse and for the dome of St. Peter's. The first definitely

Baroque architect in Rome is Maderna (d. 1629). His façade of Santa Susanna uses bold contrasts of light and shade by placing free-standing columns instead of pilasters on the façade of the church. Maderna also redesigned the nave of St. Peter's to lengthen it to the west, and planned the huge façade of the church. In these and other designs, Maderna worked on a huge scale, and his plans show a solid and serious style that seems to be in reaction against Mannerism toward a more severe classicism.

On Maderna's death, Bernini, though he was only thirty-one years old, was appointed architect of St. Peter's. His first great architectural creation is the great bronze canopy over the altar of St. Peter's. It is nearly a hundred feet high and rests on four twisted columns. The whole is of a grandeur and extravagance without restraint, and is lavishly decorated with sculpture in the round and reliefs. Among a series of churches and other works that Bernini designed, the great colonnades in front of St. Peter's are his masterpieces. They are very original in conception and are laid out on a colossal scale, and they give the great church a superb approach and setting. No sculptor or architect of the seventeenth century approached Bernini in reputation. Little wonder that when he went to the court of Louis XIV he was treated like a visiting monarch, even though his design for the Louvre was rejected.

More daring in his designs was Borromini (d. 1669). His first important work, San Carlo alle Quattro Fontane, shows great ingenuity in building an oval church and cloister on a small and irregularly shaped plot of land. Within and without, he uses curve against curve, convex against concave, so that the whole structure has a rhythmical movement. In his buildings, as in the Church of Sant' Agnese on the Piazza Navona in Rome, Borromini seems to give a tension to every shape and form though all the parts always combined into an organic whole. In his search to discover new forms he showed an inventiveness that disregarded rules, logic, or even common sense. He sometimes refused to relieve flat surfaces of walls by decoration; instead, he relieved the flatness by altering the very structure of the wall itself by an outward or inward curve—the most original of his innovations. When his Church of San Carlo was finished, a papal official wrote: "In the opinion of everybody nothing similar with regard to aesthetic merit, caprice, excellence, and singularity can be found anywhere in the world. This is testified by the number of people (Italians, Germans,

Flemings, Frenchmen, and Spaniards) who try to procure plans of the work." Borromini's influence on architecture throughout Europe was much greater than that of Bernini.

Some of Borromini's work, as the cupola and façade of the Sapienza in Rome, shows an oddity and extravagance of caprice that were taken up in northern Italy by Guarini (d. 1683), some of whose buildings seem like stage properties. Guarini loved deliberate incongruities and surprising dissonances. One zone of his structure contains no indication of what the next will reveal. His greatest tour de force was in building domes with complicated systems of ribs that appear to defy all static principles.

The Baroque style in France derives from that of Italy, but is much more reserved and restrained. The French, like the Italians, built on a colossal scale, but they did not go in for elaborate tricks of foreshortening and illusionism; and though painting and sculpture are combined with architecture in vast ensembles, the line of demarcation is always kept clear. The exuberance of Italian Baroque was usually checked; walls rarely curve, entablatures are seldom broken, pediments are straight, and plans are more simple and more nearly rectilinear. A freer play of fancy was allowed in French Baroque for the designing of fireplaces and of both the inside and the outside of doorways and windows. Here appeared scrolls, broken pediments, masks, coats of arms, and other decorative features often in luxurious profusion.

As in other fields of the arts, the French delighted in making rules for architecture. In his *Cours d'architecture* of 1675 Blondel says that architecture must follow reason rather than fantasy, and one of the manifestations of reason is orderliness. Besides reason, the student should be guided by the designs of the best Roman and Renaissance buildings. French Baroque architecture was dominated by court patronage, as that of Italy had been mostly influenced by the patronage of the church. There is an aristocratic elegance and understatement and a sophisticated moderation about French Baroque architecture which is evident in its leading monuments: Perrault's east front of the Louvre, J. B. Mansart's Church of the Invalides, and the garden front at Versailles; and, in the eighteenth century, the Petit Trianon of Gabriel and the Panthéon of Soufflot. In the last years of the reign of Louis XIV, the younger members of the royal family and of the court demanded a lighter and gayer type of interior decoration with themes of mythology treated in a more frivolous style, and playful genre pictures. Rooms were greatly reduced in size, they were designed to give more comfort and privacy, and living arrangements were made less grandiose and more convenient. Here, at the beginning of the eighteenth century, was the origin of the Rococo style; and during the remainder of the century French architecture and decoration assumed an influence all over Europe—including Italy—that had been earlier commanded by the architecture and decoration of Italy.

The Baroque style in Spanish architecture, while showing profound Italian influence, developed a floridness, exuberance, and theatricality of its own, especially in decoration. The Spanish architects loved to load surfaces with elaborate and fantastic ornament contrasted with spaces that are bare of any adornment. Especially around doors, niches, and windows, they reduplicated frames up to as many as four or five, each differing from the other. Sometimes the decoration is so loaded on that the basic design of the building is lost, and the eye wanders in bewilderment over the whole design; one is conscious only of elaboration. This style of Baroque decoration is called Churrigueresque from a family of Madrid architects and sculptors, greatest of whom was José de Churriguera. On its stronger side, Spanish Baroque architecture has a virility and force that shine through some of its capriciousness as in the magnificent façade of the Cathedral of Compostella.

Inigo Jones (d. 1662) introduced Palladian architecture into England in the early seventeenth century, but the great masters of Baroque in England were Wren and Vanbrugh. Like Shakespeare, Rembrandt, and Bach, Wren (d. 1723) never went to Italy, but he did spend time in France, where he met Bernini and saw his plans for the Louvre. Wren's St. Paul's Cathedral, in its originality of structural engineering and in the beauty of its proportions and decorative detail, is one of the great achievements of the Baroque, and is hardly surpassed by any Baroque church in Italy. Vanbrugh (d. 1726), in palaces like Castle Howard and Blenheim Palace, caught successfully the note of lofty grandeur for which the Baroque stood. Pope, however, made fun of the grandeurs of Blenheim Palace:

> "Thanks sir," cried I, "'tis very fine
> But where d'ye sleep or where d'ye dine?
> I find, by all you have been telling,
> That 'tis a house, but not a dwelling."

Everywhere in England there is evidence of Italian and French influence, though the handling of these foreign architectural idioms is usually fresh and original, and is always done with much restraint and reserve. In a curious way the old lived on beside the new; in 1637 a Baroque porch with twisted columns was added to the Oxford University Church, and, at the same time, a vestibule and staircase were built at Christ Church College in perpendicular Gothic.

Finally in Germany and Austria, the introduction first of Baroque and then of Rococo architecture was due to Italians and Frenchmen who came to fill commissions of churchmen and nobles. But these German-speaking lands produced a number of great architects of their own, including Fischer von Erlach (d. 1723), Lukas von Hildebrandt (d. 1745), Jakob Prandauer (d. 1726), and Balthasar Neumann (d. 1753). Their churches and palaces were built on an enormous scale, have a kind of forced drama, and show a proud disregard for both expense and material. They enjoyed rich decorative effects; these, and the vast size of their buildings, give a dynamic and theatrical effect not found elsewhere in Baroque architecture. The Austrian and German Baroque architects designed complicated interiors that work a kind of spatial counterpoint not unlike the musical counterpoint of Bach. Germany and Austria were the only important countries that used the Rococo, essentially a form of interior decoration, for the exteriors of their buildings, as for example the palace of the Zwinger in Dresden. In the Rococo phase of German and Austrian Baroque, the decorative forms become increasingly daring, even fantastic, and the colors used became lighter with much use of white, gold, pink, pale blue, and yellow. Whereas the Baroque was usually somber, heavy, and passionate, the Rococo becomes airy, delicate, and even playful, and has the tempo of the minuet and the delicacy of porcelain. Both Baroque and Rococo are full of movement, vivacious, and voluptuous. The creative fancy of these German and Austrian architects and decorators went beyond anything else in Europe. They reached into ever new forms, inventing complicated plans and decorative schemes that astonish by their constant change of direction and their dancing movement. Most surfaces are covered with ornaments; capitals and cornices seem, as one writer says, "to froth and quiver." Bunches of flowers, foliage, and figures are scattered on arches, walls, and ceilings. The whole effect is raised to a Dionysiac level of intensity. Yet the plan and the decoration are so skilfully managed that usually the main structural values are not lost. In their complicated effects Baroque and Rococo produced an architect's and artist's architecture, as the fugue is musician's music. But it was also for the common man whom it would overwhelm and mesmerize.

3. Literature

The Baroque in literature, as in art, emphasized mass and size. It achieved majestic, sublime, and, at the same time, dynamic effects. Like the literature of Mannerism it was full of doubts and conflicts, though these were generally relaxed into a sense of balance and optimism. In the Baroque there are sharp contrasts of gross sensuality and mystical religious exultation, of materialism and spiritualism, of naturalism and formalism, of passion and reason, of the elegant and the grotesque, but, unlike the Age of Mannerism, such contrasting qualities are usually resolved into harmonious unities and held within the framework of strict organization. The conflicting currents of the Baroque were the expression of an age of violent contrasts: on the one hand, there were amazing triumphs of experimental science and, on the other, the horrors of religious wars and of witchcraft persecutions. In its strong and positive assertiveness, Baroque literature lays great emphasis on force and power; as Hobbes declared, "I put for a general inclination of all mankind a perpetual and restless struggle for power that ceaseth only in death." All of the fields of Baroque achievement in art, literature, and music give the impression of a tremendous power of imagination at work and a constant yearning to reach into the infinite in order to reconcile it to the finite. There is also in the Baroque a re-emphasis on classical forms; and there is much evidence of a desire to impose on the tumultuous and conflicting feelings of the artist or poet or composer something of classical restraint, proportion, and balance. This emphasis on classic form and on a certain reserve is most marked in France. In general, the literature of the Baroque Age has more respect for older forms than do the art and music of the period.

The writers show less of the extreme individualism displayed in the Age of Mannerism; and their interest is more clearly focused on discovering general patterns of social conduct, and on the analysis of fixed types of human beings. Their characters in poetry and the drama are delineated in terms of outstanding traits universally recognizable. It is not the writer's business, said Dr. Johnson, "to number the streaks of the tulip." Human nature was absorbingly interesting but only in its universal aspects. Authors wrote both to entertain and to teach; and the literature of the Baroque Age is filled with a didactic purpose and with ethical concerns. Interest was centered not only in man rather than in nature, but also in the city rather than in rural life. Mme de

Sévigné is typical of the period in feeling that it is a great handicap to be compelled to live in the country.

The Baroque reaches for the lofty and the sublime in all the arts, and it delights in celebrating majesty and heroic ideals. Poetry, which in the Age of Mannerism had lost some of its musical quality, is now again marked by emphasis on rhythm and rhyme, and on alliteration and assonance. The poet again tries, as he had in the Age of the High Renaissance, to create a hypnotic state in the mind and heart of his reader. Many of the poets seemed to long for a majestic music that would bring all heaven, and all creation under it, before the eyes. The world of the senses is often deeply explored and its imagery used to describe the spiritual life. The favorite literary metaphors of the Baroque are of lilies and roses, of blood drops like rubies, of tears like pearls or wine or milk, of ecstasies, of flaming hearts, of wounds, and of the grave. Whereas the metaphors of Mannerist writers were often abstract and recondite, those of Baroque writers were usually specific and concrete. Sometimes, the symbols are interchangeable; tears turn into pearls, pearls into lilies, and lilies into innocent babes.

The literature of the Age of the Baroque appealed less to the mass of men than that of the preceding age; especially is this true in the drama. The plays of Lope de Vega and Shakespeare were for the masses; those of Corneille, Racine, and Calderón appealed only to the upper classes and intellectuals. The plots were usually complicated. In the earlier drama, great emphasis was laid on the main plots, and, if subplots were used, they were definitely of minor consequence. Each scene was fairly distinct and was subordinated to the principal theme, and the characters stood out clearly. In Baroque plays the plots are often complicated, and the meaning of the whole play only begins to become clear toward the end, with often a surprise in the last scene. So the principal theme is not always evident, and an obvious logical development of the plot is avoided. This, along with the subject matter and the learning displayed in Baroque plays, shows that the audiences were restricted to the upper classes. Baroque writers were very critical of earlier plays, which they accused of showing vulgar taste, stupid plots, unbelievable incidents, ranting speeches, and incredible and eccentric characters.

The Baroque style in painting, sculpture, and architecture had its origin in Italy, but in letters it was largely the creation of France; however, there were some very great achievements in Baroque literature

that were French in neither origin nor inspiration. The heavy censorship in Italy, much less marked in art and music than in literature,
seems to have been one of the chief reasons why Italy produced few
outstanding men of letters in the Baroque Age. The greatest of her
writers was Galileo who, in both Latin and Italian, wrote in a powerful and direct prose style that helped to make his works known among
scientists and philosophers all across Europe. Much the same is true of
the prose writings of Bruno, Campanella, and Vico, but their writing
had almost no effect on the style of imaginative literature in Italy or
elsewhere.

Many French historians of literature insist on separating seventeenth-
century "French Classicism" from the whole movement of the Baroque
Age, making it something that is *sui generis*. But this is like separating
English Norman architecture from the Romanesque architecture of the
Continent. There are decided differences in the Baroque in various
states but French "classical" literature, like the painting of Poussin
and the music of Couperin, should be seen inside the larger framework
of the Baroque Age. Actually, the French literature of the later seventeenth century represents the largest body of distinguished writing
produced by the Age of the Baroque, and though there are giants in
other countries, like Milton, nowhere else are there at once so many
great writers as in France. France in the seventeenth century was the
leading political, economic, and military power in Europe, and, at the
same time, the cultural center of the Western world. Her government
was a despotism that aimed at controlling the church, the economy,
and culture—a world, as men said, of "one faith, one law, one king,"
where political absolutism, Gallicanism, mercantilism, and a state-
patronized and directed classicism in art and literature were the order
of the day. And French attained the position of a universal language.
It was the instrument of diplomacy, and the vernacular of high society
and fashion; and educated persons from one end of Europe to the
other knew French.

The roots of French Baroque literature go back to the first half of
the seventeenth century. Here were the rationalism of Descartes and
the reforms of Malherbe, Vaugelas, and Guez de Balzac, followed
shortly by the first great plays of Corneille and the founding, in 1635,
of the French Academy. Descartes (d. 1650) insisted on the use of
reason and evidence in thought, and his writings represented a new
dispensation in organization, clarity, and precision. Descartes wrote

mostly in the vernacular, not in Latin, and his appeal was wide and made to all men who felt inclined to use their own minds. Malherbe (d. 1628), a curious mixture of pedant and artist, insisted on reason, logic, and clarity; and on simplicity and purity of diction in the writing of verse. He took an ordinance survey of Parnassus, and set out to liquidate the affairs of the previous age. So he was critical of the exaggerations and affectations of the Mannerist Précieux writers as well as of those who used Latin and Greek words in French verse and who, as Malherbe declared, "used the language as though it were their own." His standard was that of usage. Malherbe's own verse is not always distinguished, but as a critic he was very influential. What Malherbe took away in variety, exuberance, and emotionalism, he restored in firmness, structure, and reserve. He also made the six-foot alexandrine line a standard for the French seventeenth century. Guez de Balzac (d. 1654) accomplished some of the same results in diverting prose from disorder, individual whimsy, and discursiveness to precision. His writings, which were chiefly on political and ethical questions, are composed in a lofty and Ciceronian style, with the balancing of fine periods and a harmonious equipoise of the various parts of each sentence and paragraph. He made French prose eloquent by giving it a lofty cadence. Balzac's sentences form a stately procession—not, like Rabelais's a joyous riot, or, like Montaigne's, a capricious and lazy sauntering.

Vaugelas (d. 1650) was a grammarian who insisted that each word must have a single and exact meaning, and that the French language needed clarifying and simplifying. These reformers, Malherbe, Balzac, and Vaugelas, set up as the standard of language reason and the speech of the cultivated gentleman, the *honnête homme*—a language free from pedantry, affectation, slovenliness, and bombast. They would banish from letters the barbarian, the peasant, the child, and anything that offered local color. They strove in speech for the universal, and a style that had balance, reason, and order. The French Academy, as founded by Richelieu, was to "make French, already more perfect than any living tongue, succeed Latin as Latin succeeded Greek." By issuing a dictionary, the Academy aimed to create a language "free from ambiguities, serious, sweet and consistent, chaste in its vocabulary, judicious in its figures, friendly to elegance but fearful of affectation, able to temper boldness by good taste." Authorities for the dictionary were good usage in the court and the salons, and reason—with a preference

for reason, that is, logical consistency. What the effort of all the reformers did was largely to strip the language of the colorful and the
picturesque, and to strengthen the abstract and rational elements, to rob
poetry to pay prose. At the same time, the influence of the salons was
to make thought clear, witty, but often shallow.

While all this discussion of literary rules and the form of the language was going on, Corneille (d. 1684) in 1636 astonished the world
with the first successful Neo-Classical tragedy, *Le Cid*. The upper
classes and the intellectuals were all greatly impressed with the play,
but many critics blamed the author for violating, to a slight extent,
the unities of time and place. Corneille defended himself, but in his
later plays he applied the rules meticulously, although not without
some strain. Corneille conceived tragedy as a portrayal of the conflict
of man's will and some strong passion. He always showed his early
Jesuit training in his continuing belief in free will: man's reason
should direct his choice of action, and then his will should put this
action into effect. Somewhat like Marlowe, Corneille's concern is with
the superlative, the extraordinary, and the tremendous, and he has
little interest in the average human being. His diction fits well his
heroic subjects, for it is eloquent and grandiose, though sometimes
bombastic and grotesque. There is a remarkable firmness and virility
in Corneille's verse, and his abstract vocabulary is perfectly suited to
his ideas. Some passages of his plays rise to a climax like a storm, and
then break on the ear with a crash of sound that is of the essence of
Baroque literary art. His characters are clearly drawn with bold rather
than subtle strokes. Through his best tragedies he shaped the French
Baroque drama. In his last years Corneille was embittered by the rapidly rising reputation of Racine and by financial troubles; he never later
equaled his four great tragedies, *Le Cid, Horace, Cinna,* and *Polyeucte*.

The critical tradition of Malherbe was continued by Boileau (d.
1711). Though known for his varied poetic works, especially a mock
epic, *Le Lutrin,* and *Satires* and *Epistles* in the style of Horace, Boileau
made his greatest impress through his *Art of Poetry*. Here he warns
the writer to go back to nature so as to get away from the artificialities
and affectations of Mannerist writing, from preciosity, bombast, and
burlesque. Boileau's models of "following nature" are especially the
writings of his three close friends, La Fontaine, Racine, and Molière.
But in observing nature he bids the writer to see also how nature is
treated by the ancient writers. Here Boileau prefers, as did the whole

period from Petrarch on, the Roman writers to the Greek. The urbanity and majesty of the ancient Romans made them more congenial than the Greeks, who, for all their sublimity, were too unequal, too individualistic, and often too close to the multitude. The "nature" which Boileau wants the writer to observe is that of the court and the city— the world of the best usage. He felt the servile idolatry of the classics shown by the Pléiade needed to be transformed into a reasonable appreciation; and, in the same way, the critical works of Aristotle, Longinus, Horace, and of late Renaissance Italy should not be accepted blindly. Reason, nature, and antiquity combined in complete harmony would give birth to superb literary productions. Common sense is the guiding principle of all Boileau's work. His most original creations are his satires, but his most influential work, though it is largely derivative, is his *Art of Poetry*. Boileau's later years were embittered by a quarrel with Perrault, in which Boileau defended the superiority of the ancient writers against Perrault's support of the higher excellence of modern writers. The defenders of the moderns delighted in pointing out the faults of classical writers from Homer on down; they insisted that the classical ideal is un-Christian, and that the law of progress defies the contention that the ancients cannot be surpassed in form and style, especially since modern literature shows they have been surpassed. Finally, there is a patriotic appeal made by the moderns, namely, that it is a foolish affectation to prefer ancient and foreign civilizations to the great national culture of France. This "Quarrel between the Ancients and the Moderns" was repeated in other countries in the eighteenth century. At his best, Boileau was the great lawgiver of Baroque literary classicism, and his influence was profound all over Europe until his sway was broken by the Romantics.

As Boileau was the defender of authority in literature, Bossuet (d. 1704), a bishop, was its defender in religion and politics. Bossuet's eminence comes rather from his qualities as a stylist than from either the depth or range of his thought. But he is undoubtedly one of the greatest prose stylists of the Baroque Age. It is a style that shows great variety, but is always fitted to his subject. Bossuet seems to have had little vanity or personal ambition, and he always gives the impression of speaking sincerely. His style is spirited in his sermons, flexible and penetrating in his controversial writings, and sublime in his funeral orations. At the heart of this style, as in that of Milton, there is a harmonious blending of Greco-Roman antiquity and of the Bible and the Church Fathers. Bossuet's command of language is sonorous, lofty, and magnificent. The love of psychological analysis seen in Bossuet's sermons runs all through the literature of seventeenth-century France and is most clearly shown in La Bruyère's *Characters* and the *Maxims* of the Duc de la Rochefoucauld. The most complete expression of Bossuet's genius is in his funeral orations that have the cadence of a great organ as it fills the vaults of a lofty church. At its best, Bossuet's style gives the same grand, majestic, and even sublime impression that one receives from Bernini's colonnades at St. Peter's and from Bach's *B Minor Mass.*

Judging from most of the French literary production of the seventeenth century, one would hardly expect to find such a witty and whimsical genius as La Fontaine (d. 1695). He called himself "the butterfly of Parnassus," and he flitted from one subject to another and from one patron to the next. La Fontaine's impracticality and absentmindedness were already legendary in his own lifetime. A sharp-eyed witness of the life about him rather than a judge, his *Tales* and his more famous *Fables* show his deep insight into the ways of men and of animals. The convention, in his *Fables,* of having animals speak flouted not only the doctrine of verisimilitude of the critics, but also Descartes's idea that animals are only automatons. Besides, the human beings brought in do not belong to the court or the city, but are of the peasant and lower classes. There are one hundred and forty fables —varying in length from a few to a few hundred lines. La Fontaine uses a great variety of verse even within one fable. Like Boccaccio, he invented few of his tales, but his treatment of each is entirely his own. His language is usually the French of the soil, rich and colorful, more like that of the sixteenth century than of his own time. He is full of the poetry of common things such as one sees in Dutch landscape and genre painting, or, in La Fontaine's own France, in the work of the Le Nain brothers. The form of his *Fables* is usually first a suggestion of background or landscape, then a swift narrative (usually with some dialogue), a denouement often in one line, and finally some maxim of worldly wisdom. In these little dramas, which present persons of every status from courtier to peasant, there is a great cross section of mankind. "Everyone," he said, "speaks in my work, even the fishes." The one thing that most clearly relates La Fontaine to his age is the brilliant finish and polish of his style. Few poets in European literature have been better craftsmen.

For a sophisticated, theatergoing public that was becoming wearied of Corneille's giants of the will, a new type of tragedy was supplied by a younger man, Racine (d. 1699). As a youth Racine was educated at Port Royal from whence came his Jansenist belief in predestination which he later combined with the Greek idea of fate, derived from a close study of the plays of Sophocles and Euripides. His first great success was *Andromaque,* where a love interest is substituted for Corneille's heroics. This was followed by six other plays on classical and oriental subjects; the culmination of this extraordinary series of masterpieces was his *Phèdre,* a profound tragedy of jealousy and remorse. As an expression of passion on a grand scale, *Phèdre* has never been surpassed in any literature. As the role of Hamlet is the ambition of every English-speaking actor, that of Phèdre is the highest goal of every French actress. Then, at the age of thirty-nine, Racine retired from composing for the stage, not to return to dramatic writing until twelve years later, when he produced two remarkable biblical plays, *Esther* and *Athalie,* for the pupils at Mme de Maintenon's school at St. Cyr. His plays take the action of a complicated situation at the very climax; and unlike Corneille he seems to have felt no restraint in keeping within the unities of time, place, and action. He always simplifies the action and uses only a small number of characters. Racine used the alexandrine verse form with a music and a range of emotional expression which no other French poet ever equaled. Beneath the highly polished formalities of his plays, there is a profound penetration of human psychology. Racine's heroes and heroines speak in a language of exquisite balance and control which often produces a mysterious music of wonder and awe; but one feels that just below the surface lie the savage fury of chaos and the subversion of all that reason ordains. He is especially perceptive in his portrayal of women caught in the coils of love. He treats love in all its manifestations, from passion to devotion and on to hatred, including jealousy, flirtation, tenderness, and ecstatic rapture. Racine can pass easily from high sustained utterance to easy familiarity, and from the sublime to the ironic or the humble. And, everywhere, his style matches his thought. "Not a verse," says Lemaître, "but explains in rapid words, and words strong as the thrust of a sword, the illusions, the suffering, the egotism, the folly, and the mischief of love." Racine is one of the two or three greatest literary geniuses of the Baroque Age. His style is equally distinguished for its precision, its beauty, and its restraint. His apparent simplicity is the result of a consummate artistry. His inventiveness in constructing plots, his psychological penetration, and the high excellence of his poetry led Strachey to say that Racine has "the right to walk beside Sophocles in the highest places of eternity."

When Louis XIV asked Boileau, "What great writer has most honored my reign?" Boileau replied, "Molière, sir." Molière (d. 1673) was the son of a substantial middle-class family. He received a thorough training in the classics, and, either at school or later, learned to read Italian and Spanish. In 1642, the year the Puritans closed the theaters in England, Molière began his career as an actor. Later, like Shakespeare, he came to be manager, producer, and playwright. Louis XIV liked him and gave him aid and patronage. He wrote thirty-nine plays, which range from ballets, court entertainments, and farces to full-fledged comedies. Some of his plays are in verse, others in prose. Molière is always something of a moralist; he castigates hypocrisy, pedantry, pretentiousness, dishonesty, perverted values, and injustice. Like Chaucer and Cervantes, he hates people who will not face facts. He is always urbane and his satire is usually good-humored rather than bitter. He declared comedy should be merry and moral, inciting laughter as a prelude to reflection. Molière's attitude is the soul of good sense; as Sainte-Beuve said of Shakespeare, "He dwelt at the center of human nature." His comedies are usually based on one single comic or incongruous idea as hypocrisy, avarice, or pretentiousness. He created a great gallery of unforgettable characters, and the comic element in his plays is usually more rooted in character than—as with Shakespeare—in the situation. Molière's plays show much less classical influence than the tragedies of Corneille and Racine, and he drew more from medieval farces, Spanish comedies, and the Italian *commedia dell' arte* than from classical writers. Molière used a language exactly suited to the character being portrayed, as did La Fontaine; and, as he presented many middle- and lower-class types his language is not always elegant. His writing is sometimes too hasty; on occasion, he clears up a complicated predicament by introducing an unmotivated event; and his minor characters are often not properly individualized. On the other hand, Molière had a profound insight into human nature, and he could penetrate a whole situation and present it in a phrase or even in a gesture. Like the greatest imaginative writers, he was able to live temporarily inside the skins of others. His greatest plays are *Tartuffe, Le Misanthrope, Les femmes savantes, Don Juan, L'Avare* and *Le Malade imaginaire*. He died directly after a performance of the last, in which he had played the leading role. Molière's fine human qualities have appealed to all peoples, and he has been translated into many languages. He is the father of the modern comedy of manners, as Cervantes is the father of the modern novel.

Next to France, England produced the largest number of outstanding writers during the Baroque Age. Typical of the Early Baroque in English letters are the *Essays* and other writings of Francis Bacon, the *Sermons* and *Devotions* of Donne, and the religious poetry of Crashaw. Bacon (d. 1626), in his English writings, moved toward a much greater simplicity of style than that earlier used by the Elizabethans, and toward a sententious and Ciceronian style of eloquence. His essays were written in imitation of those of Montaigne, but they show much greater concentration and organization, thereby illustrating the contrast between Mannerism and the Baroque.

The poems of John Donne (d. 1631) are mostly in a Manneristic style, but his prose writings show a return to classical integration and a carefully cadenced style. Donne's sermons set forth, in dark terror, all the conflicts of the soul. He mixes the sublime and the loathsome but carefully builds up his effects to imposing climaxes. His metaphors are among the most brilliant in English letters. Donne's sentences have a sonorous quality, a great richness, and a calculated symmetry; words, phrases, and sentences are carefully balanced one against the other, and in relation to the whole composition. He gives the impression of tremendous power of emotion under strict control. Crashaw (d. 1649), a convert to Catholicism who spent much of his life on the Continent, represents the essence of the Catholic Baroque spirit in literature. His most famous verses are in long poems devoted to the name of Jesus, to the Magdalen's tears, and to the ecstasies of St. Theresa of Avila. He is the most daring of the metaphysical poets in his imagery, and his poetry still contains elements of Mannerism. His long religious poems are uneven but they rise at times to an electric fervor and an ecstatic grandeur. Crashaw's lines are decked with red, purple, and flame color, like a church decorated for the Feast of the Most Precious Blood. His lines are full of tears and fire, of vision and rapture, and a mystical intensity. Nowhere else in the Baroque period is poetry so close to works like the "St. Theresa" of Bernini.

The greatest genius of the Baroque in England is Milton (d. 1674). As no other writer, he combined the Renaissance and the Reformation, and he showed always about an equal devotion to the classics and the

Bible. Milton was a Puritan, whose deity was the God of the Old Testament rather than of the New; but behind this Puritan was the son of the Italian Renaissance who equaled, if he did not surpass, the finest minds of that movement. His early poems, as "L'Allegro" and "Il Penseroso," are in the harmonious style of the High Renaissance, while "Lycidas" is Manneristic. During the middle period of his life, when he was devoting his talents to defending the Puritan cause, he wrote almost no poetry. The prose of this period is polemical and uneven, but full of passages of a soaring eloquence, as in the *Areopagitica,* where he combines the loftiest majesty of style with real exultation of spirit. Milton's greatest work was written in the period after the Restoration, when he was out of favor at court, blind, and in failing health. To this period belong *Paradise Lost, Paradise Regained,* his two great epics, and *Samson Agonistes,* a classical tragedy. Here, Milton, writing in sublime blank verse, tried to do for English poetry what Virgil had done for Latin verse. He shows everywhere an unrivaled grasp of the intricacies of metrical music, and in trying "to justify the ways of God to men" he renders the infinite in terms of the finite. Milton's poetry is very scholarly, but it is scholarship distilled into poetry. In this he resembles Virgil and, among the English poets, Thomas Gray. He was steeped in classical mythology, philosophy, and poetry, and in the literature of the Italian and French Renaissance. Likewise, he was familiar with English poetry from Chaucer through Spenser, whom he especially admired, to Donne. Out of these rich stores he created his own lofty and majestic style with the vigor of a Baroque architect.

In *Paradise Lost* Milton is closest to Virgil, especially in his use of verse paragraphs, where one line runs into the next, in the manipulation of the musical value of words, and in interjecting his own personality, as Homer does not. He could hardly reproduce Virgil's Latin because English lacks the multiplicity of case endings and verb forms and the variability of word order possessed by Latin, but he succeeded remarkably in producing something like the organ roll of the *Aeneid. Samson Agonistes,* a classical play with choruses, recounts the blind poet's despair, and the victory of his will and mind over fate and matter. The play is the tragedy of a hero like himself, blind and surrounded by Philistines. The only rounded character in the drama is that of Samson, and the work, though it contains some sublime poetry, lacks the tension of true drama.

Milton looked to Italy as the great mother of modern culture. But

Dryden (d. 1700), who was twenty-three years younger, turned to France for a similar inspiration. No writer of the Baroque Age was more versatile, for Dryden excelled in play-writing, literary criticism, translation, poetic satire, and lyric poetry. His prose introductions and essays form the first considerable body of criticism in English. His taste was very catholic, yet surprisingly sure. He appreciated Shakespeare as a great genius and, at the same time, admired the French writers of his own age, though he dared to point out some of their limitations. Dryden has been called "the father of modern English prose." It is a clear and rational style which lacks not only Milton's splendid passages but also Milton's cumbersomeness in the less inspired parts of his writing. His style is precise, lucid, and dignified, and goes right to the heart of the matter under consideration. In comparison with Milton's, it is more direct and unadorned, and with fewer words of Latin origin. Dryden defined good style as "the art of clothing and adorning thought in apt, significant, and sounding words." Ciceronian periods give way to clipped sentences, juxtaposed rather than linked, and essentially conversational in structure. His style shows the influence of rationalism and of scientific writing that became more marked in the prose of the eighteenth century. The tendency of the time is well set forth in a statement of the Royal Society that "rejected all forms of undesirable ornaments of speech" and favored "a close, naked, and natural way of speaking."

Dryden's dramas, written largely for money, were in prose and in blank and rhymed verse. His best tragedy, *All for Love,* a version of the story of Antony and Cleopatra, and his finest comedy, *Marriage à la Mode,* lack the distinction of his critical prose writing, his satires, and his lyric poetry. As a satirist, Dryden ranks with Pope and Byron as one of the greatest, particularly in his satiric portraits. This type of occasional poetry, no matter what its quality, loses much of its interest when the circumstances that produced it are largely forgotten. His satire, the best of which is *Absalom and Achitophel* (in support of Charles II against the Whigs) is vigorous and incisive, yet detached—almost an editorial commentary on men and events, an intellectual utterance emotionally suffused so as to persuade a public audience. Dryden is the first English poet to give satire a high polish. Earlier English satirists had believed that the style should be rugged and somewhat uncouth. His model was chiefly Juvenal, though Juvenal did not bring into his poems contemporaries as did Dryden. Unlike Pope, whose satire became more petty and spiteful, Dryden's prose is controlled; like contemporary writing in

France, it is restrained by the models of the best ancient and modern writers, and by the rules of the critics. Dryden's quest for control extended to his system of metrics, and the closed heroic couplet (two lines of iambic pentameter, rhyming, and forming a complete unit of thought) became his favorite poetic form; and it remained a favorite for at least two generations after his death.

Dryden came nearest to achieving the heights of Baroque grandeur, majesty, and sublimity in his Pindaric odes, especially in his "Song of St. Cecelia's Day" and "Alexander's Feast." Here a series of strophes of no fixed structure succeed one another; the whole, however, is handled with great ease and surety of touch. Both poems were later set to music by Handel in a magnificent blend reflecting the very quintessence of Baroque art and music.

In the Baroque Age, Holland produced her greatest man of letters, Vondel (d. 1679), who was for Holland what Camoëns was for Portugal, and what Mickiewicz was to be for Poland. Vondel wrote a great deal of lyric poetry, but his fame rests chiefly on a series of poetic dramas, mostly on biblical and religious subjects. They are composed in alexandrine verse in five acts with choruses between the acts. In his plays on religious subjects, Vondel took as the basis of his work the medieval mystery and morality plays, and combined with this the example of ancient drama and the rules of the critics in regard to choice of subject, verisimilitude, and the dramatic unities. In his later years, he became a Catholic, though this did not alter his style. Like Milton, Vondel was influenced by the French Mannerist poet, Du Bartas. In his masterpiece, *Lucifer,* he chose a subject which was free from too many set circumstances, and which allowed him to invent situations and characters. Vondel is more human and more tender than Milton, but his verse at times reaches the same sublime heights. Had he written in one of the major languages, instead of in Dutch, Vondel would be known as one of the great figures in European letters.

While Racine was writing in France, and Milton in England, Calderón (d. 1681) was producing a series of remarkable plays in Spain. Calderón is much more subdued and restrained than Lope de Vega, and, unlike Lope de Vega, he did not write for a popular audience, but primarily for the court. His style still contains elements of Mannerism, especially in farfetched figures of speech, and in the occasional bringing into his plays of exaggerated and distorted characters the possibility of whose existence does not convince the reader. He composed about a hundred and twenty plays, some of whose plots he borrowed from Lope de Vega, and also a number of one-act religious pieces. Calderón had a genius for constructing complicated plots, but the main lines of the story are never lost. He has less range of interest and less spontaneity than Lope de Vega, and he uses a greater economy in the number of characters he introduces. Calderón's drama is one of thought and ideas rather than of passion. His plays—both tragedies and comedies—show an intense devotion to the Catholic church, an absolute and unquestioning loyalty to the Spanish monarchy, and an exaggerated feeling for all points of honor. *Life Is a Dream,* Calderón's most famous play, defends the freedom of man's will, teaches that, if this life is only a dream, what we do in this dream determines our place in the reality to which we awaken at death. By using his powers of reason and will, the hero saves himself from bestiality on earth and wins salvation in heaven. Goethe found Calderón's plots to be miracles of construction, but thought his characters often lacked clarity of outline. Calderón is a great master of verse form, and his plays are highly polished. Their careful concentration of effect, their skilful structure—though they do not observe the unities—relate them to the plays of Corneille and Racine. Some of Calderón's characters are exaggerated and talk in hyperbole, for which reason Shelley and a number of the German Romantics, who admired him, saw in him a thwarted Romantic. His heroines are always beautiful, chaste, eloquent, and resourceful; and his heroes exaggeratedly chivalrous and amorous, wearing their hearts on their sleeves and carrying their hands on their swords. The father is always austere and unyielding; the maidservants are always roguish, and the valets cowardly and comic. And the mother is usually dead. The verse is always facile, and the moral is almost always the same—a vindication of some point of honor, or else of loyalty to the king or the church. Yet because of the ingenuity of the plots there is much variety. Not for nothing had Calderón studied casuistry with the Jesuits. Chastity and points of honor were to him what virtue was to the Jesuit theologians—subjects for intricate inquiry as to the application of a general rule to all conceivable cases. He was always able to exploit common Spanish sentiments with a complete confidence in the response of his hearers. On the other hand, he is so very Spanish and so much of his own time that he has been hard for foreigners to appreciate.

The Rococo phase of Baroque literature, much of which lies in the first half of the eighteenth century, shows the same characteristics as

Rococo art. Like the Baroque, the Rococo is strongly under classical influence and the rules of the critics. But it is far lighter in touch and more elegant and more sophisticated. Baroque eloquence gives way to Rococo wit. Whereas Milton wrote *Paradise Lost* to "justify the ways of God to men," Pope wrote his mock epic, *The Rape of the Lock,* only "to divert a few young ladies." Milton was conscious of writing in the tradition of Homer and Virgil, while Pope, in order to set the mood of his poem, prefaced it with lines from the Roman wit Martial. The refinement of Pope's heroic couplets, in contrast to the sublime tone of Milton's blank verse, suggests the difference between the sharp clarity of the harpsichord and the majestic tones of the organ.

Pope (d. 1744), like other English writers of his time, Swift, Hume, and Johnson, was a staunch Tory—aristocratic, monarchical, and very dubious of easy and utopian solutions of public problems. Pope excelled in lyric poetry, in translation, in satire, and in the poetic essay; yet the essence of his style is best seen in *The Rape of the Lock.* Pope's poetic style, which seems so much his own, owes a great deal to four English poets who were often his models: Chaucer, Spenser, Milton, and, above all others, Dryden. In the *Dunciad,* a long and ambitious satire, Pope created, as in Dante's *Inferno,* a convenient limbo into which to commit his personal enemies and detractors. Pope worked off and on at the piece for thirty years; and the final result, while venomous, is extraordinarily witty and clever. In his *Essay on Man,* his most ambitious work, and in his *Essay on Criticism* he gave succinct statements to many of the ideas of his time. Pope is, in these works, in nowise original, but either in English or in translation, he helped to spread many of the commonplaces of eighteenth-century thought.

In the preface to the *Essay on Man* Pope said he "will steer betwixt the extremes of doctrine seemingly opposite," and he strove to harmonize social rank with equality, self-love with benevolence, reason with passion, and partial ill with universal good. In the *Essay on Criticism,* he followed Horace and Boileau, and to a less extent the earlier Italian critics in pointing out the disruptive tendency of individual whim, the disciplinary value of tradition, the infallibility of the ancients, the necessity of study and thought as preparation for creative effort, and the obligation to keep the parts of a work in strict subordination to the whole. Both essays abound in sparkling epigrams, but they are also full of contradictions. They show clearly the essence of Pope's style, which lies in a brilliant, brittle, clear-cut, and incisive phrasing. His verbal marksmanship is unmatched, he is usually elegant, with a studied ease, and he rarely lacks both sparkle and dignity. Of Pope's popular translation of the *Iliad* (he also translated the *Odyssey*) Bentley, the great classical scholar, said, "A pretty poem, Mr. Pope, but you must not call it Homer's." *The Rape of the Lock,* which Hazlitt dismissed as "the triumph of the insignificant," shows Pope's preoccupation with the trivial, a characteristic of the Rococo. The poem is a marvelous picture of the frivolities of the age and is very close in style to some of the paintings of Boucher and Fragonard. During his own lifetime Pope came to be acknowledged everywhere as the greatest poet in Europe.

Carducci once said that "there never was a period less poetical than the first fifty years of the eighteenth century." But he should have added there are few periods whose prose was of higher quality. The influence of science and rationalism on prose style is already evident in Dryden and other prose writers at the end of the seventeenth century. The prose of the sixteenth and most of the seventeenth century was either modeled on Latin and often majestic though also cumbrous, or it had been assimilated to poetry and was fanciful and turgid. What this prose urgently needed was clarity, lucidity, and precision, and the ability to convey ideas to the common man, who was now a member of the reading public. Two important new forces, those of democracy and science, are chiefly responsible for the change in prose style in the early eighteenth century. At the end of the seventeenth century, Fontenelle spoke of the need for "order, neatness, precision and exactness" in books and in the press, while Sprat, the historian of the Royal Society in England, urged writers to reject "all the amplifications, digressions and swellings of style" so as to bring "all things as near mathematical plainness as they can, preferring the language of artisans, countrymen and merchants before that of wits and scholars." As a result of such agitation the average length of sentences was cut in half. And, symptomatic of the rapid growth of the reading public, there was a striking increase in newspapers and periodicals. These tremendous shifts in style and readership form the background for the works of Swift and Voltaire.

Swift (d. 1745), England's greatest prose satirist, tried deliberately to combine clarity and strength in his writing. Dryden, as a satirist, chiefly attacked parties and sects, and Pope directed his shafts mostly against persons, but Swift attacked all mankind. His writing has a studied simplicity, a biting economy of phrase, a great clarity of exposition and argument, and an over-all style that cuts like steel. Back of his fury and venom, there lay always a fundamental sincerity, a positive belief in reason and sound sense, and a growing hatred of sham and oppression, so deep as to end in insanity. Swift's moods ranged from black grumblings and bitter invective to delightful buffoonery and exquisite playfulness; at times his wit is dazzling. Swift's poetry, which is mostly occasional verse, is quite inferior to his prose. Dryden is said to have remarked to Swift, "Cousin Swift, you will never be a poet." The *Battle of the Books* and the *Tale of a Tub* are brilliant prose satires on the aesthetic and religious shams and pedantry of scholars and divines. Swift's general attitudes and his lucid prose style are best seen in *Gulliver's Travels,* a biting satire on the pettiness, follies, and vices of his age. The work is full of magnificent and malignant irony, centered chiefly on such topics as education, politics, religion, war, and commerce. Swift's own definition of prose style, "proper words in proper places," is nowhere better exhibited. Somerset Maugham, who like many others regards Swift's prose style as the finest in English letters, advises a young person who wants to learn to write well to practice reading twice a paragraph of Swift, then, closing the book, to try to reproduce it in his own words. "Keep repeating this," declares Maugham, "and you will become an effective writer."

What Swift was to Britain, Voltaire (d. 1778) was to the whole of Europe. As a young man, after receiving a thorough classical training from the Jesuits, he spent several years in England; here he knew, among others, Pope and Swift and came into contact with the ideas of Bacon, Locke, and Newton. This English sojourn was pivotal in Voltaire's life, and, through him, in the whole movement of ideas in the Enlightenment. From his English visit, Voltaire returned to the Continent, soon to become the great prophet of deism, skepticism, and belief in intellectual and religious freedom. Few men in modern literature have been so versatile. During his long life, Voltaire wrote enough to fill over ninety volumes: lyrics, dramas, epics, history, literary criticism, political and religious tracts, and over twelve thousand letters that have survived and as many or more that have disappeared. In no single form of literature did Voltaire attain first rank, partly because he wrote too rapidly, and partly because, though he had a quick and sharp mind, he had no great profundity. Voltaire developed no system of thought of his own; he was a destroyer of old systems rather than the maker of any new one. It has been said that "his mind was a chaos of clear ideas." He valiantly smashed old idols, but was unable to set up new ones. He believed in benevolent despotism, and in the unities for the drama; indeed, he was a conservative or a moderate liberal in nearly everything except religion. But he somehow furnished much of the drive and fire that later went into the French Revolution. Amidst the vast output of his pen the story *Candide* is the best known. No book, in a comparable number of pages, contains so much devastating wit. It is perhaps the world's masterpiece of skepticism, a skepticism, however, that is not a work of easy cynicism, for behind it lies a genuine moral earnestness. Voltaire attacks the follies of war, the injustices of religious persecution and of stupid governments, and the avarice of men. His final advice is to live quietly, and "cultivate your own garden."

Voltaire was first and last a great propagandist. "Crush the infamous thing" was his motto, by which he meant crush superstition and intolerance. Many of his plays and stories are dramatized or novelized pamphlets. The main features of his style are its swiftness, its clarity and smoothness, its graceful wit, and its nervous vitality. The sentences fly to the mark like poisoned arrows. Voltaire is the ablest manipulator of what his age called *le style coupé,* the clipped style which had succeeded to the long sentences and involved constructions of the Baroque Age. As few men in history, Voltaire interested millions of men in his ideas, and so he became one of the great emancipators of the human spirit from the barriers and burdens of stupid authority and ignorance.

4. Music

The Age of the Baroque was a golden period in the history of music. No other period can boast of a greater variety of new forms, or of an equal number of great composers, or of a summation comparable to that represented by the achievement of Bach and Handel. As in art and letters, the music of the Baroque Age shows a love of grand and vast plans and sumptuous and resplendent effects. The composers loved massive sonority, ornament, movement, color, and strong contrasts. Such contrasts were emphasized by sectional construction and change of key along with shifts of tempo and texture, as, for example, chordal passages contrasted with others of contrapuntal part-writing. In performance the Baroque musicians show a great passion for technical virtuosity. Composers and performers are no longer interested in economy of means; rather they are bent on spending lavishly everything they possess, and elaborate display is of prime importance to them. As in art and literature, the composers tried to give the illusion that there is no barrier between heaven and earth, between the church militant on earth and the church triumphant in heaven, and they approach the spiritual through the sensual.

The Baroque period is marked by a continuation and elaboration of polyphonic writing which culminates in the music of Bach; but alongside of this there was, in both vocal and instrumental music, a striking development of monody. For the first time, instrumental music has an equal importance with vocal music; and there is a final establishment of major and minor keys. The three great stylistic currents that run through the Baroque Age are, first, the development of a monodic style in the opera, which likewise affected such forms as the oratorio and the cantata and left a deep impress on instrumental composition. Second, there is the phenomenal growth of new forms of instrumental music, the beginnings of which first clearly appeared in sixteenth-century Venice; out of this current came the sonata in its various forms, the suite, the overture, and the concerto. And, finally, there began with Frescobaldi a development of organ music—elaborated primarily in Germany—out of which were evolved the fugue, the chorale prelude, the toccata, and other forms of organ composition. Side by side, thus, there grew three styles, one of accompanied melody, one of a concerto style, and one of a contrapuntal style.

In all these changes, Italy took the lead. The two greatest composers of the Baroque Age, Bach and Handel, were not Italians, but it was Italy that was in nearly every case the initiator. It is typical that Schütz in Germany and Sweelinck in Holland were pupils of the Italian Gabrieli and that the German Froberger perfected his art in study with another Italian, Frescobaldi. Music seems to have suffered less than literature or even art from the oppressive tyranny of the governments and the heavy hand of the Counter Reformation. Princes and prelates patronized and supported brilliant innovations in music, and during the seventeenth century in Italy almost the whole of modern music was taking shape. Opera and oratorio, at first scarcely distinguished, grew with Monteverdi and Carissimi; and from their style of song sprang much of vocal music until the time of Schubert. Corelli set the standard of violin playing for the future and gave vogue to the instrumental form that was destined to develop into the sonata. Frescobaldi established a new style of organ composition. Moreover, apart from the activity of her many composers, Italy was the land where music was most eagerly cultivated and most bountifully supported by the upper classes; indeed it would seem that cities like Venice, Rome, and Naples were music mad in the seventeenth century.

The first great composer of Baroque Italy, Monteverdi (d. 1643), has the distinction, through a very long life, of writing in the style of three periods. Some of his church music is in the calm and noble style of the High Renaissance; some of his madrigals, with their expressive use of dissonance, belong to the experimental style of Mannerism; and his operas are definitely Baroque. Against his conventional critics, Monteverdi defended himself by declaring that audacities of harmony are justified if they serve as a faithful expression of words and mood. Monteverdi's first opera, *Orfeo,* was composed hardly a decade after the first experimental opera of Peri had been performed in Florence, yet it is far removed in style from the origin of the form. Whereas the first operas had used only four instruments for the accompaniment, the score for Monteverdi's *Orfeo* called for thirty-six; and instead of introducing, as in the first operas, no instrumental numbers, Monteverdi used twenty-six individual movements for instrumental ensembles. Then he bound the scenes of his opera together by the repetition of short refrain passages. The instruments of Monteverdi's orchestra were divided into categories so that each emotion evoked from the orchestra its own individual tone-coloring. His style of writing for voices and the manner of orchestral coloring were brilliantly used to heighten the emotional effect. All the involved contrapuntal feeling is gone and the accompaniment has taken on a chordal harmonic form. His later operas, as the *Coronation of Poppea,* were written for the first opera house built in Europe, which was opened in Venice in 1637. The solo songs of Monteverdi were divided into recitatives to further the action and arias of a more varied melodic character to comment on the situation and to interpret the whole mood of a scene; this became a common custom in opera and oratorio.

After Monteverdi, Italy produced many opera composers, and the opera became throughout the peninsula, and then all over Europe, a popular form of entertainment. The tendency was to heighten the scenic effects with all sorts of technical devices that brought gods riding on chariots out of clouds, dragons spewing flames, and figures rising from the sea. Music was written to allow the singers to show off their technique in the *bel canto* style; and the essential dramatic elements were often lost in displays of scenery, costume, and technical virtuosity. The oratorio followed the opera in the use of recitative, arioso (a recitative in a less dry form), aria, chorus, and orchestra. Often the oratorio was divided in the middle by a sermon. Sometimes the part of narrator was added, as later in Bach's passion music. As in many other fields of Baroque music, the finest achievements in any given form were made only in the eighteenth century by Bach and Handel. The finest Italian master of oratorio was Carissimi (d. 1674), whose works are characteristically Baroque with big and sometimes double or triple choruses, powerfully rhythmic recitatives, and glowing arias. Carissimi's style shows greater restraint, less capriciousness, and irregularity than the contemporary style of opera. Closely related to the oratorio, whose subject was religious, was the secular cantata for soloists and orchestra. Both were Italian inventions whose popularity spread across Europe.

Opera, with its combination of dramatic poetry, acting, stage decoration, costuming, and music, became perhaps the most characteristic musical realization of the Baroque. Among a large galaxy of Italian opera composers who followed in the century after Monteverdi, the most outstanding was Alessandro Scarlatti (d. 1725), most of whose operas were presented first in Naples, which, along with Venice and Rome, was one of the leading centers for opera in Italy. Scarlatti brought together many of the styles of his predecessors and helped to fix a form for opera. The overture was elaborated and written in three sections, an allegro, followed by an adagio, and then an allegro usually of a fugal character. This arrangement of a quick, a slow, and a quick movement survived long after Scarlatti's time. The plot was only an excuse, and the main musical effort was to show off vocal talents. The recitatives were either accompanied by an occasional chord on the harpsichord, or by a group of stringed instruments. The arias, for which the audience waited impatiently, were frequently written in a *da capo* form where the conclusion repeats the introduction in an *aba* form. The singers were expected to embellish their arias as written with improvisations, a style which demanded the greatest technical capacity. Scarlatti's operatic style was widely imitated not only in Italy but throughout Europe.

Many critics made fun of opera; it was an outrage to common sense, utterly puerile and irrational. So thought Boileau, La Bruyère, Addison, and many others. But opera caught on, not only in Italy, but also in Dresden and other cities in Germany, in Vienna, Paris, Madrid, London, and in other centers. Not a king or a grand duke but must have his theater, his scenic artists, his composers; his maestro, ballet master, and prima donna. Everywhere people raved over opera, a pattern to which many arts made their contribution—a feast of sound, color, and rhythmic motion, enchantment for both the eye and the ear, and a great novel form of emotional appeal. The opera, in turn, had a great influence on all types of instrumental music, moving these toward monody.

Instrumental music had begun to have an independent life of its own in the sixteenth century, but the seventeenth century is the first great period of musical writing for both solo instruments and instrumental ensembles, and here Italy took the lead by inventing a series of new musical forms like the sonata, the suite, the overture, and the concerto; by showing how musically to exploit the possibilities of varied instruments; and finally by perfecting old instruments and inventing new ones, especially those of the violin family. Musicians became more attentive to the individuality of various instruments such as the organ and the harpsichord and to their tonal qualities and technical possibilities. It became the custom in Italy to string together a series of short compositions and to call the whole, depending on what instruments were used and where the work was to be performed, a *sonata da camera,* a *sonata da chiesa,* a suite, a partita, or an overture. The various sections of such a composition differ in mood and rhythm. Usually the parts are in the same key, and many of them are dances contrasting in rhythm and arranged in sequence. These various musical forms had different origins, but as they developed, the forms tended to fuse. The invention and perfecting of the violin family—violin, viola, cello, and double bass—brought a great change in instrumental music. The violin, especially, had a more brilliant and carrying tone than the old viols, and it satisfied the Baroque taste for faster tempi, greater sonority, much technical agility, more florid embellishments, and for a sharper defining of rhythms. Besides, the violin could be made to speak eloquently, brilliantly, and soulfully as almost no other instrument, and it is nearest in sound to the human voice. Other instruments of the orchestra were likewise improved by gaining a large range and by increased sonority. All this allowed the orchestra to create more sonority, variety, and contrast.

The Baroque orchestra grew and took shape to meet two needs: one was the necessity of increasing the number of players, especially string players, in an ensemble where the performance was to be given in a large building; the other arose from the advisability of having something like a standard organization so that work performed in one city could be repeated elsewhere. It was the development and spread of opera as a public spectacle that made these requirements urgent. By the later seventeenth century, the orchestra was well established as a medium for independent instrumental performance entirely apart from its function in theater, church, or palace. Besides exploiting the orchestra, the Italians developed music to bring out the idiomatic qualities of smaller instrumental ensembles in the *sonata da camera,* the *sonata da chiesa,* and the duo and trio sonata. They also showed how to exploit the possibilities of the organ and the harpsichord. Indeed, in every field of music, during the Baroque Age, the Italians were the innovators and teachers for the rest of Europe. They opened up new stylistic roads in music in quite a number of directions.

Few composers have, with so small an amount of music, left so deep a mark on musical history as Corelli (d. 1713), the first great composer of orchestral music. He wrote no vocal music, but confined his composing to violin and harpsichord and trio sonatas. The trio sonata came to be a favored form among Baroque composers. The two high-singing violins could weave their contrapuntal patterns, held together by the harmonies of the harpsichord, with no danger of obscuring the lines or making the sonority too dense. Corelli also composed twelve superb *concerti grossi,* written in a lofty and elegant style; on these his great reputation chiefly rests. All these instrumental works are divided into distinct sections called movements, each with its own tempo. A frequent number of movements is four, in the succession of slow, fast, slow, fast. In general, movements are thematically independent, and each movement has only one theme. Both monody and polyphony are used. Corelli, though his works never range beyond the violin's third position, greatly expanded the possibilities of the new violin family. He traveled extensively in western Europe, and his works (some of which were published after his death) became widely known. By his use of major-minor tonality and modulations within a movement Corelli established principles of tonal architecture subsequently elaborated by Vivaldi, Bach, and Handel. As in much Baroque music, the performers were supposed to add ornaments to the notes as written; these often took the form of trills and arpeggios. Sometimes these ornamentations were written out, and published with the music.

Corelli's leadership was continued by Vivaldi (d. 1743), the first great virtuoso on the violin and a prolific composer. Most of his life was spent as musical director of an orphanage in Venice, though he made long and frequent trips in Italy and beyond, and finally died in Vienna. His output was enormous; besides motets, oratorios, cantatas, and nearly forty operas, Vivaldi wrote many duo and trio sonatas and over four hundred and fifty concertos for various combinations of instruments; and he was the first great creator of solo concertos. His *concerti grossi* were, however, like most of those of the period, for a small group of instruments—usually several violins and a harpsichord—playing against the mass of the orchestra, which itself was made up of strings, as it was not common to include woodwind instruments in *concerti grossi*. Alessandro Scarlatti had, in his later works, introduced into his orchestral writing more music for the flute; Vivaldi continued this and used, more than previously, the oboe and bassoon, though these woodwinds were usually used in orchestral works other than *concerti*.

Outside Italy, throughout western Europe, the Italian influence in music, in the seventeenth century, was primary. The dominant figure in French music, Lully (d. 1687), was an Italian by birth, and, though he always laid an emphasis on his writing of French music as distinct from Italian, his style of composition, though more restrained, is still close to that of seventeenth-century Italy. Music was much favored at the French court; in the time of Louis XIV there were no fewer than eight distinct musical groups employed at Versailles. Music of every sort was to be heard: opera and ballet; orchestra and chamber music for soirées, dances, Sunday concerts; and church music in the royal chapel. Lully held the favor of Louis XIV by his playing of the violin and the harpsichord, and by his pantomiming which made "Le Grand Monarque" laugh until the tears rolled down his face. Lully was also a born flatterer; he knew how to hold the King's favor, and used his influence to keep other musicians from competing with him. He co-operated with Molière in arranging ballets and comedies, but usually Lully was both composer and general director at once. Lully's opera overtures, like most of those of the Baroque period, could be played as separate compositions. His *French Overture* began with a slow, rather pompous section, followed by a lively fugal section, and concluded with another slow section. Much of Lully's music has a ceremonial formality about it, a dignity and majesty tempered with grace befitting the Age of Louis XIV. Besides his operas and orchestra works, including *ballets de cour,* Lully wrote a number of powerful and effective religious motets. His music is always restrained and usually as stylized as the gardens of Versailles; it is sometimes monotonous, and unrelieved by any flash of spontaneous feeling. Lully translated into music some of the rhetorical splendor of Racine's plays and Mansart's architecture. The words of his opera were not to be made unintelligible by the music, nor was the opera to be interrupted by many lengthy arias in the Italian manner. Vocal utterance was modeled on the style of speech used in classical tragedies. Ballets were extensively used as interludes or as parts of a scene, and usually, at the end of the opera, there was a great choral section. Though rather a second-rate musician, Lully was a great organizer and a prolific writer. More gifted than Lully was his contemporary, Charpentier (d. 1704), who studied in Italy with Carissimi and, on his return, espoused the Italian style of opera. Lully long kept Charpentier in minor positions. His greatest works are his religious masses, motets, and oratorios which capture the grandeur of the Baroque as well as any music written before Bach. Charpentier showed that church music could be as dramatic and intense as opera and that vocal music must be interesting as music regardless of the importance of the text.

England lagged behind France in musical development partly because the country was involved in a protracted series of wars and violent political changes. The one artistic musical form developed in the early seventeenth century was the "masque," as typical of England as was the *ballet de cour* of France. No great musical genius, however, appeared until Purcell (d. 1695) in the second half of the seventeenth century. Though he died at the age of thirty-seven, Purcell wrote an opera and much instrumental music of a high order, including incidental music for plays, settings for the poems of his friend Dryden, cantatas, anthems, sonatas for chamber orchestra, and compositions for the organ and for the harpsichord. In Purcell's music there is an interesting blend of Italian, French, and native English musical forms and traditions. He got unusual effects by using both modal and tonal scales, by failing to resolve certain dissonances, and by moving from major to minor scale within one composition. Unfortunately for English music, no composer appeared after Purcell to maintain the national tradition against the overwhelming popular preference for Italian, French, and German music.

In northern Europe, the new impulses from Italy were evident around 1600. Sweelinck (d. 1621) of Amsterdam, a fellow countryman of Franz Hals and Vondel, was a great composer for the organ. He also wrote many choral works and compositions for the harpsichord, but his organ music is by far the most distinguished part of his work. It shows a new freedom in the bass pedal parts, and a great understanding of the idiomatic potentialities of the organ. Sweelinck created the giant organ fugue and variations on psalm tunes and chorales that had a long and glorious history. Among his pupils were Praetorius and a number of Germans; the great seventeenth- and eighteenth-century school of German organists stems largely from Sweelinck.

The first German composer to be trained in Italy was Hassler (d. 1612), who studied in Venice with Andrea Gabrieli. On his return, he wrote madrigals, chorales, motets, and organ compositions, all of which show the influence of Italian forms. His much younger and more gifted fellow countryman, Schütz (d. 1672), studied with Giovanni Gabrieli in Venice. He wrote the first German opera, *Dafne,* to a text by Opitz, a work that is unfortunately lost. Schütz's greatest achievement is found in his great choral works, madrigals, motets, and oratorios. Most of his active years were spent as master of the Chapel of the Elector of Saxony at Dresden. In 1628 he returned to Italy on a visit to Monteverdi, whom he greatly admired. Schütz's style fused Italian and German styles. His work shows great melodic invention and a striking use of pictorial motives suggested by the text. In his most famous choral work, *The Seven Last Words,* the narrative portions are set as solo recitatives over a *basso continuo,* while the words of Jesus, in free and highly expressive monody, are accompanied by *continuo* and strings. There are choral passages at the beginning and end, and the whole work breathes an atmosphere of intense and mystical devotion. Others of his choral works are handled in varied styles. In all this he was an important precursor of Bach.

Throughout the seventeenth century, Protestant Germany produced a series of great organ composers, who developed a number of forms of composition for the organ, and for solo and choral singing with the organ. Among these masters the most outstanding before Bach were Pachelbel (d. 1706), Buxtehude (d. 1707), Kuhnau (d. 1722), and Böhm (d. 1733). They perfected two species of organ compositions, the toccata and the organ chorale. The toccata aimed to produce the effect of an improvised performance; it used free and varied rhythms, sudden sharp changes of texture, and a contrived uncertainty in the harmonic flow of the music. Contrasting sections were often introduced of strictly imitative counterpoint. The two motives of impulse and order were used, with a wonderful sense of movement and climax, in monumental organ compositions, the greatest of which, before Bach, were those of

Buxtehude. The toccata was wonderful for displaying a performer's technique and skill, especially in virtuosity in playing the pedal stops. The term "organ chorale" was loosely applied to any organ composition based on a chorale melody. Many varieties of treatment were possible, a favorite one with some composers being the fugue form. Along with all this remarkable development of organ composition in Germany, especially in Protestant northern Germany, went a great improvement in organ construction. The organs gained in clarity and brilliance, and at the same time produced a more homogeneous ensemble. In addition, organs offered better means of bringing any single voice of the ensemble into a prominent position. Thus the organ was able both to present elaborate counterpoint, and to accompany a melody, as required.

The summation of a century of Baroque music in its manifold forms is found in the music of Bach and Handel. Both were born, only about eighty miles apart, in the same year, 1685, of middle-class, North German, Protestant families. Both perfected old forms rather than invented new ones. In this respect, they are different from many of the composers of the later sixteenth and seventeenth centuries, and also from those of the later eighteenth century, as Gluck, Haydn, and Beethoven, all of whom strove to create a new aesthetic creed and to work great changes in the art of music. In this respect, Bach and Handel resemble Palestrina, who also realized the ultimate possibilities of a long-familiar style and was thus unlike the opera reformers of 1600, and Monteverdi, who started on an adventurous journey into unknown lands of musical expression. Though both Bach and Handel were German, each showed a profound study of the musical styles of other countries. Bach (d. 1750) was provincial in that he spent his whole life in a number of posts in central Germany and was only locally known, whereas Handel (d. 1759) traveled widely in Italy and elsewhere, was well known, and was buried in Westminster Abbey. Bach was very much of a family man, the father of twenty children, the result of two marriages. Nine of Bach's children survived him, and four of these won fame as composers. Handel never married. Bach's life was largely concerned with small ventures, whereas Handel's career centered upon big financial undertakings, some of which brought him temporary ruin. Both were devoutly and genuinely religious; both became blind near the end of their lives. Handel wore a lordly and man-of-the-world attitude, whereas Bach, though occasionally hot-tempered, was generally very humble and self-effacing. Bach's favorite forms of composition were in church music, religious cantatas

and sacred organ music, and he has never been surpassed in his interpretation of the Bible and the Christian creed so far as persuasiveness,
penetration, and fervor are concerned. Handel's favored forms were
large and dramatic operas, oratorios, and cantatas. Whereas Bach used
the chorale form extensively in his composing, Handel almost never
employed it. Bach is the greatest of all composers for the organ, whereas
Handel, who was recognized as the leading virtuoso organist in
Europe, wrote very little organ music. Each was a great master of both
choral and instrumental music. Bach's music is of an impersonal nature,
while Handel is frequently regarded as the first composer to show his
personality in his musical writing. Bach's music is usually polyphonic
and Handel's is mostly homophonic, though each man was a great
master of Baroque polyphony. Bach's vocal music leans toward an
instrumental style, whereas Handel shows a style of vocal writing more
fitted to the possibilities of vocal expression. Both composers liked regular rhythms but Bach often uses a stronger and more driving beat.
Bach's harmony, on the whole, is more complex than that of Handel.
Bach is more severe in style and more angular, more profound, and less
easy to understand than Handel.

Bach's ingenuity as a contrapuntalist has never been excelled. This is
revealed in a superb series of works for organ, harpsichord, and for
large and small instrumental ensembles. Bach's highest mastery in this
field is, perhaps, best shown in his *Art of the Fugue* and his *Musical
Offering,* written on a theme given him by Frederick the Great. His
harmonic richness and inventiveness are on the same high level as his
capacity as a contrapuntalist. According to some critics, Bach consistently used a set of musical forms to express different moods. This can
be more easily traced in his vocal music, where the meaning of the text
is emphasized by the repeated use of musical phrases. For instance, sorrow is expressed by a descending chromatic phrase as in the "Cruci-
fixus" of the *B Minor Mass.* Certain words, such as eternity, quiet, sorrow, joy, ascend, and fall, are usually presented in the same musical
terms. This style did not originate with Bach, but he used it more consistently than any other composer.

Bach's varied styles show a profound and thorough mastery of the
best musical writing of Italy, France, England, and his own Germany.
He was evidently always eager to study the scores of other composers,
and he made great efforts to hear other performers, especially on the
organ. Everywhere Bach takes up the achievements of his forerunners

and brings their forms to a higher level of expression. The collected edition of Bach's works seems to represent an activity worthy of a number of great geniuses rather than of one. He wrote over three hundred church cantatas, of which about two-thirds are still extant, two "Passions," the superb *B Minor Mass,* four short masses, some motets, and four hundred chorales set in four-part harmony. His harpsichord and organ compositions, and his chamber and orchestra music, though not in any category as extensive as his choral compositions, exist in great quantity and variety. Everywhere he shows an unheard-of technical ingenuity and resourcefulness. Few men in any field of artistic activity had such a tremendous output and one of so uniformly high quality. Bach's contributions to many departments of musical composition are considered so important that choirs, organists, pianists, violinists, and cellists all look to his music as the supreme test of their performing skill. Bach erected fantastic edifices of sound that seem to climb to the stars, but everything is carefully wrought, and it all stands on a solid foundation of granite. Everywhere a cool and masterful intellect is united with the deepest sensibility. When Bach died he was well known only in Leipzig, where he had conducted the St. Thomas choir for over thirty years, and all his published music could have been put into one volume, instead of the fifty-nine volumes of the present still incomplete edition of his works. His burial place was soon forgotten, and he was nearly unknown until his music began to be rediscovered in the nineteenth century.

Handel's style, like that of Bach, represents a synthesis of Italian, German, and English styles; he was much less influenced by French musical style than Bach. Two trips to Italy deeply impressed Handel with the style of Italian opera, oratorio, and orchestral writing. This probably accounts for the fact that his writing is predominantly homophonic, though he remained fond of contrasts of all sorts in tempo and volume, and in polyphonic and homophonic sections. As Bach used certain musical phrases to represent various ideas and emotions, Handel as regularly chose certain keys to fit the mood of a given composition. Handel lacks Bach's thoroughness and concentration, though he is a more facile writer and sometimes seems to possess a titanic strength not given to Bach. Beethoven said of Handel, "Go and learn from him how to achieve great effects with simple means." And Haydn declared, on hearing the Hallelujah Chorus in Westminster Abbey, "He is the greatest of us all!" Contemporaries spoke of Handel's later oratorios as written in "his big bow-wow manner." Handel's output as a composer, though not as large as Bach's, is nonetheless huge. It includes forty-six operas, mostly in an Italian style. They contain much fine music but suffer from the fact that he had very poor librettists, many of whose lines are pompous and inane. This was also the case with most of his thirty-two oratorios, which he wrote after he found only financial failure in the opera. In turning from opera to oratorio and cantata he turned for support from the aristocracy to the growingly influential middle class. Except for the *Messiah,* little of Handel's vocal music is now much performed, though there has been some effort to revive these works. As an instrumental composer, Handel wrote a great variety of magnificent works, including suites and other compositions for the harpsichord; sonatas for violin, oboe, flute, and recorder, all with figured bass accompaniments; sonatas for small groups of instruments; some superb *concerti grossi;* suites called *Water Music* and *Fireworks Music;* and, finally, both Italian and French types of overtures. No one before Handel ever achieved such power, such force, such brilliance and fullness with such naturalness and apparent simplicity of construction. If Handel lacks Bach's mysterious, awe-inspiring emotional power, Bach's capacity to look into the hidden depths of the soul and to unlock the inner secrets of religion and of beauty, Handel still is one of the giants in the whole history of music. The achievement of Bach and Handel sums up the Baroque Age in music as the achievement of no pair of artists or writers can sum it up in art or in literature.

While the two giants, Bach and Handel, were scaling the heights of Baroque expression, other composers in France, Germany, and Italy— paralleling what was taking place in art and letters—moved into a Rococo phase. This graceful, charming, and light-hearted daughter of Baroque represents the Baroque in art, literature, and music in miniature. It leaves out all the sublime, passionate, and powerful traits, it accentuates all that is ornamental, elegant, and refined, and it achieves a new touch of fragile beauty and light-hearted sophistication. Like the exquisite Meissen porcelain, a dainty prettiness and a subtle elegance pervade Rococo expression in the arts. This is the spirit of Watteau, of Pope, and of Couperin.

François Couperin (d. 1733) was the greatest member of a large musical family in France. Like Lully earlier, he enjoyed the backing of the French monarch, and was organist at the Royal Chapel at Versailles and at one of the large churches in Paris. In his own time, he was also famous as a virtuoso on the organ and the harpsichord and as a teacher.

In 1716, Couperin published his *Art of Playing the Harpsichord,* which helped to spread his fame. His works consist of compositions for the harpsichord, the organ, for combinations of instruments, and religious works for voices. Couperin's most characteristic works are his charming pieces for the harpsichord—dainty, miniature compositions to which he gave such titles as "Regrets," "Tender Langours," "Sister Monica," and "Rose Bushes." He is an early writer of program music. His *style galant* emphasizes pointed rhythms and clearly defined melodies set above a simple and symmetrical accompaniment. Couperin's delicate and sentimental art is close in spirit to the painting of Watteau.

Rameau (d. 1764) made his reputation primarily as a musical theorist rather than as a composer. He did not write his first opera until he was fifty; and he showed therein—as well as in his chamber music and in his compositions for the harpsichord—that he was a highly gifted composer; his operas, unfortunately, suffered from the wretched librettos to which they were written, which led his contemporary, Voltaire, to remark, "What is too silly to be said is sung." Some of his finest and freshest music is in his exquisite opera-ballet, *Les Indes galantes.* Here the orchestration is brilliantly colorful, the harmonies varied and rich, the rhythmic patterns constantly supple, and the solos and choruses ingeniously contrasted. Rameau was the first composer who consistently used orchestral instruments to obtain effects of tone color, in which he anticipates Gluck. He was, first, attacked by those who said his operas varied too much in style from those of Lully; later, he was assailed by proponents of Italian opera—a row that was paralleled in a number of countries. Rameau likewise annoyed the critics by his strange and daring instrumental tricks, both in writing for groups of instruments and in his descriptive compositions for the harpsichord. Rameau's *concerts spirituels,* beginning in 1725, and arranged for the general public (to take place in the twenty-four days of the year when opera was forbidden) were the first modern type of public concert performances. In 1722 Rameau had published his *Treatise on Harmony,* the first of a series of important works on this subject which he was to bring out. In these, he provided the bases of musical science up to the beginning of the twentieth century.

Domenico Scarlatti (d. 1757), whose active years were spent in Naples and Madrid, wrote operas, masses, and motets; but he is chiefly remembered for his more than five hundred harpsichord sonatas—short compositions, usually in one movement, which may modulate through several keys. These sonatas take from two to six minutes to perform.

They are usually divided in the middle, with both halves repeated. They begin with some effective melodic or rhythmic idea and then proceed to something different in the same or another key; in the second half there is usually a contrasting mood, and sometimes a different key and tempo. The endings of the first and the second half are ordinarily alike. Scarlatti's modulations are frequently sudden and striking. The disposition of keys foreshadows the later sonata of the Neo-Classical period. A favorite virtuoso device of these masterpieces in miniature is the crossing of the hands at lightning speed. The effective performance of his sonatas demands a high degree of technical skill. Scarlatti was the greatest harpsichord virtuoso of his day; once, as a man in his twenties, he competed with the young Handel; Handel clearly won on the organ, but the competition for the harpsichord performance was declared a draw. Scarlatti used a melodic and harmonic treatment that displayed, as did no other composer, the special qualities of the harpsichord. His little gems are no longer music that might have been played on a lute or an organ or a group of string instruments as well as on a harpsichord. And these charming and effervescent short pieces, full of an infinite variety of expression, sound as fresh as the day they were created.

5. Conclusion

Whitehead, in speaking of the great triumphs of science in the seventeenth century, characterized this hundred years as the "Century of Genius." The phrase may equally well be applied to the arts. If Ruskin and Burckhardt regarded the achievement of the Baroque Age as a degeneration from the high level of accomplishment of the Renaissance, today the tendency would be in the direction of considering Baroque achievement equal if not superior to that of the High Renaissance. The work of Bernini and Rubens, of Racine and Milton, and of Bach and Handel, and of many of their contemporaries is quite unmatched by anything that came earlier. And even the Rococo—a later phase and rather an afterglow of the Baroque—is still a time of fresh creation and unique accomplishment. The achievement of Pope, Watteau, Couperin, and other contemporaries has a distinct quality and flavor of its own that makes it seem a kind of Baroque in miniature. So, all in all, the whole Baroque period from about 1600 to about 1750 has now come to be recognized as one of the richest and most varied periods in the history of the arts.

Chapter VI

NEO-CLASSICISM
AND ROMANTICISM
1750–1830

1. Background

Between 1300 and 1750 each change of style had succeeded—with much overlapping—the preceding style. Now, however, two styles, Neo-Classicism and Romanticism, developed side by side, each style taking something from the other, but remaining nonetheless distinctive. The Romantics were inclined to borrow classical subjects, usually Greek ones, and then handle them in their own way. To take two examples, Keats is Neo-Classical in his "Ode to a Grecian Urn," but medieval and Romantic in his "Eve of Saint Agnes"; and the same architects would design buildings in both classical and Gothic styles. Both Neo-Classicism and Romanticism arose near the middle of the eighteenth century as a stylistic reaction against the frivolities and whimsies of the Rococo, which they finally set aside though never fully displaced. This accounts for the complicated mixture of styles in the arts in the century between about 1750 and 1850.

Neo-Classicism in art and letters, like the earlier styles considered here, arose from a new and deeper examination of the heritage of classical antiquity. Fresh sources of beauty were found in Roman art, but the greatest new revelation came in a further study of the artistic and literary heritage of Greece. This has led some historians to call the classical revival the "Greek Revival." This, however, is too limited a view, for, especially in the fine arts, there is a fresh infusion of ideas derived from new discoveries in Roman art and a fresh estimate of some of its distinguishing qualities. The earlier study of Greek civilization had emphasized its calm Olympian qualities, and the Apollonian aspects of its culture. Now, especially in literature, the Dionysian and somewhat untamed qualities of Greek letters came to the fore, notably in the handling of classic subjects by the Romantic poets.

The sources of Neo-Classicism came from no single country, but in the rediscovery of aspects of ancient civilization in which quite a number of nations played a role. Fénelon's *Télémaque,* in the midst of the Baroque Age, had given a new glamor to the world of ancient Greece. In 1734 the Society of Dilettanti was formed in England, chiefly to further archeological investigations of ancient civilization. The society sent students to Italy and Greece and financed important publications on ancient art. In the 1760's appeared the first volumes of Stuart and Revett's *Antiquities of Athens,* and, shortly before this, a study of the ruins of Palmyra and Baalbec by two other Englishmen was published. In 1769 appeared a volume of *Ionian Antiquities.* About the same time, the Royal Academy was founded in England, and from the beginning it was strongly Neo-Classical in outlook. Also, furniture and architectural designs in both France and England moved away from the Rococo to the more severe lines we associate with the styles of Louis XVI in France and of Adam and Hepplewhite in England. It was in this period that Wedgwood began to make his Neo-Greek porcelains, many of them with classical designs by the sculptor and engraver, Flaxman. During these years, Piranesi (d. 1778) delighted the intellectuals by his dramatic etchings and engravings of ancient Roman and Greek buildings (especially the Greek temples at Paestum), where there was a great exaggeration in the scale of ancient buildings, and where few opportunities for emphasizing the picturesque aspects of his subjects were lost. Amid his pictures of classical urns, statues, shattered columns, and the ruins of temples, baths, and amphitheaters—all beset with dark shadows and haunted figures of beggars and thieves—there were working a great imaginative vehemence and a feeling for the grandiose and the sublime qualities of ancient Roman architecture. Piranesi represented, indeed, a fascinating combination of Neo-Classical and early

Romantic styles. During this period the ruins of Paestum, Pompeii, and Herculaneum, the Baths of Titus in Rome, and Hadrian's villa at Tivoli were being systematically excavated and some of the finds were being published.

The general direction of thought is shown by the teaching of the German scholar Gesner, first at Leipzig, then at Göttingen. He defended the study of the Greek and Latin classics against the Pietists, who denounced all classical writers as "foul pagans"; against rationalists, who said the classics were out of date and useless; and finally against the grammarians, who taught the classics only from a grammatical point of view and kept the students writing stupid rhetorical exercises in Greek and Latin. Gesner taught his students enough of the classical languages to enable them to read extensively in the literature so as to discover the style and ideas of the great classical writers. In 1755 Winckelmann published his first great study of ancient art. His view of Greek art was more ideal than historical. To Winckelmann the Greeks were a race of glorious idealists raised above the accidents of time and place, and their art was the greatest man had ever achieved. Though he was murdered in middle life and never got to Greece, his enthusiastic writings caused fresh breezes from the Aegean to sweep throughout Europe. The publications about Greece became numerous. In 1788 Barthélemy published his *Voyage of the Young Anacharsis in Greece;* here is presented a highly idealized picture of Greek antiquity that charmed the imagination of men for half a century. Other important dates in early Neo-Classicism were the publication in 1762 of Raphael Mengs's *Reflections on Beauty* and the completion by Canova, in 1779, of his "Daedalus and Icarus," and by David, in 1784, of his "Oath of the Horatii."

In 1763 Grimm observed: "For some years now the forms of ancient times are much in favor. Taste has benefited thereby, and everything is 'à la Grecque'; exteriors of buildings, their interior decoration, furniture, fabrics and jewelry. Thanks to this we now have beautiful and noble forms instead of the eccentricities which offended us ten or twelve years ago." The Rococo is giving way to Neo-Classical. But Goethe, though he was deeply influenced by Neo-Classicism, made fun of the artists and students who crept over the mighty ruins of antiquity taking elaborate measurements and then fancied themselves the very keepers of art because they knew the exact size of the gigantic achievements of the ancients.

The attitude of the artists and writers influenced by Neo-Classicism was to fix their attention on the universal in man. Reason, it was assumed, is identical in all men, and anything which is limited to men of a special age, race, or tradition is of little value in comparison to what has influenced men in all times and places. Neo-Classicism, thus, was against individualism and originality. It was, said Dr. Johnson, the labor of Socrates "to turn philosophy from the study of nature to speculations upon life, but the innovators [i.e., the Romantics] I oppose are turning attention from life to nature. They seem to think we are placed here to watch the growth of plants or the motion of the stars. Socrates was of the opinion that we are here to learn how to do good and avoid evil." What is best in man, according to Dr. Johnson, is his capacity not to follow his "original" feelings but to attain a rational understanding of a high ideal set by what Matthew Arnold later called "the best that has been thought and said." The aim of the benefactor of mankind is not to proclaim new truths, but to purge men's minds of provincialism and prejudice and to fix attention on truths that have always prevailed. The local, the temporary, and the particular are to be excluded; and an austere simplification that deals only in what is basic and universal in man should be the subject matter of art and literature. This had been, of course, the basic tradition of classicism for centuries, but the Neo-Classical writers and critics gave it a fresh emphasis—all of which stands in striking contrast to the rising propaganda of Romanticism. The Neo-Classical antipathy to originality and to private intuition in matters of taste is analogous to the Deist's dislike of enthusiasm. As Hume said, "Above all avoid enthusiasm." Both the Neo-Classicist and the Deist saw in history a long decline from a superior state of things. Art, literature, and religion had all begun well, and all had been corrupted. The way of salvation, thus, was not in advance but in reversion. Seneca had said that the mark of a well-regulated mind is that it can call a halt where it will and can dwell at peace within itself. How different all this was from the Romantic credo! The results of Neo-Classicism are more evident in the arts than they are in literature and music. Neo-Classicism worked toward a great simplification of style: decoration in architecture was reduced to a minimum and, in all the fine arts, simplicity and clarity of outline were emphasized.

Romanticism, which had its rise at the same time as Neo-Classicism, represented much more than new artistic, literary, and musical styles, though that is our main interest here. Romanticism brought forth, at the same time, new attitudes toward man and nature in nearly all phases of life. It was a reorientation, along many lines, as fundamental as that of the Renaissance, and its results are still being worked out. A strong reaction against the rationalism of the seventeenth and eighteenth centuries steadily gathered force as time proceeded. It was first evident in the great growth of Pietism in seventeenth-century Germany, followed in the eighteenth century by the rise and spread of Methodism in England. The Pietists and the Methodists belittled human reason and laid great emphasis on developing the personal and emotional aspects of religion. Another source of Romanticism was Locke's empiricism. To Locke knowledge comes from sensation and from reflection on sensation. Thus Locke's emphasis is on individual experience and upon sensory experience, and on the idea that such truth as may be known is to be found primarily in and through the particular, and, finally, that truth is to be arrived at by imaginative and emotional faculties rather than by reason. Locke's theory is thus individualistic, subjective, and with emphasis on emotions. As Sterne said, "Clear sensibility, eternal fountain of our feelings; all comes from Thee!" It was only a step from this to Rousseau's idea that man was naturally good and had been corrupted by society. Remove the social fetters and the natural man will inevitably fulfil himself, and realize a golden age.

These religious and philosophical currents were in the eighteenth century accompanied by a deliberate cultivation of emotionality and sensibility, and the belief that it is emotion rather than reason that is basic in man's nature. Goethe has Faust trying to define God, and the hero ends by saying that reasoned definitions are vain; all is feeling:

> Call it Bliss! Heart! Love! God!
> I have no name to give it.
> Feeling is all in all;
> The name is sound and smoke,
> Obscuring heaven's pure glow.

Only emotion can capture the inner relations of things, and know their significance. Reason alone, said Wordsworth, viewed "all objects in disconnection, dead and spiritless." August Wilhelm Schlegel had much the same idea in mind when he wrote, "Whereas reason can only comprise each object separately, feeling can perceive all in all at one and the same time." The Romantics loved to emphasize the "organic," that is, seeing things as wholes and with all their relations understood. This was paralleled by a new praise of the simple life and the virtues of the common man and the noble savage, neither of whom had been affected by the artificialities of corsets, dancing masters, and French Baroque and Rococo elegance. The routine of social life inevitably spells frustration for the artist, the writer, the musician, and the philosopher. So Romanticism inclines to all that is individualistic, subjective, and free. The Romantic hero is usually an egocentric individual devoured by melancholy or boredom, or a fiery rebel against society and its rules, authorities, and traditions.

Along with this great emphasis on man's emotion as being even more important than his reason, there ran a new concern for the life of the lowly. Robinson Crusoe in the later seventeenth century was a common man, one of the first of a long line in literature. How different he was from the heroes of the plays of Racine, and the classical idea that "the actions of mean and base personages tend in very few cases to any good example." The plays, novels, and poems of the later eighteenth century are filled with the life of the lowly. It appears in Lessing, Diderot, Richardson, Burns, Wordsworth, and a host of others. Richardson's letters of instruction to "handsome girls who were obliged to go out to service, how to avoid the snares that might be laid against their virtue" were the origins of *Pamela,* and heroines like Pamela dulled the glitter of the Baroque and Rococo gallants. There were often tears in their eyes. When Richardson's second heroine, Clarissa, died, a wail of lament spread across the whole continent of Europe. It rose to a flood in Germany, where all the currents of Romanticism cut their deepest channels. Thus, there came back into literature little children, humble folk, the beggar, the idiot, and natural objects—trees, flowers, and even inanimate things which could not say, with Descartes, "Cogito, ergo sum." Earth could be strange again; there might be heaven in a wild flower!

The Romantics saw new things in nature, especially the reflection of their own moods, and they much preferred wild nature to the formalities of classically laid out gardens. Nature meant a good order in the universe; it also meant the rejection of the artificialities of upper-class decorum. The wisdom to be acquired by a close communion with nature is summed up by Wordsworth:

> One impulse from a vernal wood
> May teach you more of man,
> Of moral evil and of good
> Than all the sages can.

The landscape, as Amiel said, "became a state of the soul." Most of the Romantics found nature benign and good, though a few, as Leopardi and Alfred de Vigny, thought nature either negative or cruel and evil. As artists and as men, the Romantics resented the impoverishment of the imagination and the emotions that came as the result of the great achievements of experimental science accompanied by the striking growth of rationalism. In an atmosphere that suffered from an excess of dry, white light, the poets and artists summoned their resources to return to what they considered the great realities of existence. The whole spirit of Romantic revolt against science and rationalism is sharply summed up by Wordsworth, who speaks of a man so scientifically minded, and therefore so dehumanized, that he would "peep and botanize on his mother's grave." The nature the Romantics cherished was that described by "Ossian": "It was the essence of misty vagueness and melancholy, a primitive wildness, sounding with waterfalls, and with mossy stones that look like old graves." They loved the mysterious forest, solitude, stillness, and night, moonlight, clouds which journey afar into dreams, and twilight which effaces sharp outlines; all of these stimulated their imaginations. It is a spirit like that of the Savoyard vicar in Rousseau's *Émile,* who sees God in the sunset, or of Beethoven's great song, "God in Nature." As Wordsworth says in "Tintern Abbey,"

> A presence that disturbs me with the joy
> Of elevated thoughts; a sense sublime
> Of something far more deeply interfused,
> Whose dwelling is the light of setting suns,
> And the round ocean and the living air,
> And the blue sky and in the minds of man;
> A motion and a spirit that impels
> All living things, all objects of all thought,
> And rolls through all things. Therefore am I still
> A lover of the meadows and the woods.

This rediscovery of the consoling and inspiring force of nature was one of the great creations of Romanticism. Its effects were summed up

by Matthew Arnold in 1850, in his verses on the occasion of Wordsworth's death:

> He found us when the age had bound
> Our souls in its benumbing round;
> He spoke, and loos'd our heart in tears.
> He laid us as we lay at birth
> On the cool flowery lap of earth;
> Our foreheads felt the wind and rain.
> Our youth returned: for there was shed
> On spirits that had long been dead,
> Spirits dried up and closely furl'd
> The freshness of the early world.

Finally, the Romantics looked for new subject matter in art and
literature. They turned to the Middle Ages, so full of color and adventure, and to writers like Dante, Shakespeare, and Cervantes who
had achieved greatness without the rules of Aristotle. Their craze for
the medieval even led to forgeries such as those of Macpherson and
Chatterton in Britain and of some Czech poets in Bohemia. New subjects were also found in the Near and Far East, and from the world
of the noble savages of the Americas. Though classical subjects were
not entirely neglected, most of the Romantics would have agreed with
Hugo when he exclaimed, "At last, Olympus and Parnassus are for
rent!" The Romantics hated all rules including those of the Baroque
critics; as Keats declared:

> A thousand handicraftsmen wore the mask
> Of poesy. Ill-fated, impious race!
> That blasphemed the bright lyrist to his face,
> And did not know it,—no, they went about,
> Holding a poor, decrepit standard out,
> Mark'd with most flimsy mottoes, and in large
> The name of one Boileau.

Romanticism thus represented the reaction of emotion against reason,
of nature against artificiality, of simplicity against the complex, and
of faith against skepticism. Romanticism was filled with a new enthusiasm for nature and for distant civilizations. It discovered the
noble savage, the virtuous Greek, the Chinese sage, and the devout
medieval knight. Whatever its object, the Romantic urge was one of
longing and of antagonism to the present, which was regarded various-

ly as an age of Rococo frivolity or of unimaginative rationalism or of ugly industrialism and bourgeois complacency. Romanticism thus meant the meeting of many currents that gathered force during the eighteenth century, and its essence is not easy to define. It was not a philosophy but a sort of emotional religion, as nebulous as it was ardent. It penetrated sensitively into the psychic, into dreams and longings, into the unconscious and the mysterious, into those regions in which men sense intuitively rather than know by reasoning. The poet becomes a seer; he is wiser than he knows. His art is divinely inspired. Artists are a higher caste, not by birth, but by insight. The Romanticist is filled with infinite longing often without goal, limit, or object; he strives for the infinite. As good a definition of Romanticism as any is that of Josiah Royce: "Trust your genius; follow your noble heart; change your doctrine whenever your heart changes, and change your heart often. Such is the practical creed of Romanticism." Or, as Goethe's friend Lenz wrote in 1776, "It was my heart that counselled me to do it, and my heart cannot err." The word "Romantic" had been used in English and French since the seventeenth century to describe medieval legends or ideas that were remote or strange. It was first used in a more modern sense in relation to a new style of English gardening that came in during the later eighteenth century, and the word then spread from England onto the Continent.

2. Art

Neo-Classicism in art, like the Baroque, began in Rome, where, around the middle of the eighteenth century, under the patronage of Cardinal Albani, Winckelmann was writing and Raphael Mengs was painting. Few theorists and critics in the history of art have had a wider influence than that of Winckelmann (d. 1768). He examined every aspect of ancient Greek art he could find, usually in Roman copies or adaptations; in his *History of Ancient Art* of 1764 he laid down rules of proportion which, in sculpture, should govern the size of the eyes and eyebrows, of collar bones and all parts of human anatomy, the proper relative importance of hands and feet and of balance and pose, and a large number of other details. Winckelmann had also steeped himself in Greek literature and history and he declared that the essential qualities of Greek civilization and art were "a noble simplicity and tranquil loftiness," "a beautiful proportion, order, and harmony." "The depths of the sea are always calm however wild and stormy the surface." As Pater said, "He catches the thread of a whole sequence of laws in some hollowing of the hand or dividing of the hair." Though Winckelmann was never in Greece and saw almost no original Greek art, he thought the art of Greece vastly superior to that of Rome, and he admonished artists and writers to steep themselves in Greek art and literature. Though he missed many things in Greek civilization, Winckelmann was the first to see, as an organic whole, the glory of Greek life, litera- ture, and art. The culture of ancient Greece was, he believed, due to a unique combination of circumstances. Ancient Greece was to him a world of beautiful bodies and of the sun, where the mind of the phi- losopher and the eye of the artist were alike attuned to beauty, a land where a kindly climate and a glorious landscape brought all nature to its most perfect development and led on the hearts of man to a natural joyousness. His theories about Greek civilization are a strange tangle of classical idealism and Romantic emotions. Winckelmann also invented the word and the idea of *Kunstgeschichte* ("art history"). His influence on art was enormous and universal, though his influence on literature was largely confined to Germany. Winckelmann disliked Bernini and nearly the whole of Baroque and Rococo art; and he preached the doctrine that painting, sculpture, and architecture should be renewed by adopting the simple and noble style of the Greeks.

Winckelmann's influence paralleled a series of publications on Greek architecture; and in the second half of the eighteenth century it is evi- dent that Greek models, or Roman copies of them, were affecting painting, sculpture, and architecture. An early disciple of Winckel- mann was the painter Raphael Mengs (d. 1779), whose style marks the transition from Baroque and Rococo to Neo-Classicism. Mengs, close friend and devoted follower of Winckelmann, strove to combine classical form, the drawing of Raphael, and the color of Titian. His own painting is lifeless and dull, but in his own time he was lavishly admired and hailed as the initiator of a new style.

The first gifted painter in the Neo-Classical style was the French- man David (d. 1825). He began his career as a pupil of Boucher but soon moved away from a Rococo style. A long sojourn in Rome filled him with enthusiasm for ancient art and the principles of Winckelmann. His first painting to attract attention was the "Oath of the Horatii" of 1784. Here he shows himself a master draftsman and a painter of lofty idealism. David was soon caught up in the wave of revolutionary enthusiasm that swept France after 1789, and, alongside the paintings on classical, mythological, and historical subjects that he continued to produce, he was commissioned by the Revolutionary governments to do vast compositions like "The Tennis-Court Oath." By this time, his classical enthusiasm led him to draw all his figures in the nude, and to clothe them afterward. David next became the official painter to Napoleon; in addition to a distinguished series of portraits, he portrayed large scenes like "The Coronation of Napoleon." In much of David's work the modeling is in linear abstractions, the forms are of a metallic hardness, and usually the figures stand motionless as if frozen; the whole effect is often that of a tinted bas-relief. The Romantics said they had to turn up their coat collars when they passed a painting by David or his school lest they catch cold! Toward the end of his life, David saw some casts of the Parthenon marbles and realized that, had he known the best of Greek art earlier, his own work would have had more vitality. David's portraits and the historical scenes of his own time, however, in both design and color have much more vitality than his paintings on classical subjects. He was always a great master of composition, and he restored to European painting some of the monumentality that it had largely lost in the Rococo period.

The most distinguished of David's pupils, who long outlived him, was Ingres (d. 1867). His work, though often deficient in color and mechanical in composition—especially in some of his huge paintings—was, through its matchless drawing, a continuing comment on the weakness of the painters of the Romantic school. Like David, and the lesser painters of the Neo-Classical school, Ingres was less interested in imitating nature than in trying to realize a generalized and abstract ideal of beauty. It is this that created such an interest in Ingres among the Post-Impressionist painters, especially Cézanne.

Parallel with this development of Neo-Classical painting, Romantic painting was slowly unfolding. In what the historians of art and literature call the Pre-Romantic period, that is, before 1800, some painters showed their search for a new style in their attention to landscapes, frequently painting twilight and nocturnal scenes where they exploited the enchantment of shadows. It is interesting to notice that the beauties of night and twilight appealed, likewise, to writers like Young in England, Novalis in Germany, and Alfred de Musset in France, and to the composer Chopin. The Pre-Romantic painters also preferred autumn and winter, with their overtones of decay and death, to spring and summer as subjects. In the same way, they made a cult of ruins, of storms, of avalanches, of tempests, and of shipwrecks. In opposition to classicism they turned for subjects to the Middle Ages with its cathedrals and crusades, to the Orient, and to wild and untamed scenery. At the same time they brought back into painting an emphasis on rich color. After the antireligious actions of the French Revolution, the Romantic painters chose religious subjects and so played a role in the great religious revival of the early nineteenth century.

The two leading artists who showed some of these Romantic tendencies before the French Revolution were Fuseli (d. 1825), a Swiss who lived in England, and the English mystic, Blake (d. 1827). Fuseli, known chiefly for his drawings, used fantastic subjects, such as witches at night and nightmares, in which he is a precursor not only of Romanticism but also of Surrealism. He did a series of illustrations for Shakespeare and for Milton's *Paradise Lost*. Blake's paintings and engravings show a preference for subjects from the Bible and from medieval life and thought. His style is a curious blending of the sublime and the puerile. Both Fuseli and his follower, Blake, though unusual in their choice of subjects and in the strange lighting used in their pictures, nonetheless employed classical forms derived from Greek sculpture or the art of Michelangelo. A third Pre-Romantic artist of much greater genius was Goya (d. 1828). His style is a blending of those of the High Renaissance and the Baroque with an amazing realism of his own. Goya lives as a great colorist and, in his drawings and etchings, as a superb creator of caricatures. A group of German painters working in Rome, the Nazarenes, developed a style of religious painting based on Italian art before the High Renaissance. Their pastiches are without originality or life. Later their work inspired that of the Pre-Raphaelite Brotherhood in England.

The main current of Romantic painting is found in France. Before the French Revolution, Greuze (d. 1805) painted sentimental pictures like the "Paralytic Looked After by His Children," and the "Broken Pitcher"; and some of the later work of Fragonard made the same obvious appeal to the emotions. At the same time, Hubert Robert (d. 1808) exploited the poetry of classical ruins, many of them in France; he also painted Gothic ruins, and wreckage made by storms in the gardens of Versailles or by fires and demolitions in Paris. During the French Revolution, an antiquary, Lenoir, gathered together from ruined churches a great museum of medieval sculpture which he called the "Museum of French Monuments"; his collection became a revelation of the beauty of medieval art to a whole generation of Frenchmen then growing up. At the same time, the great gathering of Renaissance painting in the Louvre, much of it looted by Napoleon's agents, revealed to a rising generation of artists the glories of the Venetian painters and of Rubens. Lenoir's collection was broken up in 1816 when the monuments were returned to their original places, but soon the great state museums, for the first time, began to exhibit medieval art. The Louvre opened a gallery of Romanesque and Gothic sculpture in 1824, and, three years later, the superb collection of German primitives assembled by the Boisserée brothers was bought by the King of Bavaria for the Pinakothek of Munich. During this period, most of the governments of western Europe began great programs of restoring medieval buildings, and the completion of the Cathedral of Cologne became a national project to which Germans of all faiths contributed.

The first outstanding achievement of a new generation of French painters was the "Raft of the Medusa" by Géricault (d. 1824), shown in the Paris Salon of 1819. Here was a painting full of movement and color and an open defiance of the tinted bas-reliefs of the school of David. The violent movement, the irregular and unsymmetrical composition, and the strong contrasts of light and shade—though prefigured by "The Pesthouse of Jaffa" by David's pupil, Gros—were so at variance with the artistic traditions of the time that the picture was everywhere regarded as marking a revolution. No wonder that one of David's pupils said to another pupil, "What hand can defend the School of David?" Géricault died at the age of thirty-three, his enormous promise unrealized. In the Salon of 1824 appeared some of the landscapes of Constable, of Corot, and of Delacroix (d. 1863), whose dramatic "Massacre of Chios" the followers of David regarded as "the massacre of painting." Delacroix was, at the time, only twenty-five years old. His painting was already full of action and contrast, and showed the influence of Rubens and Rembrandt, whom Delacroix ranked above Raphael. The *Globe,* a periodical strong for Romantic theories, praised Delacroix for making pictures "truer to life and less academic."

At this time both literature and art were waging war on classical standards in the name of a new definition of beauty. Delacroix never went to Italy, apparently because he feared the influence of Italian painting on his own style. But, while still young, he spent some months in England, studying the methods of painting of his English contemporaries, and he made a long stay in North Africa, where the glowing colors and patriarchal way of life left a deep impression. Delacroix always regarded color as the essential element of painting, whereas David, Ingres, and the Neo-Classical painters considered drawing the heart of painting. For thirty years, Delacroix, who was a careful craftsman and a prodigious worker, continued to paint as though he were fighting. The Neo-Classical painters delighted in pointing out faults in Delacroix's drawing and the rough and uneven surfaces where the paint was put on in broad, slashing strokes, "as though painted with a drunken broom." Delacroix loved remote and often exotic subjects; thoroughly Romantic is his remark, "The most real things I paint are the illusions I create." Among Delacroix's greatest achievements are four great mural paintings he left: one in a chapel of Saint Sulpice, others in the libraries of the Senate and of the Chamber of Deputies, and finally the central panel of the ceiling of the Gallery of Apollo in the Louvre. Though less known than some of his other paintings, these are perhaps his best works. His work is uneven, but on the whole of such a high quality that with him Romanticism in painting became a major achievement. According to Gautier, Delacroix "formed with Victor Hugo and Hector Berlioz the trinity of Romantic art." And Delacroix remains the best representative painter of Romanticism, not only in France, but in Europe.

One of the great achievements of early nineteenth-century Romantic painting was in the field of landscape art. The Neo-Classical painters were even more indifferent to landscape than had been many of the painters of the Baroque Age; they centered their attention on the human figure, and minimized the setting. A revival of the great landscape painting that had flourished in Holland in the seventeenth century began in England in the later eighteenth century. Among a number of painters of landscape, some of whom were water-colorists, the leader was Gainsborough (d. 1788). Having studied the landscapes especially of Hobbema and Rubens, he discovered that he got a live and vibrant effect by applying color in small patches of unmixed hues that are blended by the eye rather than on the palette. Gainsborough found a magic world of beauty in the English countryside. Unfortunately he could find few purchasers of his landscapes, and so many of them remained as sketches done for his own pleasure. They were not views painted directly from nature but compositions designed to evoke and reflect a mood. His discoveries were taken up by younger men, chief of whom were Constable and Turner.

None of the great English landscape painters looked at the world through the eyes of any past artist; each saw the world of nature in his own way. Constable (d. 1837) never went to the Continent, and traveled little in Britain. Most of his life was spent in his native district of Suffolk, and he once said, "I am born to paint my dear old England." For him, the subject was less important than the handling of light and shade. He never hunted, as did Turner, for the exceptional. A river bank or a group of trees under changing skies, and clouds always ready to pour their rain on the eternally green fields—these were all he required to evoke a picture full of poetry and loveliness. Constable's color was often put on in smears and dots and in scrapings of the palette knife. The effect was vibrant and alive, far removed from the smooth shiny surfaces of Neo-Classical painting. In mood and spirit Constable is close to Wordsworth, who declared he would "choose incidents and situations from common life, and would relate them in language really used by men" while he wished, "at the same time to throw over them a certain coloring of the imagination, whereby ordinary things should be presented to the mind in an unusual aspect."

Turner (d. 1851) was much more of an experimenter than Constable, and more Romantic in temperament. He traveled widely on the Continent and became a great admirer of the style of Claude Lorrain. In Turner's later works the forms are dissolved in light, and he seems to be a precursor of Monet and the Impressionists. Turner's subjects were often as dramatic as his color and lighting; whatever title he used for his pictures, it was the grandeur of sunlight and shadow, of mountain and sea, and the vast forces of nature that were at the center of his interests. A German Romantic landscape painter, Friedrich (d. 1840), like Turner, sought unusual lighting effects and contrasts, but he was a less gifted painter than either Constable or Turner. Friedrich's landscapes are interesting chiefly because they reflect many of the moods of German Romantic poetry and music.

While Constable and Turner were becoming known in France, a native school of French landscape painters was at work. Most notable of these was Corot (d. 1875). Though Corot is a leading figure of French Romanticism there is nothing feverish or excessive in his work; he is always well balanced and calm. His early landscapes made in Italy and in various parts of France are remarkable for their fine sense of values and their sensitive and subtle lighting. His later landscapes, where the forms are often left undefined in a sort of haze and the trees are masses in which one cannot distinguish the leaves, are less interesting than either his earlier landscapes or his relatively few paintings of human figures. The new world of beauty opened up by the English and French landscape painters of the early nineteenth century was one of the greatest achievements of the whole Romantic movement.

Sculpture showed the same stylistic currents as painting, though most of the sculptors worked in the Neo-Classical tradition. Canova (d. 1822) occupied in sculpture the place earlier held in painting by David. In his youth, he had been deeply influenced by Winckelmann and Raphael Mengs. His style was also one of a natural reaction against the extravagances of the Baroque and Rococo and an attempt to return to the style of ancient classical sculpture. The aims set were repose of body, impassivity of countenance, and simplicity of composition. Christian subjects were considered less capable of the highest artistic expression than those of classical mythology and history. Canova became the favorite of popes and princes and attracted many sculptors to Rome and to Italy from all over Europe and America. Many of Canova's oversized nudes, with their slick surfaces and relaxed muscles, give the appearance of having been modeled from cadavers. Yet the elegance and sweetness of some of his productions, as in his "Pauline Bonaparte as Venus," have lingering echoes of the Rococo. In their refined sensuality, some of Canova's nudes remind one of Ingres and, in literature, of Keats's "Ode to Psyche" and Poe's "To Helen." Among a large number of sculptors influenced by the Neo-Classical style of Canova, the most important was a Dane, Thorvaldsen (d. 1844), whose work is sometimes graceful but rarely very vital. Neo-Classicism in sculpture remained the dominant trend during the first half, and more, of the nineteenth century in every country, including the United States.

Parallel with Neo-Classicism in sculpture, went a return to the style of Gothic and High Renaissance sculptural styles. During the eighteenth century there had been a revival of Gothic and Renaissance motifs in interior decoration—clocks, chairs, printed cotton fabrics, and wallpaper. Architecture and sculpture were also influenced by these currents. Sculpture was to be influenced by Romanticism less than were painting and architecture. As Gautier wrote: "Of all the arts, that which lends itself least to the expression of the Romantic idea is sculpture. It seems to have received in Antiquity its definite form. What can the sculptor do without his gods and heroes of mythology? Every sculptor is, perforce, classical." More important than this is the fact that it is difficult for sculpture to capture the infinitude, the mystery, and the movement which are at the heart of Romanticism. These could be more easily realized in painting, poetry, and music. The greatest sculptor in the Romantic style was the Frenchman Rude (d. 1855). Like others of his time, he reacted against Neo-Classical aloofness from actuality, and showed a closer observation of nature. Some of the forms used by Rude were Neo-Classical, but he broke with that tradition by the infusion into his designs of great animation and movement, in which he was influenced by Gothic and Renaissance sculpture. His most renowned achievement is the group, "The Departure of Volunteers," on the Arch of Triumph in Paris. The figures are either nude or dressed in Roman armor, but the closely knit composition is instinct with life and movement, the most superb embodiment of which is the Goddess of War flying above the whole group. Rude's sculpture was of great influence on the sculptural styles of the later nineteenth century, on Carpeaux, Rodin, and even Bourdelle, where the sculptors, like Rude himself, gradually moved away from Neo-Classical traditions.

In the second half of the eighteenth century, architecture, like painting and sculpture, turned away from the Baroque and Rococo, and, out of a fresh consideration of classical styles, began to create new architectural forms. For the first time in art there had come to be a clear-cut consciousness of the nature of style, especially of historic styles. Heretofore, the idea in any given period was that there was only one style of art—or at most two—an older one that was bad and a new one that was good. In the later eighteenth century, there appeared, almost simultaneously, a desire to find new forms for architecture in a reconsideration of certain historic styles and, a little later, an urge to create an entirely new style largely freed from all relation to any past architectural style. The revival of classical styles, one current of this age of change, differs from earlier revivals of classical art in the degree of accuracy of its imitation and adaptation. Ever since the Early Renaissance there had been a great enthusiasm for all forms of Roman art, and something of both the spirit and vocabulary of the classical past had been recaptured, especially in sculpture and architecture. But both the spirit and the form of Roman art had been modified to suit the changing taste of one period after another. Now, under Neo-

Classicism, which appeared in the latter half of the eighteenth century, success is justified by archeological accuracy, and, at the same time, a Greek inspiration challenges and often supplants the Roman.

The rediscovery of the qualities of Greek art stems in part from the writing of Winckelmann and, to an even larger degree, from the influence of a long series of publications on Greek architecture already referred to. These new works, with their elaborately engraved plates, evoked much interest during the middle and later eighteenth century. Hitherto the fund of knowledge concerning ancient buildings, aside from the details of the classic orders, was surprisingly small, and at the same time there was a marked tendency not to consider ancient architecture except as it was set forth in a few treatises, especially those of Vitruvius, Alberti, and Palladio. It now became the fashion of both amateurs and professional architects to own the sumptuous new publications on ancient architecture. Educated men came to know the houses and public buildings of Pompeii and Herculaneum and their decoration, the Greek ruins of Athens, Southern Italy, and Asia Minor, and the great Roman buildings of Syria, Dalmatia, and of Rome itself as they had not been known before. Among the most popular of these books were the series of volumes by Piranesi which gave a new and glamorous version of Roman architecture and of the Greek monuments at Paestum. In all his plates, the classical buildings are greatly exaggerated in size in comparison with the small human figures set beside them, and thus they seem to be the work of giants. Flaxman confessed that he found "the ruins of Rome less striking than I had become accustomed to suppose after seeing the prints of Piranesi." Piranesi always insisted that Roman architecture was superior to Greek. Through the publications of Piranesi and others it was found that Roman architecture was much more varied than had been supposed. In many of these eighteenth-century books on classical architecture, it was not considered enough to present these ruins as they were; the authors attempted to restore what they thought were the original appearances of the buildings. Later on, during the Greek Revolt, Byron and many of the great Romantic poets made all things Greek very popular and helped to create an artistic furor which it was impossible to withstand.

At the same time that Winckelmann was attacking the unclassical aspects of Baroque and Rococo art, there arose an extended attack on the whole Baroque tradition in the name of reason in a pair of works of a French priest, Laugier. His *Essay on Architecture* (1753) and *Observations on Architecture* (1755) were very widely circulated. Laugier not only attacked the Baroque style and the light and whimsical graces of Rococo but went on to set up positive principles of architectural style based on use and reason. He opposed the employment of classical orders as decoration; he would not allow the employment of pilasters and attached columns; and he insisted that columns should only be used to support part of the basic structure. "One should never," he declared, "put anything in a building for which one cannot give a solid reason." He also believed that new and unhistorical forms could be used in architecture, such forms to be based on the application of reason and logic to the problem in hand. Later other architectural writers, such as Boulée (d. 1799) and Ledoux (d. 1806), sketched designs for buildings that used no historical architectural forms but were built up of globes, pyramids, and squares. In this, they are the forerunners of later functional architecture. Laugier goes on to present elaborate plans for a whole city, where gates, streets, and squares are to be laid out, not to honor royalty, but for convenience as functional parts of the machinery of city life. Residential quarters should be placed in well-ventilated situations; hospitals should be placed upstream from a town so that polluted drainage would flow away from them; and he goes on to particularize about many other details. Finally, Laugier regarded Greek architecture as superior to Roman. The influence of these writers and designers is hard to estimate, but it seems to have been great. Sir John Soane, the great revolutionary architect of England at the beginning of the nineteenth century, kept a large supply of Laugier's essays and gave copies to his friends and assistants. Boulée and Ledoux designs also had wide circulation.

Among the first achievements of the classical revival were the severe and beautifully proportioned buildings of Gabriel (d. 1782) in France. He used rectangular openings and a simple combination of columns and pilasters. Both in his exteriors and in his interior designs, there is a quiet refinement and a studied simplicity in moldings and decoration. The same reaction against the Rococo was shown in other countries; and everywhere in later eighteenth-century architecture and interior decoration there appeared rectangular forms, simplicity of surface and decoration, and archeological accuracy of detail. The effect is often cold and dry. These were shown in the Panthéon in Paris and the later Madeleine; the Brandenburg Gate in Berlin, modeled on the

monumental entrance to the Acropolis in Athens; and in the buildings
of Robert Adam in England. The straight line everywhere replaced
the Rococo curve. Refinement and repose were sometimes sought at
the expense of strength and vitality. Moldings and other decorations
frequently looked pulled out and thin, as though smallness were somehow itself a virtue.

As the Neo-Classical style continued into the early nineteenth century it became much heavier and more monumental, and the style
known as "Empire" tried to recapture Roman magnificence and
grandeur. Among the great monuments of early nineteenth-century
classical revival are the Arch of Triumph in Paris; Schinkel's Old
Museum in Berlin—Schinkel designed buildings both in classical and
in Gothic style as did many other architects of the time—and a series
of buildings designed by Von Klenze in Munich; the British Museum
and Soane's Bank of England in London; and the Capitol in Washington. Many of the nineteenth-century classical revival buildings use
the heavy Doric order, columns without bases. But just as classical
architecture had appeared in many forms—especially Roman architecture—the classical revival architecture exists in confusing and prolific
variety. Some is Greek in inspiration, some Roman, and some mixes
elements from both historic traditions. After 1800, the Neo-Classical
movement in architecture spread over the entire Western world with
a surprising speed. Some looked upon classical architecture as the expression of republicanism; others, as Napoleon, considered it the architecture of imperial power. In great public buildings, in smaller business
buildings, and in private houses, the style was studied and exploited
until architects came to have an excellent sense of what the style could
do and do well. There is a dignity and restraint, a wise fitness of form
to use, and a severe harmony that combine to create buildings of extraordinary beauty. The achievements of Neo-Classical architecture of the
period from 1750 to 1850, both in Europe and the United States, still
await a proper understanding and appreciation.

While the Neo-Classical style was slowly unfolding in every country
from Spain to Russia, a Gothic revival was also under way. The
apologists for this revival, especially in England and Germany, believed, wrongly, as we now know, that Gothic was in each country
not a foreign style as were all classical styles but a national creation.
Later, in the midst of the great Christian revival that followed the
excesses of the French Revolution, the apologists for Gothic presented

the style as Christian in contrast to the pagan styles of Greece and Rome. In England, the Gothic style had never died out. Wren, Vanbrugh, and other Baroque architects designed some buildings in the Gothic style. Vanbrugh, though he had designed Blenheim Palace, for his own house introduced a castellated round tower and other Gothic features. Horace Walpole introduced a new taste for Gothic in his Strawberry Hill. Here were crenelations mounted irrelevantly on top of exterior walls and, within, elaborate fan vaulting made not of stone but of lath and plaster with mirrors placed here and there among the multiple ribs of the ceiling. Fireplaces and wall paneling were carefully copied—often in plaster—from engravings of medieval tombs and choir screens. With Walpole, as with most of the Gothic revival of the eighteenth century, the interest lay in decorative features of Gothic, and in any possible picturesque qualities, but not at all in the structural principles of Gothic. Gothic details were used as a stage setting and were often frankly a sham. The eighteenth-century taste for Gothic in England was undoubtedly stimulated by the vogue of the Gothic novel. Books like *The Haunted Priory, The Bleeding Nun of Lindenberg,* and Walpole's own *Castle of Otranto* presented lurid stories laid in settings of baronial halls and decayed abbeys with mysterious trap doors, sliding panels, creaking gates, and sepulchral voices. The heroines were innocent and delicate, the heroes reckless and dashing.

Coming over into the early nineteenth century, one discovers that the true nature of Gothic is becoming better understood, and buildings such as the Parliament Buildings in London, designed by Barry and Pugin in Perpendicular Gothic in the 1830's, are more geniune and show a real understanding of the essential qualities of Gothic style. The Neo-Gothic style continued to be popular in the nineteenth century, and while some fine churches and public buildings were built, they are on the whole inferior both to the contemporary Neo-Classical buildings and to the Gothic buildings in the twentieth century. This seems to have been due to the long study and association of classical forms since the fifteenth century and thus a much better understanding of what could be done with classical designs than of how to use Gothic forms. And not until the twentieth century was Gothic architecture handled with anything like sureness of touch.

An unfortunate aspect of the simultaneous revival of both classical and Gothic architectural styles was that other historical styles, from

Egyptian on down, were also revived and were often badly mis-
handled; and the various styles were often hopelessly mixed together.
In the eighteenth-century royal gardens at Kew in England, William
Chambers built a large number of garden pavilions. The majority of
these were Neo-Classical, but they also included a Chinese House of
Confucius, an Alhambra and a Mosque in Islamic style, a Gothic
cathedral, a huge "Chinese pagoda" (which alone survives), and,
finally, some elaborate artificial classical ruins. At Chateaubriand's
country house, La Vallée aux Loups, which was originally a small
brick house, an early nineteenth-century owner built a portico supported by two columns of black marble and two caryatids of white
marble; of it he said, "I remembered I had passed through Athens!"
At one end of the house, he added simulated medieval battlements.
The eclecticism of later nineteenth-century art was already under way.
Today, the house is a government lunatic asylum.

3. Literature

Romanticism left a much deeper impression on literature than on the
fine arts. It is a strange paradox that the writers of the century between
1750 and 1850 often showed a much greater knowledge and understanding of classical literature—they were steeped especially in Greek
letters—than was evident among the writers of any earlier period.
These writers drew copiously from the many themes and forms of the
classical writers; but the fundamental moods of classical literature,
those of harmony, restraint, and repose, they usually rejected. In classical literature, it was the Greek heritage and the dynamic Dionysiac
element that poets like Goethe and Shelley and many of their contemporaries most admired and imitated. As nearly all the important
writers of the period were profoundly affected by the basic attitudes
of Romanticism, it is hard to find many men of letters who may be
classed as Neo-Classical as we use the concept in the fine arts. The
four most outstanding of these Neo-Classical writers were Chénier,
Hölderlin, Alfieri, and Landor, none of them men of the first rank.

The mother of Chénier (d. 1794) was a Greek who taught him the
language as a child. He forged for himself a Greek soul, and he looked
at nature and humanity from an ancient point of view. Though his
language is French, much of his thought is Greek; and even when his
ideas belong primarily to the modern world, they are expressed in a

classic Greek form. His idyls, eclogues, elegies, epistles, and odes are thoroughly Greek in spirit, and some of his shorter lyrics read like translations of Greek originals. His finest works are his pastoral idyls in the style of Theocritus and, next, his love elegies modeled on the Roman poets, Tribullus, Propertius, and Ovid, whom Chénier surpasses in intensity of emotion. With his delicate taste, he could transmute effects from the classics without ever seeming merely to copy them. His poetry somewhat resembles that of Keats, though it lacks the fundamental Romanticism even of Keats's poems on Greek subjects. Chénier was guillotined; his career as a poet ended in midstream.

The German poet Hölderlin, though he lived until 1843, ceased writing in 1802, when he became insane. He drew his inspiration from Greece, and his best verses have some of the timeless quality of antiquity. The dominant themes of his poetry show a passionate love of everything Greek and a pantheistic belief in the oneness of man and of nature which show an attachment to some of the ideas of Romanticism. His poetry is uneven, but the best of his classic odes are breathtaking. Hölderlin had a great penetration into human motives, and this, with the beauty of form of his lyrics, long outlived Romanticism and has been a vital force in the literature of the twentieth century.

Predominantly Roman in inspiration, Alfieri (d. 1803) was a proud, passionate, and undisciplined Italian noble. Largely self-taught, he steeped himself in Latin literature, especially in Seneca, and in Plutarch's *Lives;* and, at the age of fifty, he taught himself Greek. His favorite theme in his twenty-two tragedies is resistance to tyranny; he was always an ardent believer in personal and political liberty, and he wanted to teach men to be strong, upright, magnanimous, and worthy of freedom. His tragedies are the best ever written in Italian. Alfieri pruned away all features not essential to the essence of his plays. He avoided local color, used only a few characters, worked within the three dramatic unities, and observed the ideas of decorum in his choice of royal and princely characters. His style is both condensed and harsh, even archaic in effect; his vigor, at times, degenerates into bombast and his conciseness often leads to obscurity; but at his best, there is a Roman force, directness, and simplicity in his effects.

The verse and prose of Landor (d. 1864) are more like the best Greek literature than is the work of any other English writer of the time. Some of the great English classical scholars, such as Bentley and Porson and their successors, had taught Landor to see that behind

Latin literature lay the greater literature of Greece, and many of his lyrics and his *Imaginary Conversations* are close imitations of Greek poetry and prose. The subjects of the *Imaginary Conversations* range from ancient Greece to his own day, but the style is taken mainly from Plato and Lucian. In his shorter lyrics Landor combines compression of statement and high polish of form with an intensity of content that is all very close to the Greek lyric.

The story of Romanticism in literary style falls naturally into two periods, one of Pre-Romanticism from the middle of the eighteenth century, or earlier, and one of Romanticism proper, the dividing point coming about 1790 or 1800. The eighteenth-century lead in starting new literary currents, which, from varied sources, converged later into the main stream of Romanticism, was taken by British and German writers, though the most influential Pre-Romantic author was the French-speaking Swiss, Rousseau. No single Pre-Romantic writer, however, presented all the aspects of later Romanticism; each developed one or sometimes more of the concepts that were to appear in new combinations later on.

A new emphasis was laid on emotion. To be virtuous and free one must listen to the heart rather than to reason, and, in relations with others, one needs sympathy even more than rational understanding. There is, at the same time, a growing attack on all rules in literature and a belief that individual genius is more important than taste or any form of conformity. New sources of literary material were discovered from the Middle Ages, among Oriental peoples, and in the noble savages of North America. The ancient poetry of the Germanic and Celtic peoples—including the forged works of "Ossian"—medieval lyric poetry, chivalric romances, and the plays of Shakespeare, which were without benefit of the rules of Aristotle, all came into vogue. In this re-evaluation of literary traditions there is always a strong movement that, for patriotic reasons, turns to national traditions rather than to the literary legacy of Greece and Rome. The Pre-Romantic writers clearly preferred a style that was fresh and direct rather than one that was polished and sophisticated. And finally, they praised the wisdom and happiness of those in the middle and lower classes, especially of the peasants on the land who lived a simple life. Indeed, nearly everything that earlier classically minded ages had either rejected or ignored now came into fashion as subjects for literary treatment and as moods to be cultivated by the writer.

The Pre-Romantic writers were very unequal in talent and very diverse in temperament. Moreover, they worked largely in isolation from one another and, unlike the later Romantics, did not form groups, recognize any leadership, or issue periodicals. For example, in the two decades between 1756 and 1776, there appeared, independently, Joseph Warton's *Essay on Pope,* Diderot's *Essays on Dramatic Poetry,* Young's *Conjectures on Original Composition,* the letters of Lessing on the wonders of Shakespeare, Hurd's book on chivalry, and Goethe's defense of Shakespeare. Usually two currents appeared side by side; on the one hand were the critics and theoretical writers, on the other were the poets, playwrights, and authors of novels. A few writers belonged to both groups.

The Warton brothers, in a series of critical works, praised medieval and Renaissance English poetry, especially that of Spenser. In the *Pleasures of Melancholy,* Thomas Warton wrote:

> Oh lead me, Queen sublime, to solemn glooms
> Congenial with my soul, to cheerless shades,
> To ruin'd seats, to twilight cells and bowers. . . .
> Beneath yon ruin'd abbey's mossgrown piles
> Oft let me sit at twilight hour of eve,
> When through some western window the pale moon
> Pours her long-levelled rule of streaming light.

Everything medieval was exalted, at the same time, in Hurd's *Letters on Chivalry and the Poetry of the Middle Ages,* and the public was treated to Percy's popular anthology, *Reliques of Ancient English Poetry,* where the chief role is played by the ballads. About this time appeared Young's *Conjectures on Original Composition,* which maintained that great poetry comes not from following rules but from the promptings of the heart of a genius. And to add to the enthusiasm for all things medieval and primitive, a Swiss, Mallet, published in 1755–56 an anthology of French translations of early Scandinavian poetry; this work was soon known all over Europe, and the poems were widely imitated, especially in England and Germany.

During the same period in Britain, a series of imaginative works showed the changes in literary tastes. As early as 1726 to 1730, Thomson (d. 1748) had published his pastoral verses *The Seasons* with long and elaborate descriptions of country landscapes. It is hard to believe that Thomson's work is contemporary with that of Pope, so very different are the men in both mood and style. In the next decade, Edward

Young (d. 1765) composed his long dissertations in verse, *Night Thoughts,* praising the virtues of solitude and the beauties of the night and the poetry of tombs. Young delighted in thrilling, mortuary images—

> The knell, the shroud, the mattock, and the grave;
> The deep damp vault, the darkness, and the worm.

The book was translated twenty-four times and into twelve languages. Richardson (d. 1761) showed the virtues of the middle class and an effective way to treat emotional situations in his novels in the form of letters, *Pamela* and *Clarissa Harlowe.* And the Scotch writer Macpherson (d. 1796) produced his famous forgeries *Fingal* and *Temora,* which were supposed to have been composed by a blind Celtic bard, "Ossian." To many of his contemporaries the poems of Ossian seemed to represent the work of a northern Homer, supposedly of the third century A.D. Their settings are filled with the poetry of twilight and moonlight, of waterfalls, and of generally mournful landscapes. Dr. Johnson loathed the writings of Macpherson, and said, "Any man might write such stuff forever, if he would abandon his mind to it"; but the younger writers, both in Britain and on the Continent, adored and imitated him. All of these theoretical and imaginative works circulated widely on the Continent, either in the original or in translations.

At home in Britain, other writers, who were to be less known on the Continent, renewed English literature with new themes and new styles of writing: Gray with his "Runic Odes," inspired by ancient Scandinavian literature, and his "Elegy in a Country Churchyard," which combined the praise of the lowly with the poetry of the tomb; Beattie with "The Minstrel" in praise of the communion with nature in a mood that prefigures Wordsworth; Cowper and Crabbe with pictures of the daily life of those close to the soil; Blake with his mystic reveries; and, finally, Burns with his love of the lowly and of animals. A number of attitudes of Romanticism are summed up in Burns's lines:

> Gie me, ae spark o' nature's fire,
> That's a' the learning I desire;
> Then, tho' I drudge thro' dub an' mire at pleugh or cart,
> My muse, tho' hamely in attire, may touch the heart.

At the same time, novelists and playwrights, following the lead of Richardson, produced a series of novels and plays on middle- and lower-class life, full of sentiment and tears. A number of novelists, such as

Horace Walpole and Mrs. Radcliffe, fed a taste for Gothic tales of dark castles, midnight escapes, and shining heroism, all given a somewhat sensational medieval setting. Mrs. Radcliffe adds other Romantic notes: "Nature and beauty," she declares, "soften the heart like notes of sweet music, and inspire that delicious melancholy that no person who has felt it once would resign for the gayest pleasures." As a result of these critical and imaginative works, literary taste in Britain profoundly changed during the course of the eighteenth century, and the way was prepared for the great flowering of letters that appeared with Wordsworth, Coleridge, and Scott, and a little later with Byron, Shelley, and Keats.

Parallel with this change in the intellectual and literary climate of Britain, and deeply influenced by it, were a series of similar changes in the German literary landscape. German Pre-Romanticism is slightly later in its development than the parallel movement in England, and nearly everywhere it shows English influence. About the middle of the eighteenth century there began a remarkable revival of German literature, which, for several centuries, had not been outstanding and which, in the earlier eighteenth century, had been dominated by French models. The general cultural situation in Germany differed from that in England and France. Class differences were more marked; pedantry prevailed in cultural circles; and the whole atmosphere was more conservative, stuffier, and more set against any new ideas. The upper classes used only French and despised the vernacular which, in turn, was divided into a multitude of dialects with no one clearly dominant.

The *Messias* by Klopstock (d. 1803), a story of the last years of the life of Jesus written somewhat in the style of Milton, was widely heralded as a new beginning in German letters—a beginning that moved German letters away from French Baroque classicism. There soon appeared a greater genius, Lessing (d. 1781), the first German writer in centuries to attract attention beyond the borders of his own country. Lessing is difficult to classify as a Neo-Classicist or a Romantic, but, in two particulars, he gave the Romantic movement in Germany a new direction. In his remarkable critical writings, he glorified the style of Shakespeare and insisted that Shakespeare came nearer to following the meaning of Aristotle's ideas on the drama than Corneille or Voltaire. And in his middle and later life, he wrote a series of plays on middle-class life, greatest of which was *Minna von Barnhelm,* based on similar English plays, on the middle-class French dramas of Diderot, and, above all, on the early novels of Richardson.

In his *Laokoon,* Lessing attacked the Renaissance and Baroque theory of *ut pictura poesis*—that poetry and painting were alike. He, in turn, maintained their essential difference. His critical writings had a great influence on Germany and, then, on the rest of Europe. And from his time on, Germany produced, for several generations, the most important of European critical writings on literature. The breaking-away from French literary ideas was in part stimulated by the brilliant victories of Frederick the Great over France in the Seven Years' War. Thus, in Germany, Lessing both helped to break the tyranny of French critical ideas and showed, more clearly than earlier German writers, how to give new directions to creative literature. In 1750, when Lessing began to write, Germany had little vital literature; thirty years later it had a flourishing literature. Goethe had published his *Götz* and his *Werther,* and Schiller had published his *Robbers,* and other works of nearly equal importance had appeared. And, in twenty more years, writers like Scott and Coleridge in England and Mme de Staël in France were proclaiming the greatness of German literature and philosophy. The resistance toward recognizing this renaissance of German letters was, however, still strong. Frederick the Great, in the midst of this great revival, jeered at the whole thing. "In order to convince yourself of the bad taste that reigns in Germany," he wrote, "you have only to frequent the theater. There you will see the abominable plays of Shakespeare, and the whole audience transported with delight by these absurd farces, fit only for the savages of Canada. They sin against every rule of the drama. Now we have a *Götz* appearing, a detestable imitation of those wretched English plays, and the pit applauds it enthusiastically."

Among a number of German writers who contributed to the growth of Romanticism in Germany, the next most outstanding leader is Herder (d. 1803). In a series of essays and of longer critical works, Herder is much more militant than Lessing. Instead of critical analysis, we now find glowing appreciations as well as bitter denunciations. Herder insists on the supreme rights of genius that should work independently of models. And he contrasts the spontaneous "natural poetry" of the Bible, Homer, Shakespeare, "Ossian," and folk poetry with the poetry based on rules. Here Herder was influenced by the primitivism of Rousseau, but he went beyond Rousseau in making a penetrating analysis of Western culture which he divided into two main streams— one coming from the Mediterranean, which was serene, balanced, and very form-conscious, and an equally valuable one coming from the Germanic north, which was cloudy, meditative, form-breaking, and boundlessly striving. No two literatures, moreover, can ever be alike when they spring from different surroundings; and any attempt to model one literature too closely on another is unnatural and pernicious. Everywhere in literature there should be emotion, spontaneity, and originality. German literature and culture should seek its development primarily from its own sources, and then from sources, as those of England, that are in harmony with its own.

Herder's essays, *German Way and German Art,* of 1773 have been called the Manifesto of German Storm and Stress. In his *Voices of the Nations in Song,* Herder published an anthology of European folk songs inspired by Percy's collection. And in Herder's greatest work, *Ideas on the Philosophy of the History of Mankind,* he made the first basic analysis of nationalism and, at the same time, laid down a program for reviving national feeling through schools, books, and newspapers using the national language. Herder's leading disciple was Goethe, to whom, as a young man, he introduced the glories of Gothic art (which he wrongly believed to be German in origin), of folk literature, of Shakespeare, and of "Ossian." To the young and impressionable Goethe, Herder quoted Young, who had declared, "Genius can set us right in composition, without the rules of the learned," and again, "The less we copy the renowned ancients the more we shall resemble them." Shakespeare, to Herder, was the typical Heaven-inspired genius whose work was not regulated by rules but created out of the fulness of the poet's own being. There was hardly a branch of thought Herder did not enrich, though his writing did lack clarity and precision and tended to be fragmentary and incomplete. But the wide range of Herder's thought and his daring originality made him a dominant influence on the growth of Romanticism in Germany.

The most gifted member of a group of poets at Göttingen who drew inspiration from Klopstock, Lessing, and Herder was Bürger (d. 1794). His famous ballad, "Lenore," inspired by the English ballads in Percy's *Reliques,* with its witches dancing in the moonlight, seemed to embody many of the ideas of the Pre-Romantic theorists in verses that attained something of Shakespearean sublimity. In the original and in countless translations Bürger's ballad made the tour of Europe. More than any work that had come out of German Romanticism it awakened foreign interest to the changes in German literature. It exerted a more widespread influence than perhaps any other short poem in the literature of the world. And certainly it helped everywhere to call the Romantic movement into life.

Herder had a great influence on a group of younger German writers whose work is collectively called the *Sturm und Drang* school, a name taken from the title of a play by a minor member of the group. Their work marked a revolt of youth against what they considered the deadening cold of rationalism, of antiquated rules in literature, and of intolerable traditions and conventions in life. Among these young writers the favorite words were "originality," "genius," and "freedom," and their favorite writer was Rousseau. Hence the term *Geniezeit* is often used for their period. These writers eagerly flouted traditional literary canons and attacked much of the social, moral, and political order. They had a titanic defiance of all authority, a sense of union with nature, a great enthusiasm for more primitive ages, an interest in the common people and the whole culture and idiom of the masses. They were given to spontaneous outbursts of feeling and passion, which they often expressed extravagantly. This sort of emotional revolt was in the air in Germany. At Göttingen, two good burghers, bursting with health, are said to have greeted each other with the remarks, "Have you shed any tears today?" and "How are your heart pangs?" Klinger, the author of the play *Sturm und Drang,* wrote: "I am torn by passions which would crush everything around me. Each moment I should like to pulverize the whole human race, and then fling myself into the chaos!" Strange currents of occultism flourished at the same time in Germany, especially esoteric sects like the Rosicrucians and the Illuminati, who denounced both the orthodox Catholics and Protestants and the rationalistic followers of the French philosophes. They wished to eradicate abuses, and to spread charity, tolerance, and the love of God. To get converts, they sometimes used hypnotism.

The first notable achievement of *Sturm und Drang* was a play, *Götz von Berlichingen* of 1773, by the young Goethe (d. 1832). The play is based on a tale of the revolt of a minor noble of the sixteenth century against centralized authority. The hero is a great-hearted champion of individual freedom struggling against the wiles of petty courtiers, and dying for a lost cause. All the dramatic unities are disregarded; the scene changes fifty-five times, involving over thirty different stage settings. From a number of angles, the play is a monstrosity. As Herder said of all this looseness of construction, "Shakespeare has quite spoiled you!" Yet the play has a vividness which comes from persons of all classes speaking a stirring and realistic language; it all gives a picture of an age glowing with life. The next year, Goethe amazed his age with the publication of his novel *The Sorrows of Young Werther* wherein a sensitive and morbidly introspective youth pours forth in letters the story of his hopeless love for his friend's betrothed, and then commits suicide. The basic conflict underlying Werther's *Weltschmerz* is between existing conditions and an unwillingness to accept any restraints. The world does not understand Werther and wounds him at every turn. Such *Weltschmerz*, which the French called *mal du siècle*, toward the end of the eighteenth century became so common as to seem almost epidemic. The work was widely read in Germany and immediately translated into a number of European languages. The novel threatened to swamp the common sense of Europe, as translations, imitations, and parodies appeared in every European language. At one stroke it gave Goethe an international reputation. Indeed, Goethe's *Werther* is the first European book to be translated into Chinese. Goethe, at the same time, began to publish a long series of lyric poems to which he continued to add in later life; these lyrics are among the greatest achievements of the whole age in European letters. But none of Goethe's other early plays, though they are superior in quality to his *Götz,* attracted the same attention.

Schiller (d. 1805), a second member of the *Sturm und Drang* group and a poet ten years younger than Goethe, first won fame through his play *The Robbers* of 1781. The play, inspired in part by his reading of Shakespeare and Rousseau, is full of youthful fire and fury, tempered by idealism, and portrays a noble-minded hero who defies the law as leader of a robber band. Schiller's hero is an individualist, an idealist, and a man of feeling who fights cynical rationalism and materialism. In the play, the tyranny of princes and of social conventions is roundly denounced. *The Robbers* is definitely the work of a man who understands the theater and stage effects better than Goethe did at the beginning of his career as a dramatist. The dramatic power of the play is very marked; it can hold an audience today as can no other of Schiller's plays. Though it contains some exaggeration and bombast, it has scenes of unforgettable beauty and grandeur. "If ever we may expect a German Shakespeare, this then is the man," wrote one of the leading critics of the day. The play established Schiller's reputation, not only in Germany, but in all Europe. By temperament Schiller was a preacher and reformer, though at the same time he was always a great literary artist.

Schiller's next plays, especially *Don Carlos* of 1787, are much better organized than his earlier works; Schiller declared it was necessary to find a midde ground between the English Renaissance drama and that of the French seventeenth century. *Don Carlos* is usually regarded as marking the end of *Sturm und Drang* and the beginning of a more restrained period in German letters.

Somewhat earlier, in 1775, Goethe accepted a call to an important position at the court in Weimar, and a different spirit began to pervade his writing. This change was partly due to the fact that greater responsibilities matured his outlook on life; to the restraining influences of an able woman, Frau von Stein; to his extended scientific studies in botany and anatomy in which he discovered that the great changes in nature take place by slow evolution, not by revolution; and to his deeper study of classical letters and civilization (partly inspired by reading Winckelmann), which culminated in his famous Italian sojourn of 1786 to 1788. Schiller now came more under Goethe's influence, and under that of classical civilization. Also, the philosophy of Kant, Schiller's study of the Dutch Revolt and of the Thirty Years' War, and the events of the French Revolution all taught Schiller that not only do tyrants endanger freedom, but that shortsighted rebels are an equal threat to liberty. Schiller became convinced that men should never strive merely for an outward liberty but also for an inner freedom, that is, the will power to restrain themselves. Without such restraint in individuals even the most successful outer revolution is doomed to failure. Schiller also plunged into a deeper study of Greek and Latin and French classical literature; he translated parts of Euripides and Virgil, and the whole of Racine's *Phèdre,* into German blank verse. Though both Goethe and Schiller maintained many of their earlier ideas and attitudes, their writing became less exuberant. German literary historians have called these middle and later years of Goethe and Schiller the "Classical Age" of German literature. This, however, should not obscure the fact that, though both writers modified the style and subject matter of their works, they still belong to the great movement of European Romanticism; for behind all their thinking lay a deep distrust of rationalism and of Newton's concept of a world machine and a profound belief in a dynamic and organic view of man, of nature, and of the universe. Even the most classical poem of Schiller, "The Gods of Greece," a lament for all the world has lost in replacing the supernatural world of ancient Greece by a lifeless scientific materialism, is Romantic in its basic point of view.

The growing restraint in Schiller's views and the greater influence of classical literature are apparent in the second half of *Don Carlos,* completed in 1787. Schiller's first play in blank verse shows a marked shift of interest from the hero's egotistical quarrel with his father to the career of a nobleman who is engaged in an idealistic fight for the principle of human freedom. As a result of this sudden shift in emphasis, the play lacks unity. In subsequent plays—three plays on the life of Wallenstein, and *Maria Stuart, The Maid of Orleans, The Bride of Messina,* and *William Tell*—Schiller displays a unity of effect and a solidity of structure in both style and thought that give him first rank among German dramatists. Though Schiller wrote some substantial historical prose works, and held the position of a professor of history at the University of Jena, he did not, in his historical plays, hesitate to alter the facts. In *Maria Stuart* his sympathy is overwhelmingly with Mary Stuart, and he is unfair to Elizabeth; and in *The Maid of Orleans* the heroine at the end, quite against the facts of history, dies gloriously on the field of battle. In *The Bride of Messina* Schiller goes so far in imitating Sophocles as to use a chorus. Besides his plays and prose histories, Schiller wrote a series of important critical and philosophical essays, and some of the finest lyrics in the German language. His early death in 1805 cut him off in the midst of his most creative years.

The change to a more sober and classical view of man's destiny in Goethe's writings is evident in the last scenes of his *Egmont,* begun in 1775 and finished in Italy in 1787. Egmont does not die futilely as did Götz and Werther, for he realizes that in his death he is one of the liberators of Holland. *Iphigenie,* which appeared the same year as *Egmont,* was Goethe's first work in blank verse. He used the story of Euripides very freely, and strove successfully for a synthesis of ancient Greece and modern Germany in both style and idea. Though Goethe was now much occupied with managing the theater at Weimar, his literary and scientific output was enormous. *Tasso* tells Goethe's version of the life of the unbalanced Italian poet and of Antonio, the realistic diplomat and courtier; with each of these two Goethe in turn identifies himself. The play is classic in form, and of great psychological penetration in its analysis of character. *Iphigenie* and *Tasso,* with their simplicity of plot and characterization, their restraint, the harmonious flow of their verse, and their insistence on humane ideals, represent a striking reappropriation of much of the essence of Greek literature. The *Roman Elegies* are outspokenly pagan in content and classical in form; also classical in a Homeric style is the tale of simple village life, *Hermann und Dorothea.* Goethe was a prolific writer, and he continued to pour out lyrics, plays, and novels up to the very end of his long life in 1832. His last two great works are *Wilhelm Meister,* a novel which appeared in two parts, years apart, and his great philosophic drama, *Faust,* the first part of which was published in 1808, while the second half appeared only in 1832. In the second part of *Faust,* as Dante said in the *Paradiso,* Goethe tried "to put into words things difficult even to think." Goethe opposed the course that Romanticism took with the younger writers, feeling that its irresponsible and unbridled outbursts, its vagueness, its lack of stamina, and its easy surrender to Catholicism were signs of weakness and morbidity.

The most important figure in Pre-Romanticism in France, and the most influential writer of the whole of European Pre-Romanticism was Rousseau (d. 1778). Out of a very disordered life—in nearly every undertaking he emerged as unsuccessful, living much of the time on the fringes of society—Rousseau evolved the concept that man is by nature good and has been corrupted by society and its institutions. Hence, he voiced his belief in instinct, emotion, and sentiment as superior to reason, his passion for wild nature, his ideal of the simple life, his disdain for most human institutions, and his morality of the heart. In 1750, Rousseau first attracted attention by his *Discourse on the Influence of Learning and Art,* which undertook to show that so-called progress in letters, society, and civilization had only served to pervert the initial goodness of man. His most characteristic works, which contain most of his basic ideas, are *Émile,* a treatise on education; *La nouvelle Héloïse,* a novel that painted the perfect love and shows the influence of Richardson; and *Confessions,* where he exhibits his instability and lack of balance. Rousseau had a greater range of influence than any writer of the eighteenth century, and his voluminous writings affected literary style, general aesthetics, ethics, political and social ideas, education, psychology, and religious thought. As a stylist, he worked a revolution, using words less as counters for ideas than as means of evoking emotions. Though he wrote entirely in prose, Rousseau should be regarded as a poet rather than as a philosopher.

Goethe, in his autobiography, said of Rousseau and Diderot, "They pointed to nature and urged us to turn from art and follow her." Diderot (d. 1784), a year younger than Rousseau, shared some of the same ideas. He belongs in the history of Romanticism because of his development of the novel and short story, and also of the drama of middle-class life, called in France *la comédie larmoyante* and in Germany *das bürgerliche Trauerspiel*. In both cases, the initial influence came from England. It is interesting to note that Diderot wrote an "Éloge de Richardson," and that, in turn, Lessing translated Diderot's middle-class plays into German. There is also a hearty realism in Diderot that relates him to Rabelais and to Balzac. Like Rousseau, he believed in sentiment and nature, and the natural goodness of man. To him all knowledge is entirely based on the senses and all truth is relative. He began as a cautious Deist, and ended as a frank materialist and an atheist. Diderot's style is one of great verve, a mixture of vividness and rapidity, though his work was too often hurried and uneven.

The last two French writers of Pre-Romanticism, Mme de Staël and Chateaubriand, belonged to a younger generation than Rousseau and Diderot, and both became influential after the storm of the French Revolution had abated, and Napoleon had restored order to France. Mme de Staël (d. 1817) was, in part, detached from the French scene; she was born of Swiss parents and was married to a Swedish nobleman. This gave her a more broadly European rather than strictly French outlook. Later, when the German critic August Wilhelm Schlegel became the tutor of her children, and she had traveled in Germany, she fell under the influence of the ideas of German Romanticism. She wove many of Rousseau's ideas and some of her own into several Romantic novels that were widely read all over Europe. Her greatest influence on Romanticism, however, came from her critical works. In *De la littérature* she attacked the tyranny of classical literary doctrines and set up the ideal of relativism in literature, pointing out, as had Herder, the great differences in national literary traditions. Mme de Staël preferred the literature of northern Europe to that of the South; the qualities of the northern literature, she declared, are courage, melancholy, metaphysical brooding, and mysticism—all shown in "Ossian," Shakespeare, and Milton. She also lays a new emphasis on the relations of literature to manners, religion, and laws, and, in turn, the effects of literature on these same social forces. She is definitely with the moderns in setting the achievements of Rome above those of Greece, and those of the French eighteenth century above the accomplishments of the French seventeenth century, because, in each case, one is later than the other. Finally, Mme de Staël insisted that modern literature must be national and Christian, that it must become aware of its roots in the Middle Ages, and that neither rules nor models should cramp spontaneity and individuality.

Mme de Staël's contrast between the literature of the North and the South of Europe is carried further in *De l'Allemagne,* a study of contemporary German culture of unusual penetration and sympathy. She points out the vagueness and the lack of structure in German literary works but shows also their superiority in psychological insight and in the portrayal of human passions. And she insists that the German writers have much to teach the rest of Europe. Her influence on the course of Romanticism, both in France and in Slavic Europe, was profound; and she helped, more than any other writer, to Europeanize modern thought. At the time she was writing there occurred first the great French emigration, and then, later, the movement of the armies of central and eastern Europe into France, where they remained as an army of occupation until 1817. Both of these movements brought a great mingling of ideas from west to east and from east to west, and, like the influence of Mme de Staël, helped to give an even greater cosmopolitanism to the literature of the early nineteenth century than that known during the eighteenth.

Chateaubriand (d. 1848) began as an ardent admirer of Rousseau. Then the excesses of the French Revolution and years of exile brought his conversion to Catholicism; as he says, "I wept and I believed." He changed his political and religious ideas, but he retained his early orientation to other phases of Romanticism, such as his belief in emotion and his love of the primitive and of wild nature, and his interest in the remote, Oriental, or Gothic. During the French Revolution, Chateaubriand visited the United States and spent some time in England. On his return to France, he published, in 1801–2, *Atala,* a story of life in the American wilderness; *René,* a tale of his own experience; and *The Genius of Christianity,* a glowing tribute to Catholicism. In this, and in most of his later works, Catholicism is presented as the mother of the arts and sciences and the defender of civilization. Dante and Milton are glorified above all poets, and Gothic art is the supreme artistic manifestation of all history. The success of these works and the backing of Napoleon suddenly made him the leading literary figure in France. Later, he broke with Napoleon and became a legitimist; then, after 1815, he fell out with the returning Bourbons.

Always an ambitious, restless, and emotional man, he was perpetually dissatisfied. This aspect of his temperament he best expressed in *René,* a short novel that resembles Goethe's *Werther*. In all his works, Chateaubriand's style is melodious and majestic, full of the echoes of "old, unhappy far-off things." Especially does he excel in descriptions of nature as it affected his moods: "I descend into the valley, I go up into the mountains searching, with all the force of my desires, the ideal object. I embrace it in the winds, I believe I hear it murmuring in the rivers, but everything is an imaginary phantom, both the stars in the sky and life in the universe." His style has a musical quality, a somewhat morbid charm, and a great seductiveness. Many of the later French Romantic writers derive some of their manner from Chateaubriand.

Romanticism lasted so long that it outlived one generation after another; and by the end of the eighteenth century many new writers had come, or were coming, to the fore. As we have seen, 1790 or 1800 is a convenient dividing point between Pre-Romanticism and the Romantic schools of England, Germany, and France. Characteristic of this second great phase of Romanticism in literature is the tendency to form groups of writers, or at least partnerships, as exemplified in the close relation of Schiller and Goethe in the last decade of Schiller's life. Sometimes these groups issued manifestoes, or at least published journals, which helped to spread their ideas. There followed often a marked quarrel between the "Romantics" and a rear guard of "Classicists." A few of the greatest writers remained, as in the Age of Pre-Romanticism, relatively isolated—for example, Lamartine, Manzoni, Leopardi, and Keats—but they form rather the exception.

Britain had been the first country where Romanticism unfolded, and, while they were no longer so clearly the precursors as before 1790, the British Romantic writers were among the most outstanding in Europe. Active around 1800 were Wordsworth, Coleridge, and Scott, to be followed in a few years by the three younger men, Byron, Shelley, and Keats. By 1790, in England and Germany (in contrast with France) the forces of Neo-Classicism had been greatly weakened by critical writings and by positive achievements in imaginative literature, so that in both countries the Romantic writers held the field with little opposition. The British writers seem to have had little taste for revolutions, abstract critical defenses of new ideas, or manifestoes, though Wordsworth and Coleridge did issue a manifesto, the *Preface to Lyrical Ballads,* and Coleridge, after a long stay in Germany, came back to England to write important critical treatises and essays.

Wordsworth (d. 1850) was slow in finding and defining his style. He wrote some dull poetry, but at his best his work supplies a more powerful aid to the imagination than is to be found in the poetry of far greater poets. Few poets have ever so transformed, with the light of a higher existence, the commonplaces of everyday existence. In his choice of subjects—mostly simple matters of daily concern—and in his use of the language of the common man, Wordsworth, as none of his predecessors, opened up a vast new world of beauty. His closeness to nature and his feeling of harmony between nature and man were among all the Romantic writers, so marked that Matthew Arnold declared, "Nature herself seems to take the pen out of his hand and to write for him." As Wordsworth himself wrote:

> To me, the meanest flower that blows can give
> Thoughts that do often lie too deep for tears.

Coleridge (d. 1834), long in close association with Wordsworth, had more the temperament of a German Romantic. This drew him toward German literature and philosophy about which he came to know more than any important writer outside Germany. And like some of his German contemporaries, he left many of his poems and prose works incomplete, and he proposed other projects which he never even began. Indeed, Coleridge left only one finished poem of perfect quality, "The Rime of the Ancient Mariner." This and two of his uncompleted poetic works, "Christabel" and "Kubla Khan" are among the most evocative of English poems. Few poems so well embody the romantic love of the exotic and the romantic spirit of wonder; both are filled with a haunted and a haunting beauty. Coleridge's inability to complete his works, together with the penetrating and inspiring quality of his ideas, led Lamb to refer to him as the "archangel somewhat damaged." In his *Biographia literaria* and other critical works Coleridge brought English thought into touch with the best of German literary criticism and German idealist philosophy; and he was an influence on a large group of writers that included Hazlitt, De Quincey, Mill, Carlyle, and Emerson. Like Wordsworth, Novalis, and many other writers, Coleridge welcomed the French Revolution only to turn against it all later and to become a thoroughgoing conservative.

Scott (d. 1832) needed no conversion to conservatism for he was from the beginning a lover of the old ways and imbued with a deeply ingrained loyalty to his country, his king, and his religion. As a young man, Scott was greatly influenced by German Romanticism; he translated Goethe's *Götz* and several of Bürger's ballads into English. His first reputation was won by his metrical romances written between 1805 and 1815. Their easy and fluent style, their colorfulness, and their lack of depth all worked toward making them popular. Scott next turned to a favorite Romantic form, the historical novel, with its great possibilities of evoking the splendors and picturesque sides of the Middle Ages, of the Renaissance, and of the seventeenth and eighteenth centuries. Scott was a born storyteller, though in the delineation of character he is more successful in presenting eccentrics, comic characters, and peasants than he is in the portrayal of leading figures. Scott's novels were translated into many languages and were the most read of all the flood of historical novels that marked the Romantic movement. Outside Britain, he shared with Byron the greatest reputation of any English writer later than Shakespeare and Milton.

A still younger group of English Romantic writers, Byron, Shelley, and Keats, had not lived through the French Revolution as adults. Byron and Shelley revived the ardent faith in mankind and the hatred of all forms of tyranny that had marked many of the Pre-Romantic writers, and even Keats shared much of their humanitarian ardor.

From his picturesque and checkered life, Byron (d. 1824) developed a poetic image which fascinated the whole of Europe. Both the man and his poetry show strange combinations that seem to lie at the heart of Romanticism—combinations of strength and weakness, of sincerity and affectation, of genuine heroism and of mock heroics. Byron's heart was romantically passionate and democratic, his head cool, classical, and aristocratic. The Byronic hero, who always reflects something of its author, is a picturesque but somber character, compounded of crime, remorse, and magnanimity. Byron's narrative poems and his dramas appealed, as did Napoleon's exploits, to people who lived drab lives and who wished to experience a release from convention, if only in literature. The three great forces in his influence were first his titanism, that is, his rebellious self-assertion that made the whole world his confessional; his penetrating, satiric, and mocking spirit; and finally his stand as a liberator along democratic and nationalist lines. *Don Juan* remains Byron's greatest and most characteristic work. It is a brilliant picture of life in many lands, furnished with a running commentary on all sorts of subjects, a commentary that is both sardonic and serious. In mood, it shows an increase in sincerity as the poet grew older. All of life is here, and many conventions are brilliantly castigated. It is, indeed, a kind of epic of modern life in which the author is keen to discern the false and the corrupt. Byron's influence in his own age was greater than that of any literary figure, except perhaps Goethe; and from Spain to Sweden and Russia Byronism penetrated deeply into literature.

Shelley (d. 1822), like Byron, was a political radical and in revolt against many of the conventions of his time, and, like Byron, he spent most of his active years as an exile out of England. The mood of many of Shelley's poems resembles the Platonism of Spenser. He speaks of Intellectual Beauty, Liberty, Love, and the Spirit of Nature. His delight was always in the abstract and the ideal rather than in the concrete and the tangible. The ruling passion of Shelley's soul was to free life from misery and evil; he called poetry one of "the instruments with which high spirits call the future from its cradle." Shelley sounds a high ecstatic note in his verse oftener than any other English Romantic poet, and at times he seems perilously close to madness. In his greatest works, as in the drama *Prometheus Unbound,* in "Adonais," a lament for Keats, and in the "Ode to the West Wind," there is a brilliant poetic iridescence that justifies Browning's name for Shelley, "the sun-tread-er." Shelley's genius was too ethereal and too peculiar to himself, and thus too unrepresentative of mankind, to give him the influence both in Britain and abroad possessed by writers like Scott and Byron.

Keats (d. 1821), like the French poet Gautier, was "a man for whom the physical world exists." As a youth, Keats borrowed Leigh Hunt's copy of Spenser's *Faerie Queene,* and Keats says he "went through it as a young horse through a spring meadow, romping." This opened up to the youthful poet the wonders of sixteenth-century English poetry which remained, perhaps, the deepest influence on his verse. Keats's genius was concrete and direct; unlike Shelley he was not much at home among abstractions. He adored sensuous beauty and knew how to create it; yet, beyond this, perhaps because he died at twenty-five and had no opportunity to develop them, he had no philosophic and hu-manitarian interests. In spite of great passages in his longer poems, especially "Hyperion," his fame still rests on his shorter lyrics: a series of sonnets, and the odes "To a Nightingale," "To Autumn," "To Melancholy," and "On a Grecian Urn," the last Neo-Classical in form and mood. The flawless beauty of these shorter pieces not only shows the depth of Keats's inspiration but also reflects his careful craftsmanship. Though he had little influence outside England, at home his was the greatest single influence upon the poetry and painting of Victorian England.

Before the close of the eighteenth century, a new generation of German writers, now known as the "German Romantic school," was beginning to publish. By this time, the achievements of earlier German writers had, in both theory and practice, established a lyric poetry that was spontaneous and a type of novel and drama free from rules. A group of writers formed a loosely knit school, first at Jena, then at Berlin. These included: the Schlegel brothers, Novalis (d. 1801), Tieck d. 1853), and Wackenroder (d. 1798), the philosopher Schelling (d. 1854), and, finally, the theologian Schleiermacher (d. 1834). Among their literary accomplishments are the critical writings of the Schlegel brothers; poems of theirs and of Novalis; legendary plays of Tieck, unactable and never performed; and some novels and short stories. Much of their work remained incomplete and fragmentary; they seemed to lack the capacity to conclude anything. Their attitudes harked back to the extreme individualism—even anarchy—of *Sturm und Drang*. They seemed to be in a frantic search for anything that would take them away from reality. Their great enthusiasm for medieval subjects shows a yearning to get away from the world they knew and to return to a time of the simplicity, spontaneity and innocence of man's lost childhood.

There are, they maintained, no rules in art or life valid for all times and nations. Each century and each country, indeed each individual, is entitled to its own standards, likes, and dislikes. These writers would have nothing to do with the separation of artistic genre as set forth in the *Laokoon*. Poetry, music, painting, and sculpture are all interchangeable manifestations of the artistic spirit. Tieck wrote poems that have no meaning beyond their verbal music; others described paintings in words and found colors to match music. One of the favorite themes was that music was the greatest of the arts, and that all the arts try to approach the purely emotional quality of music. These writers differed, however, from the earlier *Sturm und Drang* school in favoring Catholicism and political reaction. Having discovered that the Enlightenment and the French Revolution had not made men good, they jumped to the conclusion they had made men bad. They were often unable to find a middle ground between absolute anarchy, on the one hand, and absolute submission to Catholicism and political despotism, on the other.

The new German Romantic school had a great aversion to all classicism, rationalism, and liberalism, including any interest in these shown by Schiller and Goethe. They loved the instinctive, the irrational, and the subconscious; and they often found in the Catholic and chivalric Middle Ages a sort of "beautiful isle of nowhere" that never existed. They cultivated dreams, and infinite aspirations toward an ideal "blue flower." They were very moody, wildly pouring forth their griefs and passions, their joy and despair. They wanted to be absolutely free and unfettered in their lives as well as in their works, and they rejected the ideas of Kant and Goethe that there must be rules in life. No harmonious balanced characters here, but colors, melody, fantasy, and a chaos of moods and inspirations. The inability of these unstable geniuses to adjust themselves to hard realities led to the *Weltschmerz* of endless conflicts, gloom, and despair. The most valuable part of their writing lay in the field of literary criticism and in their remarkable translations of foreign literatures, above all August Wilhelm Schlegel's translations of many of the plays of Shakespeare. The Schlegel brothers, especially Friedrich (d. 1829), opened up the beauties of all medieval literature and that of Renaissance Italy, Spain, and England, and even the literature and wisdom of India.

Of many holding to the same views, though in a less exaggerated form, was a second group at Heidelberg which included Arnim (d. 1831) and Brentano (d. 1842). These two published a celebrated collection of German popular songs, *The Boy's Wonderhorn,* which helped to increase the taste for popular legends and folk poetry. A third group at Stuttgart, of whom the principal members were Uhland (d. 1862) and Körner (d. 1862), wrote poetry that was less complicated, ironic, and metaphysical than that of the Berlin group and was closer to the interests of the mass of the German people. All were strongly patriotic.

A number of writers of the German Romantic school belonged to no group. This includes the two great playwrights Kleist (d. 1811) and Grillparzer (d. 1872). Kleist's plays are filled with romantic ideas: the love of night, the influence of the subconscious and of dreams, the high emotionality of the leading characters, and the declamatory language used. Kleist possessed real dramatic genius, but his outlook on life is morbid; and his plots are often far-fetched. There is on earth no absolute justice and no absolute love, and his characters perish in heroic striving after one or the other. Kleist was, also, a master of the short story, which he told with superb artistry and concentration. Grillparzer is far more objective. He borrowed from the simpler style of Goethe's *Tasso* and *Iphigenie* and suffused his plays with a delicate, but not overdone, romantic melancholy. Unlike most of the writers of the German Romantic school he is able to get out of himself sufficiently to construct a variety of convincing characters. The novelist Jean Paul (d. 1825) wrote long novels of strong sentimental appeal, written in a loose and colorful style. The public loved his tales because of his interest in the life of the common people, his loving portrayal of the little things of life, his whimsical humor akin to tears, his fine feeling for nature, and his pity and emotionality. The fact that his heroes talk and dream incessantly (and rarely act) and that there is a fairy-tale unreality in his plots, all of which bother the modern reader, seem to have represented no handicaps to his popularity in Germany and England. His contemporary, E. T. A. Hoffmann (d. 1822), cultivated the fantastic tale where everything is strange, contradictory, enigmatic, and mysterious. He exploited the gruesome and the supernatural and got telling effects, as did Poe and Kafka later, by juxtaposing the supernatural and the real.

Among the finest flowers of later German Romanticism were the exquisite narrative poems and the lyrics of Heinrich Heine (d. 1856), some of the most important of which appeared in his famous *Book of Songs* of 1827. These became favorites of the Romantic song composers. Heine's perpetual cynicism and his ardent faith in political liberty herald the rise of a new literary movement in Germany, that of Young Germany. The total literary production of the German Romantic school from 1790 to about 1830 was enormous, but few of the works of the younger men are really outstanding. In this last group must be included some of the critical writings of the Schlegel brothers, Kleist's finest play, *The Prince of Homburg,* a number of short stories and fairy tales, and the poems of Heine.

The strength of classical rules in France retarded the growth of a Romantic school there. In 1815 the literary currents still remained essentially classical, and Pre-Romanticism had brought to the fore fewer writers than in England and Germany. Nowhere, except perhaps in Italy, did the Greco-Roman tradition have such a hold on poetry and the theater. The strong influence of the critical writings of Mme de Staël, a translation of August Wilhelm Schlegel's study of the drama, Sismondi's *Literatures of the South of Europe,* and translations of

Shakespeare, Byron, Scott, Goethe, Schiller, and "Ossian," together with the experiences of the emigration and the Napoleonic Wars, all brought into France, after about 1810, strong foreign influences. Most of these new influences were either medieval or from northern Europe, and these gradually replaced the imitation of antiquity. These new currents were discussed in a number of literary groups (some of them called "Cénacles") and in several new literary journals, most important of which was the *Globe* (1824–30).

Soon, as was the custom in France, literary manifestoes began to appear. One in 1822 by Stendhal, *Racine et Shakespeare,* praised the English poet above the French classic writer. Stendhal was the first important French writer to call himself a Romantic. As early as 1818 he wrote in a letter, "I am a furious Romantic, I am for Shakespeare against Racine, and for Byron against Boileau." In France, as elsewhere, changes in style began to occur long before there was a very clear realization of their historic significance. Slowly the poor quality of French poetry produced since the seventeenth century became more evident. Personal sentiments and emotions and serious thoughts, especially as they concerned the living world, had been pushed aside in favor of a cold and abstract style. Romanticism, in turn, had a profound belief in the emotional and expansive power of the individual. And it emphasized the particular, where classicism had emphasized the universal. Individual sentiment, passion, and genius became the order of the day; this favored lyric poetry more than it did the drama. The whole approach to art is now through the senses and imagination rather than through reason. In his manifesto Stendhal makes ennui and servile imitation the notes of classicism, and his plea is for liberty of expression for the artist and for a literature more closely related to life. "Classical literature," he concludes, "is that which pleased our grandfather; Romantic literature is that which pleases us."

Another manifesto was Sainte-Beuve's brilliant history of sixteenth-century French poetry, through which French writers were brought into touch again with a glorious poetic tradition that had preceded the age of literary rules. And in 1827 Hugo published his *Preface to Cromwell,* which glorified the plays of Shakespeare and set them up as a model for the regeneration of the French theater. The *Preface to Cromwell* was a veritable trumpet blast. Full as it is of gross historical errors and of bombast, it seemed at the time a successful attack on the rules of classical taste. It was, in any case, clever propaganda with its appeals to the examples of Ariosto, Cervantes, Rabelais, and, above all, Shakespeare. All literature is divided into three periods: a primitive period when poetry is lyric, then ancient civilization when it is epic, and finally the modern period, the age of the drama. The only thing original about this famous preface is its assertion that art must contain a contrast between the ugly and the beautiful. Meanwhile, the early poems of Lamartine, Hugo, and Alfred de Vigny, the first historical novels of Mérimée and others, and the plays of Dumas and Hugo had aroused the reading public to a pitch of excitement.

All the forces of classicism in the French Academy, the schools, and the press opposed the efforts of the younger men. Nowhere in Europe did the war beween Neo-Classicism and Romanticism become so dramatic. It finally came to a battle in 1830 when the Neo-Classicists tried to drive Hugo's *Hernani* off the stage of the Comédie Française. Hugo, by this time, had come to be recognized as the leader of the new forces. All the young poets and novelists joined in the fray, their ranks swelled by the painter Delacroix, the composer Berlioz, and their followers. The theater was, in France, one of the great strongholds of classicism and a struggle against any innovation was sure to be made there. The Romantics wanted a type of drama free from classical rules of all sorts, and one that would truly reflect the ideas and emotions of living men. The dramatic unities were disregarded, along with the old rules of versification and the old limitations on the vocabulary. Gautier later said that those who had not lived through the 1820's could never understand the enthusiasms of the time. It was an intoxicating atmosphere of tumultuous revolt and wild creative energy, a great war of liberation where poems were read in painters' studios, Delacroix and his friends sang Hugo's ballads, and Berlioz admired Shakespeare even more than did Hugo. The Romantics won their cause just a few months before the royal troops were defeated in the street fighting of July, 1830. By this time, Lamartine, Hugo, and some of the other writers who had after 1815 rallied to "the throne and the altar," had discovered that their Bourbon rulers did not resemble Charlemagne or Saint Louis or any of the heroes of the admired Middle Ages, and that the living French aristocracy had little of the glamor of old-time chivalry. By 1830, these illusions were mostly past, and the younger men had identified their literary aspirations with the political ideals of democracy, for, as Hugo declared, "Romanticism is liberalism in literature."

The full flowering of the French Romantic movement lies between

1820 when Lamartine published his *Premières méditations* and 1843 when Hugo's last important Romantic tragedy failed. By 1830 there was still no general agreement as to what exactly Romanticism was. To the young journalist Thiers the movement stood for "nature and truth"; to the scientist Ampère it was "opposed to imitation"; for the historian Sismondi it was "the faithful image of modern civilization"—a view shared by Stendhal; and for Hugo it was "liberalism and freedom in literature." As this movement affected the generation of 1830 in France, it manifested itself in an attempt to renew poetry, the drama, the novel, the fine arts, and music, after all of these had seemingly exhausted themselves in the sterilities of classical formalism.

Although the great fight between Neo-Classicists and Romanticists during the Restoration (1815–30) came over the drama, the most remarkable achievement of the young Romantic school, during this period, was in the lyric poetry of three young men, Lamartine, De Vigny, and Hugo. With his *Méditations poétiques* of 1820 Lamartine (d. 1869) created something of a sensation. Nothing could have been drier or more sterile than the poetry of the period of the Napoleonic empire, the last stand of dessicated classicism. This explains why Lamartine's poetry caused such a stir. Even a man of the *ancien régime* like Talleyrand tells us that he was so moved by these verses that he was unable to sleep the night he read them. Writing fifty years later, Sainte-Beuve said, "One passed suddenly from a poetry that was dry, thin, and poor to a poetry from the heart, overflowing and divine." Lamartine's inspiration was centered in the inspiring and consoling forces of nature, religion, and love. He likes to set his poems on the borders of a lake at the twilight hour or in the moonlight. Lamartine's attitude toward nature is that of a vague pantheism, and he evokes his personal moods against the backgrounds of Burgundy and Savoy. There were a simple, flowing style, a meditative sweetness, and a confessional quality about his verses that struck fresh notes, though his poems seem now to lack both strength and intensity. In his *Nouvelles méditations* of 1823, written after his marriage, the melancholy gives way to the celebration of a happy love in a sunny landscape. This second series of verses has more polish though less spontaneity than the first; but these two volumes of poetry represent the first outstanding achievements of the French Romantic school. Many of the same moods appeared in a third collection of 1830, *Les harmonies poétiques et réligieuses*. The technical qualities of Lamartine's poetry showed a suave harmony, a softness of tone and outline, a fresh spontaneity, and a preference for floating and soaring imagery. Sometimes Lamartine displays an airy insubstantiality like that of Shelley. And not since the Pléiade had there appeared in French any poetry so subjective.

Alfred de Vigny (d. 1863) published small volumes of poetry in 1822, 1824, and 1826. His spirit is proud, profoundly sincere, pessimistic, and stoical. The poet had been disappointed in life and love, but his complaint is in general and abstract terms. Man is destined to endless striving and endless failure. He should accept his fate with resignation and in silence. Every man is solitary and in isolation. De Vigny is the most sincere and most bitterly logical of all the descendants of Goethe's *Werther* or Chateaubriand's *René* or Byron's *Manfred*. Men are hostile or indifferent; nature is cold and impassive; and God, if he exists, is silent. The earlier classical ages had seen in nature fauns, dryads, and shepherds. The Romantics saw only themselves, and hence each one saw something different. Many of De Vigny's moods, however, resemble those of Leopardi in Italy. De Vigny liked to clothe his ideas in descriptive poems, some of whose subjects were from the Bible. His historical novel, *Cinq-Mars,* of the time of Louis XIII, and his tragedy *Chatterton* (1835) are among the finest and least dated works of the French Romantic school. De Vigny wrote only thirty poems and, owing to his reserve and detachment, Sainte-Beuve said he dwelt "in an ivory tower." His style is very polished and condensed; he was a meticulous craftsman.

As Voltaire dominated much of the literature of eighteenth-century France, so does Victor Hugo (d. 1885) dominate much of that of the nineteenth century. This most gifted of all French poets had, as a child, declared, "I want to be Chateaubriand or nothing." Hugo first attracted attention in 1822 by the publication of a volume of lyric poems. Other volumes of poems followed in 1826 and 1829. In each new volume the verses were orchestrated with a more magnificent sweep and amplitude. Huge proclaimed that, in his wide choice of words, he had "put the red bonnet [of the Revolution] on the old dictionary." He declared he would call a pig by its name. Even through the French Revolution and the Empire, poets had been forced to avoid many ordinary words because they were low. Audiences, at the theater, would hiss if they heard words like "room" or "handkerchief" or "horse." Correct diction ruled that "spouse" was preferable to "husband," because "husband" signified merely a domestic relationship while "spouse" conveyed the idea of a contract hallowed by society. Negroes were to be called "mortals blackened by the suns of Guinea." Instead of "priest" and "bell" it was better to use "pontiff" and "bronze." A revolution in poetic diction was overdue.

In his verse forms, Hugo was an innovator, especially in his use of *enjambement,* that is, the carrying of a thought without a break through more than one line of poetry. Even these earliest verses of Hugo are marked by a great imaginative force, and at times by a magnificent handling of the French language. Personally, the writer was often petty, fickle, and quarrelsome; and time was to show that the poet was greater than the man and the thinker. But Hugo was still in this early phase the White Knight leading the Romantic forces—their most vivid and fearless figure and their natural leader. In these early volumes of verse it became evident that Hugo could do anything with rhythm and that in language and metaphor he was destined to open wide horizons. His imaginative power shows in the number and novelty of his images, his myth-making faculty, his treatment of the elements of nature as living forces, and his ability to evoke immensity. In sonority and tone color, in his handling of the resources of French language and rhetoric, and in his enormous range of vocabulary, time was to prove Hugo unmatched in the whole realm of French verse. His worst faults were to lie in his lack of selection, his lack of taste, and his overexuberance. Before he finished, Hugo had exemplified in his poems, plays, and novels every mode and quality, and nearly every virtue and fault, of the whole Romantic movement.

4. Music

In music, as in art and literature, the century following 1750 was marked by both Neo-Classicism and Romanticism. But whereas in art and letters, the two styles ran side by side, in music the Romantic phase succeeded a classical period. In all three fields, art, literature, and music, the rise of Neo-Classicism was in part a reaction against the light-hearted frivolities of the Rococo period, and in part a discovery of new techniques of expression. Classicism in music, as it appeared in the second half of the eighteenth century, was marked by greater clarity and simplicity of structure, the development of the sonata form, an emphasis on a homophonic style and on a type of melody that is often folklike in its simplicity, a much lessened use of counterpoint and harmonic complexity, a great development of instrumental as against vocal music, more attention to the use of instrumental color, and finally the increased employment of dynamic shading, that is, of crescendo and diminuendo. At the same time the new pianoforte came in alongside the harpsichord, although it only slowly replaced it. The rise of the piano encouraged a new type of keyboard composition.

The style of the great Baroque masters, Bach and Handel, came to seem too heavy and far too complex. One now desired less display of skill and greater simplicity and naturalness of style. The rise in power and influence of the middle class helped to popularize tuneful music. Philosophy, science, art, and literature all take more account of the general public rather than of a group of aristocrats and connoisseurs. At the same time, there came to be more interchange among the musical styles of the nations of western Europe. There was an overlap between the old and the new. Works typical of the new era, as Pergolesi's *La serva padrona* and Sammartini's first symphonies, for example, were written in the 1730's at the same time as Bach's *B Minor Mass,* and earlier than Handel's *Messiah.* By 1740, however, changes in style became generally noticeable. Stress was now laid on melody as the main factor of composition, and everything else became subservient. This new love of melody drew much from folk songs and dance tunes. Such melody needed a different type of both development and accompaniment than that used earlier; contrapuntal complexity could find little place in this new type of strictly melodic material.

The sonata form was developed as the basis for nearly all instrumental music: the symphony, the solo concerto, types of chamber music, and the solo keyboard composition. In contrast to the Baroque sonata, which usually began with a slow movement, the newer type of sonata usually opens with an allegro movement. The first movement, written in what became known as the sonata form, starts out with one theme followed by a contrasting theme; these are, then, developed in a central section, and the movement ends with a recapitulation. The second movement of a sonata is usually in a slow tempo. The third movement is often in the form of a minuet; it is sometimes omitted, as was commonly the case in the solo concerto. The fourth and final movement is ordinarily in a lively tempo.

Perhaps the most important contribution of the Neo-Classical period to music was the symphony, which used the sonata form and four contrasting movements, and, also, new types of orchestration and a new

manner of performance. In the seventeenth century the term "symphony" had been applied to various kinds of instrumental music, but
especially to the overture, with its contrasting movements of fast, slow,
and fast. By about 1770, the symphony had developed into an independent instrumental form quite unconnected, as had been the overture, with
the opera. There was added the minuet between the second and last
movements so that, by the later eighteenth century, the symphony in
four contrasting movements was the common form. By this time, it had
come to replace the *concerto grosso* and the orchestral suite as well as the
overture of the Baroque period as the leading type of music for the orchestra. The new symphonies are homophonic in style, and, where counterpoint is used, it is usually incidental. The nucleus of the parts of the
composition is in the themes used. The thorough bass disappears, and all
the parts are written out.

The second half of the eighteenth century also saw a standardization
of the orchestra both in the instruments used and in their grouping. The
development of the symphony took place simultaneously in at least
three centers: at Milan, where the chief composer was Sammartini (d.
1775); at Vienna, where Gluck, J. C. Bach, and Mozart (pupils of Sammartini) were leading composers; and at Mannheim, where the leading
composer was Johann Stamitz (d. 1757). Of these three centers, Mannheim, in western Germany, was perhaps the most important historically.
Here occurred a fusion of Italian and German currents. The Mannheim group practiced many of the innovations later used by Haydn—
and once attributed to him—such as the sonata form as a constructional
formula, the great prominence given the violins in the orchestra, the
addition of a minuet to make four movements, the elimination of the
basso continuo, the increased importance of the melody, and the use of
a simple harmonic rather than a contrapuntal style, and finally the employment of various instruments to give special and definite tone color.
A contemporary writer described the effect of the playing of the Mannheim orchestra in rhapsodic phrases: "Its 'forte' is thunder; its 'crescendo' a waterfall; its 'diminuendo' a crystal clear brook murmuring in
the distance; its 'pianissimo' a breath of spring."

At the same time, the new pianoforte was coming more into use and
a new style of composing and playing was being developed—for harpsichord, clavier, and piano—by Carl Philipp Emanuel Bach (d. 1788). He
used the same principles of thematic development and harmonization
used in the orchestral compositions of the Mannheim school. His themes

are often highly emotional. C. P. E. Bach's style fused the Rococo *style galant,* with its graceful and gay tunes, and the sentimental style of *Empfindsamkeit,* which had as its aim the expression of "passions in the way they rise out of the soul." It was a compromise between expressions of the intellect and the feelings of the heart. Most of C. P. E. Bach's piano sonatas are works in three movements. He also wrote a famous treatise, *On the True Art of Playing Key-board Music,* which for decades fixed the general ideas about the technique of harpsichord, clavier, and piano playing. In his music, as in most instrumental music, the bass loses all trace of leadership and contrapuntal independence and becomes, as do the other parts, only a background for the melody. At the same time, orchestral music gives most of the essential material to the strings and uses the wind instruments for reinforcing and for filling in the harmonies. Later in the eighteenth century, the wood winds and the brasses came to be given more important and more independent parts. Haydn was deeply influenced by the music of the Mannheim school and by that of C. P. E. Bach, who in turn declared that Haydn was "the only man who understood my work." Of C. P. E. Bach, Mozart said, "He is the parent and we are the children."

While these great changes in the style of instrumental music were going on, there was taking place a reform of the opera in which a number of composers played a role. The opera had begun as a means of setting forth the words in a drama in a style that was supposed to represent a Greek play. But gradually this dramatic intention was set aside, and librettos and opera music had come to be written to show off elaborate and quite undramatic vocal display. The singers made arbitrary demands on writers and composers, compelling them to put in showy arias without concern for either dramatic or musical propriety. Moreover, to the score as written, singers added all sorts of spectacular embellishments, which were often tasteless displays of vocal acrobatics.

A return to a simpler style was begun by a number of Italian composers who were employed at courts where French taste in the opera predominated. The consummation of this movement is seen in some of the later operas of Gluck (d. 1787). Gluck had received a good classical education paralleling his training as a musician, and, somewhere along the way, he had fallen under the influence of the writings of Winckelmann. His first operas were in a showy Italian style, but in 1762 he produced in Vienna a work in a new manner, *Orfeo ed Euridice.* This was followed in a few years by his *Alceste*. In the preface to this last opera, Gluck declared:

I resolved to avoid all those abuses which had crept into Italian opera through the vanity of singers and the compliance of composers. I endeavoured to reduce music to its proper function, that of seconding poetry without weakening it by superfluous ornament. My object was to put an end to abuses against which good taste and good sense have long protested in vain. My chief endeavour should be to attain a grand simplicity, and consequently I have avoided making a parade of difficulties at the cost of clarity.

In these later operas, Gluck used only a few characters, and avoided subplots and intrigues. One gets an interesting contrast of the Baroque and Neo-Classicism by comparing an oratorio of Handel with one of the later operas of Gluck. The first is grandiose and colossal; the second is marked by a just and balanced beauty, by a perfectly measured accent, and by an effect that is close to what Winckelmann had declared was the essential genius of Greek art. The role of the chorus was emphasized by Gluck; the distinction between recitative and aria was much reduced, and the recitative was accompanied by the orchestra, not by the harpsichord alone. The overture was closely related to the opera and was intended to prepare the audience for the mood of the work that followed. The orchestration varied according to the words and spirit of the drama. Gluck also wrote some charming comic operas in rather a Rococo style. His enemies insisted that one of the reasons he liked simpler music in his serious operas was that he was a clumsy musical craftsman, and Handel had said that Gluck "knew no more counterpoint than my cook." On the other hand, Handel's music had a profound influence on that of Gluck, and he came to achieve some of the breadth, simplicity, and vigor of Handel's style without, however, imitating the Baroque grandeur of Handel. Gluck's audiences insisted on happy endings, and still preferred elaborate vocal displays. So his reform, and his beautiful and remarkable operas had little immediate effect, though he did have some influence on Mozart; and his style was carried into the nineteenth century by Cherubini, Spontini, Berlioz, and Weber.

The Neo-Classical music of the later eighteenth century is largely summed up in the writing of Haydn and Mozart. They represent their period as Orlandus Lassus and Palestrina represent the height of the High Renaissance, and as Bach and Handel sum up the Age of the Baroque. Haydn and Mozart were in addition good friends, though Mozart was a whole generation younger than Haydn. Mozart's style was deeply influenced by that of Haydn. At the same time, Haydn very early and very generously recognized Mozart's genius, and was in turn influenced by Mozart. Haydn told Mozart's father, after hearing some new quartets of his son, "Your son is the greatest composer known to me either personally or by reputation." And Haydn refused an invitation to write an opera for Prague, where Mozart's *Don Giovanni* had lately been produced, because, he said, "it would be difficult for anyone, no matter who, to equal the great Mozart." Haydn's growth to artistic maturity was much slower than Mozart's, who toured as a child prodigy and, while still a child, began to compose. When Mozart died at thirty-five, Haydn, who lived to the age of seventy-seven, had not yet written many of his best works. The two men had very contrasting personalities. Mozart was precocious, and always unsettled and impractical in the affairs of life. Haydn was a calm and very self-possessed man, simple in manner, whose life and affairs were well regulated from beginning to end. Both men grew up in Austria, which in the eighteenth century seemed to possess more musical interest and musical talent than any state in Europe. All the great Austrian noble families had private orchestras, and even private opera houses. Every manservant in a great household was expected to play an orchestral instrument. In every little town there was a music master who could, on short notice, call together a group of musicians for parties, weddings, and funerals. The whole country was steeped in music.

Haydn (d. 1809) was the gifted inheritor of a very fruitful period of experimentation and new discoveries in instrumental music. He had little education except what he got as a boy when he was a member of the choir of St. Stephen's Cathedral in Vienna. When his voice changed and he lost his position in the choir, he supported himself with various odd jobs. During this period, he made a thorough study of C. P. E. Bach's clavier compositions, and also of the standard theoretical works on music. After several appointments with musical organizations, he joined the staff of musicians maintained by Prince Esterhazy, with whose family he maintained connections for the rest of his life. In this household he came to be the musical director and had a group of skilled players for whom he wrote much of his music. The collection of musicians in this household of a great prince gave him an orchestra with which he could experiment, and for which it was his duty to furnish compositions of many types. Besides about twenty-five orchestral players, Haydn had a dozen or so singers for the opera, all recruited from the best talent available. There were two theaters in the palace, one for opera and another for plays by marionettes, and two large concert halls. In his later life, Haydn made long stays in Vienna, Paris, and London, where he had become very well known through the publication of his works. All in all, his musical output was enormous, including over a hundred symphonies, nearly the same number of string quartets, over fifty clavier sonatas, and an equal number of concertos and other works for various groups of instruments. In addition, he wrote some operas, which are no longer performed; a series of masses; and two great oratorios, *The Creation* and *The Seasons*. These two oratorios show, more clearly than any of his works, Haydn's deep religious faith and his love of nature.

Throughout his long life, Haydn was a constant experimenter, and there is an enormous variety in his work. His early symphonies, which are short and mostly for strings, his early clavier pieces, and quartets, hardly seem to have been written by the same man who produced his later works. Through his career as a composer there is a steady development, though from the beginning his musical style reflects a warm-hearted, vigorous, and enthusiastic man. Haydn gathered together a series of experimental forms from earlier German music and, to a less extent, from the earlier music of Italy and France, and wove a fabric of beautiful and rich expressiveness. He inherited the beginning of the sonata and symphony forms, the organization of the modern orchestra based on strings but with some wind and percussion instruments, the establishment of a clear line of demarcation between the style of chamber and orchestral music, and a type of monophonic writing. Every one of these traditions he carried further, and so perfected them that he seemed to be the originator of them all. For this reason, Mozart gave him the name of "Papa Haydn."

Haydn cared little for Rococo elegancies and frivolities. His nature was both too solid, and too simple and homespun for that. He loved good, straightforward themes in the style of folk songs and square-cut dance rhythms which give his music a fresh and open-air quality. He was a peasant in origin, and he never lost contact with the simple and the direct in the life about him. This rustic simplicity, which is always in the background of his work, is shown not only in the music itself but in the names he gave some of his works, as the "Lark" and the "Frog" quartets, and the "Surprise" and the "Clock" symphonies.

By far his finest work is that done in his later life, much of it when he was past sixty. By this time, Haydn had, through much experimentation and through the stimulating influence of his younger contemporary Mozart, achieved a style of great fluency, variety, and depth. In his orchestral writing, he came to employ more wind and percussion instruments and to exploit them in new and telling combinations. The twentieth century has come to regard his string quartets as his finest achievement. In his later symphonies and string quartets the first two movements are usually long and serious; the third movement, often a minuet, is shorter and offers relaxation; while the last movement is an allegro or presto—in sonata or rondo form, or a combination of the two —overflowing with high spirits and sometimes with tricks and surprises. He varies the texture by occasional use of skilfully handled counterpoint. Haydn's two great oratorios, inspired by hearing the works of Handel performed in England, are primarily orchestral pieces enlarged by soloists and a chorus. There is more Rococo influence and more of a theatrical quality, in his church music, especially his masses, than in any other of his works. His church music, like that of Mozart, seems to match the contemporary Austrian Baroque church architecture with its love of dramatic effects. The masses employ a full orchestra with drums and trumpets and are written in the style of the opera and symphony. Haydn once remarked, "Since God has given me a cheerful heart, he will forgive me for serving Him cheerfully." Haydn's later compositions achieve a truly classical form in the perfect blending of the work of the mind and that of the heart, though occasionally an emotional surge breaks through the classical composure. In this, one may discern the first indications of Romanticism. There is no indication, however, that Haydn had a consciousness of self-expression which became one of the most marked qualities of the Romantic composer. In these later works, all technical problems are completely solved, and the ideas fit the musical forms perfectly. There is a just balance in everything, and there is nothing in excess. Haydn did more than any other composer to establish the form and style of the classical sonata and of the symphony, and, at the same time, he has been called "the father of the string quartet." His genius was primarily for instrumental music, for which he had a profound understanding, and in which he was a consummate craftsman.

Though Mozart (d. 1791) was twenty-four years Haydn's junior, he died eighteen years before Haydn. His music harks back to the airy graces of the Rococo, of which he is in some ways the greatest genius;

yet it often has the dignity and depth of the best of the Neo-Classical tradition. Betwen the ages of six and fifteen young Mozart toured as an infant prodigy on the clavier. Soon, he also became a good organist and violinist as well. In his concerts, as a child prodigy, he not only played prepared compositions but also performed fluent sight readings and brilliant improvisations. He composed minuets at six, a symphony soon before his ninth birthday, an oratorio at eleven, and an opera at twelve. Because of the careful musical training he received from his father and his wide travel as a child, Mozart was brought into early contact with all the musical styles of his time. With amazing aptitude, he absorbed them all, and then improved on his models. His own work thus came to be a synthesis of the musical ideas of his time. Unlike Haydn, however, he seems to have had little interest in nature or in folk music. Mozart's later life was restless and unhappy, and he never found congenial posts; after being for a time in the employ of the Archbishop of Salzburg, he gave up the position and supported himself as a virtuoso, composer, and teacher in Vienna.

Curiously enough, the increasingly unhappy conditions of Mozart's life seem to have left relatively few marks on his music. Some of his greatest and most radiant works were done at a time when his existence was made wretched by debts and other hardships. His music flowed out of an ideal realm, and, like Raphael and Keats, he was the pure creator who could freely invent with an apparently effortless perfection. Among the most important influences on Mozart were the compositions of Johann Christian Bach, whom he met in London and whose music he much admired; the writings of Haydn, with whom he had formed a deep and abiding friendship; and, later, the music of Johann Sebastian Bach. The mature style of Mozart blended Italian grace, French clarity, and German warmth and depth of emotion as that of no other composer. Especially did he synthesize the styles of Italian and German music. Italian music was directed primarily toward entertainment, while German music aimed at a deeper expression of thought and emotion. Though the forms preferred by the Italians were the opera and cantata, instrumental music was by no means neglected. On the other hand, in the eighteenth century the Germans had developed marvelously all types of instrumental music. The Italians preferred monody, while the Germans still used a great deal of polyphony. German music had little influence in Italy, but Italian music had great influence in Germany and the rest of Europe. Never were Italian grace and elegance and German depth and strength so combined as in the music of Mozart.

The sum total of Mozart's works, over six hundred separate compositions, seems beyond the capacity of any man who died at thirty-five. He excelled in all types of music—string quartets and quintets, trios, symphonies, and other orchestral compositions, piano sonatas, piano and violin sonatas, and operas. And in every field his work is superb, much of it unequaled in the whole history of music. In one summer, the thirty-third of his life, he composed his three greatest symphonies, the one in E flat, another in G minor and, perhaps his most remarkable one, in C major, the "Jupiter." The last contains some of Mozart's most advanced and stimulating writing, part of it experimental and foreshadowing music developments that came later. Never is there here, or in his other music, any distortion or straining for effect; it all has what Matthew Arnold called the mark of greatness in poetry—inevitability. Much the same may be said of Mozart's other compositions. In his Italian and German operas dramatic and musical elements are perfectly blended. These operas are among the most effective and charming works ever written, and they had a great influence on the writing of later composers, such as Rossini, Weber, and even Wagner. Mozart gained for the opera, especially for the *opera buffa,* to which he gave great perfection of form, something like the place that the plays of Schiller and Goethe won for the drama.

Mozart left no type of music known in his day unadorned: church music (masses and motets), concertos, symphonies, *divertimenti* and serenades, chamber music of all types, piano sonatas, sonatas for violin and piano, and serious and comic operas. Shown clearly in his operas, but running through much of the rest of Mozart's work, is the emotional factor of love. He is concerned only secondarily with religious or ethical questions, or with the heroic and the pathetic. But love, from the purest and most exalted sentiment to the most outspoken sensuality, is never far from his mind. This is one of the factors that make his music more varied and complex than that of Haydn. Most of the best of all these types of composition were the work of the last ten years of his life, between the ages of twenty-five and thirty-five. Surprisingly enough, Mozart was never a conscious theorist and rarely expressed his ideas about music as an art. His grasp of the principles of composition for different media seems to have been intuitive rather than intellectual. All in all, Mozart is the summation of the Neo-Classical Age of music as Bach and Handel were of Baroque music. Mozart's musical style had the classical perfection that ruled out later improvement or even adequate continuation.

Beethoven (d. 1827), by the mighty force of his genius, carried music from classicism to Romanticism. He may be compared with Mozart as Michelangelo may be compared with Raphael. Michelangelo had taken the forms of classical design and extended them into forms essentially new in the Sistine ceiling and the Medici tombs. In the same way, Beethoven took the classical forms of Haydn and Mozart, broke out of their boundaries, and changed their content so as to achieve a new style. And like Michelangelo in relation to classical artistic forms, Beethoven brought a new sense of scale to classical instrumental forms. With Beethoven, classical forms are greatly extended: the sonata, the symphony, and the string quartet are doubled or tripled in length. The sonority takes on a corresponding increase of force and depth; the themes are characterized by a greater warmth of feeling and often a demoniac power; new chords and new chord progressions are used, and there are more chromaticism, and more fluid modulation; and sudden and striking contrasts are often introduced. The contrasts of themes and tonalities have the force of dramatic conflicts unknown before, conflicts finally dissolved in a triumphant synthesis. As the contemporary novelist E. T. A. Hoffmann wrote, "Beethoven's music sets in motion the lever of fear, of awe, of horror, of suffering, and awakens just that infinite longing which is the essence of Romanticism." What the German Romantic writers were saying about music seemed to be realized by Beethoven. According to these writers, music is the greatest of the arts because it produces the most ecstatic effect and best supplies the soul with its desire for indefinite and infinite longing. The other arts are never able to express their message fully as does music, which best opens unknown realms to man, realms which have nothing to do with the world about him.

As a youth Beethoven received his first instruction from his father and other teachers at his birthplace, Bonn. Later he studied with a number of teachers in Vienna (among whom Mozart may have been one) and likewise had some lessons with Haydn. He then made his living by giving concerts and lessons, and by publishing his music. Unlike Haydn and Mozart, Beethoven was forthright in dealing with patrons and publishers, and never in his life did he force himself to write at someone's command. He was always reasonably well off and left a substantial estate at his death. Beethoven was extremely individualistic and poorly adjusted to the world about him. His manners were gauche, his movements were awkward, and he was quite disdainful of all shams and artificialities. Though he was arrogant, highly sensitive and passionate, and afraid of ridicule, he had a lively and robust sense of humor which often appears in his music. Indeed, nearly all of Beethoven's music, more than that of any composer before him, gives the impression of being a direct expression of his personality. This musical individualism is one of the most Romantic elements in his work. Beethoven's failure to marry and his growing deafness, which began to be evident in 1798 and became nearly total by 1820, increasingly shut him off from the world and turned him in on himself.

The range of Beethoven's work is great; it included nine symphonies, eleven overtures, incidental music to plays, one violin and five piano concertos, sixteen string quartets and other chamber music, ten violin and five cello sonatas, thirty-two piano sonatas and many sets of variations for the piano, an oratorio, an opera, two masses, and a great many songs. Beethoven's music, like the writings of Shakespeare, gives expression to all human experience. The range is from profound meditation and dark despair to the highest exuberance of joy, and from repose to a Promethean energy and a Dionysian ecstasy. Vincent d'Indy divides Beethoven's compositions into three periods, a period of "imitation" when he is still largely under the influence of earlier composers; a second period of "externalization" when Beethoven dares to go forth to do battle for his new ideas; and, finally, a period of "reflection" when he moves into a mysterious realm of his own and invents a series of unprecedented innovations in traditional forms. In the first period, when Beethoven is close to the style of Haydn, he begins to break away from his predecessors. His sonatas have four movements instead of three as was sometimes the case with earlier composers, and, in some of his first sonatas, the classical minuet is replaced by a more robust scherzo. In his first quartets and symphonies, too, he shows his individuality in the character of the themes, the unexpected turns of phrase, and the unconventional modulations.

It is in Beethoven's second period, from about 1803 to 1816, that he wrote the works that have always been most popular. By this time, Beethoven was recognized as the leading concert pianist of Europe, and he was in great demand in Vienna for concerts and for teaching. This period includes the symphonies from the third through the eighth, some of the greatest piano sonatas, the violin concerto, his greatest piano concertos, *Fidelio* (his only opera), and some of his finest quartets. His deafness was increasing, and he was often in deep despair and contemplated suicide. But he said, "I will take fate by the throat; it shall not bend me completely to its will." It is in this period that Beethoven first exploits fully the uses of the piano. The instrument had been invented by the Italians in the early eighteenth century but was slow in coming into general use. The piano's range of expression was very great, and as it is the easiest of all instruments to play, it gradually became a favorite of the middle classes. Beethoven now supplied the instrument with music of magical richness and beauty.

There is no more characteristic work of Beethoven's second period than his Third Symphony, originally dedicated to Napoleon and then, when Napoleon made himself emperor, to the "memory of a great man." The movements are much longer than in any previous symphony. It moves from defiant courage in the first movement to black despair in the funeral march of the second. In the third movement there is an indomitable resurgence of hope, and in the last movement there is a theme that, in a number of Beethoven's other works, is associated with Prometheus. The Third Symphony is an early example of Beethoven's love of variations on a theme, which became one of the most characteristic features of his style. His variations are melodic, rhythmic, and harmonic, and they become really a thematic development rather than the usual repetition in various forms of the same musical idea. In the form and length of the Third Symphony, and its revolutionary orchestration, he created something unlike anything that had been done before. As a result, it took a while for the symphony to be understood even by the most cultivated part of the public. As came to be seen later, the amazing feature of the Third Symphony—and this remains true of much of the music of Beethoven's middle period—is the way one theme seems inevitably to follow from the one before. There is a steady dynamic growth which moves from one climax to another, and the whole is organized into a superb musical unity. This quality of inevitability, which Mozart seems to have achieved with utter ease, came to Beethoven only after a long struggle. His notebooks show the slow and painful methods of the growth of his compositions from the first sketches to the final creation.

In these works of the years 1803 to 1816, the old forms are expanded to unprecedented proportions by the multiplication of themes, by the long, varied, and complex developments, and by the lengthened codas, which sometimes take on the dimensions of a second development section. Beethoven often conceals the dividing lines between the several parts of a movement, recapitulations are varied, new themes arise ingeniously out of earlier themes, and the whole progresses with a driving and organic character that plays with, and at the same time defies, the precise patterns of classical music. These changes are more marked in the sonatas and quartets than in the symphonies of this period.

In his final period, 1816 to 1827, Beethoven wrote the Ninth Symphony with its choral ode in the final movement, the *Missa Solemnis,* and his last five string quartets. He was now living in a soundless world; he retreated within himself and became more difficult even for his closest friends. Musically, he seems to have become entirely detached from the bonds of this world and to be living in the boundless reaches of eternity. Beethoven's music now has a more contemplative character; the former passionate urge to communicate has subsided, and its place is taken by a sense of peace and calm affirmation. His style also has become more abstract; he uses more contrapuntal devices, and his handling of the old forms is much freer—for example, Opus 131 has seven movements. He now works out themes and motifs to their ultimate implications. We seem to hear the composer as he meditates on his themes, finding continually new depths and slowly leading into worlds where the music becomes a sort of mystic revelation. Few of Beethoven's contemporaries understood the works of these last years, and his influence on them stems chiefly from the compositions of his middle period.

While Beethoven was at the height of his fame, two much younger men, Von Weber and Schubert, were likewise finding new paths in Romanticism in music. We see in both these composers what was to be common in the later Romantic style in music. The rhythms are less marked and less varied than in classical music; and more attention is paid to lyrical melody, to new harmonic techniques, and to instrumental color. The outlines of tonality are less sharply marked. New chords and chord progressions and modulations are exploited. More use is made of the brasses and wood winds in the orchestras, and contrapuntal forms are little used. Kinship between the inner life of the composer and nature, already evident in Haydn's choral works and in some of the compositions of Beethoven, as the "Pastoral" Symphony, becomes more marked. From Haydn's *Creation* and *Seasons* and from Beethoven came the growing Romantic delight in painting the world of nature; from Mozart and Beethoven came the Romantic interest in depicting the personal emotions of the composer; and from Beethoven was derived

the means of expressing Romanticism's limitless aspirations and its passionate search for the ideal.

Von Weber (d. 1826), though he died at thirty-nine, left a good many
piano and orchestral works. But he is best known for his three operas,
Der Freischütz, Euryanthe, and *Oberon.* Their subjects are derived from
German folklore and old legends and, to heighten dramatic interest,
supernatural forces are freely used. The last two operas suffer from their
poor librettos, and Weber thus is best known through his *Freischütz.*
Here he is the founder of German Romantic opera and the precursor of
the modern music drama. The story is centered on a man who has sold
his soul to the devil for some magic bullets which will permit him to
win a shooting contest and, thereby, the lady he loves. The devil is
cheated, the hero is saved, and the opera ends happily. The dark forest
background is depicted in various forms by the orchestra, sometimes in
the light of daytime, sometimes in the moonlight. Choruses, dances, and
songs of the peasants mingle with arias in an Italianate style. Much use
is made of folk, or folklike, melodies, and of recurrent themes that
begin in the overture and run through the whole opera. This was a
device that was not entirely new, but had never been used so effectively
before, and it was later taken over by Wagner in his music dramas. *Der
Freischütz* has the atmosphere of much German Romantic literature and
painting in that it is filled with the spirit of old Germanic legends and
folk tales, with a close communion with nature and with simple homely
things from the life of the German people. The success of *Der Freischütz* was immediate, and the opera has remained in the usual opera
repertory. Weber's influence on Berlioz and Wagner and a number of
other composers was profound. Wagner began his career as a conductor
in Dresden with a performance of Weber's *Euryanthe,* and he was the
main speaker at the time of Weber's reburial in Dresden in 1844.

Under the shadow and deeply under the influence of the great Beethoven in Vienna, lived Schubert (d. 1828), a much younger man, and
one of a quite different temperament. To us, he seems the very personification of the musical spirit of Old Vienna. No composer ever excelled
Schubert in his inexhaustible flow of melody, which has the natural
attractiveness and warmth of sentiment of folk song and is consistently
endowed with simplicity, directness, and nobility. Much of his music
was written for the living room of the Viennese house rather than for
the theater or concert hall. Like Beethoven, Schubert held no position
with theater, church, or court; and he made a very humble livelihood,

first as a schoolteacher, then through the publication of some of his works and by selling his manuscripts to musical societies. Thus, like Beethoven he did not compose to order, but only as his genius prompted him. He was the center of a small circle of musical and artistic young men who used to meet in their homes or in a beer hall, where usually Schubert's music had its first performances. Although by no means unknown in his native city, Vienna, he never received wide recognition or much money. Many of his immortal songs he sold for a dollar or two, and he was usually in debt. But his Bohemian life seems not to have made him unhappy or interfered with his composing. He died at the age of thirty-one, and on his tombstone is inscribed, "Music has here buried a rich treasure but still fairer hopes."

Schubert's works include nine symphonies, twenty-two piano sonatas, and a large number of short piano compositions, trios, quartets, and quintets, six masses, some operatic works, and over six hundred songs. In all these works he was not only a superb writer of melodies; he was also a very original harmonist, chiefly in his use of modulations where he achieved an unusual color and richness of expression. Schubert must have been a modest man, for though he was a master of contrapuntal effects, he made arrangements shortly before his death to study with a professor of counterpoint. His piano works show that he realized fully the possibilities both of the enlarged pianos of his time with their increased sonority and of the development of new techniques of playing. In the period after 1815 the piano clearly became the supreme Romantic instrument. Schubert's piano music shows a mixture of classical and Romantic elements. His sonatas are based on the patterns of Haydn and Mozart, but his fantasies, impromptus, and other short piano compositions show the influence of Beethoven. He excelled in melodic invention rather than in thematic development and his style is poetic and lyric rather than inventive or profound. Schubert's orchestral works use the conventional orchestration of Haydn and Mozart, and his symphonies are in the spirit of the classical symphonic form. Schubert lacked Beethoven's originality both in the use of new orchestral color and in thematic development, his themes being usually only repeated or transposed. His harmonies and modulations, however, are original, and give his music its special quality. His achievement is none the less remarkable when it is remembered that he never had adequate opportunity to try out his effects with an orchestra.

Schubert's greatest achievement lies in his more than six hundred songs. For texts he turned to the wealth of German verse produced by Goethe and his younger contemporaries. In that sense Schubert's achievement depended on an earlier development of German verse. At the same time, his enrichment of the piano accompaniment, until it became as important as the vocal part and supported and intensified the meaning of the poetry, was possible only because of the enhanced sonority attained by the piano. Some of his songs repeat the same music for each stanza, others are "through-composed" and the music changes with each stanza. The variety of moods in these songs is seemingly endless. Everywhere the music shows great sensitivity to the text. Often the very first bars of a song will evoke the poetic atmosphere of the whole work. Beyond this, Schubert shows unending resource in the color of his modulations, in enlarging or condensing phrases, and compensating this through variations in melody or rhythm. The German song was centuries old, and Schubert's achievement was based on a long earlier history, but to him belongs the credit of raising the song to a great art form.

5. Conclusion

Neo-Classicism and Romanticism in art and letters had begun together about the middle of the eighteenth century, and they long continued to run parallel. But Romanticism in music followed rather than paralleled classicism in music; and Romanticism in music only appeared at a time when this movement was reaching its climax in art and literature. This account extends only to about 1830, yet, as the nineteenth century proceeded, Neo-Classicism and Romanticism in art and literature continued side by side, and they both went on well into the twentieth century—all this in spite of the rise of Realism in painting and literature in the 1840's and the subsequent development of Functionalism in architecture. Thus, the movements in the art and literature became more complex; the new came in alongside of the old without, however, supplanting it. In music, Romanticism, which appeared late on the scene with Beethoven and Schubert, produced a series of great figures, such as Berlioz, Schumann, Mendelssohn, Chopin, Liszt, and Wagner, and still dominated music at the opening of the twentieth century. There are, thus, in the period 1750 to 1830 and beyond, parallels in the nature of the arts, but not in their timing.

BIBLIOGRAPHY

CHAPTER I

STYLE

M. Schapiro, "Style" in A. L. Kroeber (ed.), *Anthropology Today* (Chicago, 1953); articles "Style" and "Form" in J. T. Shipley (ed.), *Dictionary of World Literature* (new ed.; New York, 1953); "Style" in W. Apel (ed.), *Harvard Dictionary of Music* (Cambridge, 1950); R. Wellek and A. Warren, *Theory of Literature* (new ed.; New York, 1956); P. van Tieghem, *La littérature comparée* (Paris, 1931); H. Levin, "Literature as an Institution," *Accent,* 1946; W. Witte, "The Sociological Approach to Literature," *Modern Language Review,* 1941; A. C. Sewter, "The Possibilities of a Sociology of Art," *Sociological Review,* 1935; R. Wellek, "The Parallelism between Literature and the Arts," *English Institute Annual,* 1941; H. Focillon, *La vie des formes* (Paris, 1936; 2d English ed. rev.; New York, 1948); A. Hauser, *Social History of Art* (new ed.; 2 vols.; New York, 1957) and "Style and Its Changes," *Philosophy of Art History* (New York, 1959), pp. 207–36; W. Sypher, *Four Stages of Renaissance Style* (New York, 1955); R. Lee, "Ut pictura poesis," *Art Bulletin,* 1940; H. Lévy, *Wölfflin* (Paris, 1936); and A. Werner, "New Perspectives on the Old Masters," *Arts Yearbook,* 1957.

GENERAL

J. Delorme, *Chronologie des civilisations* (Paris, 1949); S. H. Steinberg, *Historical Tables, 58 B.C.–A.D. 1955* (4th ed.; London, 1956); A. Mayer, *Annals of European Civilization, 1501–1900* (London, 1949); A. W. Mitchell,

Historical Charts of the Humanities (New York, 1939); T. Munro, *The Arts and Their Interrelations* (New York, 1949); A. von Martin, *Sociology of the Renaissance* (London, 1944); A. Soreil, *Introduction à l'histoire de l'esthétique française* (new ed.; Brussels, 1955); W. K. Ferguson, *Renaissance in Historical Thought* (Boston, 1948); H. O. Taylor, *Thought and Expression in the Sixteenth Century* (2 vols.; New York, 1920); N. A. Robb, *Neoplatonism of the Italian Renaissance* (London, 1935); D. J. McGinn and G. Howerton (eds.), *Literature as a Fine Art* (Evanston, Ill., 1959); E. G. Gardner (ed.), *Italy: A Companion to Italian Studies* (London, 1934); A. Tilley, *Modern France: A Companion to French Studies* (Cambridge, 1922); R. L. Ritchie (ed.), *France: A Companion to French Studies* (5th ed.; London, 1953); E. A. Peers (ed.), *Spain: A Companion to Spanish Studies* (5th ed.; London, 1956); and J. Bithell (ed.), *Germany: A Companion to German Studies* (5th ed.; London, 1955).

ART

GENERAL

Art Index (1933 ff.; lists articles); M. W. Chamberlin (ed.), *Guide to Art Reference Books* (Chicago, 1959); G. von Schlosser, *Die Kunstliteratur* (Vienna, 1924); E. L. Lucas (ed.), *Harvard List of Books on Art* (new ed.; Cambridge, Mass., 1952); *Encyclopedia of World Art* (New York, 1959 ff.); L. Hourticq (ed.), *Harper's Encyclopedia of Art* (2 vols.; New York, 1937); D. D. Runes and H. G. Schrickel (eds.), *Encyclopedia of the Arts* (New York, 1946); E. Bénézit, *Dictionnaire des peintres, sculptures, dessinateurs, et graveurs* (3 vols.; Paris, 1924); N. Pevsner (ed.), *Pelican History of Art* (many vols.; London, 1950 ff.); R. Goldwater and M. Treves, *Artists on Art* (3d ed.; New York, 1958); E. G. Holt (ed.), *Documentary History of Art* (2 vols.; New York, 1957–58); H. Gardner, *Art through the Ages* (4th ed.; New York, 1959); P. Lavedan, *Histoire de l'art,* Vol. II (2d ed.; Paris, 1950); D. M. Robb and J. J. Garrison, *Art in the Western World* (2d ed.; New York, 1942); E. H. Gombrich, *Story of Art* (new ed.; New York, 1958); W. Fleming, *Art and Ideas* (New York, 1955); B. S. Myers, *Art and Civilization* (New York, 1957); E. M. Upjohn and others, *History of World Art* (2d ed.; New York, 1958); L. Venturi, *History of Art Criticism* (New York, 1936); F. P. Chambers, *History of Taste* (New York, 1932); K. Gilbert and H. Kuhn, *History of Esthetics* (rev. ed.; Bloomington, Ind., 1953); H. Wölfflin, *Principles of Art History* (New York, 1929); A. A. Hatzfeld, *Literature through Art: A New Approach to French Literature* (Oxford, 1952); E. Panofsky, *Renaissance and Renascences in Western Art* (2 vols.; Stockholm, 1960) and *Studies in Iconology* (New York, 1939); N. Pevsner, *Academies of Art* (Cambridge, 1940); A. Blunt, *Artistic Theory in Italy* (new ed.; Oxford, 1959); A. Chastel, *L'art italien* (2 vols.; Paris, 1956); W. Weisinger, "Renaissance Theories of the Revival of the Fine Arts," *Italica,* 1943; W. Paatz, *Die Kunst der Renaissance in Italien* (Stuttgart, 1953); A. Blunt, *Art and Architecture in France, 1500–1700* (London, 1953); and J. J. Timmers, *History of Dutch Art and Life* (London, 1959).

PAINTING

F. R. Shapley and J. Shapley, *Comparisons in Art* (New York, 1957); K. Clark, *Landscape into Art* (2d ed.; London, 1956); H. W. Janson and D. J. Janson, *Picture History of Painting* (New York, 1957); D. M. Robb, *Harpers History of Painting* (New York, 1951); F. J. Mather, *Western European Painting of the Renaissance* (New York, 1939); J. White, *Birth and Rebirth of Pictorial Space* (London, 1957); C. Gould, *An Introduction to Italian Renaissance Painting* (London, 1957); B. Berenson, *Italian Painters of the Renaissance* (many editions); F. M. Godfrey, *Early Italian Painting, 1250–1500* (London, 1958) and *Later Italian Painting, 1500–1800* (London, 1958); E. T. De Wald, *Italian Painting, 1200–1800* (New York, 1961); O. Hagen, *Patterns and Principles of Spanish Art* (Madison, 1936); E. Harris, *Spanish Painting* (New York, 1937); a series of studies by R. Wilenski: *Dutch Painting* (New York, 1955), *Flemish Painters, 1430–1830* (2 vols.; The Hague, 1959), and *French Painting* (Boston, 1936); and the series of Skira volumes: *Italian Painting* (3 vols.), *Flemish Painting* (2 vols.), *Spanish Painting* (2 vols.), and *Dutch Painting* (1 vol.). In addition Skira has published a long series of volumes on "Great Centuries of Painting."

SCULPTURE

G. H. Chase and C. R. Post, *History of Sculpture* (New York, 1925); C. R. Post, *History of European and American Sculpture* (2 vols.; Cambridge, Mass., 1921); and L. Rothschild, *Sculpture through the Ages* (New York, 1942).

ARCHITECTURE

R. Sturgis, *Dictionary of Architecture* (3 vols.; New York, 1901–3); three works by M. S. Briggs: *Short History of the Building Crafts* (Oxford, 1925), *The Architect in History* (Oxford, 1927), and *Everyman's Encyclopedia of Architecture* (London, 1959); B. Fletcher, *History of Architecture* (17th ed.; London, 1956); T. Hamlin, *Architecture through the Ages* (2d ed.; New York, 1953); N. Pevsner, *Outline of European Architecture* (5th ed.; London, 1957); G. Scott, *The Architecture of Humanism* (2d ed.; New York, 1924); R. Wittkower, *Architectural Principles in the Age of Humanism* (2d ed.; London, 1952); B. Allsopp, *History of Renaissance Architecture* (London, 1959); Q. Hughes and N. Synton, *Renaissance Architecture* (London, 1962); J. Summerson, *Architecture in Britain, 1530–1830* (London, 1953); B. Kaye, *Development of the Architectural Profession in Britain* (London, 1959);

P. Lavedan, *Histoire de l'urbanisme,* Vol. II (Paris, 1952); and R. H. Schol-
field, *Theory of Proportion in Architecture* (Cambridge, 1938).

LITERATURE

GENERAL

Year's Work in Modern Language Studies (1929 ff.); *Yearbook of Comparative and General Literature* (1951 ff.); *Revue de la littérature comparée*
(1921 ff.); *Comparative Literature* (1949 ff.); C. S. Brown (ed.), *Reader's
Companion to World Literature* (New York, 1956); L. Magnus (ed.), *Dictionary of World Literature* (2d ed.; London, 1927); J. T. Shipley (ed.),
Dictionary of World Literature (New York, 1953) and *Encyclopedia of Literature* (2 vols.; New York, 1946); S. H. Steinberg (ed.), *Cassell's Encyclopedia
of Literature* (2 vols.; London, 1953); H. R. Keller (ed.), *Reader's Digest
of Books* (new ed.; New York, 1945); F. N. Magill (ed.), *Masterplots* (8 vols.;
New York, 1955–60); R. W. Horton and V. F. Hopper, *Backgrounds of
European Literature* (New York, 1954); W. P. Friedrich and D. H. Malone,
Outline of Comparative Literature (Chapel Hill, N.C., 1954); N. Ségur,
Histoire de la littérature européenne (5 vols.; Paris, 1948–52); H. Peyre, *Les
générations littéraires* (Paris, 1948); L. Magnus, *History of European Liter-
ature* (London, 1934) and *European Literature in the Centuries of Romance*
(London, 1918); B. B. Trawick, *World Literature,* Vol. II (New York, 1955);
P. van Tieghem, *Histoire littéraire de l'Europe et d'Amérique de la Renais-
sance à nos jours* (2d ed.; Paris, 1946; English translation of an earlier edition,
New York, 1930); P. van Tieghem (ed.), *Répertoire chronologique des lit-
tératures modernes* (Paris, 1937); J. M. Cohen, *History of Western Literature*
(London, 1956); A. C. Ward, *Landmarks in Western Literature* (London,
1932); C. Laird (ed.), *The World through Literature* (New York, 1951);
J. B. Priestley, *Literature of Western Man* (London, 1959); J. H. Horn (ed.),
Literary Masterpieces of the Western World (Baltimore, 1953); E. Neff,
Revolution in Poetry, 1600–1900 (New York, 1940); H. F. Hopper and B. D.
Grebanier, *Essentials of European Literature* (3 vols.; New York, 1953);
R. Wellek, "Periods and Movements in Literary History," *English Institute
Annual,* 1941; R. Wellek and A. Warren, *Theory of Literature* (new ed.;
New York, 1956); A. L. Guérard, *Preface to World Literature* (New York,
1940); A. Brett-James, *Triple Stream: English, French, and German Liter-
ature, 1531–1930* (Cambridge, 1953); G. Murray, *The Classical Tradition in
Poetry* (Cambridge, Mass., 1927); G. Highet, *The Classical Tradition* (Ox-
ford, 1949); D. Bush, *Classical Influences in Renaissance Literature* (Cam-
bridge, Mass., 1952); P. O. Kristeller, *Classics and Renaissance Thought*
(Cambridge, Mass., 1956); C. Brooks (ed.), *Tragic Themes in Western
Literature* (New Haven, 1955); C. M. Bowra, *From Virgil to Milton* (Lon-

don, 1945) and *Heroic Poetry* (Oxford, 1952); C. S. Brown, *Music and Literature* (New York, 1948); W. G. Howard, "Ut pictura poesis," *PMLA,* 1909; and M. Valency, *In Praise of Love: Introduction to Love Poetry of the Renaissance* (New York, 1958).

ANTHOLOGIES

M. Van Doren (ed.), *Anthology of World Poetry* (New York, 1939) and *Anthology of World Prose* (New York, 1939); M. Mack and others (eds.), *World Masterpieces* (2 vols.; New York, 1956); S. Thompson (ed.), *Our Heritage of World Literature* (New York, 1938); J. W. Cunliffe (ed.), *Century Readings in European Literature* (New York, 1925); E. H. Weatherly and others (eds.), *Heritage of European Literature* (2 vols.; Boston, 1948); D. J. McGinn and G. Howerton (eds.), *Literature as a Fine Art* (Evanston, Ill., 1959); H. H. Blanchard (ed.), *Prose and Poetry of the Continental Renaissance* (2d ed.; New York, 1955); and H. Haydn and J. C. Nelson (eds.), *Renaissance Treasury* (New York, 1953).

LITERARY CRITICISM

A. H. Gilbert (ed.), *Literary Criticism* (2 vols.; New York, 1940–41); J. H. Smith and E. W. Parks (eds.), *The Great Critics* (3d ed.; New York, 1951); W. J. Bate (ed.), *Criticism, the Major Texts* (New York, 1952); F. Brunetière, *Evolution de la critique* (6th ed.; Paris, 1914); W. K. Wimsatt and C. Brooks, *Literary Criticism, a Short History* (New York, 1957); R. Wellek, *History of Modern Criticism* (2 vols.; New Haven, 1955); L. Cooper, *The Poetics of Aristotle* (Ithaca, 1956); J. E. Spingarn, *Literary Criticism in the Renaissance* (2d ed.; New York, 1908); C. S. Baldwin, *Renaissance Literary Theory and Practice, 1400–1600* (New York, 1939); V. Hall, *Renaissance Literary Criticism* (New York, 1945); J. W. Atkins, *English Literary Criticism* (3 vols.; Cambridge, 1943–51); I. Babbitt, *The New Laokoön* (Boston, 1910); M. T. Herrick, *The Fusion of Horatian and Aristotelian Literary Criticism* (Urbana, Ill., 1946); and L. L. Schücking, *Sociology of Literary Taste* (London, 1944); cf. also bibliography for chapter iv.

DRAMA

P. Hartnoll (ed.), *Oxford Companion to the Theater* (2d ed.; Oxford, 1957); E. Bentley (ed.), *Classic Theater* (4 vols.; New York, 1958–62); A. Nicoll, *World Drama* (New York, 1950); K. Macgowan and W. Melnitz, *The Living Stage* (New York, 1955); J. Gassner, *Masters of the Drama* (3d ed.; New York, 1954); A. Nicoll, *Development of the Theater* (3d ed.; New York, 1948) and *Masks, Mimes, and Miracles* (New York, 1931); and V. H. Cartmell, *Play Outlines of One Hundred Famous Plays* (New York, 1952).

NATIONAL LITERATURES

Italy: F. de Sanctis, *History of Italian Literature* (2 vols.; New York, 1959);
E. H. Wilkins, *History of Italian Literature* (Cambridge, Mass., 1954); R. A.
Hall, Jr., *Short History of Italian Literature* (Ithaca, 1951); H. Hauvette,
Littérature italienne (6th ed.; Paris, 1924); J. Fletcher, *Literature of the
Italian Renaissance* (New York, 1934); G. R. Kay (ed.), *Penguin Book of
Italian Verse* (London, 1958); L. E. Lind (ed.), *Lyric Poetry of the Italian
Renaissance* (New Haven, 1954); and M. T. Herrick, *Italian Comedy of the
Renaissance* (Urbana, Ill., 1960).

France: D. C. Cabeen, *Critical Bibliography of French Literature* (New
York, 1947 ff.); P. Harvey and J. Heseltine (eds.), *Oxford Companion to
French Literature* (Oxford, 1958); S. D. Braun (ed.), *Dictionary of French
Literature* (New York, 1961); W. A. Nitze and E. P. Dargan, *History of
French Literature* (3d ed.; New York, 1938); R. Jasinski, *Histoire de la lit-
térature française* (2 vols.; Paris, 1947); J. Bédier and P. Hazard, *Littérature
française* (new ed.; 2 vols.; Paris, 1948); G. Mason, *Concise Survey of French
Literature* (London, 1959); G. Brereton, *Short History of French Literature*
(London, 1954); P. G. Castex and P. Surer, *Manuel des études littéraires fran-
çaises* (2 vols.; Paris, 1954); G. Brereton, *Introduction to French Poets* (London, 1956); H. Hatzfeld, *Literature through Art* (Oxford, 1952); P. van
Tieghem, *Petite histoire des grandes doctrines littéraires en France* (Paris,
1950); W. F. Patterson, *Three Centuries of French Poetic Theory* (Ann
Arbor, Mich., 1935); H. Peyre, *L'influence des littératures antiques sur la littérature française moderne, état des travaux* (New Haven, 1941); G. Brereton
and A. Hartley (eds.), *Penguin Books of French Verse* (2 vols., 1957–58).

Spain: G. T. Northup, *Introduction to Spanish Literature* (new ed.; Chi-
cago, 1960); E. Mérimée and S. G. Morley, *History of Spanish Literature*
(New York, 1930); G. Brenan, *Literature of the Spanish People* (Cambridge,
1951); R. S. Boggs, *Outline History of Spanish Literature* (Boston, 1937);
E. T. Turnbull (tr.), *Ten Centuries of Spanish Poetry* (Baltimore, 1955); and
J. M. Cohen (ed.), *Penguin Book of Spanish Verse* (London, 1956).

Germany: W. P. Friederich, *Outline History of German Literature* (new
ed.; New York, 1961); J. G. Robertson, *History of German Literature* (3d ed.;
London, 1959); E. Rose, *History of German Literature* (New York, 1960);
G. Whitehouse, *Short History of German Literature* (3d ed.; London, 1959);
G. E. Spenlé, *La pensée allemande de Luther à Nietzsche* (Paris, 1934); F. O.
Nolte, *German Literature and the Classics: A Guide* (Cambridge, Mass.,
1935); A. Closs, *Genius of the German Lyric* (London, 1938); and L. W.
Forster (ed.), *Penguin Book of German Verse* (London, 1957).

England: Bateson, *Concise Cambridge Bibliography of English Literature*
(Cambridge, 1960, based on a 5-vol. work, 1941–57); P. Harvey (ed.), *Oxford
Companion to English Literature* (3d ed.; Oxford, 1946); W. Davin and R.

W. Chapman (eds.), *Annals of English Literature, 1475-1950* (new ed.; London, 1961); A. C. Baugh (ed.), *Literary History of England* (New York, 1948); H. Craig (ed.), *History of English Literature* (Oxford, 1950); B. Dobrée (ed.), *Introductions to English Literature* (2d ed.; 5 vols.; London, 1950); L. Leavy, *Contemporary Literary Scholarship* (New York, 1958); T. G. Tucker, *The Foreign Debt of English Literature* (London, 1907); J. A. Thompson, *The Classical Background of English Literature* (London, 1948); and D. Bush, *Mythology and the Renaissance Tradition in English Poetry* (Minneapolis, 1932).

MUSIC

GENERAL

E. C. Krohn, *History of Music: An Index to the Literature in Musicological Publications* (St. Louis, 1952); R. D. Darrell (ed.), *Schirmer's Guide to Works on Music* (New York, 1951); G. Haydon, *Introduction to Musicology* (Chapel Hill, N.C., 1959); J. A. Westrup, *Introduction to Musical History* (London, 1955); W. D. Allen, *Philosophies of Music History* (New York, 1939); H. Leichtentritt, *Musical Form* (Cambridge, Mass., 1951); E. Blom (ed.), *Grove's Dictionary of Music and Musicians* (5th ed.; 9 vols.; London, 1954; and supplementary vol., London, 1961); W. Apel (ed.), *Harvard Dictionary of Music* (new ed.; Cambridge, Mass., 1955); *Baker's Biographical Dictionary of Musicians* (5th ed.; New York, 1958); J. A. Westrup and F. L. Harrison (eds.), *Collins' Music Encyclopedia* (London, 1959); P. Scholes (ed.), *Oxford Companion to Music* (9th ed.; Oxford, 1955); N. Dufourcq (ed.), *Larousse de la musique* (3 vols.; Paris, 1957); F. Michel and others (eds.), *Encyclopédie de la musique* (3 vols.; Paris, 1958 ff.); E. Blom (ed.), *Everyman's Dictionary of Music* (rev. ed.; London, 1954); O. Thompson, *Tabulated Biographical History of Music* (New York, 1936); A. L. Bachrach (ed.), *The Great Masters* (4 vols.; London, 1957-58); A. T. Davidson and W. Apel (eds.), *Historical Anthology of Music* (2 vols.; Cambridge, Mass., 1950); C. Parrish and J. F. Ohl (eds.), *Masterpieces of Music before 1750* (New York, 1951, all compositions recorded on 3 records by Haydn Society); C. Parrish (ed.), *Treasury of Early Music* (New York, 1958); H. Riemann, *Musikgeschichte in Beispielen* (4th ed.; Leipzig, 1929); O. Strunk (ed.), *Source Readings in Music History* (New York, 1950); H. L. Clarke, "Toward a Musical Periodization of Music," *Journal of American Musicological Society,* 1956; and H. Leichtentritt, "Aesthetic Ideas as the Basis of Musical Styles," *Journal of Aesthetics and Art Criticism,* 1945.

HISTORY OF MUSIC

J. A. Westrup and others (eds.), *New Oxford History of Music* (11 vols.; Oxford, 1956 ff.); K. Nef, *Outline of the History of Music* (New York, 1939); A. Einstein, *Short History of Music* (4th ed.; New York, 1954); C. Sachs,

Our Musical Heritage (New York, 1948); H. A. Miller, *History of Music* (2d ed.; New York, 1953); H. C. Colles, *Growth of Music* (3d ed.; London, 1956); B. C. Cannon and others, *Art of Music: A Short History* (New York, 1960); H. Leichtentritt, *Music, History, and Ideas* (Cambridge, Mass., 1954); T. M. Finney, *History of Music* (rev. ed.; New York, 1947); D. N. Ferguson, *History of Musical Thought* (3d ed.; New York, 1959); H. D. McKinney and W. R. Anderson, *Music in History* (2d ed.; New York, 1957); P. H. Lang, *Music in Western Civilization* (New York, 1941); A. Harman and others, *Man and His Music* (4 vols.; London, 1958–59); D. J. Grout, *History of Western Music* (New York, 1960); P. Garvie (ed.), *Music and Western Man* (London, 1958); G. Kinsky (ed.), *History of Music in Pictures* (New York, 1930); M. Pincherle, *Illustrated History of Music* (New York, 1959); P. Collaer and A. Van der Linden, *Atlas historique de la musique* (Paris, 1960); P. Lang and O. Bettman, *Pictorial History of Music* (New York, 1961); R. Stevenson, *Music before the Classic Era* (London, 1955); D. J. Grout, *Short History of Opera* (2 vols.; New York, 1947); A. Loewenberg, *Annals of Opera, 1597–1940* (2 vols.; Geneva, 1955); E. E. Lowinsky, "Music History and Its Relation to the History of Ideas," *Music Journal,* 1946; and A. Einstein, *The Italian Madrigal* (3 vols.; Princeton, 1949).

C. S. Brown, *Music and Literature: A Comparison* (Athens, Ga., 1948) and *Tones into Words: Musical Compositions as Subjects of Poetry* (Athens, Ga., 1953); C. Sachs, *History of Musical Instruments* (New York, 1940); K. Geiringer, *Musical Instruments* (Oxford, 1945); and W. Apel, *Notation of Polyphonic Music, 900–1600* (4th ed.; Cambridge, Mass., 1949).

C. Parrish and J. F. Ohl, *Masterpieces of Music before 1750* (3 records, Haydn Society); *History of Music in Sound* (1953 ff.; 10 vols., with pamphlets containing music scores, published by Oxford University Press); *History of Music in Sound* and the *Decca Archiv Production* (a long series of records of music from Gregorian chant through Mozart and later).

CHAPTER II
Nature of the Renaissance

P. Helton (ed.), *The Renaissance* (Madison, Wis., 1961); D. Hay, *The Renaissance* (Cambridge, 1961); F. Chabod, *Machiavelli and the Renaissance* (Cambridge, Mass., 1958), especially the bibliography; *Renaissance News,* 1948 ff.; *Studies in the Renaissance,* 1954 ff.; *Journal of the Warburg Institute,* 1937 ff.; W. K. Ferguson, *The Renaissance in Historical Thought* (Boston,

1948); K. M. Setton, "Some Recent Views of the Italian Renaissance," *Report of the Annual Meeting of the Canadian Historical Association,* 1947; E. F. Jacob and A. S. Turberville, "Changing Views of the Renaissance," *History,* 1931–32; J. Huizinga, "Le problème de la Renaissance," *Revue des cours et conferences,* 1938–39; L. Thorndike, "Renaissance or Pre-renaissance?" *Journal of the History of Ideas,* 1943; three articles by H. Baron, "A Sociological Interpretation of the Early Renaissance in Florence," *South Atlantic Quarterly,* 1939; "The Historical Background of the Florentine Renaissance," *History,* 1938; and "Toward a More Positive Evaluation of the 15th Century Renaissance," *Journal of the History of Ideas,* 1943; four articles by H. Weisinger, "Renaissance Theories of the Revival of the Fine Arts," *Italica,* 1943; "The Self-Awareness of the Renaissance" and "Who Began the Revival of Learning?" *Papers of the Michigan Academy,* 1944; and "The Renaissance Theory of Reaction against the Middle Ages," *Speculum,* 1945; D. B. Durand and H. Baron, "Tradition and Innovation in the 15th Century Renaissance," *Journal of the History of Ideas,* 1943; P. O. Kristeller, "Humanism and Scholasticism in the Italian Renaissance," *Byzantion,* 1945; A. Chastel, *Art et humanisme au temps de Laurent le Magnifique* (2d ed.; Paris, 1961); two works by W. H. Woodward, *Vittorino da Feltre and Other Humanist Educators* (Cambridge, 1897) and *Studies in Education, 1400–1600* (Cambridge, 1906); S. H. Thomson, "Pro saeculo XIV," *Speculum,* 1953; P. O. Kristeller, "Place of Classical Humanism in Renaissance Thought," *Journal of History of Ideas,* 1943; Bedarida (ed.), *Pensée humaniste et tradition chrétienne, XVᵉ–XVIᵉ siècles* (Paris, 1950); G. Post and others, "The Medieval Heritage and the Humanist Ideal," *Traditio,* 1955; W. J. Bowsma (ed.), *Interpretation of Renaissance Humanism* (Washington, 1959); and W. K. Ferguson, "The Interpretation of the Renaissance: Suggestions for a Synthesis," *Journal of the History of Ideas,* 1951.

ART

E. Panofsky, *Renaissance and Renascences in Western Art* (2 vols.; Stockholm, 1960); O. Sirén, *Giotto and Some of His Followers* (2 vols.; Cambridge, Mass., 1917); J. Mesnil, *Masaccio* (The Hague, 1927); G. Fiocco, *Mantegna* (Paris, 1938); E. Tietze-Conrat (ed.), *Mantegna* (London, 1955); K. M. Clark (ed.), *Piero della Francesca* (Oxford, 1951); A. Chastel, *Botticelli* (New York, 1958); L. Goldscheider (ed.), *Botticelli* (Vienna, 1937); P. Hendy and L. Goldscheider, *Giovanni Bellini* (Oxford, 1945); J. Walker, *Bellini and Titian at Ferrara* (London, 1956); J. Pope-Hennessy (ed.), *Italian Renaissance Sculpture* (London, 1958); G. H. Crichton, *Nicola Pisano* (Cambridge, Mass., 1938); R. Krautheimer, *Ghiberti* (Princeton, 1956); H. W. Janson, *Donatello* (2 vols.; Princeton, 1957); H. Folnesics, *Brunelleschi* (Vienna, 1915); and P. H. Michel, *La pensée de L. B. Alberti* (Paris, 1930).

LITERATURE

J. A. Symonds, *The Revival of Learning* (3d ed.; London, 1897) and *Italian Literature* (2d ed.; London, 1898), Vol. I; P. van Tieghem, *La littérature latine de la Renaissance* (Paris, 1944); E. Garin, *Der italienische Humanismus* (Berne, 1947); F. Schevill (ed.), *First Century of Italian Humanism* (New York, 1928); E. H. R. Tatham, *Petrarch* (2 vols.; London, 1925-26); a long series of admirable studies on Petrarch by E. H. Wilkins reprinted in a number of volumes, cf. especially his *Life of Petrarch* (Chicago, 1961); T. E. Mommsen, "Petrarch's Conception of the Dark Ages," *Speculum,* 1942; E. H. Wilkins, "Survey of Renaissance Petrarchism," *Comparative Literature,* 1950; A. Chastel, *Art et humanisme à Florence au temps de Laurent le Magnifique* (Paris, 1959); W. K. Ferguson, "Revival of Classical Antiquity or the First Century of Humanism, a Reappraisal," *Report of the Annual Meeting of the Canadian Historical Association,* 1957; F. N. Jones, *Boccaccio and His Imitators* (Chicago, 1910); H. Hauvette, *Boccace* (Paris, 1914); E. G. Gardner, *Dukes and Poets in Ferrara* (London, 1904); P. Grillo, *Two Aspects of Chivalry, Pulci and Boiardo* (Providence, 1942); E. W. Edwards, *"Orlando furioso" and Its Predecessor* (Cambridge, 1924); L. Einstein, *Pulci* (Berlin, 1902); M. P. Gilmore, *The World of Humanism, 1453-1517* (New York, 1952); and F. Schevill, *The Medici* (New York, 1949).

MUSIC

Music Index, 1949 ff.; *Musical Quarterly,* 1915 ff.; *Musica Disciplina,* 1946 ff.; G. R. Reese, *Music in the Middle Ages* (New York, 1940) and *Music in the Renaissance* (New York, 1949); E. Lowinsky, "Music in the Culture of the Renaissance," *Journal of the History of Ideas,* 1954; M. F. Bukofzer, *Studies in Renaissance and Baroque Music* (New York, 1950) and "Changing Aspects of Medieval and Renaissance Music," *Musical Quarterly,* 1958; S. Levarie, *Guillaume de Machaut* (New York, 1954); C. van den Borren, *Études sur le XVᵉ siècle musicale* (Antwerp, 1941); M. F. Bukofzer, "Dunstable," *Musical Quarterly,* 1954; C. van den Borren, *Dufay* (Brussels, 1926); E. Krenek, *Ockeghem* (New York, 1953); B. Murray, "New Light on Obrecht," *Musical Quarterly,* 1957; and P. O. Kristeller, "Music and Learning in the Early Italian Renaissance," *Journal of Renaissance and Baroque Music,* 1947.

CHAPTER III

ART

H. Wölfflin, *Classical Art* (reprint; London, 1952); C. Gould, *Introduction to Italian Renaissance Painting* (London, 1957); and R. Wittkower, "The Arts in Western Europe," *New Cambridge Modern History,* Vol. I (Cambridge, 1957).

PAINTING

S. J. Freedberg, *Painting of the High Renaissance in Rome and Florence* (Cambridge, Mass., 1961); K. M. Clark, *Leonardo da Vinci* (Cambridge, 1939); L. Goldscheider (ed.), *Leonardo da Vinci* (2d ed.; London, 1944); J. P. Richter (ed.), *Literary Works of Leonardo da Vinci* (2 vols.; Oxford, 1939); O. Fischel, *Raphael* (2 vols.; London, 1948); W. Suida (ed.), *Raphael* (2d ed.; London, 1948); C. de Tolnay, *Michelangelo* (6 vols.; Princeton, 1947 ff.); C. Morgan, *Michelangelo* (New York, 1960); L. Goldscheider (ed.), *Michelangelo* (London, 1959); G. M. Richter, *Giorgione* (Chicago, 1947); J. Babelon, *Titien* (Paris, 1950); H. Tietze (ed.), *Titian* (2d ed.; London, 1950); C. Ricci, *Correggio* (New York, 1930); G. Gronau (ed.), *Correggio* (Stuttgart, 1907); E. Panofsky, *Dürer* (2 vols.; 3d ed.; Princeton, 1948); and P. Ganz, *Holbein* (New York, 1958).

SCULPTURE

G. H. Huntley, *Andrea Sansovino* (Cambridge, 1935). (For Michelangelo cf. "Painting" above.)

ARCHITECTURE

O. H. Förster, *Bramante* (Vienna, 1956); G. Clausse, *Les San Gallo* (3 vols.; Paris, 1900–1902); and W. W. Kent, *Peruzzi* (New York, 1925).

LITERATURE

E. G. Gardner, *King of Court Poets* (Ariosto) (London, 1906); A. H. Gilbert (tr.), *Ariosto's "Orlando furioso"* (2 vols.; New York, 1954); J. Cartwright, *Castiglione* (2 vols.; London, 1908); M. T. Herrick, *Italian Comedy of the Renaissance* (Urbana, Ill., 1961); A. H. Gilbert, *Machiavelli's "Prince" and Its Forerunners* (Durham, 1939); F. Chabod, *Machiavelli and the Renaissance* (Cambridge, Mass., 1958); J. Huizinga, *Erasmus* (New York, 1952); J. Plattard, *Life of Rabelais* (London, 1930); M. Bishop, *Ronsard* (New York, 1940); A. W. Satterthwaite, *Spenser, Ronsard and du Bellay, a Comparison* (Princeton, 1960); R. V. Merrill and R. J. Clements, *Platonism in French Renaissance Poetry* (New York, 1959); H. Keniston, *Garcilaso de la Vega* (New York, 1922); W. C. Atkinson (tr.), *Camoëns' "The Lusiads"* (London, 1952); A. F. G. Bell, *Camoëns* (Oxford, 1923); C. M. Bowra, *From Virgil to Milton* (Oxford, 1945); F. Gundolf, *Opitz* (Munich, 1923); H. Morris, *Elizabethan Literature* (Oxford, 1959); R. Tuve, *Elizabethan and Metaphysical Imagery* (Chicago, 1947); J. Buxton, *Sidney and the English Renaissance* (New York, 1954); H. S. V. Jones, *A Spenser Handbook* (New York, 1930); C. S. Lewis, *Allegory of Love* (Oxford, 1936); H. Levin, *The Overreacher* (Marlowe) (Cambridge, Mass., 1952); and E. K. Chambers, *Shakespeare* (2 vols.; Oxford, 1930).

MUSIC

A. Hughes and G. Abraham, "Ars Nova and the Renaissance, 1300–1540," *New Oxford History of Music,* Vol. III (Oxford, 1959); A. T. Merritt, *Sixteenth Century Polyphony* (Cambridge, Mass., 1939); G. Reese, *Music in the Renaissance* (New York, 1954); E. E. Lowinsky, "Music in the Culture of the Renaissance," *Journal of History of Ideas,* 1954; N. de Robeck, *Music of the Italian Renaissance* (London, 1928); L. C. Delpuech, *Josquin des Près* (St. Quentin, 1945); W. Boetticher, *Orland de Lasso* (Kassel, 1958); C. van den Borren, *Roland de Lassus* (Brussels, 1944); H. Coates, *Palestrina* (New York, 1938); E. H. Fellowes, *Byrd* (2d ed.; Oxford, 1948); G. M. Woodward, "German Hymnody," *Proceedings of the Musical Association,* Vol. XXXII; A. Einstein, *The Italian Madrigal* (3 vols.; Princeton, 1949); F. Lesure, *Musicians and Poets of the French Renaissance* (New York, 1955); E. H. Fellowes, *The English Madrigal Composers* (Oxford, 1921); G. S. Bedbrook, *Keyboard Music from the Middle Ages to the Baroque* (London, 1949); and J. Jacquot (ed.), *La musique instrumentale de la Renaissance* (Paris, 1955).

CHAPTER IV

GENERAL

There is no general work on Mannerism in the arts, except the work of G. R. Hocke, *Der Mannerismus* (2 vols.; Hamburg, 1957), though it omits music. Following are some good introductions to the subject of Mannerism; most of them are concerned with one or another special aspect of Mannerism, but some of the basic concepts of the subject are usually also treated: W. Sypher, *Four Stages of Renaissance Style* (New York, 1955), pp. 100–180; A. Blunt, "Mannerism in Architecture," *Journal of the Royal Institute of Architects,* 1949, and "The Précieux and French Art" in D. J. Jordan (ed.), *Saxl: A Volume of Memorial Essays* (London, 1957); E. B. Borgerhoff, "Mannerism and Baroque," *Comparative Literature,* 1953; W. Friedlander, *Mannerism and Anti-Mannerism in Italian Painting* (New York, 1957); E. H. Gombrich, "Renaissance Idea of Artistic Progress," *Actes du XVIIe Congrès internationale d'histoire de l'art* (The Hague, 1955); N. Pevsner, "The Architecture of Mannerism," *The Mint,* 1946; T. Rousseau, Jr., "Triumph of Mannerism," *Art News,* 1955; M. Treves, "*Maniera,* History of a Word," *Marsyas,* 1941; and I. L. Zupnick, "The Aesthetics of the Early Mannerists," *Art Bulletin,* 1953.

ART

PAINTING

F. M. Clapp, *Pontormo* (New Haven, 1916); S. J. Freedberg, *Parmigianino* (Cambridge, Mass., 1950); F. Hartt, *Giulio Romano* (2 vols.; New Haven,

1958); and A. K. McComb, *Bronzino* (Cambridge, Mass., 1928). The fullest discussion of Michelangelo is C. de Tolnay, *Michelangelo* (5 vols.; Princeton, 1954 ff.) and one-volume studies: C. H. Morgan, *Michelangelo* (New York, 1960); R. J. Clements, *Michelangelo's Theory of Art* (New York, 1961); H. Tietze, *Tintoretto* (New York, 1948); L. Dimier, *La peinture française au XVIᵉ siècle* (Paris, 1942; earlier English version, New York, 1904); S. Béguin, *L'École de Fontainebleau: Le Mannerisme* (Paris, 1961); P. Keleman, *El Greco Revisited* (New York, 1961); H. E. Wethey, *El Greco and His School* (2 vols.; Princeton, 1962); and G. Glück, *Brueghel* (London, 1936).

SCULPTURE

The works on Michelangelo referred to above; E. Dhanes, *Jean Boulogne* (Brussels, 1956); Cellini, *Autobiography* (many editions); P. du Colombier, *Goujon* (Paris, 1949); and C. Terrasse, *Pilon* (Paris, 1930).

ARCHITECTURE

R. Wittkower, *Architectural Principles in the Age of Humanism* (2d ed.; London, 1953) and "Michelangelo's *Bibliotheca Laurenziana*," *Art Bulletin,* 1934; J. S. Ackerman, *Architecture of Michelangelo* (2 vols.; New York, 1961); F. Hartt on Giulio Romano referred to above; G. Lukomskii, *Vignola* (Paris, 1927); Tuckermann (tr.), *Five Orders of Architecture* (Vignola's treatise) (New York, 1891); R. Pane, *Palladio* (Turin, 1948); Palladio's treatise is available in an eighteenth-century English translation by Leoni; R. T. Bloomfield, *Three Hundred Years of French Architecture, 1494–1794* (New York, 1936); and A. Blunt, *Art and Architecture in France, 1500–1700* (London, 1953).

LITERATURE

E. Hutton, *Aretino, Scourge of Princes* (New York, 1922); W. Boulting, *Tasso* (New York, 1909); E. Roditi, "Tasso," *Journal of Aesthetics and Art Criticism,* 1948; K. M. Lea, *Italian Popular Comedy* (2 vols.; Oxford, 1934); P. Duchartie, *La commedia dell'arte* (Paris, 1955); P. E. Robertson, *Commedia dell'arte* (Natal, 1960); J. Plattard, *D'Aubigné* (Paris, 1935); I. Buffum, *D'Aubigné's "Les Tragiques"* (New Haven, 1951); L. Lavaud, *Desportes* (Paris, 1936); E. Magne, *Voiture et l'Hôtel de Rambouillet* (2 vols.; Paris, 1929–30); M. Magendie, *Astrée* (Paris, 1929) and *Le roman français au XVIIᵉ siècle* (Paris, 1932); W. J. Entwistle, *Cervantes* (London, 1940); L. Nelson, "Góngora and Milton," *Comparative Literature,* 1954; R. Schevill, *The Dramatic Art of Lope de Vega* (Berkeley, 1918); W. Rose, *Men, Myths, and Movements in German Literature* (London, 1931); V. M. Jeffery, *Lyly and the Italian Renaissance* (London, 1929); T. M. Parrott, *Shakespeare: A Handbook* (new ed.; New York, 1955); W. H. Clemen, *The Development of Shake-*

speare's Imagery (London, 1952); J. B. Leishman, *The Monarch of Wit* (Donne) (London, 1951), and also F. J. Warnke, *European Metaphysical Poetry* (New Haven, 1961).

MUSIC

A. Einstein, *The Italian Madrigal* (3 vols.; Princeton, 1949); C. Grey and P. Heseltine, *Gesualdo* (London, 1926); L. Schrade, *Monteverdi* (New York, 1950); D. J. Grout, *Short History of Opera* (2 vols.; New York, 1947); and N. Pirrotta, "Temperaments and Tendencies in the Florentine *Camerata*," *Musical Quarterly,* 1954.

THE QUEST FOR RULES

E. Mâle, *L'art religieux après le Concile de Trente* (Paris, 1932); N. Pevsner, *Academies of Art* (Cambridge, 1940); A. Blunt, *Artistic Theory in Italy, 1450–1600* (2d ed.; Oxford, 1959); E. G. Holt, *Documentary History of Art* (2 vols.; New York, 1958); L. Venturi, *History of Art Criticism* (New York, 1936); K. Gilbert and H. Kuhn, *History of Esthetics* (rev. ed.; Bloomington, Ind., 1953); J. L. Meyers, *Learned Societies* (Liverpool, 1922); F. A. Yates, *French Academies in the 16th Century* (London, 1947); R. A. Hall, Jr., *The Italian "Questione della lingua"* (Chapel Hill, N.C., 1942); J. E. Spingarn, *History of Literary Criticism in the Renaissance* (2d ed.; New York, 1912); V. Hall, Jr., *Renaissance Literary Criticism* (New York, 1945); C. S. Baldwin, *Renaissance Literary Theory and Practice* (New York, 1939); B. Weinberg, *History of Literary Criticism in the Italian Renaissance* (2 vols.; Chicago, 1961); B. Hathaway, *The Art of Criticism in the Late Renaissance in Italy* (Ithaca, N.Y., 1961); J. H. Smith and E. W. Parks (eds.), *The Great Critics* (3d ed.; New York, 1951); A. H. Gilbert (ed.), *Literary Criticism, Plato to Dryden* (New York, 1940); H. B. Carlton, *Castelvetro's Theory of Poetry* (Manchester, 1913); H. Riemann, *Geschichte der Musiktheorie* (2d ed.; Berlin, 1920); and O. Strunk (ed.), *Source Readings in Music History* (New York, 1950).

CHAPTER V

ART

GENERAL

A. Neumeyer, "Baroque," in D. Runes (ed.), *Encyclopedia of the Arts* (New York, 1946); W. Stechow, "Definitions of Baroque in the Visual Arts," *Journal of Aesthetics,* 1946, and "The Baroque," *ibid.,* 1955; E. C. Hassold, "The Baroque as a Basic Concept of Art," *College Art Journal,* 1946; J. P. Martin, "The Baroque from the Viewpoint of the Art Historian," *Journal of Aesthetics,* 1955; J. Lees-Milne (ed.), *Baroque Europe* (London, 1962); W. Sypher, *Four Stages of Renaissance Style* (New York, 1955), pp. 180–297;

H. Wölfflin, *Principles of Art History* (New York, 1932); W. Weisbach (ed.), *Die Kunst des Barock* (Berlin, 1924), pictures; P. Smith, *History of Modern Culture* (2 vols.; New York, 1930–34); D. Ogg, *Europe in the 17th Century* (8th ed.; London, 1960); G. N. Clark, *The 17th Century* (2d ed.; Cambridge, 1947); P. Hazard, *The European Mind, 1680–1715* (London, 1953); E. d'Ors, *Du Baroque* (Paris, 1935); V. L. Tapié, *Age of Grandeur* (London, 1960); R. Fry, "Baroque," *Burlington Magazine*, 1921; G. Evans, "The Baroque Harmony of Space and Form," *Gazette des beaux arts,* 1952; B. Croce, *Storia della età barocca in Italia* (2d ed.; Bari, 1946); D. Mahon, *Studies in Seicento Art and Theory* (London, 1947); E. Mâle, *L'art religieux après le Concile de Trente* (Paris, 1923); R. Wittkower, *Art and Architecture in Italy, 1600–1750* (London, 1958); T. H. Fokker, *Roman Baroque Art* (2 vols.; Oxford, 1938); J. Lees-Milne, *Baroque in Italy* (London, 1959); C. Ricci (ed.), *Baroque Architecture and Sculpture in Italy* (London, 1922), pictures; R. Schneider, *L'art français XVIIᵉ siècle* (Paris, 1925); A. Blunt, *Art and Architecture in France, 1500–1700* (London, 1954); L. Réau, *Histoire de l'expansion de l'art français* (4 vols.; Paris, 1924–35); L. Vitet, *L'Academie royale de peinture et de sculpture* (Paris, 1880); H. Gerson and E. H. ter Kuile, *Art and Architecture in Belgium, 1600–1800* (London, 1960); B. S. Allen, *Tides in English Taste* (new ed.; 2 vols.; New York, 1959); S. Sitwell, *German Baroque Art* (London, 1928); N. Powell, *From Baroque to Rococo* (London, 1959); W. Weisbach, *Spanish Baroque Art* (Cambridge, 1941); J. Lees-Milne, *Baroque in Spain and Portugal* (London, 1960); and G. Kubler and M. Soria, *Art and Architecture in Spain and Portugal, 1500–1800* (London, 1959).

PAINTING

F. J. Mather, *Western European Painting of the Renaissance* (New York, 1939); B. Rogerson, "Art of Painting the Passions," *Journal of the History of Ideas,* 1953; R. W. Lee, "Ut pictura poesis," *Art Bulletin,* 1940; W. Martin, *Dutch Painting, 1650–1697* (London, 1951); J. Dupont and F. Mathey, *The Seventeenth Century, from Caravaggio to Vermeer* (Geneva, 1952); A. Pigler, *Barock Themen* (2 vols.; Berlin, 1956); F. M. Godfrey, *Later Italian Painting, 1500–1800* (London, 1958); A. K. McComb, *The Baroque Painters of Italy* (Cambridge, Mass., 1934); E. K. Waterhouse, *Baroque Painting in Rome* (London, 1937); W. Friedlaender, *Mannerism and Anti-Mannerism in Italian Painting* (New York, 1957); G. Rouchès, *La peinture polonaise à la fin du XVIᵉ siècle* (Paris, 1913); R. Hinks, *Caravaggio* (London, 1953); B. Berenson, *Caravaggio* (London, 1953); W. Friedlaender, *Caravaggio Studies* (Princeton, 1955); G. Isarlo, *La peinture en France au XVIIᵉ siècle* (Paris, 1960); A. Chastel (ed.), *Poussin* (2 vols.; Paris, 1960); P. Courthion, *Claude Lorrain* (Paris, 1932); M. Rothlisberger, *Claude Lorrain* (2 vols.; New Haven, 1961); E. Tapier, *Velásquez* (New York, 1948); R. Fry, *Flemish Art* (London,

1927); M. Rooses, *Rubens* (2 vols.; London, 1904); B. A. Stevenson (ed.), *Rubens* (Oxford, 1934); L. van Puyvelde, *Van Dyck* (Paris, 1959); L. Gowing, *Vermeer* (London, 1952); N. S. Trivas (ed.), *Hals* (New York, 1941); A. Bredius (ed.), *Rembrandt* (Vienna, 1936); J. Rosenberg, *Rembrandt* (2 vols.; Cambridge, Mass., 1948); and H. Focillon (ed.), *Rembrandt: Paintings, Drawings and Etchings* (London, 1960).

SCULPTURE AND ARCHITECTURE

V. V. Stech, *Baroque Sculpture* (London, 1961); E. Maclagan, *Italian Sculpture of the Renaissance* (Cambridge, Mass., 1935); R. Wittkower (ed.), *Bernini, Sculptor* (London, 1955); M. S. Briggs, *Baroque Architecture* (London, 1913); G. Scott, *The Architecture of Humanism* (new ed.; New York, 1954); G. Cattani, "Baroque et Rococo," *Critique,* 1957; P. Askew, "Relation of Bernini's Architecture to the Architecture of High Renaissance," *Marsyas,* 1950; P. Zucker, "Space and Movement in Baroque City-planning," *Journal of Architectural Historians,* 1955; E. Hempel, *Borromini* (Vienna, 1924); H. I. Triggs, *Garden Craft in Europe* (London, 1913); S. Crowe, *Garden Design* (London, 1958); J. C. Shepherd and G. A. Jellicoe, *Italian Gardens of the Renaissance* (2d ed.; London, 1953); G. Masson, *Italian Villas and Palaces* (London, 1959) and *Italian Gardens* (London, 1961); A. Marie, *Jardins français classiques* (Paris, 1944); H. Leclerc, *Les origines italiennes de l'architecture théatrale moderne* (Paris, 1946); J. Scholz (ed.), *Baroque and Romantic Stage Design* (New York, 1950); A. H. Mayor, *The Bibiena Family* (New York, 1945); F. Kimball, "Classicism, Academism, and Creation in 17th Century French Architecture," *Scritti di storia dell'arte in onore di Lionello Venturi* (2 vols.; Rome, 1956); P. Bourget and G. Cattani, *J. H. Mansart* (Paris, 1960); J. N. Summerson, *Architecture in Britain, 1530–1830* (London, 1953); E. F. Sekler, *Wren and His Place in European Architecture* (London, 1956); R. Wittkower, "Palladianism in England," *Listener,* 1950; T. H. Burrough, *South Germany Baroque* (London, 1956); J. Bourke, *Baroque Churches of Central Europe* (London, 1958); H. Sedlmayr, *Fischer von Erlach* (Vienna, 1956); and E. Kaufmann, *Architecture in the Age of Reason* (Cambridge, Mass., 1955).

ROCOCO

Article "Rococo" in D. D. Runes and H. G. Schuckel (eds.), *Encyclopedia of the Arts* (New York, 1946); M. Osborn (ed.), *Die Kunst der Rokoko* (Berlin, 1929), pictures; A. Schönberger and H. Soehner, *Age of Rococo* (London, 1960); G. de Traz, *The Eighteenth Century, Watteau to Tiepolo* (Geneva, 1952); F. Kimball, *The Creation of the Rococo* (Philadelphia, 1943); L. Guillet, *Watteau* (4th ed.; Paris, 1943); M. Gauthier, *Watteau* (New York, 1960); P. Lavallée, *Boucher* (Paris, 1942); G. Wildenstein (ed.), *Fragonard* (London, 1960); R. B. Beckett, *Hogarth* (London, 1946); F. Antal, *Hogarth and His Place in European Art* (London, 1961); M. Levy, *Painting in 18th*

Century Venice (London, 1959); and A. Morassi (ed.), *Tiepolo* (2 vols.; New York, 1955).

LITERATURE

GENERAL

R. Alewyn, "Baroque in Literature" in J. Shipley, *Dictionary of World Literature* (New York, 1953); R. Wellek, "Concept of Baroque in Literary Scholarship," *Journal of Aesthetics,* 1946; H. Hatzfeld, "The Baroque from the Viewpoint of the Literary Historian," *Journal of Aesthetics,* 1955; H. Hatzfeld, "The Baroque Problem in Romance Literatures," *Comparative Literature,* 1949; D. McCarthy, "The European Tradition in Literature from 1600 Onwards" in E. Eyre (ed.), *European Civilization,* Vol. VI (London, 1939); M. W. Croll, "The Baroque Style in Prose," in *Studies in Honor of F. Klaeber* (New York, 1929); A. Adam, *Histoire de la littérature française au XVIIe siècle* (5 vols.; Paris, 1948–56); R. Bray, *La formation de la doctrine classique en France* (Paris, 1927); G. de Reynold, *Le XVIIe siècle* (Montreal, 1944); J. Rousset, *La littérature de l'âge Baroque en France* (Paris, 1953); D. Mornet, *Histoire de la littérature française classique* (Paris, 1942); A. Bailly, *L'école classique français* (6th ed.; Paris, 1958); R. Picard, *Les salons littéraires, 1610–1789* (Paris, 1943); R. Lebègue, *Nouvelles études malherbiennes* (Paris, 1947); G. Guillaumie, *J. L. de Balzac et la prose française* (Paris, 1927); I. Buffum, *Studies in the Baroque* (New Haven, Conn., 1957); V. Cerny, "Le Baroque et la littérature française," *Critique,* 1956; M. Turnell, *The Classical Moment* (London, 1947); H. C. Lancaster, *History of French Dramatic Literature in the 17th Century* (9 vols.; Baltimore, 1929–42); T. E. Lawrenson, *The French Stage in the 17th Century* (Manchester, 1957); G. Couton, *Corneille* (Paris, 1958); L. Lockert, *Studies in French Classical Tragedy* (Nashville, Tenn., 1958); G. C. May, *Tragédie cornélienne, tragédie racinienne* (Urbana, Ill., 1948); P. Butler, *Classicisme et Baroque dans l'œuvre de Racine* (Paris, 1959); G. Brereton, *Racine* (London, 1951); H. Peyre, "Phèdre," in C. Brooks (ed.), *Tragic Themes in Western Literature* (New Haven, Conn., 1955); D. Mornet, *Molière* (Paris, 1943); D. B. Lewis, *Molière* (London, 1959); H. Gillot, *La querelle des anciens et modernes en France* (Paris, 1914); R. F. Jones, *Ancients and Moderns* (St. Louis, 1936); H. Baron, "The 'Querelle' of the Ancients and Moderns as a Problem of Renaissance Scholarship," *Journal of the History of Ideas,* 1959; R. Bray, *Boileau* (Paris, 1942); P. Clarac, *La Fontaine* (Paris, 1943); M. Guiton, *La Fontaine* (New Brunswick, 1961); J. Calvet, *Bossuet* (Paris, 1941); B. Willey, *The 17th Century Background* (London, 1934); A. D. McKillop, *English Literature from Dryden to Burns* (New York, 1948); A. Warren, *Crashaw* (Baton Rouge, La., 1939); R. C. Wallerstein, *Crashaw* (Madison, Wis., 1959); G. Williamson, "The Rhetorical Pattern of Neo-Classical Wit," *Modern Philology,* 1935–36; J. B. Leishman, *The Monarch of Wit* (Donne) (London, 1951); M. Y. Hughes (ed.), Milton, *Complete*

Poems and Major Prose (New York, 1957); D. Saurat, *Milton* (2d ed.; London, 1944); K. M. Burton, *Restoration Literature* (London, 1958); D. N. Smith, *Dryden* (London, 1950); C. R. Noyes (ed.), *Poetry of Dryden* (Boston, 1950); A. J. Barnouw, *Vondel* (New York, 1925); M. Sloman, *Dramatic Craftsmanship of Calderón* (Oxford, 1958); L. Reynaud, *Histoire générale de l'influence française en Allemagne* (Paris, 1914); A. Moret (ed.), *Anthologie du lyrisme baroque en Allemagne* (Paris, 1957); C. von Faber du Faur (ed.), *German Baroque Literature: A Catalogue* (New Haven, 1958); J. C. Schoolfield, *The German Lyric of the Baroque in English* (Geneva, 1961); J. Mark, "Uses of the Term, Baroque," *Modern Language Review,* 1938; and L. Nelson, *Baroque Lyric Poetry* (New Haven, Conn., 1961).

ROCOCO

F. C. Green, *Minuet, Survey of French and English Literary Ideas in the 18th Century* (London, 1935); R. P. McCutcheon, *Eighteenth Century English Literature* (Oxford, 1949); J. E. Butt, *The Augustan Age* (New York, 1950); B. Dobrée, *English Literature in the Earlier 18th Century* (Oxford, 1959); R. K. Root, *The Poetical Career of Pope* (Princeton, 1938); R. P. Parkin, *Poetical Workmanship of Pope* (Minneapolis, Minn., 1955); R. Quintana, *Swift, an Introduction* (Oxford, 1955); L. Réau, *L'Europe française* (Paris, 1938); H. N. Brailsford, *Voltaire* (London, 1936); and G. Lanson, *Voltaire* (rev. ed.; Paris, 1960).

MUSIC

Article "Baroque" in W. Apel (ed.), *Harvard Dictionary of Music* (Cambridge, Mass., 1950); M. Bukhofzer, *Music in the Baroque Era* (New York, 1947) and "The Baroque in Music History," *Journal of Aesthetics,* 1955; P. L. Frank, "Some Remarks about Periods in Music History," *American Musicological Society Journal,* 1955; J. H. Müller, "Baroque," *Journal of Aesthetics,* 1954; M. Bukhofzer, "Renaissance versus Baroque Music," *Bulletin of the American Musicological Society,* 1948; W. Fleming, "Element of Motion in Baroque Art and Music," *Journal of Aesthetics,* 1946; S. Clercx, *Le Baroque et la musique* (Brussels, 1948); "Baroque Interpretation of Music," in E. Blom (ed.), *Grove's Dictionary of Music and Musicians* (5th ed.; 9 vols.; London, 1954); R. Rolland, *Musicians of Former Days* (New York, 1915); D. J. Grout, *Short History of Opera* (2 vols.; New York, 1947); N. Pirrotta, "Temperaments and Tendencies in the Florentine *Camerata,*" *Musical Quarterly,* 1954; L. Schrade, *Monteverdi* (New York, 1950); E. J. Dent, *Alessandro Scarlatti* (new ed.; New York, 1960); E. van der Straeten, *History of the Violin* (2 vols.; London, 1933); A. J. Hutchings, *The Baroque Concerto* (London, 1960); W. S. Newman, *The Sonata in the Baroque Era* (Chapel Hill, N.C., 1959); M. Pincherle, *Corelli* (New York, 1956) and *Vivaldi* (London, 1958); N. Demuth, *French Opera from Its Origins to the*

Revolution (London, 1960); H. Punières, *Lully* (2d ed.; Paris, 1927); A. K. Holland, *Purcell* (2d ed.; London, 1948); J. A. Westrup, *Purcell* (London, 1937); H. J. Moser, *Schütz* (St. Louis, Mo., 1960); A. T. Davidson, *Bach and Handel* (Cambridge, Mass., 1957); P. Spitta, *Bach* (new ed.; New York, 1951); K. Geiringer, *Music of the Bach Family* (Cambridge, Mass., 1951) and *The Bach Family* (New York, 1954); H. David and A. Mendel (eds.), *The Bach Reader* (New York, 1959); N. Flower, *Handel* (2d ed.; London, 1958); H. Weinstock, *Handel* (2d ed.; New York, 1959); G. E. Abraham (ed.), *Handel, a Symposium* (Oxford, 1954); and W. Dean, *Handel's Dramatic Oratorios and Masques* (Oxford, 1959).

ROCOCO

Article "Rococo" in W. Apel (ed.), *Harvard Dictionary of Music* (Cambridge, Mass., 1950); A. Carse, *The Orchestra in the Eighteenth Century* (New York, 1950); W. Mellers, *François Couperin* (Paris, 1951); C. Girdlestone, *Rameau* (London, 1957); and R. Kirkpatrick, *Domenico Scarlatti* (Princeton, 1953).

CHAPTER VI

GENERAL WORKS

B. S. Allen, *Tides in English Taste (1619–1800)* (2 vols.; Cambridge, Mass., 1937); W. J. Bate, *From Classic to Romantic Premises of Taste in 18th Century England* (Cambridge, Mass., 1946); W. J. Hipple, *The Beautiful, the Sublime, and the Picturesque in 18th Century British Aesthetic Theory* (Carbondale, Ill., 1957); F. Novotny, *Painting and Sculpture in Europe, 1790–1880* (London, 1960).

NEO-CLASSICISM

GENERAL WORKS

A. O. Lovejoy, "Parallel between Deism and Classicism," *Modern Philology,* 1932; R. Canat, *La renaissance de la Grèce antique, 1820–50* (Paris, 1911); L. Lawrence, "Stuart and Revett, Their Literary and Architectural Careers," *Journal of the Warburg Institute,* 1938–39; and H. T. Parker, *The Cult of Antiquity and the French Revolutionaries* (Chicago, 1937).

ART

G. Pauli (ed.), *Die Kunst des Klassizismus und der Romantik* (Berlin, 1925), pictures; L. Hautecoeur, *Rome et la renaissance de l'antiquité à la fin du XVIIIe siècle* (Paris, 1912); L. Bertrand, *La fin du classicisme et le retour à l'antique* (Paris, 1897); C. Hussey, *The Picturesque* (London, 1927); C. Justi, *Winckelmann* (3d ed.; 3 vols.; Leipzig, 1923); H. C. Hatfield, *Winckelmann and His German Critics* (New York, 1943); G. Bagnani, "Winckelmann and the Second Renascence, 1755–1955," *American Journal of Archeology,* 1955; H. Focillon, *Piranesi* (Paris, 1918); A. H. Mayor, *Piranesi* (New York, 1952); J. Seznec, *Essais sur Diderot et l'antiquité* (Oxford, 1957); J. Maret, *David* (Monaco, 1943); J. Locquin, *La peinture d'histoire en France, 1747–85* (Paris, 1912); J. Alazard, *Ingres* (Paris, 1950); G. Wildenstein (ed.), *Ingres* (New York, 1954); E. Bassi, *Canova* (Bergamo, 1943); H. R. Hitchcock, *Early Victorian Architecture in Britain* (2 vols.; New Haven, Conn., 1954) and *Architecture, 19th and 20th Centuries* (London, 1958); J. Lees-Milne, *Age of Adam* (London, 1947); and D. Pilcher, *The Regency Style, 1800–30* (London, 1948).

LITERATURE

R. D. Havens, "Changing Taste in the 18th Century," *PMLA,* 1929; M. Gilman, *Idea of Poetry in France* (Cambridge, Mass., 1958); E. M. Butler, *Tyranny of Greece over Germany* (Cambridge, 1935); W. J. Keller, *Goethe's Estimate of the Greek and Latin Writers* (Madison, Wis., 1916); H. Trevelyan, *Goethe and the Greeks* (Cambridge, 1942); A. Stansfield, *Hölderlin* (Manchester, 1944); L. S. Salzberger, *Hölderlin* (Cambridge, 1952); B. H. Stern, *Rise of Romantic Hellenism in English Literature, 1732–86* (Menasha, Wis., 1940); F. E. Pierce, "The Hellenic Current in English 19th Century Poetry," *Journal of English and German Philology,* 1917; M. Elvin, *Landor* (London, 1942); P. Moreau, *Le classicisme des romantiques* (Paris, 1932); R. Canat, *L'Hellenisme des romantiques* (2 vols.; Paris, 1951–53); G. Walter, *Chénier* (Paris, 1947); P. Dimoff, *Chénier* (2 vols.; Paris, 1936); J. Fabre, *Chénier* (Paris, 1955); C. R. Miller, *Alfieri* (Williamsport, Pa., 1931); and G. Megaro, *Alfieri, Forerunner of Italian Nationalism* (New York, 1930).

MUSIC

R. Rolland, *Some Musicians of Former Days* (New York, 1915); K. Geiringer, *The Bach Family* (New York, 1954); A. Einstein, *Gluck* (New York, 1936); A. A. Albert, *Gluck* (London, 1960); E. Newman, *Gluck* (new ed.; London, 1960); K. Geiringer, *Haydn* (New York, 1946); R. Hughes, *Haydn* (London, 1956); A. Einstein, *Mozart* (Oxford, 1951); E. Bloom, *Mozart* (New York, 1949); E. Schenk, *Mozart* (New York, 1959); H. C. Landon (ed.), *The Mozart Companion* (Oxford, 1956); L. L. Biancolli (ed.), *Mozart Handbook* (Cleveland, 1954); A. H. King, *Mozart in Retrospect* (Oxford, 1955); and E. J. Dent, *Mozart's Operas* (new ed.; London, 1946).

ROMANTICISM

GENERAL WORKS

F. Baldensperger (ed.), *Romantique, ses analogues et ses équivalents, 1650–1840* (Cambridge, Mass., 1937); A. O. Lovejoy, "Meaning of Romanticism for the Historian of Ideas," *Journal of the History of Ideas,* 1941; M. H. Nicolson, *Mountain Gloom and Mountain Glory* (Ithaca, N.Y., 1959); and P. van Tieghem, *Le sentiment de la nature dans le Préromantisme européen* (Paris, 1960).

ART

P. Courthion, *Romanticism* (Geneva, 1961); L. Réau, *L'ère romantique, les arts plastiques* (Paris, 1949); R. Lanson, *Le goût du moyen âge en France du XVIIIᵉ siècle* (Paris, 1926); K. Clarke, *The Gothic Revival* (2d ed.; London, 1950); A. Addison, *Romanticism and the Gothic Revival* (New York, 1938); M. Brion, *Romantic Art* (New York, 1960); C. Tinker, *Painter and Poet: Studies in the Literary Relations of English Painting* (Cambridge, Mass., 1938); W. Friedlaender, *David to Delacroix* (Cambridge, Mass., 1952); L. Hautecoeur and others, *Le Romantisme et l'art* (Paris, 1928); G. Bazin, *Corot* (Paris, 1942); R. Escholier, *Delacroix* (3 vols.; Paris, 1926–29); E. K. Waterhouse, *Gainsborough* (London, 1958); S. J. Key, *Constable* (London, 1948); A. J. Finberg, *Turner* (2d ed.; Oxford, 1960); P. Gassier, *Goya* (New York, 1955); J. Calmette, *Rude* (Paris, 1920); and J. Fleming, *Robert Adam and His Circle* (Cambridge, Mass., 1962).

LITERATURE

R. Wellek, "Concept of Romanticism in Literary History," *Comparative Literature,* 1949; P. van Tieghem, *Le Romantisme dans la littérature européenne* (Paris, 1948); J. C. Blankenagel and others, "Romanticism, a Symposium," *PMLA,* 1946; P. van Tieghem (ed.), *Le mouvement romantique* (3d ed.; Paris, 1940), collection of texts; R. Wellek, *History of Criticism,* Vol. II (New Haven, Conn., 1955); P. van Tieghem, *Le Préromantisme* (5 vols.; Paris, 1924–48) and *La découverte de Shakespeare sur le continent* (Paris, 1937); O. Elton, *Survey of English Literature, 1780–1880* (4 vols.; London, 1920); H. N. Fairchild, *The Romantic Quest* (New York, 1931); T. Wright, *Blake* (2 vols.; London, 1929); L. A. Willoughby, *The Classical Age of German Literature* (Oxford, 1926); W. H. Bruford, *Germany in the 18th Century* (Cambridge, 1935), *Theater, Drama, and Audience in Goethe's Germany* (London, 1950), and *Culture and Society in Classical Weimar, 1775–1806* (Cambridge, 1962); P. S. Prawer, *German Lyric Poetry* (London, 1952); E. A. Blackall, *The Emergence of German as a Literary Language, 1700–75* (Cambridge, 1959); R. Ayrault, *La genèse du romantisme allemand* (2 vols.; Paris, 1961); H. B. Garland, *Lessing* (Cambridge, 1937); R. Pascal, *The German "Sturm und Drang"* (Manchester, 1953); A. Gillies, *Herder* (Oxford, 1945); H. B. Garland, *Schiller* (London, 1949); C. Thomas, *Goethe* (2d ed.; New York, 1929); B. Fairley, *A Study of Goethe* (Oxford, 1947); D. Mornet, *Le Romantisme en France au XVIIIᵉ siècle* (Paris, 1912) and *Rousseau* (Paris, 1950); E. H. Wright, *The Meaning of Rousseau* (New

York, 1929); A. M. Wilson, *Diderot, the Testing Years* (New York, 1957); D. G. Larg, *Mme de Staël* (New York, 1926); J. C. Herold, *Mistress to an Age* (Indianapolis, Ind., 1958); A. Maurois, *Chateaubriand* (Paris, 1938); M. Levaillant, *Le véritable Chateaubriand* (Paris, 1951); T. M. Raysor (ed.), *The English Romantic Poets: A Review of Research* (2d ed.; New York, 1956); C. Thorpe and others, *The Major English Romantic Poets* (Carbondale, Ill., 1957); E. Bernbaum (ed.), *The English Romantic Poets* (New York, 1950); C. H. Herford, *The Age of Wordsworth* (new ed.; London, 1930); M. H. Abram, *The Mirror and the Lamp: Romantic Theory and Critical Tradition* (Oxford, 1953); D. Perkins, *Quest for Permanence: Wordsworth, Shelley, and Keats* (Cambridge, Mass., 1957); H. House, *Coleridge* (London, 1953); H. J. Grierson, *Scott* (London, 1938); P. West, *Byron* (London, 1960); D. King-Hele, *Shelley* (New York, 1960); W. J. Bate, *Stylistic Development of Keats* (London, 1958); L. A. Willoughby, *Romantic Movement in Germany* (Oxford, 1930); O. Walzel, *German Romanticism* (New York, 1932); R. Tymms, *German Romantic Literature* (London, 1955); F. E. Pierce and C. F. Schreiber (eds.), *Fiction and Fantasy of German Romance, 1790–1830* (Oxford, 1927); A. Guerne (ed.), *Les romantiques allemands* (Bruges, 1956); W. Silz, *Early German Romanticism* (Cambridge, Mass., 1939); B. Haywood, *Novalis* (Cambridge, 1959); E. H. Zeydel, *Tieck* (Princeton, N.J., 1935); R. Marsh, *Kleist* (Cambridge, 1954); M. Brod, *Heine* (London, 1956); G. Bianquis, *La vie quotidienne en Allemagne à l'époque romantique* (Paris, 1959); R. Martino, *L'époque romantique en France* (Paris, 1944); P. Moreau, *Le Romantisme* (new ed.; Paris, 1957); F. Brunot and others, *Le Romantisme et les lettres* (Paris, 1929); N. H. Clement, *Romanticism in France* (Oxford, 1939); J. Bertaut, *Histoire de la vie littéraire, l'époque romantique* (Paris, 1951); M. F. Guyard, *Lamartine* (Paris, 1956); P. G. Castex, *De Vigny* (Paris, 1952); J. B. Barrère, *Hugo* (Paris, 1952); and A. Maurois, *Olympio, Life of Hugo* (New York, 1955).

MUSIC

A. Einstein, *Music in the Romantic Era* (New York, 1947); J. Chantavoine and J. Gaudefroy-Demombynes, *Le Romantisme dans la musique européenne* (Paris, 1954); C. Laforêt, *La vie musicale aux temps romantiques* (Paris, 1929); F. Baldensperger, *Sensibilité musicale et Romantisme* (Paris, 1925); L. Guichard, *La musique et les lettres au temps du Romantisme* (Paris, 1955); A. W. Thayer, *Beethoven* (new ed.; 3 vols.; New York, 1921); D. F. Tovey, *Beethoven* (Oxford, 1945); L. P. and R. P. Stebbins, *Von Weber* (New York, 1940); M. J. Broun, *Schubert* (New York, 1958); A. Einstein, *Schubert* (Oxford, 1951); O. E. Deutsch (ed.), *Schubert Reader* (New York, 1947); J. Barzun, *Berlioz and the Romantic Century* (2 vols.; Boston, 1950); and D. Evans, *Les romantiques français et la musique* (Paris, 1934).

SUPPLEMENTARY GENERAL BIBLIOGRAPHY, 1975

T. Munro, *Evolution in the Arts and other Theories of Culture History* (New York, 1963); R. N. Stromberg, *Intellectual History of Modern Europe* (New York, 1965); R. Huyghe, *Larousse Encyclopedia of Renaissance and Baroque Art* (New York, 1964); U. Hatje, ed., *Styles of European Art* (London, 1965); H. Read, ed., *The Styles of European Art* (London, 1965); M. C. Beardsley, *Aesthetics from Classical Greece to the Present* (New York, 1966); E. H. Gombrich, *Norm and Form, Studies in the Art of the Renaissance* (London, 1966); C. S. Singleton, *Art, Science, and History in the Renaissance* (Baltimore, 1967); P. van Tieghem, *Les influences étrangeres sur la littérature française, 1550-1880* (Paris, 1961); B. C. Cannon & others, *The Art of Music* (New York, 1960), one of the first histories of music with a separate discussion of Mannerism in music; H. Riemann, *History of Music Theory, 9th-16th Centuries* (Lincoln, Neb., 1962); P. H. Lang & O. Bettmann, *Pictorial History of Music* (London, 1964); H. Raynor, *Social History of Music* (London, 1972); W. Dunwell, *Music and the European Mind* (London, 1962), integrates music with art and literature; A. Robertson & D. Stevens, *Renaissance and Baroque Music* (New York, 1965); J. B. Coover, *Medieval and Renaissance Music on Long-playing Records* (New York, 1964); A. Geoffroy-Dechaune, *Les secrets de la musique ancienne, 16me-18me siecles* (Paris, 1964); A. L. Burkhalter, *Music of the Renaissance* (New York, 1968); F. Blume, *Renaissance and Baroque Music* (London, 1969); A. Harmon & A. Milner, eds., *Late Renaissance and Baroque Music* (New York, 1969); R. S. Lopez, *Three Ages of the Italian Renaissance* (New Haven, 1970); E. Wind, *Pagan Mysteries in the Renaissance* (new ed., London, 1967); F. Hartt, *History of Italian Renaissance Art* (London, 1971); D. S. Chambers, *Patrons and Artists in the Italian Renaissance* (London, 1971); G. Bazin, *History of World Sculpture* (New York, 1968); H. D. Molesworth, *European Sculpture from Romanesque to Neo-Classic* (New York, 1965); H. Busch & B. Lohse, eds., *Renaissance Sculpture* (London, 1969); J. Pope-Hennessy, *Italian High Renaissance and Baroque Sculpture* (3 vols., London, 1962); N. D. Shergold, *History of the Spanish Stage* (Oxford, 1967); O. H. Green, *Spain and the Western Tradition, The Castilian Mind in Literature* (2 vols., Madison, Wis., 1963-5); H. M. Priest, ed., *Renaissance and Baroque Lyrics* (Ital., Fr., & Sp. in translation, Evanston, Ill., 1962); A. Chastel, *Italian Art* (London, 1963); C. Vermeule, *European Art and the Classical Past* (Cambridge, Mass., 1964); B. Rowland, *The Classical Tradition in Western Art* (Cambridge, Mass., 1963); N. P. Stallknecht & H. Frenz, eds., *Comparative Literature, Method and Perspective* (Carbondale, Ill., 1961); H. Keutner, *Sculpture, Renaissance to Rococo* (London, 1969); R. Murray, *Architecture of the Italian Renaissance* (London, 1969); and F. Artz, *Renaissance Humanism* (Kent, Ohio, 1966).

INDEX